Lecture Notes in Computer Science 4900

Commenced Publication in 1973
Founding and Former Series Editors:
Gerhard Goos, Juris Hartmanis, and Jan van Leeuwen

Editorial Board

David Hutchison
  Lancaster University, UK
Takeo Kanade
  Carnegie Mellon University, Pittsburgh, PA, USA
Josef Kittler
  University of Surrey, Guildford, UK
Jon M. Kleinberg
  Cornell University, Ithaca, NY, USA
Alfred Kobsa
  University of California, Irvine, CA, USA
Friedemann Mattern
  ETH Zurich, Switzerland
John C. Mitchell
  Stanford University, CA, USA
Moni Naor
  Weizmann Institute of Science, Rehovot, Israel
Oscar Nierstrasz
  University of Bern, Switzerland
C. Pandu Rangan
  Indian Institute of Technology, Madras, India
Bernhard Steffen
  University of Dortmund, Germany
Madhu Sudan
  Massachusetts Institute of Technology, MA, USA
Demetri Terzopoulos
  University of California, Los Angeles, CA, USA
Doug Tygar
  University of California, Berkeley, CA, USA
Gerhard Weikum
  Max-Planck Institute of Computer Science, Saarbruecken, Germany

Stefano Spaccapietra (Ed.)

Journal on Data Semantics X

 Springer

Volume Editor

Stefano Spaccapietra
Database Laboratory, EPFL
School of Computer and Communication Science
Lausanne, Switzerland
E-mail: stefano.spaccapietra@epfl.ch

Library of Congress Control Number: 2007942739

CR Subject Classification (1998): H.2, H.3, I.2, H.4, C.2

LNCS Sublibrary: SL 3 – Information Systems and Application, incl. Internet/Web and HCI

ISSN   0302-9743
ISBN-10 3-540-77687-7 Springer Berlin Heidelberg New York
ISBN-13 978-3-540-77687-1 Springer Berlin Heidelberg New York

This work is subject to copyright. All rights are reserved, whether the whole or part of the material is concerned, specifically the rights of translation, reprinting, re-use of illustrations, recitation, broadcasting, reproduction on microfilms or in any other way, and storage in data banks. Duplication of this publication or parts thereof is permitted only under the provisions of the German Copyright Law of September 9, 1965, in its current version, and permission for use must always be obtained from Springer. Violations are liable to prosecution under the German Copyright Law.

Springer is a part of Springer Science+Business Media

springer.com

© Springer-Verlag Berlin Heidelberg 2008
Printed in Germany

Typesetting: Camera-ready by author, data conversion by Scientific Publishing Services, Chennai, India
Printed on acid-free paper   SPIN: 12215324   06/3180   5 4 3 2 1 0

The LNCS Journal on Data Semantics

Computerized information handling has changed its focus from centralized data management systems to decentralized data exchange facilities. Modern distribution channels, such as high-speed Internet networks and wireless communication infrastructure, provide reliable technical support for data distribution and data access, materializing the new, popular idea that data may be available to anybody, anywhere, anytime. However, providing huge amounts of data on request often turns into a counterproductive service, making the data useless because of poor relevance or inappropriate level of detail. Semantic knowledge is the essential missing piece that allows the delivery of information that matches user requirements. Semantic agreement, in particular, is essential to meaningful data exchange.

Semantic issues have long been open issues in data and knowledge management. However, the boom in semantically poor technologies, such as the Web and XML, has boosted renewed interest in semantics. Conferences on the Semantic Web, for instance, attract big crowds of participants, while ontologies on their own have become a hot and popular topic in the database and artificial intelligence communities.

Springer's LNCS *Journal on Data Semantics* aims at providing a highly visible dissemination channel for most remarkable work that in one way or another addresses research and development on issues related to the semantics of data. The target domain ranges from theories supporting the formal definition of semantic content to innovative domain-specific application of semantic knowledge. This publication channel should be of the highest interest to researchers and advanced practitioners working on the Semantic Web, interoperability, mobile information services, data warehousing, knowledge representation and reasoning, conceptual database modeling, ontologies, and artificial intelligence.

Topics of relevance to this journal include:

- Semantic interoperability, semantic mediators
- Ontologies
- Ontology, schema and data integration, reconciliation and alignment
- Multiple representations, alternative representations
- Knowledge representation and reasoning
- Conceptualization and representation
- Multi-model and multi-paradigm approaches
- Mappings, transformations, reverse engineering
- Metadata
- Conceptual data modeling
- Integrity description and handling
- Evolution and change

- Web semantics and semi-structured data
- Semantic caching
- Data warehousing and semantic data mining
- Spatial, temporal, multimedia and multimodal semantics
- Semantics in data visualization
- Semantic services for mobile users
- Supporting tools
- Applications of semantic-driven approaches

These topics are to be understood as specifically related to semantic issues. Contributions submitted to the journal and dealing with semantics of data will be considered even if they are not from the topics in the list.

While the physical appearance of the journal issues is like the books from the well-known Springer LNCS series, the mode of operation is that of a journal. Contributions can be freely submitted by authors and are reviewed by the Editorial Board. Contributions may also be invited, and nevertheless carefully reviewed, as in the case for issues that contain extended versions of best papers from major conferences addressing data semantics issues. Special issues, focusing on a specific topic, are coordinated by guest editors once the proposal for a special issue is accepted by the Editorial Board. Finally, it is also possible that a journal issue be devoted to a single text.

The Editorial Board comprises an Editor-in-Chief (with overall responsibility), a Co-editor-in-Chief, and several members. The Editor-in-Chief has a four-year mandate. Members of the board have a three-year mandate. Mandates are renewable and new members may be elected anytime.

We are happy to welcome you to our readership and authorship, and hope we will share this privileged contact for a long time.

Stefano Spaccapietra
Editor-in-Chief
http://lbd.epfl.ch/e/Springer/

Previous Issues

JoDS I	Special Issue on Extended Papers from 2002 Conferences, LNCS 2800, December 2003 Co-editors: Sal March and Karl Aberer
JoDS II	Special Issue on Extended Papers from 2003 Conferences, LNCS 3360, December 2004 Co-editors: Roger (Buzz) King, Maria Orlowska, Elisa Bertino, Dennis McLeod, Sushil Jajodia, and Leon Strous.
JoDS III	Special Issue on Semantic-Based Geographical Information Systems, LNCS 3534, 2005 Guest editor: Esteban Zimányi
JoDS IV	Normal Issue, LNCS 3730, December 2005
JoDS V	Special Issue on Extended Papers from 2004 Conferences, LNCS 3870, 2006 Co-editors: Paolo Atzeni, Wesley W. Chu, Tiziana Catarci, and Katia P. Sycara
JoDS VI	Special Issue on Emergent Semantics, LNCS 4090, 2006 Guest editors: Karl Aberer and Philippe Cudre-Mauroux
JoDS VII	Normal Issue, LNCS 4244, Autumn 2006
JoDS VIII	Special Issue on Extended Papers from 2005 Conferences, LNCS 4830, Winter 2006 Co-editors: Pavel Shvaiko, Mohand-Saïd Hacid, John Mylopoulos, Barbara Pernici, Juan Trujillo, Paolo Atzeni, Michael Kifer, François Fages, and Ilya Zaihrayeu
JoDS IX	Special Issue on Extended Papers from 2005 Conferences (continued), LNCS 4601, September 2007 Co-editors: Pavel Shvaiko, Mohand-Saïd Hacid, John Mylopoulos, Barbara Pernici, Juan Trujillo, Paolo Atzeni, Michael Kifer, François Fages, and Ilya Zaihrayeu

JoDS Volume X

This JoDS volume results from a rigorous selection among 26 full-paper submissions received in response to a call for contributions issued in July 2006.

After two rounds of reviews, eight papers spanning a wide variety of topics were eventually accepted for publication. They are listed in the table of contents.

We would like to thank the authors of all submitted papers as well as all reviewers who contributed to improving the papers through their detailed comments.

The forthcoming volume XI will contain extended versions of the best papers from 2006 conferences covering semantics aspects. Its publication is expected in early 2008.

We hope you'll enjoy reading this volume.

Stefano Spaccapietra
Editor-in-Chief
http://lbdwww.epfl.ch/e/Springer/

Organization

Reviewers

We are very grateful to the external reviewers listed below who helped the editorial board in the reviewing task:

Michel Adiba, Grenoble University, France
Bernhard Bauer, University of Augsburg, Germany
Davide Bresolin, University of Udine, Italy
Silvana Castano, University of Milan, Italy
Marco Comerio, University of Milano-Bicocca, Italy
Ying Ding, University of Innsbruck, Austria
Gillian Dobbie, University of Auckland, New Zealand
Guillermo Hess, University of Milan, Italy
Giancarlo Guizzardi, CNR Trento, Italy
Ian Horrocks, University of Manchester, UK
Hanjo Jeong, George Mason University, USA
Aditya Kalyanpur, IBM T.J. Watson Research Center, Hawthorne, USA
Roland Kaschek, Massey University, New Zealand
Stephen Kimani, J. Kenyatta University of Agriculture and Technology, Kenya
Andrei Lopatenko, Free University of Bozen-Bolzano, Italy
Luke McDowell, U.S. Naval Academy, USA
Salvador Mandujano, Intel Corporation, USA
Diego Milano, University of Rome "La Sapienza," Italy
Michele Missikoff, IASI-CNR, Rome, Italy
Angelo Montanari, University of Udine, Italy
Saravanan Muthaiyah, George Mason University, USA
Matteo Palmonari, University of Milano-Bicocca, Italy
Jeff Pan, The University of Aberdeen, UK
Antonella Poggi, University of Rome "La Sapienza," Italy
Alex Poulovassilis, University of London, UK
Elaheh Pourabbas, IASI-CNR, Rome, Italy
Pierre-Yves Schobbens, University of Namur, Belgium
Richard Snodgrass, University of Arizona Tucson, USA
Yong Uk Song, Yonsei University, South Korea
Alexei Tretiakov, Massey University, New Zealand
Denny Vrandecic, University of Karlsruhe, Germany

JoDS Editorial Board

Coeditors-in-Chief Lois Delcambre, Portland State University, USA
Stefano Spaccapietra, EPFL, Switzerland

Members of the Board

Carlo Batini, Università di Milano Bicocca, Italy
Alex Borgida, Rutgers University, USA
Shawn Bowers, University of California Davis, USA
Tiziana Catarci, Università di Roma La Sapienza, Italy
David W. Embley, Brigham Young University, USA
Jerome Euzenat, INRIA Alpes, France
Dieter Fensel, University of Innsbruck, Austria
Nicola Guarino, National Research Council, Italy
Jean-Luc Hainaut, FUNDP Namur, Belgium
Ian Horrocks, University of Manchester, UK
Arantza Illarramendi, Universidad del País Vasco, Spain
Larry Kerschberg, George Mason University, USA
Michael Kifer, State University of New York at Stony Brook, USA
Tok Wang Ling, National University of Singapore, Singapore
Shamkant B. Navathe, Georgia Institute of Technology, USA
Antoni Olivé, Universitat Politècnica de Catalunya, Spain
José Palazzo M. de Oliveira, Universidade Federal do Rio Grande do Sul, Brazil
Christine Parent, Université de Lausanne, Switzerland
John Roddick, Flinders University, Australia
Klaus-Dieter Schewe, Massey University, New Zealand
Heiner Stuckenschmidt, University of Mannheim, Germany
Katsumi Tanaka, University of Kyoto, Japan
Yair Wand, University of British Columbia, Canada
Eric Yu, University of Toronto, Canada
Esteban Zimányi, Université Libre de Bruxelles (ULB), Belgium

Table of Contents

Asymmetric and Context-Dependent Semantic Similarity Among
Ontology Instances 1
  Riccardo Albertoni and Monica De Martino

Query Relaxation in RDF 31
  Carlos A. Hurtado, Alexandra Poulovassilis, and Peter T. Wood

A Fine-Grained Approach to Resolving Unsatisfiable Ontologies 62
  *Joey Sik Chun Lam, Derek Sleeman, Jeff Z. Pan, and
  Wamberto Vasconcelos*

Deploying Semantic Web Services-Based Applications in the
e-Government Domain 96
  *Alessio Gugliotta, John Domingue, Liliana Cabral, Vlad Tanasescu,
  Stefania Galizia, Rob Davies, Leticia Gutierrez Villarias,
  Mary Rowlatt, Marc Richardson, and Sandra Stincic*

Linking Data to Ontologies 133
  *Antonella Poggi, Domenico Lembo, Diego Calvanese,
  Giuseppe De Giacomo, Maurizio Lenzerini, and Riccardo Rosati*

Context Representation in Domain Ontologies and Its Use for Semantic
Integration of Data 174
  Guy Pierra

Semantically Processing Parallel Colour Descriptions 212
  Shenghui Wang and Jeff Z. Pan

A Cooperative Approach for Composite Ontology Mapping 237
  Cássia Trojahn, Márcia Moraes, Paulo Quaresma, and Renata Vieira

Author Index 265

Asymmetric and Context-Dependent Semantic Similarity among Ontology Instances

Riccardo Albertoni and Monica De Martino

CNR-IMATI,
Via De Marini, 6 – Torre di Francia - 16149 Genova, Italy
{albertoni, demartino}@ge.imati.cnr.it

Abstract. In this paper we propose an asymmetric semantic similarity among instances within an ontology. We aim to define a measurement of semantic similarity that exploit as much as possible the knowledge stored in the ontology taking into account different hints hidden in the ontology definition. The proposed similarity measurement considers different existing similarities, which we have combined and extended. Moreover, the similarity assessment is explicitly parameterised according to the criteria induced by the context. The parameterisation aims to assist the user in the decision making pertaining to similarity evaluation, as the criteria can be refined according to user needs. Experiments and an evaluation of the similarity assessment are presented showing the efficiency of the method.

1 Introduction

Semantic similarity plays an important role in information systems as it supports the identification of objects that are conceptually close but not identical. Similarity assessment is particularly significant in different areas of knowledge management (such as data retrieval, information integration, and data mining) because it facilitates the comparison of the information resources in different types of domain knowledge [1,2].

Nowadays domain knowledge is often available in the form of an ontology, which reflects the understanding of a domain that a community has agreed upon. An ontology consists of different parts, including a set of concepts and their mutual relations and instances. In particular, ontologies have recently been imposed as means of organizing the *metadata* (called ontology-driven metadata) of complex information resources. According to Sheth et al. [3] ontology-driven metadata provide syntactic and semantic information about complex information resources. *Syntactic metadata* describe non-contextual information about the content (e.g. language, a bit rate, format). This offers no insight into the meaning of a document. In contrast, *semantic metadata* describe domain specific information about the content and contextual information, such as which entities take part in the production and usage of the information resource. The metadata of the resources are encoded as instances in the ontology. Therefore, the definition of a method for assessing the semantic similarity among ontology instances becomes essential in order to compare all these complex resources.

The concept of similarity among information resources is not univocal as it is affected by the human way of thinking as well as by the application domain [4]. Its evaluation cannot ignore some cognitive properties related to the human way of perceiving the similarity. In particular, we underline three main aspects. Firstly, considering that, in the naïve view of the word, similarities defined in terms of a conceptual distance are frequently asymmetric, the formulation of similarity should for many applications provide an asymmetric evaluation [5]. Secondly, it should be flexible and adaptable to different application contexts, which affect the similarity criteria. Moreover, considering that part of the domain knowledge as it is perceived by the domain expert is already formalized in the ontology and the ontologies are artefacts whose definitions require time consuming and costly processes, the similarity evaluation should be able to exploit as much as possible all the hints that have already been expressed in the ontology.

So far, most of the research activity pertaining to similarity and ontologies has been carried out within the field of ontology alignment or in order to assess the similarity among concepts. Unfortunately, these methods produce results that are inappropriate for the similarity among instances. On the one hand, similarities for ontology alignment strongly focus on the comparison of the structural parts of distinct ontologies, and their application for assessing the similarity among instances might give misleading results. On the other hand, similarities among concepts mainly deal with the lexicographic database, ignoring the comparison of the values of the instances. Apart from these, few methods for assessing similarities among instances have been proposed. Unfortunately, these methods rarely take into account the different hints hidden in the ontology, and they do not consider that the ontology entities concur differently in the similarity assessment according to the application.

To overcome the limitations mentioned above, our ongoing research is aimed at defining a framework for assessing the semantic similarity among instances. This paper proposes an asymmetric similarity assessment, where the asymmetry is explicitly adopted to stress the principle of "containment" between the two sets of characteristics of two instances representative of two information resources. The similarity between two instances tends to be greater for instances that have a higher level of containment.

The measurement of the asymmetric semantic similarity is defined by an amalgamation function. The amalgamation function combines and extends different similarities already defined in literature: it takes into account both the structural comparison between two instances, in terms of the classes that the instances belong to, and the comparison between the attributes and relations of the instances. Moreover, the framework provides a parametric evaluation of the similarity with respect to different applications. The application induces the criteria of similarity, which are explicitly formalized in the application context. An application context models the importance of the entities, which concur in the assessment of similarity, and the operations used to compare the instances. The parametric evaluation allows us to tailor the similarity assessment to specific application contexts, but also allows us to obtain different similarity assessments employing the same ontology.

The main framework contributions are:

- To exploit as much as possible the implicit knowledge stored in the ontology: the similarity assessment is set up by considering different kinds of hints in the ontology.
- To tailor the similarity assessment according to the needs arising from the specific application contexts: different similarity assessments can be defined for the same ontology, according to the criteria arising from different applications.
- To improve the decision making of the user in the similarity evaluation: as the similarity assessment is completely parameterized on context criteria, the criteria can be refined according to user needs.

This paper is an extension of an ongoing research programme whose first result has been presented previously [6]. Here, we aim to provide more information useful for exploiting our similarity evaluation: detailed illustrations of the motivations that are behind the principle of our approach are discussed and some scenarios are illustrated. In addition, the asymmetric property in the assessment is stressed and argued more deeply with each equation. The paper is organized as follows. In the first section, we illustrate the motivation and the scenario that drove us to the similarity definition. Then, after providing some useful assumptions (section 3), we discuss the main principle of the approach (section 4). The approach description is characterised by three main parts: context, ontology, data and knowledge layers according with the framework proposed by Ehrig et al. [7]. A formalization of the similarity criteria induced by the context is proposed as context layer (section 5). The ontology layer (section 6) and data and knowledge layer (section 7) are devoted to the definition of the similarity functions that characterize our approach, followed by two experiments and an evaluation of the results (section 8). At the end, we evaluate related works (section 9), underlining how they have been useful as a starting point for our research but how, contrary to the proposed framework, they do not fulfil the requirements and goal we address by our contributions.

2 Motivations and Scenarios

This section discusses the motivations that are behind the design of our approach as well as the reference scenario that has been developed with respect to this work.

2.1 Motivations

Here we provide the motivations behind our approach underlying the need of a similarity evaluation among ontology instances that takes into account the hints hidden in the ontology as well as the dependence on the context. In particular, we aim to answer the following questions:

- Why define a semantic similarity among ontology instances?
- What is the role of the implicit knowledge expressed by the ontology in setting up a similarity assessment?
- What is the role of the application context in the similarity evaluation?

Why define a semantic similarity among ontology instances?
Defining a semantic similarity among ontology instances represents a challenging priority in future research as it will pave the way for the next wave of knowledge intensive methods that will facilitate intelligent browsing as well as information analysis.

Here we do not refer to similarity as a tool for identifying possible mapping or alignment among different ontologies. Rather, we address a different problem related to the comparison of the ontology instances. We realize the importance of solving this problem from our direct research experience working in the European founded Network of Excellence AIM@SHAPE [8].

Within the NoE AIM@SHAPE, ontology has been adopted to organize the metadata of complex information resources. Different ontologies are integrated to describe 3D / 2D models (i.e. models of mechanical objects, digital terrains or artefacts from cultural heritage) as well as the tools for processing the models [9,10,11]. From our experience, we realize that the ontology driven metadata definition turns out to be outrageously expensive in terms of man-month efforts needed, especially whenever the domain that is expected to be formalized is complex and compound. The "standard ontology technology" provides reasoning facilities that are very useful in supporting querying activity as well as in checking ontology consistency, but the current technology lacks an effective tool for comparing the resources (instances). In addition to efforts to formalize the ontology, domain experts are often quite willing to provide the domain knowledge required to characterize their resources. However, they are disappointed when their efforts do not result in any measure of similarity among the resources.

Aware of this shortcoming, we address our research efforts towards investigating how to better employ the information encoded in the ontology and to provide tools that exploit as much as possible the result of the aforementioned efforts [6,12].

What is the role of the knowledge expressed by the ontology in setting up a similarity assessment?
An ontology reflects the understanding of a domain, which a community has agreed upon. Gruber defines an ontology as "the specification of conceptualizations, used to help programs and humans share knowledge" [13].
There is a strong dependence between the knowledge provided by the domain expert in order to define the ontology and his expectation of the results of the semantic similarity. Actually, the domain expert will perceive a similarity that is based on the knowledge he has provided.

The main ontology components (concepts, relations, instances) as well as its structure are representative of the domain knowledge conceptualized in the ontology. Therefore, they provide the base on which to set up the different hints to define the similarity. Classes provide knowledge about the set of entities within the domain. Properties, namely relations and attributes, provide information about the interactions between classes as well as further knowledge about the characteristics of concepts. Moreover, the class structure within the ontology is also relevant as the attributes and relations shared by the classes, as well as their depth in the ontology graph, are representative of the level of similarity among their instances. In our proposal, the similarity assessment takes advantage of all of these ontology entities, which are usually available in the most popular ontology languages. Other entities could be considered as long as more specific ontology languages are adopted.

What is the role of the application context in the similarity evaluation?
The definition of a similarity explicitly parameterized according to the context is essential because the similarity criteria depend on the application context. Two instances may be more closely related to each other in one context than in another since humans compare the instances according to their characteristics but the characteristics adopted vary with the context.

In particular, as a consequence of the explicit parameterization of the similarity with respect to the application context, it is possible to:

- Use the same ontology for different application contexts. The ontology design usually ignores the need to tailor the semantic similarity according to specific application contexts. In that case, to assess the similarity between two different applications, two distinct ontologies need to be defined instead of simply defining two contexts.
- Provide a tool for context tuning that supports the decision-making process of the ontology user. The user often has not clearly defined in his mind the set of characteristics relevant for the comparison of the instances, or his specification does not match the result induced by the information system. A parameterization of the semantic similarity measurement supports a refinement process of the similarity criteria. The parameterization provides a flexible and adaptable way to refine the assessment toward the expected results and, therefore, it reduces the gap between user-expected and system results.

2.2 Framework Scenario

We have identified two main scenarios where the proposed similarity framework is relevant: scenario 1 refers to a similarity evaluation in different application contexts exploiting the same ontology; scenario 2 refers to the iterative criteria refinement process used to properly assess the similarity in accord with the expectations of the domain expert.

In both scenarios we assume that we have an ontology describing the metadata of the resources in a complex domain and that the different resources are already annotated according to this ontology driven metadata.

Two actors play important roles in the two scenarios:

- The user who is the domain expert and who is looking for the semantic similarity. He has the proper knowledge to formulate the similarity criteria in the domain.
- The ontology engineer who is in charge of defining the similarity assessment on the basis of the ontology design and the information provided by the domain expert. He plays the role of communication channel for the requests of the domain expert, with the system defining the application context to properly parameterize the similarity assessment.

2.2.1 Scenario 1: Two Different Application Contexts

Fig. 1 illustrates the first scenario, which highlights the dependence of the similarity result on the similarity criteria induced by the application. The domain expert user formulates different similarity criteria in two different application contexts. The two sets of criteria are formalized by the ontology engineer according to the system formalization, and the evaluation is performed. Two different results of the similarity evaluation are provided by the system and represented by similarity matrices. It is evident in this scenario how two application contexts induce two different similarity matrices just by exploiting the same ontology.

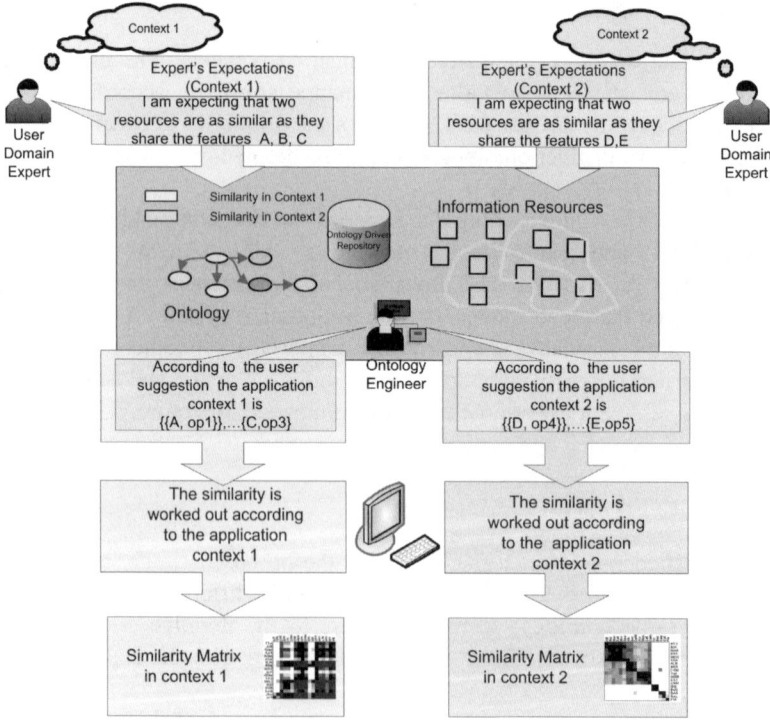

Fig. 1. Scenario 1: similarity evaluation according to different application contexts

2.2.2 Scenario 2: Similarity Criteria Refinement

This scenario is characterized by an interactive exchange of information between the two actors. The domain expert browses the repository looking for similar resources. He relies on his domain of knowledge to compare the resources, perceives the similarities among resources (which are not provided directly from the standard ontology reasoning technology), and provides some informal similarity criteria to be adopted in the similarity evaluation. The ontology engineer translates the user requests to the system: he figures out which ontology entities are relevant and how to use them during the similarity assessment. The ontology engineer runs the similarity evaluation proposed in this paper and he shows the result to the domain expert.

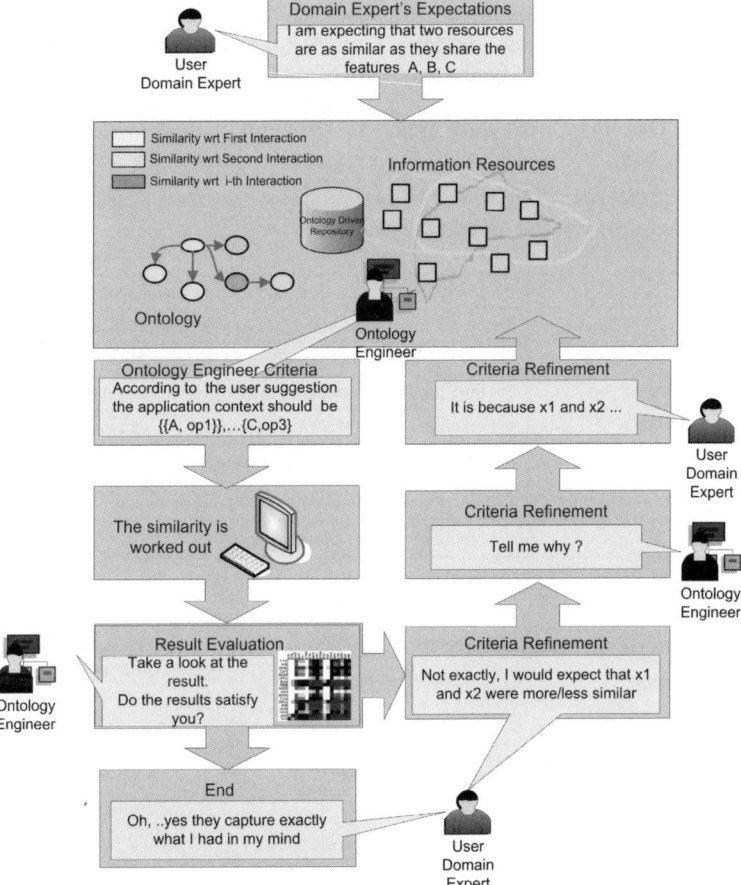

Fig. 2. Scenario 2: similarity criteria refinement

Analysing the result, the domain expert might point out some unexpected result to the ontology engineer. Then the ontology engineer refines the similarity criteria, interacting with the domain expert, until the results are correct.

We assume that usually the user expert is so familiar with the domain conceptualized in the ontology that his expectations about similarities are often implicit. Thus, he does not provide to the ontology engineer a complete set of information concerning the criteria of similarity to be used. With this assumption the criteria definition process requires further iterative refinement.

In this scenario the framework supports the iterative criteria refinement process to precisely adapt the similarity assessments to the user expectations.

3 Preliminary Assumptions

This paper proposes a semantic similarity among instances taking into account the different hints hidden in the ontology. As the hints that can be considered largely depend on the level of formality of the ontology model adopted, it is important to state clearly to which ontology model a similarity method is referring. In this paper, the ontology model with data type defined by Ehrig et al. [7] is considered.

Definition 1: Ontology with data type. *An Ontology with data type is a structure* $O := (C, T, \leq_c, R, A, \sigma_R, \sigma_A, \leq_R, \leq_A, I, V, l_C, l_T, l_R, l_A)$ *where* C, T, R, A, I, V *are disjoint sets, respectively, of classes, data types, binary relations, attributes, instances and data values, and the relations and functions are defined as follows:*

$\leq_C$	the partial order on C, which defines the classes hierarchy,
$\leq_R$	the partial order on R which defines the relation hierarchy,
$\leq_A$	the partial order on A which defines the attribute hierarchy,
$\sigma_R : R \to C \times C$	the function that provides the signature for each relation,
$\sigma_A : A \to C \times T$	the function that provides the signature for each attribute,
$l_C : C \to 2^I$	the function called class instantiation,
$l_T : T \to 2^V$	the function called data type instantiation,
$l_R : R \to 2^{I \times I}$	the function called relation instantiation,
$l_A : A \to 2^{I \times V}$	the function called attribute instantiation.

A symmetric normalized similarity is a function $S : I \times I \to [0,1]$, which satisfies the following axioms:

$\forall x, y \in I \quad S(x,y) \geq 0$ *Positiveness*

$\forall x \in I, \forall y, z \in I, S(x,x) \geq S(y,z)$ *Maximality*

$\forall x, y \in I \quad S(x,y) = S(y,x)$ *Symmetry*

An asymmetric normalized similarity is a function $\bar{S} : I \times I \to [0,1]$ that does not satisfy the symmetric axioms. The preference between symmetric and asymmetric similarity mainly depends on the application scenario; in general, there is no a-priori reason to formulate this choice. A complete framework for assessing the semantic similarity should be provided by both of them.

The preference between symmetric and asymmetric similarity mainly depends on the application scenario; often the symmetric similarity is preferred because it is mathematically closer to the inverse of distance measure than the asymmetric one. However, according to the assumption of Tvesky, often a non-prominent item is more similar to a prominent item than vice versa [14]. In this paper we chose to propose an asymmetric similarity because we think it is more informative. This informativeness is useful for example in application such as the browsing of information resources.

During the browsing, we need to identify similar resources that are representative of a searched resource and that can be used to replace it. For instance if we consider as information resources the members of a research staff, and we suppose to search for a member with a specific scientific expertise, usually a *PhD student* can be replaced by his *PhD advisor*, because the experience of a *PhD student* is usually contained in the expertise of his *PhD advisor* but the vice versa is not true. As a consequence the similarity between the *PhD student* and his *PhD advisor* is greater than the similarity between the *PhD advisor* and his *PhD student*. The symmetric similarity is not suitable to support this characteristic of containment.

Then a representative resource is the resource that includes others. A similar approach has been proposed in [15] for the retrieval of documents. We stress the relation of containment between the sets of characteristics of two information resources. The information resources are characterized by ontology driven metadata; therefore, each resource is assumed to be an instance and the similarity is defined among pairs of instances.

Definition 2: Containment between two information resources/instances. *Given two information resources x, y (represented as instances in the ontology) and their sets of characteristics (coded as instance attributes and relation values), x is contained in y if the set of characteristics of x is contained[1] in the set of characteristics of y.*

We assume that instance similarity behaves coherently with the concept of containment. Given two instances x, y, their similarity is sim(x,y)=1 if and only if the set of characteristics of x is contained in the set of characteristics of y. On the contrary, unless y is contained in x, the similarity between y and x is sim(y,x)<1. The similarity value between x and y tends to decrease as long as the level of containment of their sets of properties decreases. Of course, the containment has to consider also the inheritance between the classes: if x belongs to a sub-class of the class of y, the asymmetric evaluation is performed relying on the idea that humans perceive similarity between a sub-concept and its super-concept as greater than the similarity between the super-concept and the sub-concept [16].

4 Semantic Similarity Approach

The proposed approach adopts the schematization of the similarity framework defined by Ehrig et.al. [7]: the similarity is structured in terms of *data, ontology* and *context* layers plus the *domain knowledge* layer, which spans all the others. The *data layer* measures the similarity of entities by considering the data values of simple or complex data types such as integers and strings. The *ontology layer* considers the similarities induced by the ontology entities and the way they are related to each other. The *context layer* assesses the similarity according to how the entities of the ontology are used in some external contexts. The framework defined by Ehrig et al. is suitable for supporting the ontology similarity as well as instances similarity.

Our contribution with respect to the framework defined by Ehrig et al. is mainly in the definition of a *context layer* including an accurate formalization of the criteria in order to tailor the similarity with respect to a context and in the definition of an *ontology layer* explicitly parameterized according to these criteria. Concerning the data and domain knowledge layers, this paper adopts a replica of what is illustrated in [7]. The formalization of the criteria of similarity induced by the context is employed to parameterize the computation of the similarity in the *ontology layer*, forcing it to adhere to the application criteria.

---

[1] The containment is not meant as proper containment. In other words each set A is considered as an A subset.

The overall similarity is defined by the following amalgamation function ($\overline{Sim}$), which aggregates two similarity functions defined in the ontology layer named *external similarity* ($\overline{ExternSim}$) and *extensional similarity* ($\overline{ExtensSim}$). The external similarity performs a structural comparison between two instances $i_1 \in I_c(c_1)$, $i_2 \in I_c(c_2)$ in terms of the classes c_1, c_2 that the instances belong to, whereas the extensional similarity performs a comparison of the instances in terms of their attributes and relations.

$$\overline{Sim}(i_1, i_2) = \frac{w_{ExternSim} * \overline{ExternSim}(i_1, i_2) + w_{ExtensSim} * \overline{ExtensSim}(i_1, i_2)}{w_{ExternSim} + w_{ExtensSim}} \quad (1)$$

$w_{ExternSim}$ and $w_{ExtensSim}$ are the weights used to balance the importance of the functions. By default they are equal to 1/2.

In the section, we have illustrated a full description of the approach. In the next, the approach is detailed in three sections. In particular our definition of context layer is described in detail as well as the ontology layer where the two similarities $\overline{ExternSim}$ and $\overline{ExtensSim}$ are designed, while the description of data and knowledge layer is shortly provided.

5 Context Layer

The context layer, according to Ehrig at al. [7], describes how the ontology entities concur in different contexts. Here we adopt the same point of view. However, we aim to formalize the application context in the sense of modelling the criteria of similarity induced by the context. This design choice does not hamper the eventual definition of a generic description of context followed by an automatic determination of which criteria would have been suitable for a given context. Rather, it allows us to calculate directly the similarity acting on the criteria, especially when it is necessary to refine them. In the following we underscore the importance of this formalization.

5.1 Motivation Behind the Application Context Formalization

The application context provides the knowledge for formalizing the criteria of similarity induced by the application. The criteria are context-dependent as the context influences the choice of classes, attributes and relations that are considered in the similarity assessment and the operations used to compare them.

We describe the motivation behind the proposed formalization through an example based on the domain of academic research, considering as resources to be compared the researchers of a research institution. We chose this domain instead of a more specific area related to our research experience in the AIM@SHAPE project (such as solid modelling, 3D model reconstruction, virtual humans, etc.) as it is without doubt a more familiar field to the readers of this paper. Let us consider a simplified version of the ontology KA[2] that defines concepts from academic research (Fig. 3) and focus on the two applications "comparison of the members of the research staff according to their working experience" and "comparison of the members of the research staff with respect to their research interest".

---

[2] http://protege.stanford.edu/plugins/owl/owl-library/ka.owl

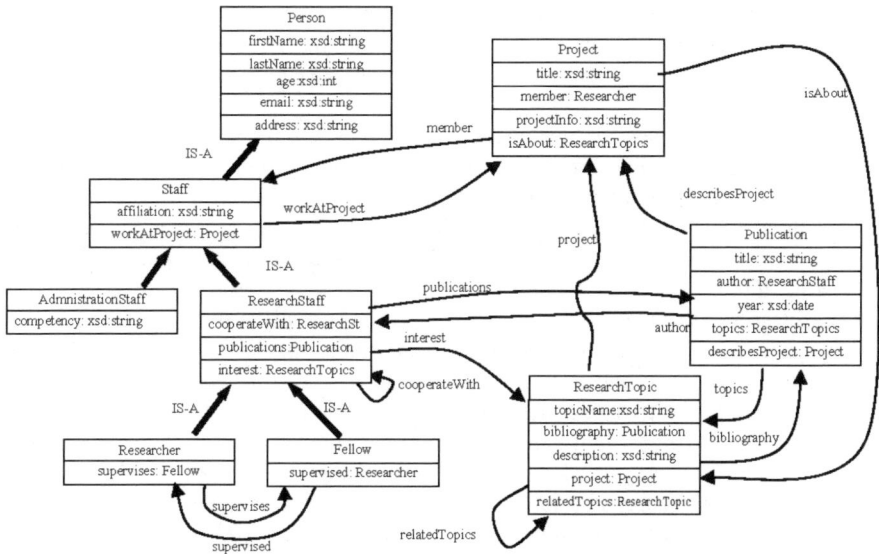

Fig. 3. Ontology defining concepts related to academic research

Two distinct application contexts may be induced according the applications:

- "Exp" induced by the comparison of the members of the research staff according to their working experience. The similarity among the members of the research staff (instances of the class *ResearchStaff*[3]) is roughly assessed by considering the member's age (the attribute *age* inherited by the class *Person*) and the number of projects and publications a researcher has worked on (the number of instances reachable through the relation *publications* and the relation *workAtProject* inherited by *Staff*).
- "Int" induced by the comparison of the members of the research staff with respect to their research interests. The researchers can be compared with respect to their interests (instances reachable through the relation *interest*) and, again, their publications (instances reachable through the relation *publications* and the relation *workAtProject*).

The following points need to be considered when analysing these examples:

1. The similarity between two instances can depend on the comparison of their related instances: the researchers are compared with respect to the instances of the class *Publication* connected through the relation *publications*.
2. The attributes and relations of the instances can contribute differently to the evaluation according to the context: the attribute *age* of the researchers is functional in the first application but it might not be interesting in the second; the

---

[3] The italics is used to explicit the reference to the entities (attributes, relations, classes) of the ontology in Fig 1.

relations *publication* and *workAtProject* are included in both application contexts but using different operators of comparison—in the first case just the number of instances is important whereas in the latter case the related instances have to be compared.
3. The ontology entities can be considered recursively in the similarity evaluation: in the context "Int" the members' research topic (instances of *ResearchTopic* reachable navigating through the relation *ResearchStaff->interest[4]*) are considered and their related topics (instances of *ResearchTopic* reachable via *ResearchStaff->interest->relatedTopic*) are recursively compared to assess the similarity of distinct topics.
4. The classes' attributes and relations can contribute differently to the evaluation according to the recursion level of the assessment: in the second application the attribute *topicName* and the relation *relatedTopic* can be considered at the first level of recursion to assess the similarity between *researchTopic*. By navigating the relation *relatedTopic* it is possible to apply another step of recursion, and here the similarity criteria can be different from the previous ones. For example, in order to limit the computational cost and stop the recursion, only the *topicName* or the instances identifier could be used to compare the *relatedTopic*.

As pointed out in the second remark, different operations can be used to compare the ontology entities:

- Operation based on the "cardinality" of the attributes or relations: the similarity is assessed according to the number of instances the relations have or the number of values that an attribute assumes. For example, in the first context "Exp", two researchers are similar if they have a similar "number" of publications.
- Operation based on the "intersection" between sets of attributes or relations: the similarity is assessed according to the number of elements they have in common. For example, in the context "Int", the more papers two researchers share, the more their interests are similar.

Operation based on the "similarity" of attributes and relations: the similarity is assessed in terms of the similarity of the attribute values and related instances. For example, in the context "Int", two researchers are similar if they have "similar" research topics.

The example shows that an accurate formalism is needed to properly express the criteria that might arise from different application contexts. The formalization has to model the attributes and relations as well as the operations to compare their values. Moreover, as stated in the fourth remark, the level of recursion of the similarity assessment also has to be considered.

5.2 Application Context Formalization

The formalization provided here represents the restrictions that the application context must adhere to. An ontology engineer is expected to provide the application context

---

[4] The arrow is used to indicate the navigation through a relation, for example $A->B->C$ means that starting from the class A we navigate through the relations B and C.

according to specific application needs. The formalization relies on the concepts of a "sequence of elements belonging to a set X", which formalizes generic sequences of elements, and a "path of recursion of length i" to track the recursion during the similarity assessment. In particular, a "path of recursion" represents the recursion in terms of the sequence of relations used to navigate the ontology.

The application context function (*AC*) is defined inductively according to the length of the path of recursion. It yields the set of attributes and relations as well as the operations to be used in the similarity assessment. The operations considered are those described in the previous section and named, respectively, *Count* to evaluate the cardinality, *Inter* to evaluate the intersection, and *Simil* to evaluate the similarity.

Definition 3: Sequences of a set X. *Given a set X, a sequence s of elements of X with length n is defined by the function* $s:[1,...,n] \to X, n \in N^+$ *and represented in a simple way by the list [s(1),...,s(n)].*

Let $S_X^n = \{s \mid s:[1,n] \to X\}$ be the set of sequences of X having length n.

Let $\cdot : S_X^n \times S_Y^m \to S_{X \cup Y}^{n+m}$ be the operator "concat" between two sequences.

Table 1 defines the polymorphism functions, which identify specific sets of entities in the ontology model.

Table 1. List of functions defining specific sets of elements in the ontology model

$\delta_a : C \to 2^A; \delta_a(c) = \{a : A \mid \exists\, t \in T, \sigma_A(a) = (c,t)\}$	set of attributes of $c \in C$,
$\delta_a : R \to 2^A$; $\delta_a(r) = \{a : A \mid \exists\, c, c' \in C\ \exists\, t \in T\ \sigma_R(r) = (c, c') \wedge \sigma_A(a) = (c', t)\}$	set of attributes of the classes which are reachable through the relation $r \in R$,
$\delta_r : C \to 2^R; \delta_r(c) = \{r : R \mid \exists\, c' \in C, \sigma_R(r) = (c, c')\}$	set of relations of $c \in C$,
$\delta_c : R \to 2^C; \delta_c(r) = \{c' : C \mid \exists\, c \in C\ \ \sigma_R(r) = (c, c')\}$	set of concepts reachable through $r \in R$,
$\delta_r : R \to 2^R$; $\delta_r(r) = \{r' : R \mid \exists\, c \in C, \exists\, c' \in \delta_C(r), \wedge \sigma_R(r') = (c', c)\}$	set of relations of the concepts reachable through r,
$\delta_c : C \to 2^C; \delta_c(c) = \{c' : C \mid \exists\, r \in \delta_r(c); \sigma_R(r) = (c, c')\}$	set of concepts related to $c \in C$ through a relation.

Definition 4: Path of recursion. *A path of recursion p with length i is a sequence whose first element is a class and whose other elements are relations recursively reachable from the class:* $p \in S_{C \cup R}^i \mid p(1) \in C \wedge \forall j \in [2, i]\ p(j) \in R \wedge p(j) \in \delta_r(p(j-1))$.

For example, a path of recursion with length longer than three is a path that starts from a class p(1) and continues to one of its relations as the second element p(2) and then to one of the relations of the class reachable from p(2) as the third element p(3), and so on. In general, a path of recursion p represents a path that is followed to assess the similarity recursively. The recursion expressed in the previous section in the context "Int" as *ResearchStaff->interest->relatedTopic* is formalized with the path of recursion [ResearchStaff, interest, relatedTopic].

Let P^i be the set of all paths of recursion with length i and P be the set of all paths of recursion $P = \cup_{i \in N} P^i$.

Definition 5: Application context AC. *Given the set P of paths of recursion, L = {Count, Inter, Simil}, the set of operations adopted as an application context is defined by a partial function AC having the signature $AC: P \to (2^{A \times L}) \times (2^{R \times L})$, yielding the attributes and relations as well as the operations to perform their comparison.*

In particular, each application context AC is characterized by two operators $AC_A: P \to 2^{A \times L}$ and $AC_R: P \to 2^{R \times L}$, which yield, respectively, the parts of the context AC related to the attributes and the relations. Formally $\forall p \in P \; AC(p) = (AC_A(p), AC_R(p))$ and $AC_A(p)$ and $AC_R(p)$ are set of pairs $\{(e_1, o_1), (e_2, o_2), \ldots, (e_i, o_i), \ldots, (e_n, o_n)\}$ $n \in N$ where e_i is, respectively, the attribute or the relation relevant to define the similarity criteria and $o_i \in L$ is the operation to be used in the comparison.

We provide two examples of AC formalization referring to the two application contexts "Exp" and "Int" mentioned in the previous section.

Example 1. Let us formalize the application context "Exp" with AC_{Exp} to assess the similarity among the members of a research staff according to their experience. We consider the set of paths of recursion {[ResearchStaff], [Research], [Fellow]} and we compare them according to age similarity and the numbers of publications and projects. Thus AC_{Exp} is defined by:

$$[ResearchStaff] \xrightarrow{AC_{Exp}} \{\{(age, Simil)\}, \{(publications, Count), (workAtProject, Count)\}\} \quad (2)$$

$$[Researcher] \xrightarrow{AC_{Exp}} \{\{(age, Simil)\}, \{(publications, Count), (workAtProject, Count)\}\}$$

$$[Fellow] \xrightarrow{AC_{Exp}} \{\{(age, Simil)\}, \{(publications, Count), (workAtProject, Count)\}\}$$

An example of AC_R is {(publication, Count), (workAtProject, Count)} while an example of AC_A is {(age, Simil)}.

Note that [Researcher] and [Fellow] belong to the set of paths of recursion considered in AC_{Exp} because their instances are also instances of *ResearchStaff*. The application context can be expressed in a more compact way assuming that, whenever a context is not defined for a class but is defined for its super class, the comparison criteria defined for a super class are by default inherited by the subclasses. According to this assumption AC_{Exp} can be expressed by:

$$[ResearchStaff] \xrightarrow{AC_{Exp}} \{\{age, Simil\}, \{(publications, Count), (workAtProject, Count)\}\} \quad (3)$$

Example 2. Let us formalize the application context "Int" to assess the similarity among the members of a research staff according to their research interest. The similarity is computed considering the set of paths of recursion {[ResearchStaff], [ResearchStaff, interest]}. The researchers are compared considering common publications, common projects or similar interests. A compact formalization for "Int" is defined by AC_{Int}:

$$[ResearchStaff] \xrightarrow{AC_{Int}} \{\{\emptyset\}, \{(publications, Inter), (workAtProject, Inter), (interest, Simil)\}\} \quad (4)$$

$$[ResearchStaff, interest] \xrightarrow{AC_{Int}} \{\{topicName, Inter\}, \{(relatedTopics, Inter)\}\}$$

In general, the operator *Count* applied to attributes or relations means that the number of attribute values or related instances is considered in the similarity assessment. For example, according to the context formalized in equation 2 (second row), two researchers, who are represented as instances of *Researcher,* are similar if they have a similar numbers of instances of *Publication* reachable through the relation *publications.*

The operator *Inter* applied to attributes or relations means that common attribute values or related instances are considered in the similarity assessment. For example, according to the context formalized in equation 4 (first row) two researchers are considered as similar if they have common project instances.

When applied to an attribute, the operator *Simil* determines that the attribute values of two instances will be compared according to a datatype similarity provided by the data layer (see the example in equation 2, first row, attribute age). When it is applied to a relation, it determines a step of recursion, in the sense that the instances related through the relation have to be considered during the similarity assessment. How these related instances have to be compared is specified by the value provided by the context function for the corresponding recursion path. Note that the researchers are compared recursively in the context expressed by equation 4. In fact the relation *interest* is included with the operator *Simil* in the first row of equation 4. This means that the instances of *ResearchTopic* associated with the researcher via *interest* have to be accessed and compared recursively when the researchers' similarity is worked out. Actually, [ResearchStaff,interest] is the path of recursion to navigating the ontology from *ResearchStaff* to *ResearchTopic* via the relation *interest.* Once the assessment has accessed the related instances, it compares them as indicated by the second row of equation 4. The interests are compared with respect to both their *topicName* and their *relatedTopic*; thus, two *ResearchTopics* having distinct *topicNames* but some *relatedTopics* in common are not considered completely dissimilar.

The image of an AC function can be further characterized by the following.

1. For a path of recursion p, AC has to yield only the attributes and relations belonging to the classes reached through p. For example, considering the ontology in Fig. 3 and the path of recursion [ResearchStaff,interest], it is expected that only the attributes and relations belonging to the class *ResearchTopic* reachable via [ResearchStaff,interest] can be identified by AC([ResearchStaff,interest]). Attributes or relations (such as *age, publications, etc),* which do not belong to *ResearchTopic,* define an incorrect application context.
2. Given a path of recursion p, an attribute or a relation can appear in the context image at most one time. In other words, given a path of recursion it is not possible to associate two distinct operations with the same relation or attribute. For example, the following application context definition is not correct as *interest* is specified twice

$$[\text{ResearchStaff}] \longrightarrow \{\{\phi\}, \{(\text{publications, Inter}), (\text{interest, Simil}), (\text{interest, Inter})\}\} \quad (5)$$

6 Ontology Layer

The ontology layer defines the asymmetric similarity functions $\overline{ExternSim}$ and $\overline{ExtensSim}$ that constitute the amalgamation function (equation 1). The "external similarity" $\overline{ExternSim}$ measures the similarity at the level of the ontology schema computing a structural comparison of the instances. Given two instances, it compares the classes they belong to, considering the attributes and relations shared by the classes and their position within the class hierarchy. The "extensional similarity" $\overline{ExtensSim}$ compares the extension of the ontology entities. The similarity is assessed by computing the comparison of the attributes and relations of the instances.

At the ontology layer additional hypotheses are assumed:

- All classes defined in the ontology have the fake class *Thing* as a super-class.
- Given $i_1 \in l_c(c_1)$, $i_2 \in l_c(c_2)$, if c_1, c_2 do not have any common super-class different from *Thing*, their similarity is equal to 0.
- The least upper bound (*lub*) between c_1 and c_2 is unique and it is c_2 if c_1 IS-A c_2, or c_1 if c_2 IS-A c_1, or the immediate super-class of c_1 and c_2 that subsumes both classes.

The aim is to force the *lub* to be a sort of "template class" that can be adopted to perform the comparison of the instances whenever the instances belong to distinct classes. Referring to the ontology in Fig. 3, it can be appropriate to compare two instances belonging, respectively, to *AdministratorStaff* and *ResearchStaff* as they are both a kind of *Staff* and *Staff* is their *lub*. However, it does not make sense to evaluate the similarity between two instances belonging to *Publication* and to *Staff*, because they are intimately different; in fact, there is not any *lub* available for them. Whenever a *lub* x between two classes exists, the path of recursion [x] is the starting path in the recursive evaluation of the similarity.

6.1 External Similarity

The external similarity ($\overline{ExternSim}$) performs the structural comparison between two instances i_1, i_2 in terms of the classes c_1, c_2 that the instances belong to: more formally $\overline{ExternSim}(i_1,i_2) = \overline{ExternSim}(c_1,c_2)$ where $i_1 \in l_c(c_1), i_2 \in l_c(c_2)$.

In this paper the external similarity function is defined starting from the similarities proposed by Maedche and Zacharias [17] and Rodriguez and Egenhofer [16]. The structural comparison is performed by two similarity evaluations:

- **Class Matching**, which is based on the distance between the classes c_1, c_2 and their depth with respect to the hierarchy induced by $\leq_C$.
- **Slot Matching**, which is based on the number of attributes and relations shared by the classes c_1, c_2 and the overall number of their attributes and relations. Then two classes having many attributes/relations, some of which are in common, are less similar than two classes having fewer attributes but the same number of common attributes/relations.

Both similarities are needed to successfully evaluate the similarity with respect to the ontology structure. For example, let us consider the ontology schema in Fig. 3 and let us compare an instance of the class *ResearchStaff* with an instance of the class *AdministrationStaff*.

They are quite similar with respect to Class Matching but less similar with respect to Slot Matching. In fact, the sets of IS-A relations joining the classes *ResearchStaff* and *AdministrationStaff* to *Thing* are largely shared. However, from the point of view of the slots, *ResearchStaff* and *AdministrationStaff* share only the attribute inherited and they differ with respect to the others. Likewise, it would be easy to show an example of two classes that are similar with respect to Slot Matching and less similar according to Class Matching.

Definition 6: ExternSim similarity. *The similarity between two classes according to the external comparison is defined by:*

$$\overline{ExternSim}(c_1,c_2) = \begin{cases} 1 & \text{if } c_1 = c_2 \\ \dfrac{w_{SM}*\overline{SM}(c_1,c_2)+w_{CM}*\overline{CM}(c_1,c_2)}{w_{SM}+w_{CM}} & \text{Otherwise} \end{cases} \quad (6)$$

where ($\overline{SM}$) is Slots Matching, ($\overline{CM}$) is Classes Matching and w_{SM}, w_{CM} are weights in the range [0,1].

For the purpose of this paper, w_{SM} and w_{CM} are defined as equal to 1/2.

6.1.1 Class Matching

Classes Matching is evaluated in terms of the distance of the classes with respect to the IS-A hierarchy. The distance is based on the concept of Upwards Cotopy (*UC*) [17]. We define an asymmetric similarity adapting the symmetric definition of CM in [17].

Definition 7: Upward Cotopy (UC). *The Upward Cotopy of a set of classes C with the associated partial order $\leq_C$ is:*

$$UC_{\leq_C}(c_i) := \{c_j \in C \mid (c_i \leq_C c_j) \vee c_i = c_j\} \quad (7)$$

It is the set of classes composing the path that reaches from c_i to the furthest superclass (*Thing*) of the IS-A hierarchy: for example, considering the class Researcher in Fig. 3 $UC_{\leq_C}$(Researcher) = {Researcher, ResearchStaff, Staff, Person, Thing[5]}

Definition 8: Asymmetric Class Matching. *Given two classes c_1, c_2 and the Upward Cotopy $UC_{\leq_C}(c_i)$, the asymmetric Class Matching is defined by:*

$$\overline{CM}(c_1,c_2) := \dfrac{|UC_{\leq_C}(c_1) \cap UC_{\leq_C}(c_2)|}{|UC_{\leq_C}(c_1)|} \quad (8)$$

$\overline{CM}$ between two classes depends on the number of classes they have in common in the hierarchy. Let us note that the Class Matching is asymmetric: for example, referring to Fig. 3, $\overline{CM}$(AdministrationStaff, Researcher) = 3/4 but $\overline{CM}$(Researcher, AdministrationStaff) = 3/5. Moreover it is important to note that

---

[5] The class Thing is not explicitly included in the **Fig. 3** but it is expected to be the super class of all the other classes, so it can be seen as superclass of Person, Project, Publication, ResearchTopic.

$\overline{CM}$ (Staff, Researcher) = 1. The rationale behind this choice of design pertains to the property of containment between instances: the instances of *Researcher* fit with the instances of *Staff*, and they can replace the instances of *Staff* at the class level.

6.1.2 Slot Matching

Slot Matching is defined by the slots (attributes and relations) shared by the two classes. We refer to the similarity proposed by Rodriguez and Egenhofer [16], based on the concept of distinguishing features employed to differentiate subclasses from their super-class. In their proposal, different kinds of distinguishing features are considered (i.e. functionalities and parts) but none coincides immediately with the native entities in our ontology model. Of course it would be possible to manually annotate the classes, adding the distinguishing features, but we prefer to focus on what is already available in the adopted ontology model. Therefore only attributes and relations are mapped as two kinds of distinguishing features.

Definition 9: Slot Matching. *Given two classes c_1, c_2, two kinds of distinguishing features (attributes and relations), and w_a, w_r, the weights of the features, the similarity function $\overline{SM}$ between c_1 and c_2 is defined in terms of the weighted sum of the similarities $\overline{S}_a$ and $\overline{S}_r$, where $\overline{S}_a$ is the Slot Matching according to the attributes and $\overline{S}_r$ in the Slot Matching according to the relations.*

$$\overline{SM}(c_1,c_2) = \omega_a \cdot \overline{S}_a(c_1,c_2) + \omega_r \cdot \overline{S}_r(c_1,c_2) \tag{9}$$

The sum of the weights is expected to be equal to 1, and by default we assume $w_a = w_r = 1/2$. The two Slot Matching similarities $\overline{S}_a$ and $\overline{S}_r$ rely on the definitions of slot importance as defined in the following.

Definition 10: Function of "slot importance" α. *Let c_1, c_2, be two distinct classes and d be the class distance $d(c_1,c_2)$ in terms of the number of edges in an IS-A hierarchy, then α is the function that evaluates the importance of the difference between the two classes.*

$$\alpha(c_1,c_2) = \begin{cases} \dfrac{d(c_1,\text{lub}(c_1,c_2))}{d(c_1,c_2)} & d(c_1,\text{lub}(c_1,c_2)) \leq d(c_2,\text{lub}(c_1,c_2)) \\ 1 - \dfrac{d(c_1,\text{lub}(c_1,c_2))}{d(c_1,c_2)} & d(c_1,\text{lub}(c_1,c_2)) > d(c_2,\text{lub}(c_1,c_2)) \end{cases} \tag{10}$$

where $d(c_1,c_2) = d(c_1,\text{lub}(c_1,c_2)) + d(c_2,\text{lub}(c_1,c_2))$.

α(c_1, c_2) is a value in the range [0,0.5]. Referring to the image in Fig. 3, α(Researcher,ResearchStaff) is equal to zero because the *lub* between *Researcher* and *Researcher* is *Researcher* itself, d(ResearchStaff,Researcher)=1 and d(Researcher,Researcher)=0. Whereas α(Researcher,Fellow) is equal to 0.5 because the *lub* is still *Researcher*, and d(Researcher,Fellow)=2.

Definition 11: Slot Matching according to the kind of distinguishing feature t. *Given two classes c_1 (target) and c_2 (base) and t, a kind of distinguishing feature (t=a* for attributes or $t=r$ for relations), let C_1^t and C_2^t be the sets of distinguishing features of type t, respectively, of c_1 and c_2; then Slot Matching $\overline{S}_t(c_1,c_2)$ is defined by:[6]

$$\overline{S}_t(c_1,c_2) = \frac{|C_1^t \cap C_2^t|}{|C_1^t \cap C_2^t| + (1-\alpha(c_1,c_2))|C_1^t \setminus C_2^t| + \alpha(c_1,c_2)|C_2^t \setminus C_1^t|} \quad (11)$$

According to the ontology in Fig. 3, considering the classes *Researcher* and *Fellow*, their sets of distinguishing features of type relation are Researcher^r ={workAtProject, cooperateWith, pubblications, interest, supervises} and Fellow^r={workAtProject, cooperateWith, pubblications, interest, supervised} and α(Fellow,Researcher)=0.5; then $\overline{S}_r$(Fellow,Researcher) = 4/5. Furthermore, this formulation of Class Matching is coherent to the containment property: considering the classes *Staff* and *Fellow*, their sets of distinguishing features of type relation are respectively Staff^r={workAtProject}, Fellow^r={workAtProject, cooperateWith, publications, interest, supervised} and α(Staff,Fellow)=0, so that $\overline{S}_r$(Staff,Fellow)=1. This means that the instances of *Fellow* can replace the instances of *Staff* because they have some quality more rather than less similar. The contrary is not true; in fact α(Fellow,Staff)=0 and $\overline{S}_r$(Fellow,Staff)=1/5. In general, whenever α=0.5 the differences between features of both classes are equally important for the matching: for example, this happens when the classes are sisters, as for *Researcher* and *Fellow*. In the case of α=0, only the features that are in c_1 and not in c_2 are important for the matching.

6.2 Extensional Similarity

The extension of entities plays a fundamental role in the assessment of the similarity among the instances: it is needed to perform a comparison of the attribute and relation values.

The extensional comparison is characterized by two similarities functions: a function based on the comparison of the attributes of the instances and a function based on the comparison of the relations of the instances.

Definition 12: Extensional asymmetric similarity *Given two instances $i_1 \in I_c(c_1)$, $i_2 \in I_c(c_2)$, $c=lub(c_1,c_2)$ and $p=[c]$, a path of recursion defined in the application context AC,[7] let $\overline{Sim_a^p}(i_1,i_2)$ and $\overline{Sim_r^p}(i_1,i_2)$ be the similarity measurements between instances considering, respectively, their attributes and their relations. The extensional similarity with asymmetric property is defined by*

$$\overline{ExtensSim}(i_1,i_2) = \begin{cases} 1 & i_1 = i_2 \\ \overline{Sim_I^p}(i_1,i_2) & Otherwise \end{cases} \quad (12)$$

---

[6] This formulation is slightly different from that provided by Egenhofer and Rodriguez: the parameters of the similarity have been reversed to be coherent with the relation between instances containment and the similarity value equal to 1.

[7] Note that $|AC_A(p)|+|AC_R(p)| \neq 0$ each time the context AC specifies at least a relevant attribute or relation for the recursion path p.

where $\overline{Sim}_I^p(i_1,i_2)$ is defined by

$$\overline{Sim}_I^p(i_1,i_2) = \frac{\sum_{a\in\delta_a(c)}\overline{Sim}_a^p(i_1,i_2) + \sum_{r\in\delta_r(c)}\overline{Sim}_r^p(i_1,i_2)}{|AC_A(p)|+|AC_R(p)|} \quad (13)$$

A first principle of the proposed extensional similarity between two instances is to consider the *lub* x of their classes as the common base for comparing them when the instances belong to different classes. Note that the index p, is a kind of stack of recursion adopted to track the navigation of relations whenever the similarity among instances is recursively defined in terms of the related instances. [x] is adopted to initialize p at the beginning of the assessment.

$\overline{Sim}_a^p(i_1,i_2)$ and $\overline{Sim}_r^p(i_1,i_2)$ are defined by a unique equation as follows.

Definition 13: Similarity on attributes and relations. *Given two instances $i_1 \in l_c(c_1)$, $i_2 \in l_c(c_2)$, $c=lub(c_1,c_2)$, $p=[c]$ (a path of recursion), X (a placeholder for the "A" or "R", $x \in A \cup R$), then let*

- $i_A(i) = \{v \in V | (i,v) \in 1_A(a), \exists y \in C \ s.t. \ \sigma_A(a) = (y,T) \wedge l_T(T) = 2^V\}$, *the set of values assumed by the instance i for the attribute a,*
- $i_R(i) = \{i' \in l_c(c') | \exists c \ i \in l_c(c) \exists c' \ s.t. \ \sigma_R(r) \in (c,c') \wedge (i,i') \in l_R(r)\}$, *the set of instances related to the instance i by the relation r,*
- *AC be the application context defined according to the restrictions defined in paragraph 0*
- $F_X = \{g : i_X(i_1) \to i_X(i_2) | g \ is \ partial \ and \ bijective\}$.

The similarity between instances according to their attributes or relations is:

$$\overline{Sim}_x^p(i_1,i_2) = \begin{cases} 1 & \text{if } (i_x(i_1) \text{ are empty sets}) \\ 0 & \text{if } (i_x(i_1) \neq \phi \wedge i_x(i_2) = \phi) \\ \dfrac{|i_x(i_2)|}{\max(|i_x(i_1)|,|i_x(i_2)|)} & \text{if } (x,Count) \in AC_x(p) \\ \dfrac{|i_x(i_1) \cap i_x(i_2)|}{|i_x(i_1)|} & \text{if } (x,Inter) \in AC_x(p) \\ \dfrac{\max_{f \in F_A} \sum_{v \in i_A(i_1)} \overline{Sim}_T^a(v,f(v))}{\min(|i_A(i_1)|,|i_A(i_2)|)} * (1-\max(0,\dfrac{|i_A(i_1)|-|i_A(i_2)|}{|i_A(i_1)|})) & \text{if } (x=a) \wedge (a,Simil) \in AC_A(p) \\ \dfrac{\max_{f \in F_R} \sum_{i \in i_R(i_1)} \overline{Sim}_I^{pNew}(i,f(i))}{\min(|i_R(i_1)|,|i_R(i_2)|)} * (1-\max(0,\dfrac{|i_R(i_1)|-|i_R(i_2)|}{|i_R(i_1)|})) & \text{if } (x=r) \wedge (r,Simil) \in AC_R(p) \\ & pNew = p \cdot s, s \in S_R^1, s(1) = r \end{cases}$$

These equations are designed to be asymmetric and to respect the properties of containment among instances: if an instance i_2 has at least the same attribute and relation values as i_1, then the extensional similarity between i_1 and i_2 is equal to one.

The approach computes $\overline{Sim}_x^p$, selecting one of the above equations according to the definition of *AC*:

- In the first case, the similarity is 1 if the set of the property values of the first instance is empty, because an instance having no characteristics is contained in all the other instances.
- In the second case, the similarity is 0 if the first instances having at least a property value are compared with an instance that does not have any value.
- The third expression is adopted if AC yields a relation or attribute associated with the operation *Count*.
- The fourth expression is adopted if AC yields a relation or attribute associated with the operation *Inter*.
- The fifth expression is adopted if AC yields an attribute with the operation *Simil*.
- The last expression is adopted if AC yields a relation with the operation *Simil*. It is important to note that each time the similarity is assessed in terms of related instances (whenever $(r, Simil) \in AC_R(p)$), the relation r followed to reach the related instances is added to the path of recursion. Thus, during the recursive assessment, the AC is always worked out on the most updated path of recursion.

In the last two expressions, the comparison of the attribute values relies on the function $\overline{Sim}_T^a$, which defines the similarity for the values of the attribute a having data type T. $\overline{Sim}_T^a$ is provided by the data layer as suggested by [7] and briefly discussed in the next paragraph.

Example of extensional similarity according with the definition 12.
We refer to the ontology in Fig. 3. We consider two instances illustrated in **Table 2**: AB and RA respectively of the classes *Researcher* and *Fellow* and their instances related to the classes *Publication, Project, ResearchTopic*. We adopt the application context AC_{int} (equation 4). We evaluate their similarity applying the equation 13.

Table 2. Example of instances of the academic research ontology

Instance ID	Instance class	Publication Instance	Project Instance	ResearchTopic Instance
AB	Researcher	P2	Pr1, Pr2	T1, T2
RA	Fellow	P2, P1	Pr1	T3

Table 3. Details of ResearchTopic instances

Instances ID	Instance class	topicName attribute	RelatedTopic instance
T1	ResearchTopic	Topic 1	
T2	ResearchTopic	Topic 2	T4
T3	ResearchTopic	Topic 3	T4
T4	ResearchTopic	Topic 4	

Their *lub* is the class *ResearchStaff* then p=[ResearchStaff] and according to the context defined in equation 4 the similarity assessment is performed considering the relations *publication*, *workAtProject* and *interest*, respectively using the operations *Inter*, *Inter* and *Simil*. Therefore, the equation 13 is an average among the three addends calculated with the formula in definition 13:

$$\overline{Sim}_{publication}^{[ResearchStaff]}(AB,RA)=1, \quad \overline{Sim}_{workAtProject}^{[ResearchStaff]}(AB,RA)=1/2, \quad \overline{Sim}_{Interest}^{[ResearchStaff]}(AB,RA)=1/4$$

The first two is calculated applying the fourth expression.

The last is calculated with the sixth expression in definition 13. It requires a more detailed argumentation.

The set of partial functions in F_X in definition 13 is employed to represent the possible matching among the set of values when the instances have relations or attributes with multiple values. In the example depicted in Table 2, the instances AB and RA are respectively related via the relation *interest* to T1, T2 and T3, then x is equal to "interest" and $i_R(AB) = \{T1,T2\}$ and $i_R(RA) = \{T3\}$. When AB and RA are compared, two possible partial and bijective functions f_1 and f_2 can be considered between the instances related to AB and RA: f_1:T1→T3 and f_2:T2→T3. The max operator selects the function which provides the matching with the highest contribution: in the example, it is f_2. Thus the sum has only one addend: $\overline{Sim}_I^{pNew}(T2, f_2(T2))$ which leads to the recursive call of the similarity assessment.

The difference in number of attributes values or related instances affects the similarity evaluation as modelled in the multiplying factors in the fifth and sixth expression of definition 13:

$$(1-\max(0, \frac{|i_A(i_1)|-|i_A(i_2)|}{|i_A(i_1)|})) \text{ and } (1-\max(0, \frac{|i_R(i_1)|-|i_R(i_2)|}{|i_R(i_1)|})).$$

These factors yield 1 if i_1 is contained in i_2; otherwise they yield the ratio between the number of properties of i_1 and the number of properties of i_2. In the example of AB and RA, looking at the Table 3, T1 and T2 are the instances of *ResearchTopic* related to AB, T3 is the instance related to RA. In this case the second factor induces a multiplying factor equal to 1/2 because half of the instances related to AB are leaved out from the matching.

The functions $\overline{Sim}_I^{pNew}(T2, f_2(T2))$ is applied to assess the similarity between AB and RA recursively with respect to the class *ResearchTopic* which are their interest. During the recursion the sixth expression in definition 13 is applied: [ResearchStaff,interest] is a new path of recursion and assigned to pNew.

Applying the application context to the new path of recursion, new criteria are listed. In particular, according to equation 4 the instances of *ResearchTopic* related to AB and RA are compared according to the values assumed by their attribute *topicName* and relation *relatedTopics*.

The similarity between T2 and T3 with respect to *topicName* is equal to 0, whereas with respect to *relatedTopic* is 1, then $\overline{Sim}_I^{pNew}(T2, f_2(T2))=1/2$. It is multiplied for the aforementioned multiplying factor thus $\overline{Sim}_{Interest}^{[ResearchStaff]}(AB,RA)=1/4$.

The overall similarity is $\overline{Sim}_I^p(AB,RA) = 7/12$.

7 Data Layer and Knowledge Layer

Data layer assesses the similarity of entities by considering the data values of simple types such as integers and strings or more complex data types such as geographical reference and shapes descriptors. The knowledge layer represents special shared ontology domains, which have their own additional vocabulary. As it can be placed at any level of the ontological complexity, it spans all the other layers.

In this paper, we adopt the data layer proposed by [7]. It relies on the distance measure proposed in [18] to assess the similarity between misspelled terms (e.g. Alignment and Allignment). Moreover, in real world data values are often affected by inconsistencies: for example there are data values that differ in representation of entity abbreviation (e.g. Genova, GE, GOA are terms referring to the same city, or IMATI-CNR-GE, IMATI-GE, GE-IMATI are terms referring to the same research institute). Contrary to the similarity assessment among misspelled terms, the management of inconsistence of data values requires a full-matching among the terms in order to obtain a satisfactory evaluation of their similarity. The aspect of different representations of abbreviation can be addressed relying on both the data layer and the knowledge layer. The knowledge layer contains explicitly information about the relation of equivalence among terms used in a specific knowledge domain. The data layer can exploit such information to evaluate the similarity among terms. The lexical similarity introduced by [18] is applied only if the terms are defined not equivalent in the knowledge layer.

8 Experiments and Evaluations

We evaluated our approach for the similarity assessment among the members of the research staff working at the Institute (CNR-IMATI-GE). An experiment was performed to demonstrate both the need for the content-dependent similarity and the importance of defining an asymmetric similarity based on the containment to select similar resources.

8.1 Experiments

Two experiments were performed considering the contexts "Exp" and "Int" mentioned in section 4.1. Eighteen members of the research staff were considered. The information related to their projects, journal publications and research interests was inserted as instances in the ontology depicted in Fig. 3 according to what was published at the IMATI web site.[8] The ontology was expressed in OWL ensuring that only the language constructs consistent with the ontology model considered in definition 1 were adopted. The resulting ontology is available at the web site [19].
Our method was implemented in JAVA and tested on this ontology.

Using the formalization of the two application contexts AC_{Int} and AC_{Exp} previously defined [equations (3), (4)], we have computed the similarity through the proposed framework. The results are represented by the similarity matrices in Fig. 4: (a) is the

---

[8] http://www.ge.imati.cnr.it, accessed the 12/05/2006.

result related to the context "Exp" and (b) is the result related to the context "Int". Each column j and each row i of the matrix represents a member of the research staff (identified by the first three letters of his name). The grey level of the pixel (i,j) represents the similarity value (Sim(i,j)) between the two members located at row i and column j: the darker the colour, the more similar are the two researchers.

Analysing the similarity matrices we can make the following statements.

- It is easy to see that they are asymmetric: for example sim(Dag,Bia)=1 while sim(Bia, Dag)<1. This confirms that the proposed model assesses an asymmetric similarity. The asymmetry result is particularly useful for comparing researchers because it behaves according to the property of containment defined in Definition 2. For example, the two results sim(Dag,Bia)=1 and sim(Bia, Dag)<1 in Fig. 4.a mean that if Bia has at least the experience of Dag, then Dag can replace Bia. The inverse is not true, and if the domain expert decides to choose Dag instead of Bia, the similarity value provides a hint about the loss inherent in this choice [for example, if sim(Bia, Dag)=0.85, then the loss is 15%].
- The comparison of the two matrices shows how they are different; it is evident that the two contexts induce completely different similarity values. For example, "Dag" results are very similar to "Bia" with respect to their experience (black pixel in Fig. 4.a), but they are not similar with respect to their research interests (white pixel in Fig. 4.b).
- During the test process we realized that the approach provides a sort of tool for context tuning, supporting us in the decision-making process to formulate the similarity criteria. From the similarity results we were able to learn and refine our criteria to obtain the expected results.

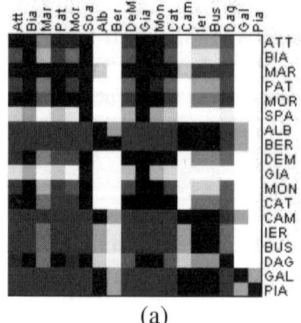
(a)

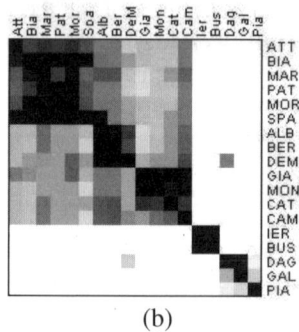
(b)

Fig. 4. (a) Similarity matrix for context "Exp"; (b) Similarity matrix for context "Int"

8.2 Evaluations

Two kinds of evaluations of the results concerning the similarity obtained with respect to research interests (Fig. 4.b) were performed.

The first evaluation was based on the concept of recall and precision, calculated considering the same adaptation of recall and precision made by [20]. More precisely, considering an entity x, the recall and precision were defined, respectively, as $(A \cap B)/A$ and $(A \cap B)/B$, where A is the set of entities expected to be similar to x and B is the set of similar entities calculated by a model. A critical issue in the similarity evaluation is to have a ground truth with respect to comparing the results obtained. We faced this problem in referring to the research staff of our institute when considering as "similar" two members of the same research group. In fact at IMATI researchers and fellows are grouped into three main research groups, and one of those is composed of three further sub-groups. Therefore, we considered the research staff as split into five groups. For each member i, A is the set of members of his research group while B is composed of the first n members retrieved by the model. We have calculated recall and precision for each group considering "n" as the smallest number of members needed to obtain a recall of 100%, and then we have evaluated the precision. The average recall was estimated to be equal to 100% with a precision of 95%. These results are quite encouraging: a recall equal to 100% demonstrates that, for each research group, the similarity is able to rank all the expected members, while a precision equal to 95% means that the average number of outsiders that need to be included to rank all group members is equal to 5%.

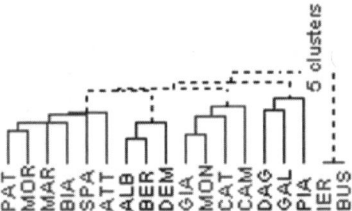

Fig. 5. The dendrogram obtained through hierarchical gene clustering

We have performed a second evaluation according to the context "Int" using a data mining application. For each researcher and fellow we have computed his similarity with respect to the other members applying our method. In this way, we associated with each research staff member a string of values, which correspond to his relative distances from the other members. The strings correspond to the rows of the similarity matrix (Fig. 4.b). Then we have applied a tool to perform hierarchical clustering among the genetic microarray [21] to the set of strings, considering each string as a kind of researcher genetic code. The dendrogram obtained is shown in Fig. 5. It recognizes the five clusters that resemble the research group structure of our institute.

9 Related Work

Semantic similarity is employed differently according to the application domain where it is adopted. Currently it is relevant in ontology alignment [22,23] and conceptual retrieval [24] as well as in semantic web service discovery and matching [25,26]. It is expected to increase in relevance in the framework for metadata analysis [27]. We discuss here related works according to their purpose and the ontology model they adopt.

Similarities in the ontology alignment. There are many methods for aligning ontology, as pointed out by Euzenat et al. [23]. Semantic similarity is adopted in this context to figure out relations among the entities in the ontology schemas. It is used to compare the names of classes, attributes and relations, determining reasonable mapping between two distinct ontologies. However, the method proposed in this paper is specifically designed to assess similarity among instances belonging to the same ontology. Some similarities adopted for ontology alignment consider quite expressive ontology language (e.g., reference [22] focuses on a subset of OWL Lite), but they mainly focus on the comparison of the structural aspects of ontology. Due to the different purposes of these methods, they turn out to be unsuitable for properly solving the similarity among instances.

Concept similarity in lexicographic databases. Different approaches to assessing semantic similarity among concepts represented by words within lexicographic databases are available. They mainly rely on edge counting-based [28] or information theory-based methods [29]. The edge counting-based method assigns terms that are subjects of the similarity assessment as edges of a tree-like taxonomy and defines the similarity in terms as the distance between the edges [28]. The information theory-based method defines the similarity of two concepts in terms of the maximum information content of the concept that subsumes them [30,31]. Recently, new hybrid approaches have been proposed: Rodriguez and Egenhofer [16] take advantage of the above methods and add the idea of features matching introduced by Tversky [14]. Schwering [24] proposes a hybrid approach to assess similarity among concepts belonging to a semantic net. The similarity in this case is assessed by comparing properties of the concept as features [14] or as geometric space [32]. With respect to the method presented in this paper, Rada et al. [28], Resnik [30] and Lin [31] work on lexicographic databases where the instances are not considered. If they are adopted, as they were originally defined, to evaluate the similarity of the instances, they are doomed to fail since they ignore important information provided by the instances, attributes and relations. Moreover, Rodriguez and Egenhofer [16] and Schwering [24] use the features or even conceptual spaces, information that is not native in the ontology design and would have to be manually added. Instead our approach aims at addressing the similarity, as much as possible, by taking advantage of the information that has already been disseminated in the ontology. Additional information is considered only to tune the similarity with respect to different application contexts.

Similarities that rely on ontology models with instances. Other works define similarity relying on ontology models closer to those adopted in the semantic web standards. D'Amato et al. [33] present a dissimilarity measure for description logics considering the expressivity of ALC, and comparing concept descriptions and individuals/instances. Hau et al. [26] identify similar services measuring the similarity between their descriptions. To define a similarity measure on semantic services explicitly refers to the ontology model of OWL Lite and defines the similarity among OWL objects (classes as well as instances) in terms of the number of common RDF statements that characterize the objects. Maedche and Zacharias [17] adopt a semantic similarity measure to cluster ontology-based metadata. The ontology model adopted in this similarity refers also to IS-A hierarchy, attributes, relations and instances. Even if these three methods consider ontology models, which are more evolved than the taxonomy or terminological ontology, their design ignores the need to tailor the semantic similarity according to specific application contexts. Thus, to assess the similarity investigated in this paper, two distinct ontologies need to be defined instead of simply defining two contexts as we do.

Contextual-dependent similarity. Some studies combine the context and the similarity. Kashyap and Sheth [34] use the concept of semantic proximity and context to achieve interoperability among different databases. The context represents the information useful for determining the semantic relationships between entities belonging to different databases. However they do not define a semantic similarity in the sense we are addressing, and the similarity is classified as some discrete value (semantic equivalence, semantic relevance, semantic resemblance, etc). Rodriguez and Egenhofer [16] integrate the contextual information into the similarity model. They define as the application domain the set of classes that are subject to the user's interest. Janowicz [35] proposes a context-aware similarity theory for concepts specified in expressive description logics such as ALCNR. As in our proposal, the last two works aim to make the similarity assessment parametric with respect to the considered context. Moreover, in contrast with our methods, they formalize the context ignoring the similarity criteria induced by the context (e.g. they ignore the need of operations) and they do not directly address the similarity among instances.

This discussion of related works shows that, apart from the different definitions of semantic similarity proposed by different parties, these definitions are far from providing a complete framework as intended in our work. They often have different purposes, they consider a simpler ontology model, or they completely ignore the need to tailor the similarity assessment with respect to a specific application context. Of course, some of the works mentioned have been particularly important in the definition of our proposal. As already mentioned, both Maedche and Zacharias [17] and Rodriguez and Egenhofer [16] have strongly inspired the part related to structural similarity. However, to successfully support our purposes, the class slots have been considered as distinguishing features. Furthermore, the methods proposed by Maedche and Zacharias [17] for Class Matching define a similarity that is symmetric, thus we have adapted the original in order to make it asymmetric.

The similarity framework proposed in this paper contributes, along with related work, toward paving the way to a tool that each ontology engineer can adopt

- to define different similarities among instances on the same ontology according to different application contexts;
- to refine the similarity criteria as long as new instances are inserted or the obtained result does not satisfy the user domain expert.

The explicit parameterization of the similarity assessment with respect to the application contexts yields a precise definition of the hints to be considered in similarity assessment as well as complete control of the recursive comparison needed to work out the similarity.

10 Conclusions and Future Work

This paper proposes a framework for assessing semantic similarity among instances within an ontology. It combines and extends different existing similarity methods, taking into account, as much as possible, the hints encoded in the ontology and considering the application context. A formalization of the criteria induced by the application is provided as a means of parameterizing the similarity assessment and to formulate a measurement more sensitive to the specific application needs.

The framework is expected to bring great benefit in the analysis of the ontology driven metadata repository. It provides a flexible solution for tailoring the similarity assessments according to the different applications: the same ontology can be employed in different similarity assessments simply by defining distinct criteria, and it is not necessary to build a different ontology for each similarity assessment. The formalization of the application contexts in terms of explicit similarity criteria paves the way to an iterative and interactive process where the ontology engineer and the domain experts can perform fine-tuning of the resulting similarity.

Nevertheless, some research and development issues are still open, such as human subject testing. Moreover, in the proposed approach the formalization of the application context affects only the similarity defined by the extensional comparison. It would be interesting to determine if the context results also in external comparison similarity. It would also be worthwhile to extend the similarity to ontology models towards OWL and to test it in more complex use cases.

Acknowledgements

This research started within the EU founded INVISIP project and partially performed within the Network of Excellence AIM@SHAPE.

References

1. Schwering, A., Raubal, M.: Measuring Semantic Similarity Between Geospatial Conceptual Regions. In: Rodríguez, M.A., Cruz, I., Levashkin, S., Egenhofer, M.J. (eds.) GeoS 2005. LNCS, vol. 3799, pp. 90–106. Springer, Heidelberg (2005)
2. Wang, H., Wang, W., Yang, J., Yu, P.S.: Clustering by pattern similarity in large data sets. In: ACM SIGMOD Conference (2002)
3. Sheth, A., Bertram, C., Avant, D., Hammond, B., Kochut, K., Warke, Y.: Managing semantic content for the Web. IEEE Internet Comput. 6(4), 80–87 (2002)
4. Medin, D.L., Goldstone, R.L., Gentner, D.: Respects for similarity. Psychological Review 100, 254–278 (1993)
5. Egenhofer, M.J., Mark, D.M.: Naive Geography. In: Kuhn, W., Frank, A.U. (eds.) COSIT 1995. LNCS, vol. 988, pp. 1–15. Springer, Heidelberg (1995)
6. Albertoni, R., De Martino, M.: Semantic Similarity of Ontology Instances Tailored on the Application Context. In: Meersman, R., Tari, Z., et al. (eds.) ODBASE-OTM 2006. LNCS, vol. 4275, pp. 1020–1038. Springer, Heidelberg (2006)
7. Ehrig, M., Haase, P., Stojanovic, N., Hefke, M.: Similarity for Ontologies - A Comprehensive Framework. In: ECIS 2005, Regensburg, Germany (2005)

8. AIM@SHAPE IST NoE No 506766, http://www.aimatshape.net
9. Albertoni, R., Papaleo, L., Pitikakis, M., Robbiano, F., Spagnuolo, M., Vasilakis, G.: Ontology-Based Searching Framework for Digital Shapes. In: Meersman, R., Tari, Z., Herrero, P. (eds.) SWWS-OTM Workshop 2005. LNCS, vol. 3762, pp. 896–905. Springer, Heidelberg (2005)
10. Papaleo, L., Albertoni, R., Marini, S., Robbiano, F.: An ontology-based Approach to Acquisition and Reconstruction. In: Workshop towards Semantic Virtual Environment, Villars, Switzerland (2005)
11. Falcidieno, B., Spagnuolo, M., Alliez, P., Quak, E., Vavalis, E., Houstis, C.: Towards the Semantics of Digital Shapes: The AIM@SHAPE Approach. In: Proceedings of the European Workshop for the Integration of Knowledge, Semantics and Digital Media Technology, London, U.K. QMUL (2004)
12. Albertoni, R., Camossi, E., De Martino, M., Giannini, F., Monti, M.: Semantic Granularity for the Semantic Web. In: Meersman, R., Tari, Z., Herrero, P., et al. (eds.) SWWS-OTM Workshops 2006. LNCS, vol. 4278, pp. 1863–1872. Springer, Heidelberg (2006)
13. Gruber, T.R.: Toward principles for the design of ontologies used for knowledge sharing? Int. J. Hum.-Comput. Stud. 43, 907–928 (1995)
14. Tversky, A.: Features of similarity. Psychological Review 84(4), 327–352 (1977)
15. Yoshida, H., Shida, T., Kindo, T.: Asymmetric similarity with modified overlap coefficient among documents. IEEE Pacific Rim Conference on Communications, Computers and signal Processing 1 (2001)
16. Rodriguez, M.A., Egenhofer, M.J.: Comparing geospatial entity classes: an asymmetric and context-dependent similarity measure. Int. J. Geogr. Inf. Sci. 18(3), 229–256 (2004)
17. Maedche, A., Zacharias, V.: Clustering Ontology Based Metadata in the Semantic Web. In: Elomaa, T., Mannila, H., Toivonen, H. (eds.) PKDD 2002. LNCS (LNAI), vol. 2431, pp. 348–360. Springer, Heidelberg (2002)
18. Maedche, A., Staab, S.: Measuring Similarity between Ontologies. In: Gómez-Pérez, A., Benjamins, V.R. (eds.) EKAW 2002. LNCS (LNAI), vol. 2473, pp. 251–263. Springer, Heidelberg (2002)
19. Sicilia, M.A.: Metadata and semantics research. Online Information Review 30(3), 213–216 (2006)
20. Rodriguez, M.A., Egenhofer, M.J.: Determining semantic similarity among entity classes from different ontologies. IEEE Trans. Knowl. Data Eng. 15(2), 442–456 (2003)
21. Hierarchical Clustering Explorer, 3.0, http://www.cs.umd.edu/hcil/multi-cluster/
22. Euzenat, J., Valtchev, P.: Similarity-Based Ontology Alignment in OWL-Lite. In: ECAI, Valencia, Spain, pp. 333–337. IOS Press, Amsterdam (2004)
23. Euzenat, J., Le Bach, T., and et al.: State of the Art on Ontology Alignment (2004), http://www.starlab.vub.ac.be/research/projects/knowledgeweb/kweb-223.pdf
24. Schwering, A.: Hybrid Model for Semantic Similarity Measurement. In: Meersman, R., Tari, Z. (eds.) ODBASE-OTM 2005. LNCS, vol. 3761, pp. 1449–1465. Springer, Heidelberg (2005)
25. Usanavasin, S., Takada, S., Doi, N.: Semantic Web Services Discovery in Multi-ontology Environment. In: Meersman, R., Tari, Z., Herrero, P. (eds.) OTM 2005. LNCS, vol. 3762, pp. 59–68. Springer, Heidelberg (2005)
26. Hau, J., Lee, W., Darlington, J.: A Semantic Similarity Measure for Semantic Web Services. In: Web Service Semantics: Towards Dynamic Business Integration, workshop at WWW 2005 (2005)

27. Albertoni, R., Bertone, A., De Martino, M.: Semantic Analysis of Categorical Metadata to Search for Geographic Information. In: Proceedings 16th International Workshop on Database and Expert Systems Applications, pp. 453–457. IEEE, Los Alamitos (2005)
28. Rada, R., Mili, H., Bicknell, E., Blettner, M.: Development and application of a metric on semantic nets. IEEE Transactions on Systems, Man and Cybernetics 19(1), 17–30 (1989)
29. Li, Y., Bandar, Z., McLean, D.: An Approach for Measuring Semantic Similarity between Words Using Multiple Information Sources. IEEE Trans. Knowl. Data Eng. 15, 871–882 (2003)
30. Resnik, P.: Using Information Content to Evaluate Semantic Similarity in a Taxonomy. In: Proc. of the Fourteenth Int. Joint Conference on Artificial Intelligence, pp. 448–453 (1995)
31. Lin, D.: An Information-Theoretic Definition of Similarity. In: Proc. of the Fifteenth Int. Conference on Machine Learning, pp. 296–304. Morgan Kaufmann, San Francisco (1998)
32. Gädenfors, P.: How to make the semantic web more semantic. In: FOIS, pp. 17–34. IOS Press, Amsterdam (2004)
33. d'Amato, C., Fanizzi, N., Esposito, F.: A dissimilarity measure for ALC concept descriptions. In: ACM Symposium of Applied Computing, pp. 1695–1699. ACM, New York (2006)
34. Kashyap, V., Sheth, A.: Semantic and schematic similarities between database objects: a context-based approach. VLDB J. 5(4), 276–304 (1996)
35. Janowicz, K.: Sim-DL: Towards a Semantic Similarity Measurement Theory for the Description Logic ALCNR in Geographic Information Retrieval. In: Meersman, R., Tari, Z., Herrero, P. (eds.) OTM 2006. LNCS, vol. 4278, pp. 1681–1692. Springer, Heidelberg (2006)

Query Relaxation in RDF

Carlos A. Hurtado[1,*], Alexandra Poulovassilis[2], and Peter T. Wood[2]

[1] Universidad de Chile
churtado@dcc.uchile.cl
[2] Birkbeck, University of London
{ap,ptw}@dcs.bbk.ac.uk

Abstract. We explore flexible querying of RDF data, with the aim of making it possible to return data satisfying query conditions with varying degrees of exactness, and also to rank the results of a query depending on how "closely" they satisfy the query conditions. We make queries more flexible by logical relaxation of their conditions based on RDFS entailment and RDFS ontologies. We develop a notion of ranking of query answers, and present a query processing algorithm for incrementally computing the relaxed answer of a query. Our approach has application in scenarios where there is a lack of understanding of the ontology underlying the data, or where the data objects have heterogeneous sets of properties or irregular structures.

1 Introduction

The conjunctive fragment of most RDF query languages (e.g., see [10,11]) consists of queries of the form $H \leftarrow B$, where the body of the query B is a graph pattern, that is, an RDF graph over IRIs, literals, blanks, and variables. The head of the query H is either a graph pattern or a tuple variable (list of variables). The semantics of these queries is simple. It is based on finding matchings from the body of the query to the data and then applying the matchings to the head of the query to obtain the answers.

Recently, the W3C RDF data access group has emphasized the importance of enhancing RDF query languages to meet the requirements of contexts where RDF can be used to solve real problems. In particular, it has been stated that in RDF querying "it must be possible to express a query that does not fail when some specified part of the query fails to match" [5]. This requirement has motivated the OPTIONAL clause, presented in the emerging SPARQL W3C proposal for querying RDF [17] and previously introduced in SeRQL [3]. The OPTIONAL clause allows the query to find matchings that fail to match some conditions in the body. In contrast to other approaches to flexible querying (e.g., [1,14]), the OPTIONAL construct incorporates flexibility from a "logical" standpoint, via relaxation of the query's conditions. This idea, however, is exploited only to a limited extent, since the conditions of a query could be relaxed in ways

---

[*] Carlos A. Hurtado was supported by Millennium Nucleus, Center for Web Research (P04-067-F), Mideplan, and by project FONDECYT 1030810, Chile.

other than simply dropping optional triple patterns, for example by replacing constants with variables or by using the class and property hierarchies in an ontology associated with the data (such as that shown in Figure 1).

In this paper, we propose the introduction of a RELAX clause as a generalization of the OPTIONAL clause for the conjunctive fragment of SPARQL. The idea is to make queries more flexible by a logical relaxation of some of the conditions that are enclosed by one or more RELAX clauses inside the body of the query. These conditions are successively turned more general so that the query is transformed and processed to successively return more general answers. We define the notion of "being more general" (or "being more relaxed") using RDFS entailment and RDFS ontologies.

1.1 RDFS Ontologies

It is common that users interact with RDF applications in the context of an ontology. As an example, OWL-QL [8] allows users to include ontologies as premises in queries, and SPARQL provides a similar facility by allowing reference to several RDF datasets [17] in a query. As we will show later, ontologies provide an important source of knowledge to support query relaxation.

Before addressing the central ideas of our approach, we give a brief description of the type of ontologies we will consider. We assume that a query is interpreted in the context of a single ontology, which is modeled as an RDF graph with interpreted RDFS vocabulary. The RDFS vocabulary defines classes and properties that may be used for describing groups of related resources and relationships between resources. In this paper we use a fragment of the RDFS vocabulary, which comprises (in brackets is the shorter name we will use) rdfs:range [range], rdfs:domain [dom], rdf:type [type], rdfs:subClassOf [sc] and rdfs:subPropertyOf [sp][1].

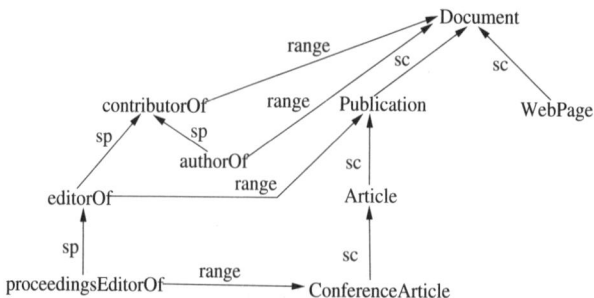

Fig. 1. An RDFS ontology modeling documents and people who contribute to them

---

[1] We omit in this paper vocabulary used to refer to basic classes in RDF/S such as rdf:Property, rdfs:Class, rdfs:Resource, rdfs:Literal, rdfs:XMLLiteral, rdfs:Datatype, among others. We also omit vocabulary for lists, collections, and variations on these, as well as vocabulary used to place comments in RDF/S data.

As an example, the ontology of Figure 1 is used to model documents along with properties that model different ways people contribute to them (e.g., as authors, editors, or being the editor of the proceedings where an article is published).

1.2 The RELAX Clause

We now explain the RELAX as an extension of the OPTIONAL clause. As an example, consider the following SPARQL-like query Q^2:

$$?Z, ?Y \leftarrow \{(?X, name, ?Z), \texttt{OPTIONAL}\{(?X, proceedingsEditorOf, ?Y)\}\}.$$

The body of this query is a graph pattern comprising two triple patterns. This query returns names of people along with the IRIs of conference articles whose proceedings they have edited. Because the second triple pattern in the body of the query is within the scope of an OPTIONAL clause, the query also returns names of people for which the second pattern fails to match the data (i.e., people who have not edited proceedings).

Now, instead of dropping the triple pattern $(?X, proceedingsEditorOf, ?Y)$ we may relax this triple pattern by using the ontology of Figure 1. As an example, though the user may want to retrieve editors of proceedings at first, she/he might also be interested in knowing about people who have contributed to publications in other roles, along with the publications themselves. Now after returning editors of conference proceedings, the user could replace the triple pattern $(?X, proceedingsEditorOf, ?Y)$ with $(?X, editorOf, ?Y)$, yielding a new, relaxed query that returns editors of publications along with their publications. Subsequently, this triple pattern can be rewritten to the triple pattern $(?X, contributorOf, ?Y)$ to obtain more general answers.

In order to save the user the effort of inspecting the ontology and rewriting the query to return more relaxed answers for the same original query, the system could perform this process automatically. This is achieved by the following query which replaces OPTIONAL with RELAX in Q:

$$?Z, ?Y \leftarrow \{(?X, name, ?Z), \texttt{RELAX}\{(?X, proceedingsEditorOf, ?Y)\}\}.$$

The idea of making queries more flexible by the logical relaxation of their conditions is not new in database research. Gaasterland et al. [9] proposed a mechanism to achieve this goal in the context of deductive databases and logic programming, and called the technique *query relaxation*.

1.3 Notion of Query Relaxation for RDF

We study the query relaxation problem in the setting of the RDF/S data model and RDF query languages and show that query relaxation can be naturally formalized using RDFS entailment. We use an operational semantics for the notion of RDFS entailment, denoted $\models$, characterized by the derivation rules

---

[2] SPARQL has SQL-like syntax; for brevity, in this paper we express queries as rules.

Group A (Subproperty)	(1) $\frac{(a,\text{sp},b)\ (b,\text{sp},c)}{(a,\text{sp},c)}$	(2) $\frac{(a,\text{sp},b)\ (x,a,y)}{(x,b,y)}$
Group B (Subclass)	(3) $\frac{(a,\text{sc},b)\ (b,\text{sc},c)}{(a,\text{sc},c)}$	(4) $\frac{(a,\text{sc},b)\ (x,\text{type},a)}{(x,\text{type},b)}$
Group C (Typing)	(5) $\frac{(a,\text{dom},c)\ (x,a,y)}{(x,\text{type},c)}$	(6) $\frac{(a,\text{range},d)\ (x,a,y)}{(y,\text{type},d)}$

Fig. 2. RDFS Inference Rules

given in Figure 2 (for details, see [10,12]). The rules describe the semantics of the RDFS vocabulary we use in this paper (i.e., sp, sc, type, dom, and range)[3].

Intuitively, as RDFS entailment is characterized by the rules of Figure 2, a relaxed triple pattern t' can be obtained from triple t by applying the derivation rules to t and triples from the ontology. As an example, the triple pattern $(?X, proceedingsEditorOf, ?Y)$ can be relaxed to $(?X, editorOf, ?Y)$, by applying rule 2 to the former and the triple $(proceedingsEditorOf, \text{sp}, editorOf)$ in the ontology of Figure 1. The different relaxed versions of an original query are obtained by combining relaxations of triple patterns that appear inside a RELAX clause.

The notion of query relaxation we propose naturally subsumes two broad classes of relaxations. The first class of relaxations includes relaxations entailed using information from the ontology and are captured by the rules of Figure 2; these include relaxing type conditions, relaxing properties using domain or range restrictions and others. The second class of relaxation consists of relaxations that can be entailed without an ontology, which include dropping triple patterns, replacing constants with variables, and breaking join dependencies.

1.4 Summary of Contributions

In this paper, we develop a framework for query relaxation for RDF. We introduce a notion of query relaxation based on RDFS entailment, which naturally incorporates RDFS ontologies and captures necessary information for relaxation such as the class and property hierarchies.

By formalizing query relaxation in terms of entailment, we obtain a semantic notion which is by no means limited to RDFS and could also be extended to more expressive settings such as OWL entailment and OWL ontologies, to capture further relaxations. Our framework generalizes, for the conjunctive fragment of SPARQL, the idea of dropping query conditions provided by the OPTIONAL construct.

An essential aspect of our proposal, which sets it apart from previous work on query relaxation, is to rank the results of a query based on how "closely" they

---

[3] We omit, for now, the RDFS rule that essentially states that blank nodes (or variables) behave like existentially quantified variables, and allows constants to be replaced with blanks or blanks with other blanks using the notion of a *map*. This notion and its use will be covered in Section 6.

satisfy the query. We present a notion of ranking based on a structure called the *relaxation graph*, in which relaxed versions of the original query are ordered from less to more general from a logical standpoint. Since the relaxation graph is based on logical subsumption, ranking does not depend on any syntactic condition on the knowledge used for relaxation (such as rule ordering in logic-programming approaches [9]). Finally, we give a query processing algorithm to compute the relaxed answer of a query, and examine its correctness and complexity.

This paper extends our earlier paper [13] in a number of ways. We have substantially developed, revised and improved the material presented there. We also make the following new contributions here: we provide proofs for all the results sketched in [13]; Section 4 includes substantial new contributions relating to the relationship between relaxations and derivations using new RDFS rules; we provide a new algorithm for computing relaxations based on the notion of the "extended reduction" of the ontology used for relaxation; and Section 5, on computing relaxed query answers, has been extended with two examples that illustrates our query processing algorithm.

1.5 Outline

The rest of the paper is organized as follows. Section 2 introduces preliminary notation. We then present our framework in a stepwise manner. Firstly, in sections 3, 4, and 5, we formalize and study relaxations that do not replace terms of the original triple pattern with variables and are captured by the rules of Figure 2; they include relaxing type conditions, relaxing properties using domain or range restrictions and others. In particular, in Section 3 we formalize the semantics of query relaxation for the aforementioned types of relaxation. Then, Section 4 discusses the problem of computing relaxations of a triple pattern and Section 5 studies query processing. In Section 6, we extend the relaxation framework to consider relaxations that replace terms of the original triple pattern with variables (e.g., replacing a literal or IRI with a variable or a variable with another variable). In Section 7 we review related work in comparison to our own work, and we give our concluding remarks in Section 8. Finally, in the appendix we present the proofs omitted in the main body of the paper.

2 Preliminary Definitions

In this section we present the basic notation and definitions that will be used subsequently in this paper. Some of these were introduced in [2,10,12,15].

2.1 RDF Graphs and RDFS Ontologies

In this paper we work with RDF graphs which may mention the RDFS vocabulary. We assume there are infinite sets I (IRIs), B (blank nodes), and L (RDF literals). The elements in $I \cup B \cup L$ are called RDF *terms*. A triple $(v_1, v_2, v_3) \in (I \cup B) \times I \times (I \cup B \cup L)$ is called an *RDF triple*. In such a triple,

v_1 is called the *subject*, v_2 the *predicate* and v_3 the *object*. An *RDF graph* (just graph from now on) is a set of RDF triples.

We consider ontologies that use RDFS vocabulary, which we will refer to as RDFS ontologies. We assume that predicates of triples in O should be in the set $\{\texttt{type}, \texttt{dom}, \texttt{range}, \texttt{sp}, \texttt{sc}\}$. Intuitively, this means that the ontology does not interfere with the semantics of the RDFS vocabulary.

We say that an ontology is acyclic if the subgraphs defined by sc and sp are acyclic. Acyclicity is considered good practice in modeling ontologies.

We write that $G_1 \models_{\text{rule}} G_2$ if G_2 can be derived from G_1 by iteratively applying the rules of Figure 2. In this paper, we also use a notion of closure of an RDF graph G [12], denoted $\text{cl}(G)$, which is the closure of G under the rules. By a result from [12], RDFS entailment (for the fragment of RDFS we use in this paper) can be characterized as follows: $G_1 \models_{\text{RDFS}} G_2$ if and only if $G_2 \subseteq \text{cl}(G_1)$.

2.2 Conjunctive Queries for RDF

Consider a set of variables V disjoint from the sets I, B, and L. A *triple pattern* is a triple $(v_1, v_2, v_3) \in (I \cup V) \times (I \cup V) \times (I \cup V \cup L)$. A *graph pattern* is a set of triple patterns. Given a graph pattern P, we denote by $\text{var}(P)$ the variables mentioned in P. In our examples, variables are indicated by a leading question mark, while literals are enclosed in quotes.

A *conjunctive query* Q is an expression $T \leftarrow B$, where B is a graph pattern, and $T = \langle T_1, \ldots, T_n \rangle$ is a list of variables which belongs to $\text{var}(B)$. (The framework formalized in this paper can be easily extended to queries with graph patterns as query heads.) We denote T by $\text{Head}(Q)$, and B by $\text{Body}(Q)$.

We next define the answer of a conjunctive query. In order to do this, we take into account that a query Q may be formulated over an RDFS ontology O, which means that Q may mention vocabulary from O and its answer is obtained from the RDF graph being queried and O. We define a *matching* to be a function from variables in $\text{Body}(Q)$ to blanks, IRIs and literals. Given a matching Θ, we denote by $\Theta(\text{Body}(Q))$ the graph resulting from $\text{Body}(Q)$ by replacing each variable X by $\Theta(X)$. Given an RDF graph G, the *answer* of Q is the set of tuples, denoted $\text{ans}(Q, O, G)$, defined as follows: for each matching Θ such that $\Theta(\text{Body}(Q)) \subseteq \text{cl}(O \cup G)$, return $\Theta(\text{Head}(Q))$. When O is clear from the context, we omit it, and write $\text{ans}(Q, G)$ instead of $\text{ans}(Q, O, G)$.

3 Formalizing Query Relaxation

We will present a relaxed semantics for queries in a stepwise manner. In Section 3.1, we present the notion of relaxation of triple patterns, and in Section 3.2 we introduce the notion of the relaxation graph of a triple pattern. This is used in Section 3.3 to define the relaxation graph of a query. In Section 3.4, we explain different types of relaxations subsumed by our framework. The relaxation graph is the basis for the notion of the relaxed answer and ranking of a query we propose in Section 3.5.

3.1 Triple Pattern Relaxation

In this section, we define the relaxation relation between triple patterns. Intuitively, a triple pattern relaxes to another triple pattern if the latter can be logically derived from the former and a given ontology. Relaxation will be defined in the context of an ontology that will be denoted by O.

Definition 1 (Triple Pattern Relaxation). *Let t_1, t_2 be triple patterns such that $t_1, t_2 \notin \mathrm{cl}(O)$, and $\mathrm{var}(t_2) = \mathrm{var}(t_1)$. We say that t_1 relaxes to t_2 (or t_2 is a relaxation of t_1), denoted $t_1 \leq t_2$, if $(\{t_1\} \cup O) \models_{\text{rule}} t_2$.*

As stated before, in this section we consider relaxations that maintain the set of variables in the original triple pattern. This is formalized in the previous definition by requiring that $\mathrm{var}(t_2) = \mathrm{var}(t_1)$. In addition, we require that $t_1, t_2 \notin \mathrm{cl}(O)$ in order to avoid relaxing to triple patterns that will be trivially true for any RDF graph being queried.

As an example, let O be the ontology of Figure 1. Then, we have that

$$(?X, \text{type}, ConferenceArticle) \leq (?X, \text{type}, Article)$$

and

$$(JohnRobert, ContributorOf, ?X) \leq (?X, \text{type}, Document)$$

among other relaxations. It is not the case, however, that

$$(?X, ContributorOf, ?Y) \leq (?Y, \text{type}, Document)$$

since the sets of variables in the two triple patterns are different.

The following proposition shows that triple pattern relaxation can be characterized in terms of the RDFS closure.

Proposition 1. *Let $\leq$ be defined using an ontology O, and t_1, t_2 be triple patterns such that $t_1, t_2 \notin \mathrm{cl}(O)$ and $\mathrm{var}(t_1) = \mathrm{var}(t_2)$. Then $t_1 \leq t_2$ if and only if $t_2 \in \mathrm{cl}(O \cup \{t_1\})$.*

It is desirable that the relaxation relation should be a partial order. The following proposition shows the conditions under which this happens.

Proposition 2. *Let $\leq$ be defined using an ontology O. Then $\leq$ is a partial order if and only if O is acyclic.*

In what follows we assume that O is acyclic. Therefore, from now on we assume that the relaxation relation is a partial order.

The *direct relaxation relation*, denoted by $\prec$, is the reflexive and transitive reduction of $\leq$. The *direct relaxations* of a triple pattern t (i.e., triples t' such that $t \prec t'$) are important in our framework, since they are the result of the smallest steps of relaxation. The *indirect relaxations* of a triple pattern t are the triples t' such that $t \leq t'$ and $t \not\prec t'$.

3.2 Relaxation Graph of a Triple Pattern

We are interested in relaxing each of the triple patterns that occurs inside the RELAX clause of a query, so we next adapt the relaxation relation to use relaxation "above" a given triple pattern. This yields the notion of relaxation graph of a triple pattern.

Definition 2 (Relaxation Graph of a Triple Pattern). *The relaxation relation (resp., direct relaxation relation) "above" a triple pattern t, denoted by $\leq_t$ (resp., $\prec_t$), is $\leq$ (resp., $\prec$) restricted to triple patterns t' such that $t \leq t'$. The relaxation graph of a triple pattern t is the directed acyclic graph induced by $\prec_t$.*

As an example, Figure 3 shows the relaxation graph of $(JohnRobert, editorOf, ?X)$, assuming that O is the ontology of Figure 1.

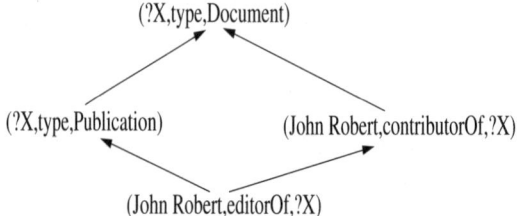

Fig. 3. Relaxation graph of the triple pattern $(JohnRobert, editorOf, ?X)$

3.3 Relaxation Graph of a Query

We now generalize triple pattern relaxation to query relaxation using the notion of the direct product of partial orders. The *direct product* of two partial order relations α_1, α_2, denoted $\alpha_1 \otimes \alpha_2$, is another partial order α such that $(a, b)\ \alpha\ (c, d)$ if and only if $a\ \alpha_1\ c$ and $b\ \alpha_2\ d$. The generalization of this definition to more than two relations is straightforward.

Definition 3 (Relaxation Graph of a Query). *Given a query Q, let $\mathsf{Body}(Q) = \{t_1, \ldots, t_n\}$. For any triple t_i not inside a RELAX clause, we overload the notation $\leq_{t_i}$ and assume that t_i relaxes only to t_i. Then, the relaxation relation "above" Q, denoted by $\leq_Q$, is defined as $\leq_{t_1} \otimes \leq_{t_2} \ldots \otimes \leq_{t_n}$. Direct relaxation, denoted $\prec_Q$, is the reflexive and transitive reduction of $\leq_Q$. The relaxation graph of Q is the directed acyclic graph induced by $\prec_Q$.*

It is important to remark that a node $(t'_1, \ldots, t'_n)$ in the relaxation graph of Q denotes the conjunctive query $\mathsf{Head}(Q) \leftarrow t'_1, \ldots, t'_n$.

As an example, consider the following query:

$$?X \leftarrow \{\mathtt{RELAX}\{(?X, \mathtt{type}, Publication)\}, \mathtt{RELAX}\{(JohnRobert, editorOf, ?X)\}.$$

Figure 4 (A) shows the relaxation graph of each of the triple patterns of the query (for the sake of space, we consider in this example only a single edge of the relaxation graph of $(JohnRobert, editorOf, ?X)$). Figure 4 (B) shows the direct product of the graphs of Figure 4 (A), which is a simplified version of the relaxation graph of the query.

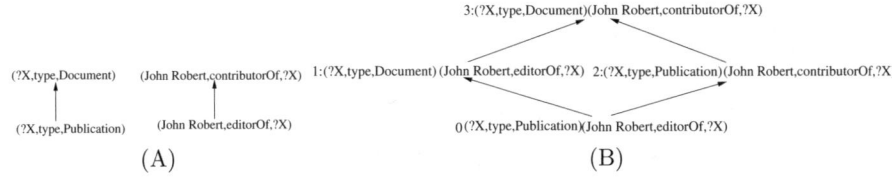

Fig. 4. (A) The relaxation graph of $(?X, \text{type}, Publication)$ and a simplified version of the relaxation graph of $(JohnRobert, editorOf, ?X)$. (B) The direct product of the graphs given in (A). Nodes are enumerated from 0 (base query) to 3 (top query).

3.4 Types of Relaxation

The notion of relaxation that we have presented in this section encompasses the following types of relaxation (the examples given use the ontology of Figure 1):

1. Type relaxation: replacing a triple pattern (a, type, b) with (a, type, c), where $(b, \text{sc}, c) \in \text{cl}(O)$. For example, the triple pattern $(?X, \text{type}, ConferenceArticle)$ can be relaxed to $(?X, \text{type}, Article)$ and then to $(?X, \text{type}, Publication)$.
2. Predicate relaxation: replacing a triple pattern (a, p, b) with (a, q, c), where $(p, \text{sp}, q) \in \text{cl}(O)$. For example, the triple pattern $(?X, proceedingsEditorOf, ?Y)$ can be relaxed to $(?X, editorOf, ?Y)$ and then to $(?X, contributorOf, ?Y)$.
3. Predicate to domain relaxation: replacing a triple pattern (a, p, b) with (a, type, c), where $(p, \text{dom}, c) \in \text{cl}(O)$. There are no domain declarations in Figure 1.
4. Predicate to range relaxation: replacing a triple pattern (a, p, b) with (b, type, c), where $(p, \text{range}, c) \in \text{cl}(O)$. For example, the triple pattern $(JohnRobert, editorOf, ?Y)$ can be relaxed to $(?Y, \text{type}, Publication)$.
5. Additional relaxations induced by additional rules from Figure 2. Combinations of rules yield additional forms of relaxation. For example, the triple pattern $(Article, \text{sc}, ?Y)$ can be relaxed to $(ConferenceArticle, \text{sc}, ?Y)$.

3.5 Notion of Ranking

An algorithm used to process a query with a RELAX clause should return a list of tuples. A condition of consistency for the algorithm is that the tuples that are computed by more specific queries should appear before the ones that are computed by more general queries. If this happens, we say that the algorithm returns its answer in *ranked order*. In this section we formalize this idea.

In order to formalize this idea, we firstly define, for a query Q' in the relaxation graph of Q, the set of tuples returned by Q' and not returned by queries below Q'. We call such a set the *new answer* of Q'. Formally,

$$\texttt{newAnswer}(Q', G) := \texttt{ans}(Q', G) - (\bigcup_{Q_i : Q_i \leq_Q Q', Q_i \neq Q'} \texttt{ans}(Q_i, G)).$$

Definition 4 (Ranking). *Consider an algorithm A that, given a query Q and an RDF graph, returns a list of tuples $L = a_1, \ldots, a_n$. We say that A returns its*

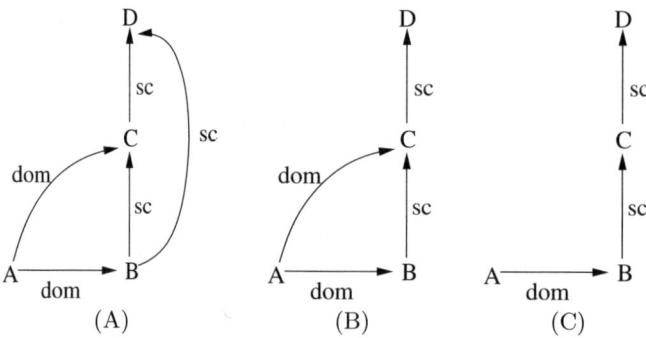

Fig. 5. (A) An ontology O. (B) The reduction $\texttt{red}(O)$ of O. (C) The extended reduction $\texttt{extRed}(O)$ of O.

tuples in ranked order if (i) the set $\{a_1, \ldots, a_n\}$ is equal to $\bigcup_{Q_i : Q \leq_Q Q_i} \texttt{ans}(Q_i, G)$, and (ii) for all pairs of queries Q_i, Q_j such that $Q_i \prec_Q Q_j$, the new answers of Q_i appear earlier in L than the new answers of Q_j.

4 Computing the Relaxation Graph

In this section, we study the problem of computing the relaxation graph of a triple pattern. In Section 4.1 we present a naive procedure to do so. Then, in Section 4.2, we show an efficient algorithm to perform this task. Finally, in Section 4.3, we study the size of the relaxation graph and the complexity of computing it.

4.1 Computing the Relaxation Graph of a Triple Pattern: Naive Algorithm

As Proposition 1 shows, it is possible to generate all the relaxations of a triple pattern t by computing $\text{cl}(O \cup \{t\})$ and $\text{cl}(O)$. However, recall that the edges of the relaxation graph are direct relaxations, and therefore the fundamental problem we need to solve is how to efficiently generate the direct relaxations of t. One may naively attempt to generate them by applying the derivation rules of Figure 2 over t and triples from the ontology $\text{cl}(O)$. We write $t, o \vdash t'$ if t' can be derived from t and $o \in \text{cl}(O)$ by the application of a single rule from Figure 2. We also write $t, o \vdash_i t'$ if rule i was the rule used in the derivation.

As an example, let O be the ontology given in Figure 5 (A). Notice that in this case $O = \text{cl}(O)$. Now, the following instantiation of rule 4

$$(B, \texttt{sc}, C), (?X, \texttt{type}, B) \vdash_4 (?X, \texttt{type}, C),$$

produces the direct relaxation $(?X, \texttt{type}, C)$ of $(?X, \texttt{type}, B)$. However, the following instantiation of rule 4

$$(B, \text{sc}, D), (?X, \text{type}, B) \vdash_4 (?X, \text{type}, D),$$

produces the indirect relaxation $(?X, \text{type}, D)$ of $(?X, \text{type}, B)$.

The example shows that the application of rules over the closure of the ontology and the triple t is not correct for computing direct relaxations of t. However, the next proposition shows that the procedure is complete for this purpose.

Proposition 3. *Let t_a, t_b be triple patterns not in $\text{cl}(O)$ such that $\text{var}(t_a) = \text{var}(t_b)$. If $t_a \prec t_b$ then there exists a triple $o \in \text{cl}(O)$ such that $t_a, o \vdash t_b$.*

As an aside, Proposition 3 along with the rules of Figure 2 allows us to classify the direct relaxations that can be obtained from a given triple pattern, which is done in Figure 6. We refer to triples having type as their predicate as *type triples*. We use a similar notation for triples with predicates dom, range, sp, and sc. A *plain triple* is a triple whose predicate term is not in the RDFS vocabulary. As an example, the figure shows that a direct relaxation of a plain triple is either a plain triple or a type triple. Notice that neither dom triples nor range triples can be relaxed.

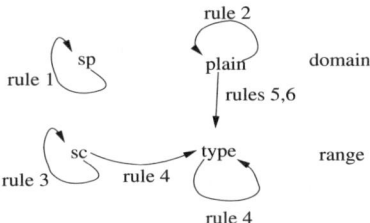

Fig. 6. Diagram of possible direct relaxations

In the remainder of the section, we present a naive algorithm to compute the relaxation graph of a triple pattern.

Firstly, let us introduce some notation to refer to the procedure just outlined that uses the RDFS derivation rules to produce relaxations of a triple pattern. We denote by $\text{applyRules}(t, O)$ all the triples generated by instantiating a rule of Figure 2 with t and a triple from O. Using O from Figure 5 (A) as an example, $\text{applyRules}((?X, \text{type}, B), O)$ generates the triple patterns $(?X, \text{type}, C)$ and $(?X, \text{type}, D)$. We will frequently abuse notation and consider $\text{applyRules}(t, O)$ simply as a set. Furthermore, since relaxations preserve variables of t, we assume we filter from $\text{applyRules}(t, O)$ triples t' such that $\text{var}(t') \neq \text{var}(t)$.

The naive algorithm works as follows. In a first step, it builds a graph that subsumes the relaxation graph of t. This graph may contain some indirect relaxations that need to be deleted in a second step. In the first step, it start by calling $\text{applyRules}(t, O)$, update the graph with new relaxations of t, and adds them to a list. It then removes a triple pattern t' from the list, update the graph with new relaxations $\text{applyRules}(t', O)$ of t' and adds them to the list. This operation is repeated until the list is emptied. A list of "visited" triple patterns can be used in order to avoid calling applyRules more than once for the same triple pattern. As each applyRules(t', O) call may generate some indirect relaxations of t', in a final step, edges associated with indirect relaxations are deleted using any standard method to compute the transitive reduction of a dag.

4.2 Computing the Relaxation Graph Incrementally

The naive procedure has a major drawback. In order to delete the indirect relaxations generated by applyRules(t, O), we need to call applyRules for all triples in the relaxation graph of t. This should be done even though the user is interested in relaxing t only one step further. In this section, we show how to transform the ontology O into a new ontology O' such that applyRules(t, O') only returns direct relaxations of t.

Now, let us return to the example of the previous subsection, where O is the ontology of Figure 5 (A). Recall that applyRules$((?X, \text{type}, B), O)$ generates the direct relaxation $(?X, \text{type}, C)$ and the indirect relaxation $(?X, \text{type}, D)$ of $(?X, \text{type}, B)$. The latter is generated using the triple (B, sc, D) of O. We say that this is a *derivable triple* since it can be derived from other two triples in cl(O). Now, observe that if we delete (B, sc, D) from O, we obtain a reduced version O' of O (which is logically equivalent to O) such that applyRules$((?X, \text{type}, B), O')$ only outputs direct relaxations. This example motivates us to delete the derivable triples of O since they produce indirect relaxations. The following proposition shows that this indeed is a good idea.

Proposition 4. *Let O be an ontology, o be a derivable triple in* cl(O) *and t, t' be triple patterns such that $t, o \vdash t'$. Then t' is an indirect relaxation of t (defined using O).*

From Proposition 4 we conclude that we should apply applyRules over the *reduction* of O instead of O. The reduction of O, denoted red(O), is the minimal ontology $O' \subseteq O$, such that cl$(O') = $ cl(O). The reduction does not contain derivable triples and can be computed as follows (applying a rule in reverse means deleting the triple deduced by the rule): (i) compute cl(O); (ii) apply rule 4 in reverse until no longer applicable; and (iii) apply rules 1 and 3 in reverse until no longer applicable. In what follows, we assume that red(O) has been precomputed. Notice that, because every predicate in a triple in the ontology should be in {type, dom, range, sp, sc}, reverse rules 2, 5, and 6 are not needed to compute the reduction.

Since red(O) is logically equivalent to O, we obtain the same relaxations using red(O) and using O. The following proposition follows directly from Proposition 3.

Proposition 5. *Let O be an ontology and t be a triple pattern not in* cl(O). *Then all direct relaxations of t (defined using O) are in the set* applyRules$(t, \text{red}(O))$.

Unfortunately, applyRules$(t, \text{red}(O))$ may still return indirect relaxations, as the following example shows. Consider the reduction red(O) shown in Figure 5 (B), where O is the ontology of Figure 5 (A). Then, with the following instantiation of rule 5

$$(A, \text{dom}, C), (?X, A, ?Y) \vdash_5 (?X, \text{type}, C)$$

applyRules$((?X, A, ?Y), \text{red}(O))$ produces the relaxation $(?X, \text{type}, C)$ of $(?X, A, ?Y)$. However, this is an indirect relaxation, since we have that $(?X, A, ?Y) \prec (?X, \text{type}, B) \prec (?X, \text{type}, C)$. Fortunately, the following proposition shows that it is not difficult to detect the triples in the reduction that cause problems.

Proposition 6. *Let O be an ontology, o be a triple in* red(O) *and t, t' be triple patterns such that $t, o \vdash t'$. Then t' is an indirect relaxation of t (defined using O) iff o can be derived by applying the rules of Figure 7 starting from* cl(O).

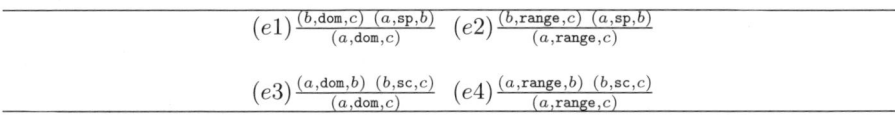

Fig. 7. Additional rules used to compute the extended reduction of an RDFS ontology

The proposition shows that we can avoid generating indirect relaxations by further reducing the ontology with the rules of Figure 7, which yields an extended reduction of an ontology O. The extended reduction, denoted extRed(O), is defined as follows: (i) compute cl(O); (ii) apply the rules of Figure 7 in reverse until no longer applicable; (iii) apply rule 4 in reverse until no longer applicable; and (iv) apply rules 1 and 3 in reverse until no longer applicable.

As an example, Figure 5 (C) shows the extended reduction of the ontology of Figure 5 (A).

Now, observe that extRed(O) may not be logically equivalent to O. However, the previous propositions show that we can still obtain all the direct relaxations of any triple pattern (defined using O) from extRed(O). We are now ready to present the main result of this section.

Proposition 7. *Let O be an ontology and t be a triple pattern not in* cl(O). *Then* applyRules$(t, \text{extRed}(O))$ *is equal to the set of direct relaxations of t (defined using O).*

Figure 8 shows an algorithm that computes the relaxation graph of a triple pattern incrementally. We assume that the extended reduction extRed(O) has been previously computed and stored. The variable Frontier keeps a list of triple patterns. The variables V and E keep the nodes and edges of the relaxation graph, respectively. Notice that, because of Proposition 7, the algorithm does not produce indirect relaxations.

4.3 Complexity

We now give a bound on the size of the relaxation graph.

Proposition 8. *Let t be a triple pattern and O be an ontology. The relaxation graph of t (using the ontology O) has $O(|\text{red}(O)|^2)$ triples.*

Input: A triple pattern t and the extended reduction $\texttt{extRed}(O)$ of an ontology O.
Output: The relaxation graph of t (using O).

$\texttt{Frontier} := \langle t \rangle$
$V := \{t\}, E := \emptyset$
While ($\texttt{Frontier}$ is non-empty)
    Delete first element u from $\texttt{Frontier}$
    $U := \texttt{applyRules}(u, \texttt{extRed}(O))$
    $V := V \cup U$
    $E := E \cup \{(u, u') : u' \in U\}$
    Add the triple patterns in U to $\texttt{Frontier}$
Return (V, E)

Fig. 8. Algorithm that computes the relaxation graph of a triple pattern

From Proposition 9, it follows that the relaxation graph of a query has $O(|\texttt{red}(O)|^{2n})$ nodes, where n is the number of triple patterns inside RELAX clauses in the query.

Proposition 9. *Let t be a triple pattern and O be an ontology. (i) Computing the direct relaxations of t takes $O(|\texttt{red}(O)|)$ steps. (ii) Computing the relaxation graph of t takes $O(|\texttt{red}(O)|^3)$ steps.*

5 Computing the Relaxed Answer

In this section, we study the problem of computing the relaxed answer of a query. We propose an algorithm that incrementally generates matchings from a query to an RDF graph and also ranks tuples in the answer.

Our query processing algorithm works by adapting the RDQL query processing scheme provided by Jena [21] to the processing of successive relaxations of a query. We assume the simplest storage scheme provided by Jena, in which the RDF triples are stored in a single table, called the *statement table*. The Jena query processing approach is to convert an RDF query into a pipeline of "find patterns" connected by join variables. Each triple pattern (find pattern in Jena's terminology) can be evaluated by a single SQL select query over the statement table. We formalize this with an operator called find that receives a triple pattern t and a statement table G and returns all matchings from t to the table.

In Section 5.1 we present our algorithm for efficiently computing the relaxed answer of a query and we prove its correctness. In Sections 5.2 and 5.3 we illustrate two examples of the execution of the algorithm. Finally, in Section 5.4, we study the complexity of the algorithm.

5.1 Algorithm

In what follows, Q is the query whose relaxed answer we intend to compute, and Q' is an arbitrary query in the relaxation graph of Q. We have that $H =$

Head(Q) = Head(Q'). For the sake of simplicity, we assume that each triple pattern in the body of Q is inside a RELAX clause. We assume that Body(Q) = $\{t_1, \ldots, t_n\}$, and Body(Q') = $\{t'_1, \ldots, \ldots, t'_n\}$. We also fix the statement table G we are querying. The answer of Q' can be computed by processing (in a pipelined fashion) a view, denoted $V_{Q'}$, defined by the following expression:

$$\pi_H(\text{find}(t'_1, G) \bowtie \ldots \bowtie \text{find}(t'_n, G)),$$

where π is the standard projection operator and $\bowtie$ is the natural join on variables shared by triple patterns. The answer of Q can be computed by a naive algorithm that traverses the relaxation graph of Q upwards, and in each step of the traversal, builds a view $V_{Q'}$, computes it, and returns those tuples which were not returned in previous steps.

Next, we propose an algorithm that avoids the redundant processing of tuples that arises with this naive approach. We define deltaFind(t'_i, G) as the set containing triples $p \in G$ such that t'_i matches p, and no triple pattern directly below t'_i in the relaxation graph of t_i, matches p. The set deltaFind(t'_i, G) can be computed similarly to find(t'_i, G) by filtering triples from the statement table. We define a *delta view* for Q', denoted $\Delta_{Q'}$, as the following expression:

$$\pi_H(\text{deltaFind}(t'_1, G) \bowtie \ldots \bowtie \text{deltaFind}(t'_n, G)).$$

The following proposition shows that new answers (Section 3.5) correspond to delta views.

Proposition 10. *Let Q be a query and G be a RDF graph. For each query Q' in the relaxation graph of Q, (i) $\text{ans}(Q', G) = \bigcup_{Q_i : Q_i \leq_Q Q'} \Delta_{Q_i}(G)$, and (ii) $\text{newAnswer}(Q', G) = \Delta_{Q'}(G)$.*

The algorithm we propose (Figure 9), called RelaxEval, performs a breadth-first traversal of the relaxation graph of Q, building and processing each delta view $\Delta_{Q'}$ in each step of the traversal. The function *level* returns the level of a triple pattern t'_i in the relaxation graph R_i of t_i. Line 3(a) outputs the new answer of each query at level k. In order to find the queries at level k of the relaxation graph, the algorithm applies the following property. The queries Q' (defined by the join expression in Line 3 (a)) that belong to the level k of the relaxation graph of Q are those satisfying $\sum_i level(t'_i, R_i) = k$.

We next prove the correctness of RelaxEval.

Proposition 11. *The algorithm RelaxEval returns its tuples in ranked order.*

5.2 Example

We next illustrate the algorithm with the following query Q (that we also presented in the example of Section 3.3):

$?X \leftarrow \{\text{RELAX}\{(?X, \text{type}, Publication)\}, \text{RELAX}\{(JohnRobert, editorOf, ?X)\}\}.$

Algorithm RelaxEval
Input: a query Q (interpreted over an ontology O), where $\text{Body}(Q) = \{t_1, \ldots, t_n\}$, a statement table G, and an integer $maxLevel$.
Output: the set of tuples $\text{ans}_{\text{relax}}(Q, G, maxLevel)$, where new answers are returned successively at each level of the relaxation graph.

1. $k := 0$, $stillMore := true$
2. For each triple pattern $t_i \in \text{Body}(Q)$, compute the relaxation graph R_i of t_i up to level $maxLevel$.
3. While ($k \leq maxLevel$ and $stillMore$) do
   (a) For each combination $t'_1 \in R_1, \ldots, t'_n \in R_n$ such that $\sum_i level(t'_i, R_i) = k$ do output $\pi_H(\text{deltaFind}(t'_1, G) \bowtie \ldots \bowtie \text{deltaFind}(t'_n, G))$
   (b) $k := k + 1$
   (c) $stillMore := $ exist nodes $t'_1 \in R_1, \ldots, t'_n \in R_n$ such that $\sum_i level(t'_i, R_i) = k$

Fig. 9. Algorithm that computes the relaxed answer of a query

For simplicity, we consider subgraphs of the relaxation graphs of triple patterns in the query, shown in Figure 4 (A). Figure 4 (B) shows the relaxation graph of the query, which is obtained by combining the graphs of Figure 4 (A).

We assume the query is interpreted in the context of an ontology O, which consists of the subgraph with edges sc and type of the ontology of Figure 1. The

Statement table G

Subject	Predicate	Object
a	type	$Publication$
b	type	$WebPage$
c	type	$Publication$
d	type	$WebPage$
$JohnRobert$	$editorOf$	a
$JohnRobert$	$editorOf$	b
$JohnRobert$	$authorOf$	c
$JohnRobert$	$authorOf$	d

(A)

Statement table for $\text{cl}(G, O)$

Subject	Predicate	Object
a	type	$Publication$
b	type	$WebPage$
c	type	$Publication$
d	type	$WebPage$
a	type	$Document$
b	type	$Document$
c	type	$Document$
d	type	$Document$
$JohnRobert$	$editorOf$	a
$JohnRobert$	$editorOf$	b
$JohnRobert$	$authorOf$	c
$JohnRobert$	$authorOf$	d
$JohnRobert$	$contributorOf$	a
$JohnRobert$	$contributorOf$	b
$JohnRobert$	$contributorOf$	c
$JohnRobert$	$contributorOf$	d

(B)

Fig. 10. (A) Statement Table G. (B) A statement table containing $\text{cl}(G, O)$, where O is the subgraph of the ontology of Figure 1 that includes only the sc and type subgraphs.

query is interpreted over the statement table G given in Figure 10 (A), whose closure $\text{cl}(G, O)$ is given in Figure 10 (B).

Figure 11 (A) shows the answers of queries in the relaxation graph of Q and Figure 11 (B) shows the answers of delta views. An answer is a set of tuples; since the query at hand has a single head variable, each tuple is a single element in our example. Figure 11 (C) shows the answer returned by RelaxEval at levels $0, 1$ and 2.

Notice that Proposition 10 (i) and (ii) hold. For instance, for query Q_3, we have

$$\text{ans}(Q_3, G) = \Delta_{Q_3} \cup (\Delta_{Q_1} \cup \Delta_{Q_2} \cup \Delta_{Q_0}),$$

and we also have

$$\Delta_{Q_3}(G) = \text{ans}(Q_3, G) - (\text{ans}(Q_1, G) \cup \text{ans}(Q_2, G) \cup \text{ans}(Q_0, G)).$$

We now illustrate how RelaxEval computes the delta view

$$\Delta_{Q_3}(G) := \pi_{?X}(\text{deltaFind}((?X, \text{type}, Document), G) \bowtie \\ \text{deltaFind}((JohnRobert, contributorOf, ?X), G)).$$

Here, deltaFind$((?X, \text{type}, Document), G)$ finds all matchings μ from $(?X, \text{type}, Document)$ to $\text{cl}(G, 0)$ such that μ is not a matching from $(?X, \text{type}, Publication)$ to $\text{cl}(G, O)$ (because $(?X, \text{type}, Publication)$ is the only triple pattern directly below $(?X, \text{type}, Document)$ in the relaxation graph of $(?X, \text{type}, Publication)$). Therefore, deltaFind$((?X, \text{type}, Document), G)$ returns the following table:

?X	type	Document
b	type	Document
d	type	Document

Similarly, deltaFind$((JohnRobert, contributorOf, ?X), G)$ computes the following table:

JohnRobert	contributorOf	?X
JohnRobert	contributorOf	c
JohnRobert	contributorOf	d

Therefore, $\Delta_{Q_3}(G) = \{d\}$.

5.3 A Further Example — Heterogeneous Database Integration

We now discuss how our algorithm for incrementally computing the relaxed answer of a query might be applied in a heterogeneous data integration setting, specifically in the integration and querying of multiple heterogeneous proteomic data resources.

Answers of Relaxed Queries	
Relaxed Query	Answer
Q_0	$\{a\}$
Q_1	$\{a,b\}$
Q_2	$\{a,c\}$
Q_3	$\{a,b,c,d\}$

(A)

Answers of Delta Views	
Delta view	Answer
Δ_{Q_0}	$\{a\}$
Δ_{Q_1}	$\{b\}$
Δ_{Q_2}	$\{c\}$
Δ_{Q_3}	$\{d\}$

(B)

Answers of RelaxEval	
Level	Answer
0	$\{a\}$
1	$\{b,c\}$
2	$\{d\}$

(C)

Fig. 11. (A) Answers of relaxed queries until level 2. (B) Delta views for the relaxed queries until level 2. (C) Tuples returned by RelaxEval per level until level 2.

Proteomic data resources are rapidly being developed globally, with the emergence of affordable, reliable methods to study the proteome. The *In Silico Proteome Integrated Data Environment Resource* (ISPIDER) project[4] is developing an integrated platform of proteome-related resources, using existing standards from proteomics, bioinformatics and e-Science. The integration of such resources is beneficial for a number of reasons. First, having access to more data leads to more reliable analyses; for example, performing protein identifications over an integrated resource reduces the chances of false negatives. Second, bringing together resources containing different but closely related data increases the breadth of information the biologist has access to. Third, the integration of these resources, as opposed to merely providing a common interface for accessing them, enables data from a range of experiments, tissues, or different cell states to be brought together in a form which may be analysed by a biologist in spite of the widely varying coverage and underlying technology of each resource.

In the ISPIDER project, we have developed an architecture which supports the combined use of Grid data access, Grid distributed querying and data integration software tools. This architecture allows us to develop an integrated global schema over heterogeneous resources and to support distributed queries posed over such a global schema. Reference [22] reports on our initial results from the integration of three distributed, autonomous proteomics resources, all of which contain information about protein and peptide identification: gpmDB[5], Pedro[6] and PepSeeker[7].

As reported in [22], building an integrated global schema over such heterogeneous proteomics resources is a lengthy and complex process. Indeed, so far, we have not performed a full integration of these three databases, but only a limited integration such that the global schema captures enough information for answering common proteomics questions. Moreover, some of the resource schemas are still under development and enhancement, which requires ongoing modification to our integration mappings and global schema.

An alternative approach, therefore, would be to undertake a "light-weight" integration of these resources, producing a global ontology that captures the

---
[4] See http://www.ispider.manchester.ac.uk
[5] See http://gpmdb.thegpm.org
[6] See http://pedrodb.man.ac.uk:8080/pedrodb
[7] See http://www.nwsr.manchester.ac.uk/pepseeker

classes and properties of the individual resources as well as their common concepts (i.e. super-classes and super-properties of the local ontology classes and properties), and to use our query processing algorithm to incrementally relax and compute the answers to queries over this global ontology.

For example, in the global ontology, there may be

- classes *PedroPeptide* and *PedroProtein*
- and properties
    - *PedroPeptideSequence*, with domain *PedroPeptide* and range Literal,
    - *PedroAligns*, with domain *PedroPeptide* and range *PedroProtein*,
    - *PedroAccessionNumber*, with domain *PedroProtein* and range Literal,

arising from the Pedro resource, which is based at Manchester (in Mass Spectrometry experiments, several Peptides result from the identification process; each Peptide aligns against a set of Proteins; a Protein is characterized by a textual description, an accession number, the predicted mass of the protein, the organism in which it is to be found, etc.).

There may be a similar set of classes and properties arising from the PepSeeker resource, also at Manchester:

- classes *PepPeptide* and *PepProtein*
- and properties
    - *PepPeptideSequence*, with domain *PepPeptide* and range Literal,
    - *PepAligns*, with domain *PepPeptide* and range *PepProtein*,
    - *PepAccessionNumber*, with domain *PepProtein* and range Literal,

In the global ontology there may be superclasses and superproperties of the above which collectively represent the information in the Manchester resources:

- superclasses *ManchPeptide* and *ManchProtein*
- and superproperties
    - *ManchPeptideSequence*, with domain *ManchPeptide* and range Literal,
    - *ManchAligns*, with domain *ManchPeptide* and range *ManchProtein*,
    - *ManchAccessionNumber*, with domain *ManchProtein* and range Literal,

This fragment of the ontology is shown in Figure 12.

We may also have properties and classes in the global ontology, arising from the publicly available gpmDB resources:

- classes: *gpmPeptide* and *gpmProtein*
- properties: *gpmPeptideSequence*, *gpmAligns* and *gpmAccessionNumber*

Finally, there may be the following classes and properties that are supeclasses or superproperties of the corresponding Manchester and gpmDB classes or properties, and that collectively represent the information in all three resources:

- superclasses: *Peptide* and *Protein*
- superproperties: *PeptideSequence*, *Aligns* and *AccessionNumber*

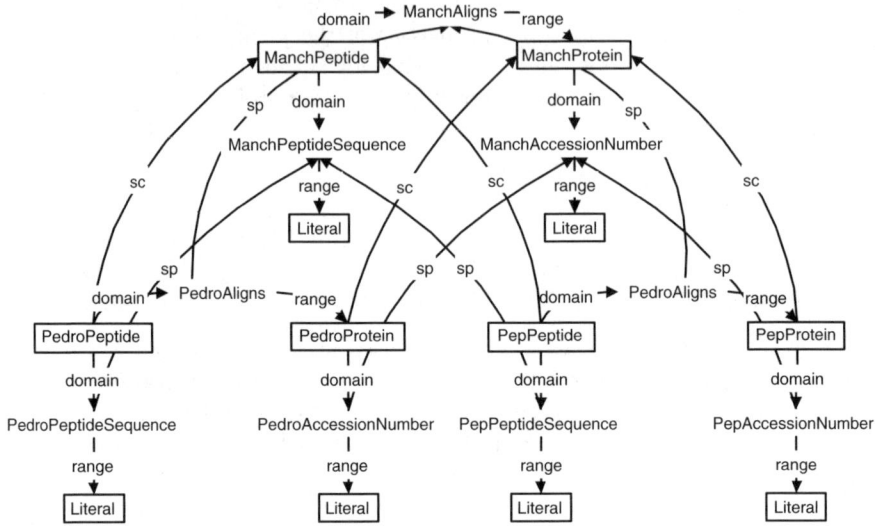

Fig. 12. Part of the Proteomics Resources Ontology

Consider now the following query posed over the global ontology by a user who is familiar with the Pedro resource:

```
?Y, ?Z <- {RELAX{(?X,PedroPeptideSequence,"ATLITFLCDR")},
           RELAX{(?X,PedroAligns,?Y)},
           RELAX{(?Y,PedroAccessionNumber,?Z)}}
```

In its non-relaxed form, this query will return the identifiers and accession numbers of proteins that have been identified within the Pedro resource as a result of experiments that have yielded the peptide "ATLITFLCDR". Such a query allows a scientist working with a protein sequence to ask if this peptide has been seen before in other proteomics experiments.

A first level of relaxation of the three literals in this query according to the sp subgraph, will result in the following relaxed query,

```
?Y, ?Z <- {RELAX{(?X,ManchPeptideSequence,"ATLITFLCDR")},
           RELAX{(?X,ManchAligns,?Y)},
           RELAX{(?Y,ManchAccessionNumber,?Z)}}
```

which will expand out the result set to include results also from the other Manchester resource, Pepseeker, without the Pedro user needing to have detailed knowledge of the schema of that resource.

A further level of relaxation of the three literals in the query according to the sp subgraph, will result in the following relaxed query,

```
?Y, ?Z <- {RELAX{(?X,PeptideSequence,"ATLITFLCDR")},
           RELAX{(?X,Aligns,?Y)},
           RELAX{(?Y,AccessionNumber,?Z)}}
```

which will now expand out the result set to include results also from the gpmDB resource, again without the Pedro user needing to have detailed knowledge of the schema of that resource.

In contrast therefore to the approach discussed in [22], in which users must pose queries against an integrated global schema, the light-weight integration and relaxed querying approach that we have outlined here would allow a more incremental construction of query results, a more exploratory approach to query answering, and also less knowledge of the global resources by users.

5.4 Complexity

The complexity of RelaxEval is given by the following proposition.

Proposition 12. *Let Q be a query, O be an ontology and G an RDF graph. Then* RelaxEval(Q, G, k) *runs in time $O(m^{2n}|G|^n)$, where m is the number of triples in* red(O)*, and $n = |$Body$(Q)|$.*

The above proposition shows that the algorithm has exponential complexity, however its complexity is polynomial in the size of the data queried for a fixed query Q (data complexity). In addition, the answer is generated incrementally and hence the processing can be halted at any level in the relaxation graph. The number of triples in red(O) provides an upper bound for k, the number of levels in the evaluation.

An improvement to the algorithm would be to process several delta views at the same time in an integrated pipelined fashion. In practice, we can improve query processing performance by further caching the results of deltaFind(t, G) for all triple patterns t that occur more than once in the query relaxation graph (such duplicate occurrences can be detected as the relaxation graphs of the individual triple patterns in the original query are being constructed).

6 Introducing Simple Relaxations

In this section, we extend the relaxation framework to consider simple relaxations that is, relaxations that replace terms of the original triple pattern with variables. In Section 6.1, we formalize simple relaxation and show how the relaxation graph can be extended with simple relaxations. In Section 6.2, we show the additional types of relaxation now captured by our framework.

6.1 Notion of Simple Relaxation

An important restriction we place in our framework is to prevent simple relaxations replacing variables of the original query. This is because such variables are needed to export results and join triple patterns in the relaxed queries. It is important to note, however, that (as we will show in the next section) this restriction does not limit the ability of our framework to relax join dependencies.

In the light of the above, we call the variables of the original query *fixed variables*, and define the notion of map that preserves such variables, along with literals and IRIs. A *map* from a triple pattern $t_1 = (a, b, c)$ to a triple pattern $t_2 = (d, e, f)$ is a function μ from terms of t_1 to terms of t_2, preserving IRIs, literals, and fixed variables, such that $(\mu(a), \mu(b), \mu(c))) = (d, e, f)$. We say that two triple patterns t_1 and t_2 are isomorphic if there are maps from t_1 to t_2 and from t_2 to t_1. Now, we define simple relaxation.

Definition 5 (Simple Relaxation). *If t_1, t_2 are triple patterns, then $t_1 \leq_{\text{simple}} t_2$ if there is a map from t_2 to t_1.*

As an example, assuming a unique fixed variable $?X$, we have $(?X, \text{type}, Article)$ $\leq_{\text{simple}} (?X, \text{type}, ?Z)$ and $(?X, \text{type}, Article) \leq_{\text{simple}} (?X, ?W, Article)$, among other simple relaxations. It is not the case that $(?X, \text{type}, Article) \leq_{\text{simple}} (?U, \text{type}, ?Z)$, since the fixed variable $?X$ is replaced.

The following proposition confirms a desired property of the simple relaxation relation.

Proposition 13. *The simple relaxation relation $\leq_{\text{simple}}$ is a partial order up to triple pattern isomorphism.*

Similarly to Section 3.2, we can define the notion of relaxation graph of a triple pattern t. It is enough to define the direct simple relaxation relation $\prec_{\text{simple}}$ (transitive and reflexive reduction of $\leq_{\text{simple}}$ up to isomorphism), and the relation $\prec_{\text{simple},t}$ (simple relaxation "above" t). The simple relaxation graph of t is the graph induced by $\prec_{\text{simple},t}$. This graph is unique up to triple pattern isomorphism. In order to obtain a clean representation of it, without loss of generality, we may assume that each non-fixed variable does not appear in more than one triple pattern.

Also notice that the simple relaxation graph of a triple pattern can be easily computed: we just need to iteratively replace terms by variables in triple patterns, taking care not to generate isomorphic triples and indirect relaxations.

The notions of relaxation graph of a triple pattern (and hence of a query) introduced in Section 3.2 can be naturally generalized to include simple relaxations in different ways. Here we sketch one possible, yet simple, extension. We add on the top of each triple pattern t in the original relaxation graph the simple relaxation graph of t, and then delete indirect edges.

As an example, consider the ontology O of Figure 1. Figure 13 (B) shows the relaxation graph of $(JohnRobert, editorOf, ?X)$ (Figure 3) extended with simple relaxations. The non-fixed variables are $?U1, \ldots, ?U10$.

Finally, we just remark that the query processing algorithm of Section 5 can be applied without any modification to the extended version of the relaxation graph as well.

6.2 Types of Simple Relaxation

The following types of relaxation can be captured by simple relaxation.

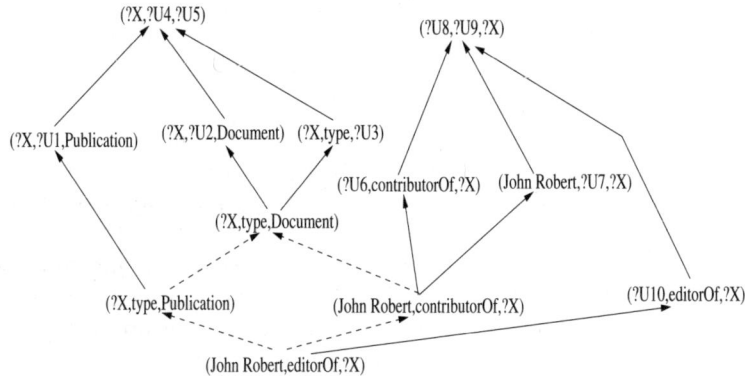

Fig. 13. Relaxation graph of the triple pattern (*JohnRobert, editorOf*, ?*X*) considering simple relaxations. The simple relaxations are shown with solid arrows.

1. Dropping triple patterns. We can model the dropping of triple patterns by introducing an "empty" triple pattern, which can be regarded as a "true" condition to which any triple pattern relaxes. In this form, relaxation generalizes the use of the OPTIONAL clause within the conjunctive fragment of SPARQL.
2. Constant relaxation: replacing a constant with a variable in a triple pattern. This can be further classified according to whether the variable replaces a property or a subject/object constant.
3. Breaking join dependencies: generating new variable names for a variable that appears in multiple triple patterns. In order to model this type of relaxation, we first transform queries by applying variable substitution. If a variable ?X appears $n > 1$ times in a query Q we replace each occurrence with a different variable and add triple patterns (?X_i, equal, ?X_j) for each pair of new variables ?X_i, ?X_j introduced. The predicate equal represents equality. Each of the equality clauses in a query can now also be subject to relaxation.

7 Related Work

Query languages based on regular expressions provide a form of flexible querying. The G$^+$ query language by Cruz et al. [6] proposes graph patterns where edges are annotated with regular expressions over labels. In this form, each graph pattern represents a set of more basic graph patterns, and therefore, a query extracts matchings that relate to its body in a variety of ways. This work considers queries over directed labeled graphs.

Kanza and Sagiv [14] propose a form of flexible querying based on a notion of homeomorphism between the query and the graph. Their data model is a simplified form of the Object Exchange Model (OEM).

Bernstein and Kiefer [1] incorporate similarity joins into the RDQL query language. This is done by allowing sets of variables in an RDQL query to be declared as *imprecise*. Bindings for these variables are then compared based on a specified similarity measure, such as edit distance.

Stuckenschmidt and van Harmelen [20] consider conjunctive queries over a terminological knowledge base that includes class, relation and object definitions. They also use query containment as a way of viewing query approximations, but are concerned about evaluating less complex queries first, so that the original query is evaluated last. They use a query graph to decide which conjuncts from the original query should be successively added to the approximate query. This is analogous to SPARQL queries in which every conjunct is optional.

Bulskov et al. [4] consider the language ONTOLOG which allows compound concepts to be formed from atomic concepts attributed with semantic relations. They define a similarity measure between concepts based on subsumption in a hierarchy of concepts. This gives rise to a fuzzy set of concepts similar to a given concept. They also introduce specialization/generalization operators into a query language that allow specializations or generalizations of concepts to be returned. They admit that combining this with similarity may make answers confusing.

In a series of papers, e.g. [18,19], Stojanovic and others have studied the problem of query refinement in information retrieval, where users tend to pose initial queries that are too short to fulfull their needs. The techniques proposed use ontologies associated with the information to analyse "amibiguities" in the user's queries as well as users' preferences in order to suggest incremental refinements to the user. For example, [19] uses a form of subsumption between queries which generates a lattice of query refinements. A form of ranking, based on user modelling and monitoring, is also provided. However, the refinements considered are, in fact, specialisations of a query, rather than generalisations as in our case. Generalisation is considered as one form of query refinement in [18]. The ontologies used in all cases, however, are not based on RDF/S.

A recent paper by Dolog et at. considers relaxing over-constrained queries on RDF [7]. The paper proposes a rewriting technique based on domain knowledge and user preferences, although these are not encoded using RDFS. The implementation of rewriting is performed using event-condition-action rules, for which the authors state that termination of execution still needs to be thoroughly investigated.

8 Concluding Remarks

Despite being a relatively unexplored technique in the semantic Web, query relaxation may have an important role in improving RDF data access. One motivation for this technique is for querying data where there is a lack of understanding of the ontology that underlies the data. Another application is the extraction of objects with heterogeneous sets of properties because the data is incomplete or has irregular structure. As an example, a relaxed query can retrieve the properties that are applicable to each resource among a set of resources having different properties. Query relaxation can also make it possible to retrieve data that satisfies the query conditions with different degrees of exactitude. Another application area where this facility could be useful is the discovery of semantic web services.

There are several areas for future work. One is the introduction of relaxation into general SPARQL queries, including disjunctions and optionals. This should also involve a generalization of the RELAX clause so that it can be applied to entire graph patterns instead of single triple patterns. Another important issue for future work is the design, implementation and empirical evaluation of algorithms for computing relaxed answers. Finally, the graph-like nature of RDF provides additional richness for a query relaxation framework, which can be exploited in future work. For example, join dependencies between triple patterns of the query can be relaxed to connectivity relationships in RDF graphs.

Acknowledgement

We gratefully acknowledge the contribution of Lucas Zamboulis in the formulation of the example in Section 5.3.

References

1. Bernstein, A., Kiefer, C.: Imprecise RDQL: Towards generic retrieval in ontologies using similarity joins. In: SAC/SIGAPP. 21th Annual ACM Symposium on Applied Computing, Dijon, France (2006)
2. Brickley, D., Guha, R.V. (eds.): RDF Vocabulary Description Language 1.0: RDF Schema, W3C Recommendation (February 10, 2004)
3. Broekstra, J.: SeRQL: Sesame RDF query language. In: Ehrig, M., et al. (eds.) SWAP Deliverable 3.2 Method Design, pp. 55+68 (2003), http://swap.semanticweb.org/public/Publications/swap-d3.2.pdf
4. Bulskov, H., Knappe, R., Andreasen, T.: On querying ontologies and databases. In: 6th International Conference on Flexible Query Answering Systems, pp. 191–202 (2004)
5. Clark, K.G. (ed.): RDF Data Access Use Cases and Requirements, W3C Working Draft (March 25, 2005)
6. Cruz, I.F., Mendelzon, A.O., Wood, P.T.: A graphical query language supporting recursion. In: ACM SIGMOD International Conference on Management of Data, pp. 323–330 (1987)
7. Dolog, P., Stuckenschmidt, H., Wache, H.: Robust query processing for personalized information access on the semantic web. In: 7th International Conference on Flexible Query Answering Systems, pp. 343–355 (2006)
8. Fikes, R., Hayes, P.J., Horrocks, I.: OWL-QL - a language for deductive query answering on the semantic web. J. Web Sem. 2(1), 19–29 (2004)
9. Gaasterland, T., Godfrey, P., Minker, J.: Relaxation as a platform for cooperative answering. J. Intell. Inf. Syst. 1(3/4), 293–321 (1992)
10. Gutierrez, C., Hurtado, C., Mendelzon, A.O.: Foundations of semantic web databases. In: 23rd Symposium on Principles of Database Systems, pp. 95–106 (2004)

11. Haase, P., Broekstra, J., Eberhart, A., Volz, R.: A comparison of RDF query languages. In: International Semantic Web Conference (2004)
12. Hayes, P.: RDF Semantics, W3C Recommendation (February 10, 2004)
13. Hurtado, C., Poulovassilis, A., Wood, P.T.: A relaxed approach to RDF querying. In: Proceedings of the 5th International Semantic Web Conference, Athens, GA, USA, pp. 314–328 (2007)
14. Kanza, Y., Sagiv, Y.: Flexible queries over semistructured data. In: 20th ACM SIGMOD-SIGACT-SIGART Symposium on Principles of Database Systems, pp. 40–51 (2001)
15. Manola, F., Miller, E. (eds.): RDF Primer, W3C Recommendation (February 10, 2004)
16. Nerode, A., Shore, R.: Logic for Applications. Springer, Netherlands (1998)
17. Prud'hommeaux, E., Seaborne, A. (eds.): SPARQL Query Language for RDF, W3C Candidate Recommendation (April 6, 2006)
18. Stojanovic, N.: Information-need driven query refinement. In: Proceedings of the IEEE/WIC International Conference on Web Intelligence, pp. 388–395 (2003)
19. Stojanovic, N., Stojanovic, L.: A logic-based approach for query refinement in ontology-based information retrieval systems. In: 16th IEEE International Conference on Tools with Artificial Intelligence, pp. 450–457 (2004)
20. Stuckenschmidt, H., van Harmelen, F.: Approximating terminological queries. In: 5th International Conference on Flexible Query Answering Systems, pp. 329–343 (2002)
21. Wilkinson, K., Sayers, C., Kuno, H., Reynolds, D.: Efficient RDF storage and retrieval in Jena. In: Proceedings of VLDB Workshop on Semantic Web and Databases (2003)
22. Zamboulis, L., Fan, H., Khalid, B., Siepen, J.A., Jones, A., Martin, N.J., Poulovassilis, A., Hubbard, S.J., Embury, S.M., Paton, N.W.: Data access and integration in the ISPIDER proteomics grid. In: Leser, U., Naumann, F., Eckman, B. (eds.) DILS 2006. LNCS (LNBI), vol. 4075, pp. 3–18. Springer, Heidelberg (2006)

A Proofs

Proposition 1. Let $\leq$ be defined using an ontology O, and t_1, t_2 be triple patterns such that $t_1, t_2 \notin \text{cl}(O)$ and $\text{var}(t_1) = \text{var}(t_2)$. Then $t_1 \leq t_2$ if and only if $t_2 \in \text{cl}(O \cup \{t_1\})$.

Proof of Proposition 1. Follows directly from the definition of relaxation. □

Proposition 2. Let $\leq$ be defined using an ontology O. Then $\leq$ is a partial order if and only if O is acyclic.

Proof of Proposition 2. (Only If) We prove the contrapositive, that is, if O is cyclic then $\leq$ is not a partial order. We prove it for the case where the subgraph O_{sc} of O induced by sc is cyclic (the proof for a cycle in the sub-property graph is similar). It is enough to prove that there exist triple patterns t_a, t_b such that $t_a \leq t_b$ and $t_b \leq t_a$. Now consider the following cycle in O_{sc}: $(e_1, \text{sc}, e_2), (e_2, \text{sc}, e_3), \ldots, (e_{n-1}, \text{sc}, e_1)$ and the following triple patterns $t_a = (c, \text{type}, e_1)$ and $t_b = (c, \text{type}, e_2)$. Because of rules 3 and 4, it can be easily verified that there exists a derivation from t_a to t_b and another derivation from t_b to t_a. Hence $t_a \leq t_b$ and $t_b \leq t_a$.

(If) Assume that O is acyclic. It can be easily verified that $\leq$ is transitive and reflexive. Therefore, it remains to prove that it is antisymmetric. Now, assume that there exist triple patterns t_a, t_b, $t_a \neq t_b$, such that $t_a \leq t_b$ and $t_b \leq t_a$. We will proceed by cases, where each case is a possible form that t_a may take in order to instantiate at least one rule. By U, V, W we denote a IRI, variable or a literal, and by a, b, c we denote IRIs and literals. Notice that t_a cannot be a dom-triple or range-triple, because in this case, the only rules that can be instantiated are rules 5 or 6, and they require the existence of a plain triple in the ontology, which is not allowed. We use the notion of linear derivation from the proof of Proposition 3.

We prove by cases.

- t_a is a type-triple. In this case, rule 4 is the only rule that t_a can instantiate, hence t_b is also a type-triple. Let $t_a = (U, \text{type}, b)$, then the there is a linear derivation of the form $(U, \text{type}, a), (a, \text{sc}, e_1) \vdash_4 (U, \text{type}, e_1), (e_1, \text{sc}, e_2) \vdash_4 (U, \text{type}, e_2), (e_2, \text{sc}, e_3) \vdash_4 \ldots (U, \text{type}, e_n), (e_n, \text{sc}, b) \vdash_4 (U, \text{type}, b)$. That is $t_b = (U, \text{type}, b)$. Therefore, there must be a path from a to b in O_{sc}. By a similar argument, we prove the existence of a path from b to a in O_{sc}, contradicting that O_{sc} is acyclic.
- t_a is an sc-triple. In this case, rules 3 and 4 are the only rules that can be instantiated by t_a. Hence t_b is either a type-triple or an sc-triple. If the former holds, then there is no derivation from t_b to t_a, a contradiction. Therefore, t_b is a sc-triple. Let $t_a = (a, \text{sc}, b)$ and let $t_b = (c, \text{sc}, d)$. In this case the internal nodes of the derivation graph are sc-triples. It can be easily verified that a path exists in $O_{\text{sc}} \cup \{(a, \text{sc}, b)\}$ from c to d that contains an edge (a, sc, b). Similarly, because there is a derivation from t_b to t_a, there must exist a path in $O_{\text{sc}} \cup \{(c, \text{sc}, d)\}$ from a to b that contains an edge (c, sc, d). It can be checked that O_{sc} has at least one cycle, a contradiction.
- t_a is an sp-triple. Only rule 1 can apply because plain triples are not allowed in the ontology. Hence t_b is an sp-triple. By a similar argument as the proof of the previous case we prove the existence of a cycle in O_{sp}, yielding a contradiction.
- t_a is a plain triple. In this case, the only rules in the derivation graph from t_a to t_b are rules 2, 4, 5, and 6. These rules only yield dom-triples, range-triples, type-triples and plain triples. However, among these, a plain triple can be derived only from a plain-triple. Hence t_b is a plain triple, and the derivation graph has only instances of rule 2. Without loss of generality, let $t_a = (a, p, b)$ and $t_b = (a, q, b)$. Using a similar argument than the one used in the previous cases, we reach the conclusion that there are paths from p to q and from q to p in O_{sp}, a contradiction. □

Proposition 3. Let t_a, t_b be triple patterns not in cl(O) such that var(t_a) = var(t_b). If $t_a \prec t_b$ then there exists a triple $o \in$ cl(O) such that $t_a, o \vdash t_b$.

Proof of Proposition 3. We define that a *derivation* from a graph G (which may have triple patterns) to a triple pattern b_n is a sequence $a_1, a_2 \vdash b_3$; $a_4, a_5 \vdash b_6$; $a_7, a_8 \vdash b_9$; ... $a_{n-2}, a_{n-1} \vdash b_n$, where each $a_i, a_{i+1} \vdash b_{i+2}$ is an instantiation of a rule and a_i, a_{i+1} either belong to G or appear as the consequent b_j of some rule where $j < i$.

A derivation is said to be *linear* if each $b_j = a_{j+1}$ and a_{j+2} belongs to G. This notion is analogous to the notion of linear proof (e.g., linear proofs in Prolog's resolution). The intuition here is that when choosing two triples to combine in a derivation, always make one be the result of a previous derived triple and the other a triple from the original graph. A linear derivation from G to b_n can be abbreviated as follows: $a_1, a_2 \vdash b_3, a_4 \vdash b_5, a_6 \vdash b_7 \ldots b_{n-2}, a_{n-1} \vdash b_n$, where each a_i belongs to G and each b_i does not. Since the RDFS rules and triples in the ontology are horn clauses, from a standard result that states that proofs for horn-clause knowledge bases are linear (Nerode and Shore Theorem [16]), the following holds: for a graph G, and a triple pattern t, we have that $G \models_{\text{rule}} t$ if and only if there is a linear derivation from G to t.

Now assume that $t_a \prec t_b$. Then there should exist a linear derivation from $\text{cl}(O) \cup \{t_a\}$ to t_b. If the derivation has more than one rule instantiation, because it is linear, we can easily prove that t_b is an indirect relaxation of t_a, a contradiction. □

Proposition 4. Let O be an ontology, o be a derivable triple in $\text{cl}(O)$ and t, t' be triple patterns such that $t, o \vdash t'$. Then t' is an indirect relaxation of t (defined using O).

Proof of Proposition 4. Let $t, o \vdash_s t'$, where s is some rule. We denote by δ this rule instantiation. Now, since o is a derivable triple, there are triples o_1, o_2 such that $o_1, o_2 \vdash_r o$. Because the predicates of the triples in the ontology should be in the set $\{\text{type}, \text{dom}, \text{range}, \text{sp}, \text{sc}\}$, $r \in \{1, 3, 4\}$. We will prove that there is a triple pattern t'' such that $t, o_1 \vdash t''$ and $t'', o_2 \vdash t'$, and hence t' is an indirect relaxation of t.

We continue the proof for each of the three cases.

- Case $r = 1$. Then without loss of generality $o_1 = (a, \text{sp}, b)$, $o_2 = (b, \text{sp}, c)$, and $o = (a, \text{sp}, c)$. Moreover, $s = 1$ or $s = 2$. If $s = 1$, w.l.g, δ is $(d, \text{sp}, a), (a, \text{sp}, c) \vdash (d, \text{sp}, c)$. That is, $t = (d, \text{sp}, a)$ and $t' = (d, \text{sp}, c)$. Hence, we have: (d, sp, a), $(a, \text{sp}, b) \vdash_1 (d, \text{sp}, b)$, $(b, \text{sp}, c) \vdash_1 (d, \text{sp}, c)$. Therefore, t'' is (d, sp, b).
- Case $r = 3$. Then without loss of generality $o_1 = (a, \text{sc}, b)$, $o_2 = (b, \text{sc}, c)$, and $o = (a, \text{sc}, c)$. Moreover, $s = 3$ or $s = 4$. If $s = 4$, without loss of generality δ is $(x, \text{type}, a), (a, \text{sc}, c) \vdash_4 (x, \text{type}, c)$. That is, $t = (x, \text{type}, a)$ and $t' = (x, \text{type}, c)$. Hence, we have that: $(x, \text{type}, a), (a, \text{sc}, b) \vdash_4 (x, \text{type}, b), (b, \text{sc}, c) \vdash_4 (x, \text{type}, c)$. Therefore, $t'' = (x, \text{type}, b)$.
- Case $r = 4$. Then without loss of generality $o_1 = (a, \text{sc}, b)$, $o_2 = (x, \text{type}, a)$, and $o = (x, \text{type}, b)$. Moreover, $s = 4$ and without loss of generality δ is $(b, \text{sc}, c), (x, \text{type}, b) \vdash_4 (x, \text{type}, c)$. That is $t = (b, \text{sc}, c)$ and $t' = (x, \text{type}, c)$. Hence, we have the following linear derivation from t to t': $(b, \text{sc}, c), (a, \text{sc}, b) \vdash_3 (a, \text{sc}, c), (x, \text{type}, a) \vdash_4 (x, \text{type}, c)$. Consequently, $t'' = (a, \text{sc}, c)$. □

Proposition 5. Let O be an ontology and t be a triple pattern not in cl(O). Then all direct relaxations of t (defined using O) are in the set applyRules(t, red(O)).

Proof of Proposition 5. Follows directly from Proposition 4. □

Proposition 6. Let O be an ontology, o be a triple in red(O) and t, t' be triple patterns such that $t, o \vdash t'$. Then t' is an indirect relaxation of t (defined using O) iff o can be derived by applying the rules of Figure 7 starting from cl(O).

Proof of Proposition 6. (If) It is enough to realize that if $o_1, o_2 \vdash_i o$, where i is some rule in Figure 7, then we have that $t, o_1 \vdash t'', o_2 \vdash t'$, and hence t' is an indirect relaxation of t.

(Only If) Assume that t' is an indirect relaxation of t. If this is the case, we will prove that either $o \notin$ red(O), which yields a contradiction, or o can be obtained by applying the rules of Figure 7 to triples of cl(O). We will do it by cases. Each case represents that $t, o \vdash t'$ is an instance of a rule i.

- $i = 1$. Then without loss of generality $t = (a, \text{sp}, b)$, $o = (b, \text{sp}, c)$ and $t' = (a, \text{sp}, c)$. Then, w.l.g the derivation δ is of the form $(a, \text{sp}, b), (b, \text{sp}, d_1) \vdash_1 (a, \text{sp}, d_1), (d_1, \text{sp}, d_2) \vdash_1 (a, \text{sp}, d_2) \ldots (a, \text{sp}, d_n), (d_n, \text{sp}, c) \vdash_1 (a, \text{sp}, c)$. Therefore, $o \notin$ red(O), a contradiction.
- $i = 2$. Because o is not a plain triple, without loss of generality $o = (a, \text{sp}, b)$, $t = (x, a, y)$ and $t' = (x, b, y)$. Then, w.l.g the derivation δ is $(x, a, y), (a, \text{sp}, d_1) \vdash_2 (x, d_1, y), (d_1, \text{sp}, d_2) \vdash (x, d_2, y) \ldots (x, d_n, y), (d_n, \text{sp}, b) \vdash_2 (x, b, y)$. Then, $o \notin$ red(O), a contradiction.
- $i = 3$. The proof is similar to the case where $i = 1$.
- $i = 4$. Then there are two cases: (i) $t = (a, \text{sc}, b), o = (x, \text{type}, a)$ and $t' = (x, \text{type}, b)$. Then, w.l.g the derivation δ is $(a, \text{sc}, b), (d_1, \text{sc}, a) \vdash (d_1, \text{sc}, b), (d_2, \text{sc}, d_1) \vdash (d_2, \text{sc}, b), \ldots \vdash (d_n, \text{sc}, b), (x, \text{type}, d_n) \vdash (x, \text{type}, b)$. Hence, $(d_n, \text{sc}, a), (x, \text{type}, d_n) \vdash (x, \text{type}, a)$, contradicting that $o \notin$ red(O). (ii) $o = (a, \text{sc}, b), t = (x, \text{type}, a)$ and $t' = (x, \text{type}, b)$. Then w.l.g the derivation δ is $(x, \text{type}, a), (a, \text{sc}, d_1) \vdash (x, \text{type}, d_1) \ldots (x, \text{type}, d_n), (d_n, \text{sc}, b) \vdash (x, \text{type}, b)$, contradicting that $o \in$ red(O).
- $i = 5$. Then without loss of generality $t = (x, a, y)$, $o = (a, \text{dom}, d)$ and $t' = (x, \text{type}, d)$. Then, w.l.g the derivation δ is of the form $(x, a, y), (a, \text{sp}, b_1) \vdash (x, b_1, y), (b_1, \text{sp}, b_2) \vdash_2 \ldots (x, b_n, y), (b_n, \text{sp}, b) \vdash_2 (x, b, y), (b, \text{dom}, c) \vdash_5 (x, \text{type}, c), (c, \text{sc}, d_1) \vdash_4 (x, \text{type}, d_1)(d_1, \text{sc}, d_2) \vdash_4 \ldots (x, \text{type}, d_m), (d_m, \text{sc}, d) \vdash_4 (x, \text{type}, d)$. Then, we have the following triples in cl(O): (a, sp, b), (b, dom, c), and (c, sc, d). Then, by rules e1 and e3, (a, dom, c) and $(a, \text{dom}, d) = o$ can be derived.
- $i = 6$. The proof is similar to the case where $i = 5$, but now we use rules e2 and e4. □

Proposition 7. Let O be an ontology and t be a triple pattern not in cl(O). Then applyRules(t, extRed(O)) is equal to the set of direct relaxations of t (defined using O).

Proof of Proposition 7. Follows directly from propositions 4 and 6. □

Proposition 8. Let t be a triple pattern and O be an ontology. The relaxation graph of t (using the ontology O) has $O(|\text{red}(O)|^2)$ triples.

Proof of Proposition 8. We denote by M_α, where $\alpha \in \{\text{type}, \text{dom}, \text{range}, \text{sp}, \text{sc}\}$, the number of α-triples in $\text{red}(O)$. We prove the proposition by cases.

- t is a type-triple. Let $t = (x, \text{type}, a)$. Notice that all derivations from t yield triples of the form (x, type, b), for some b mentioned in a sc-triple. This is because derivations use only rule 4. Therefore, the relaxation graph of t cannot have more than M_{sc} nodes.
- t is a dom-triple or a range-triple there are no derivations from t.
- t is a sc triple. The relaxation graph of t may only have sc-triples and type-triples. Assume it only has sc-triples. Then, triples cannot be more than the number of pairs of classes in $\text{red}(O)$, which is at most M_{sc}^2. Now, if the relaxation graph has also type-triples, then for each type-triple in $\text{cl}(O)$ there are at most M_{sc} type-triples in the relaxation graph. So overall we have at most $M_{\text{sc}}^2 + M_{\text{type}} M_{\text{sc}}$ triples in the relaxation graph.
- t is a sp triple. By a similar argument as in the previous case we have that there are at most M_{sp}^2 triples in the relaxation graph.
- t is a plain triple. In this case we have at most $M_{\text{sp}} + M_{\text{sp}} M_{\text{sc}}$ triples in the relaxation graph.

For each triple pattern t' resulting from an ontology relaxation there are at most a constant number of simple relaxations above t', so the generation of simple relaxation does not asymptotically increase the size of the relaxation graph. □

Proposition 9. Let t be a triple pattern and O be an ontology. (i) Computing the direct relaxations of t takes $O(|\text{red}(O)|)$ steps. (ii) Computing the relaxation graph of t takes $O(|\text{red}(O)|^3)$ steps.

Proof of Proposition 9. Part (i) This is a bound for the cost of evaluating $\text{applyRules}(t, \text{extRed}(O))$. Part (ii) follows directly from Part (i) and Proposition 8. □

Proposition 10. Let Q be a query and G be a RDF graph. For each query Q' in the relaxation graph of Q, (i) $\text{ans}(Q', G) = \bigcup_{Q_i : Q_i \leq_Q Q'} \Delta_{Q_i}(G)$, and (ii) $\text{newAnswer}(Q', G) = \Delta_{Q'}(G)$.

Proof of Proposition 10. For simplicity, we consider that Q and Q' have two triple patterns each, and both triple patterns of Q are within the RELAX clause. That is $\text{Body}(Q) = \{t_1, t_2\}$ and $\text{Body}(Q') = \{t'_1, t'_2\}$. The generalization of the proof for more than two triple pattern is direct. Also, we have that $\text{Head}(Q) = \text{Head}(Q') = H$.

For a triple pattern t' in the relaxation graph of t, let $S_t(t')$ be the set containing t_i such that $t_i \leq_t t'$.

(i) We have that $\mathtt{ans}(Q', G) = V_{Q'} = \pi_H(\mathtt{find}(t'_1) \bowtie \mathtt{find}(t'_2))$.
By the definition of $\mathtt{deltaFind}$, it can be easily verified that

$$\mathtt{find}(t'_1) = \bigcup_{t_i \in S_t(t'_1)} \mathtt{deltaFind}(t_i).$$

A similar equality can be obtained for $\mathtt{find}(t'_2)$.

Therefore, we have

$$V_{Q'} = \pi_H((\bigcup_{t_i \in S_t(t'_1)} \mathtt{deltaFind}(t_i)) \bowtie (\bigcup_{t_j \in S_t(t'_2)} \mathtt{deltaFind}(t_j))),$$

which is equivalent to

$$V_{Q'} = \pi_H((\bigcup_{t_i \in S_t(t'_1), t_j \in S_t(t'_2)} (\mathtt{deltaFind}(t_i) \bowtie \mathtt{deltaFind}(t_j))).$$

which is equivalent to

$$V_{Q'} = \bigcup_{Q_i : Q_i \leq_Q Q'} \Delta_{Q_i}(G).$$

(ii) We use (i) to replace $\mathtt{newAnswer}(Q', G)$, obtaining

$$\Delta_{Q'}(G) = (\bigcup_{Q_i : Q_i \leq_Q Q'} \Delta_{Q_i}(G)) - (\bigcup_{Q_i : Q_i \leq_Q Q', Q_i \neq Q'} \mathtt{ans}(Q_i, G))$$

But, from (i) it follows that:

$$\bigcup_{Q_i : Q_i \leq_Q Q'} \Delta_{Q_i}(G)) = \bigcup_{Q_i : Q_i \leq_Q Q'} \mathtt{ans}(Q_i, G)).$$

Hence, (ii) is equivalent to $\Delta_{Q'}(G) = \Delta_{Q'}(G)$. □

Proposition 11. The algorithm $\mathtt{RelaxEval}$ returns its tuples in ranked order.

Proof of Proposition 11. Follows directly from Proposition 10 and the fact that $\mathtt{RelaxEval}$ traverses the relaxation graph of Q in breadth-first fashion, that is, delta views of less relaxed queries are processed before delta views of more relaxed queries. □

Proposition 12. Let Q be a query, O be an ontology and G an RDF graph. Then $\mathtt{RelaxEval}(Q, G, k)$ runs in time $O(m^{2n}|G|^n)$, where m is the number of triples in $\mathtt{red}(O)$, and $n = |\mathtt{Body}(Q)|$.

Proof of Proposition 12. Follows from the fact that the size of the relaxation graph is in $O(m^{2n})$ and the execution of each delta view takes time in $O(|G|^n)$. □

Proposition 13. The simple relaxation relation $\leq_{\mathtt{simple}}$ is a partial order up to triple pattern isomorphism.

Proof of Proposition 13. It can be easily verified that $\leq_{\mathtt{simple}}$ is reflexive and transitive, and it is also reflexive and transitive up to isomorphism. So we have to prove that it is antisymmetric up to isomorphism. If it is not the case, there are two triples t_a, t_b, where t_a is not isomorphic to t_b, such that $t_a \leq_{\mathtt{simple}} t_b$ and $t_b \leq_{\mathtt{simple}} t_a$. Hence there are maps u_a from t_a to t_b and u_b from t_b to t_a and both maps preserve the fixed variables. Therefore, t_a is isomorphic to t_b, a contradiction. □

A Fine-Grained Approach to Resolving Unsatisfiable Ontologies*

Joey Sik Chun Lam, Derek Sleeman, Jeff Z. Pan, and Wamberto Vasconcelos

Department of Computing Science
University of Aberdeen, AB24 3UE, UK
{slam, sleeman, jpan, wvasconc}@csd.abdn.ac.uk

Abstract. The ability to deal with inconsistencies and to evaluate the impact of possible solutions for resolving inconsistencies are of the utmost importance in real world ontology applications. The common approaches either identify the minimally unsatisfiable sub-ontologies or the maximally satisfiable sub-ontologies. However there is little work which addresses the issue of rewriting the ontology; it is not clear which axioms or which parts of axioms should be repaired, nor how to repair those axioms. In this paper, we address these limitations by proposing an approach to resolving unsatisfiable ontologies which is fine-grained in the sense that it allows parts of axioms to be changed. We revise the axiom tracing technique first proposed by Baader and Hollunder, so as to track which parts of the problematic axioms cause the unsatisfiability. Moreover, we have developed a tool to support the ontology user in rewriting problematic axioms. In order to minimise the impact of changes and prevent unintended entailment loss, both harmful and helpful changes are identified and reported to the user. Finally we present an evaluation of our interactive debugging tool and demonstrate its applicability in practice.

Keywords: Ontologies, Description Logics reasoning.

1 Introduction

Resolving inconsistencies in ontologies is a challenging task for ontology [25] modellers. Standard Description Logic (DL) [2] reasoning services can check if an ontology is unsatisfiable (i.e., if there are any unsatisfiable concepts in an ontology); however, they do not provide support for resolving the unsatisfiability. The ability to deal with inconsistencies and to evaluate the impact of the possible modifications are of the utmost importance in real world ontology applications.

Most existing approaches either identify problematic axioms (by providing the minimally unsatisfiable sub-ontologies) [22] or weaken the target unsatisfiable

---

* This paper is an extended version of [Joey SC Lam et al., A Fine-grained Approach to Resolving Unsatisfiable Ontologies, In Proc. of the 2006 IEEE/WIC/ACM International Conference on Web Intelligence (WI-2006)]. We extend our previous work to handle general concept inclusions and cyclic definitions. This work is supported by the AKT Project (the EPSRC's grant number GR/N15764).

ontology (by providing the possible maximally satisfiable sub-ontologies) [15]. However practical problems remain: it is not clear which axioms or which parts of axioms should be repaired, nor how to repair those axioms. Let us use an example to illustrate these limitations.

Example 1. Let us assume that an ontology $\mathcal{O}$ contains the following axioms:

α_1: $A \doteq C \sqcap \forall R.B \sqcap D$
α_2: $C \doteq \exists R.\neg B \sqcap B$
α_3: $G \doteq \forall R.(C \sqcap F)$

It can be shown that the concept A is unsatisfiable, by using standard DL TBox reasoning. The existing approaches [22,15] either identify the minimally unsatisfiable sub-ontologies $\mathcal{O}_1^{min} = \{\alpha_1, \alpha_2\}$ or calculate the maximally satisfiable sub-ontologies $\mathcal{O}_1^{max} = \{\alpha_1, \alpha_3\}$, and $\mathcal{O}_2^{max} = \{\alpha_2, \alpha_3\}$. In short, either α_1 or α_2 should be removed from $\mathcal{O}$. However, it is easy to see that we do not need to remove either the whole of α_1 or α_2. In order to minimise the loss of information from the ontology, we should simply remove parts of axiom α_1, i.e., (a) $A \sqsubseteq C$, or (b) $A \sqsubseteq \forall R.B$, or part of axiom α_2, i.e., (c) $C \sqsubseteq \exists R.\neg B$, and then $\mathcal{O}$ becomes satisfiable.

Schlobach et al. [22] and Kalyanpur et al. [12] have proposed approaches, which determine which parts of the asserted axioms are responsible for the unsatisfiability of concepts. We further discuss their work in Section 7. In this paper, we extend Meyer et al.'s tableaux algorithm [15]. Our algorithm traces which parts of the axioms are responsible for the unsatisfiability of a concept (this is a novel way of achieving the same result as [22,12]). Using this algorithm, we make the following two further contributions. The first is to calculate the lost entailments of named concepts due to the removal of axioms. Whenever parts of an axiom are removed, it frequently happens that indirect or implicit entailments are lost. In order to minimise the impact on the ontology, we analyse the lost entailments of named concepts which occur due to the removal of parts of axioms. The second contribution is to identify harmful and helpful changes; this is where the fine-grained tracing information is useful to facilitate rewriting the problematic axioms, rather than removing them completely. It should be noted that inappropriately revising a problematic axiom might not resolve the unsatisfiability, and could introduce additional unsatisfiable concepts into the ontology. For this purpose we define *harmful* and *helpful* changes with respect to an unsatisfiable named concept. A harmful change cannot resolve the problem, or might cause additional unsatisfiable concepts in the ontology; a helpful change resolves the problem without causing additional contradictions, and restores some lost entailments. We believe tools based on such techniques could help users to resolve unsatisfiable ontologies. To evaluate this vision, we have created a plugin in Protégé 3.2[1]. The result of our usability evaluation demonstrate that our approach helps non-expert ontology users to resolve unsatisfiable ontologies; the

---
[1] http://protege.stanford.edu/

performance results demonstrate that our algorithms provide acceptable performance when used with real world ontologies.

The rest of this paper is organised as follows. Section 2 briefly introduces ontologies and the Description Logic $\mathcal{ALC}$. Section 3 presents our fine-grained approach to pinpointing problematic parts of axioms. The impact of removing axioms is described in Section 4. The methods for identifying harmful and helpful changes are presented in Section 5. Section 6 presents the evaluation of our implementation. The paper closes with a discussion of related work and conclusion.

2 Ontology and the $\mathcal{ALC}$ DL

An ontology formally captures a shared understanding of certain aspects of a domain: it provides a common *vocabulary*, including important concepts, properties and their definitions, and *constraints* regarding the intended meaning of the vocabulary, sometimes referred to as background assumptions. Description Logics (DLs) [1] provide the underpinning of the recent W3C standard Web Ontology Language OWL DL.[2] In this paper, we use the smallest propositionally closed DL, i.e., the $\mathcal{ALC}$ DL [23], to illustrate our approach. The techniques presented here are general enough to be used as the basis for developing similar algorithms for more expressive DLs.

An ontology $\mathcal{O}$ consists of a set $\mathcal{T}$ (TBox) of concepts and role axioms and a set $\mathcal{A}$ (ABox) of individual axioms. As this paper handles satisfiabilities in ontologies, we focus on TBox reasoning. As $\mathcal{ALC}$ TBox reasoning is not influenced by ABox reasoning [16,20], without loss of generality, we assume that ontologies consist only of TBoxes in the rest of the paper. A TBox $\mathcal{T}$ consists of a set of axioms of the form $C \sqsubseteq D$ (*general concept inclusions*, GCIs); $C \doteq D$ (*concept equivalence*) is an abbreviation of $C \sqsubseteq D$ and $D \sqsubseteq C$, where C and D are (possibly complex) concept descriptions. $\mathcal{T}$ is *unfoldable* iff the left-hand side of every $\alpha \in \mathcal{T}$ contains a named concept A, there are no other αs with A on the left-hand side, and the right-hand side of α contains no direct or indirect references to A (no cycles). We divide $\mathcal{T}$ into an unfoldable part $\mathcal{T}_u$ and a general part $\mathcal{T}_g$, such that $\mathcal{T}_g = \mathcal{T} \setminus \mathcal{T}_u$.

An interpretation $\mathcal{I} = (\Delta^\mathcal{I}, \cdot^\mathcal{I})$ consists of the domain of the interpretation $\Delta^\mathcal{I}$ (a non-empty set) and the interpretation function $\cdot^\mathcal{I}$, which maps each concept name $\mathsf{CN} \in N_C$ to a set $\mathsf{CN}^\mathcal{I} \subseteq \Delta^\mathcal{I}$ and each role name $\mathsf{RN} \in N_R$ to a binary relation $\mathsf{RN}^\mathcal{I} \subseteq \Delta^\mathcal{I} \times \Delta^\mathcal{I}$. The interpretation function can be extended to give semantics to concept descriptions (see Table 1). An interpretation $\mathcal{I}$ *satisfies* a GCI $C \sqsubseteq D$ if $C^\mathcal{I} \subseteq D^\mathcal{I}$. An interpretation $\mathcal{I}$ *satisfies* a TBox $\mathcal{T}$ if it satisfies all GCIs in $\mathcal{T}$; in this case, we say $\mathcal{I}$ is an interpretation of $\mathcal{T}$. A TBox $\mathcal{T}$ is consistent if there exists some interpretation that satisfies it. A concept C is satisfiable w.r.t. $\mathcal{T}$ if there exists an interpretation $\mathcal{I}$ of $\mathcal{T}$ such that $C^\mathcal{I} \neq \emptyset$. A TBox $\mathcal{T}$ is satisfiable if all *named* concepts in $\mathcal{T}$ are satisfiable.

---

[2] More precisely, OWL DL is a key language and is a member of the family of the OWL standard languages, which also include OWL Lite and OWL Full.

Table 1. Semantics of $\mathcal{ALC}$-concepts

Constructor	Syntax	Semantics
top	$\top$	$\Delta^\mathcal{I}$
bottom	$\bot$	$\emptyset$
concept name	CN	$\mathsf{CN}^\mathcal{I} \subseteq \Delta^\mathcal{I}$
general negation ($\mathcal{C}$)	$\neg C$	$\Delta^\mathcal{I} \setminus C^\mathcal{I}$
conjunction	$C \sqcap D$	$C^\mathcal{I} \cap D^\mathcal{I}$
disjunction ($\mathcal{U}$)	$C \sqcup D$	$C^\mathcal{I} \cup D^\mathcal{I}$
exists restriction ($\mathcal{E}$)	$\exists R.C$	$\{x \in \Delta^\mathcal{I} \mid \exists y.\langle x,y\rangle \in R^\mathcal{I} \wedge y \in C^\mathcal{I}\}$
value restriction	$\forall R.C$	$\{x \in \Delta^\mathcal{I} \mid \forall y.\langle x,y\rangle \in R^\mathcal{I} \rightarrow y \in C^\mathcal{I}\}$

Note that subsumption can be reduced to satisfiability [1]. If $\mathcal{T} \vDash C \sqsubseteq D$, then in all interpretations $\mathcal{I}$ that satisfy $\mathcal{T}$, $C^\mathcal{I} \subseteq D^\mathcal{I}$ and so $C^\mathcal{I} \cap (\neg D)^\mathcal{I} = \emptyset$. Therefore, $\mathcal{T} \vDash C \sqsubseteq D$ iff $\mathcal{T} \vDash \neg(C \sqcap \neg D)$.

3 Approach

In this section, we introduce the extended tableau algorithm from Meyer et al.[15] (this kind of tracing technique was first proposed by Baader and Hollunder [4]). Instead of removing complete axioms involved in an unsatisfiability, our algorithm captures the components of axioms responsible for a concept's unsatisfiability.

3.1 Extended Tableaux Algorithm

We assume that $\mathcal{T} = \{\alpha_1, \cdots, \alpha_n\}$, with α_i referring to $C_i \doteq D_i$ or $C_i \sqsubseteq D_i$ for $i = 1, \ldots, n$. A tableau-based algorithm decides the satisfiability of a concept C_i w.r.t. $\mathcal{T}$ by trying to construct a representation of a *model* for it, called a tree **T**. The model is an interpretation $\mathcal{I}$ in which $C_i^\mathcal{I}$ is non-empty. Each node x in the tree is labeled with a set $\mathcal{L}(x)$ of concept or role elements. The concept elements are of the form $(a : C, I, a' : C')$, where C and C' are concepts, a and a' are individual names, and I is an index-set. This means that the individual a belongs to concept C due to an application of an expansion rule on $a' : C'$. The set of axioms, which $a : C$ comes from, is recorded in the index-set I. This is done by adding i to I, which is a set of integers in the range $1, \ldots, n$. In an element of the form $(a : C, I, a' : C')$ we frequently refer to C as "the concept", and a as "the individual" (i.e., we are referring to the first concept assertion). When a concept element $(a : C, I, a' : C')$ exists in the label of a node x, it represents an interpretation $\mathcal{I}$ that satisfies C, i.e., the individual corresponding to a is in the interpretation of C. That is, if $(a : C, -, -) \in \mathcal{L}(x)$, then $a \in C^\mathcal{I}$, where "$-$" stands for any value, that is, it is a place holder. Role elements are of the form $(R(a,b), I, a : \exists R.D)$, where R is a binary relationship between individual a and b; I is the index-set; the third parameter is to record the existence of

$R(a, b)$ due to an application of an expansion rule on $a : \exists R.D$. That is, if $(R(a, b), -, -) \in \mathcal{L}(x)$, then $\langle a, b \rangle \in R^{\mathcal{I}}$.

3.2 Applications of Expansion Rules

To determine the satisfiability of a concept A in $\mathcal{T}$, the algorithm initialises a tree **T** to contain a single node x, called the root node, with $\mathcal{L}(x) = \{(a : A, \emptyset, nil)\}$. The tree is then expanded by repeatedly applying a set of expansion rules which either extend node labels or add new leaf nodes. Our extended set of expansion rules for the Description Logic $\mathcal{ALC}$ is shown in Table 2, where A_i is a named concept, C, C_1, C_2, C_i, D_i are concept descriptions, R is a role name, a and b are individuals, $RHS(\alpha_i)$ is the concept at the right hand side of α_i, and the signature $Sig(\alpha_i)$ of an axiom α_i is the set of concept and role names occurring in α_i.

Table 2. Our extended tableaux expansion rules for $\mathcal{ALC}$

$U_{\doteq}^+$-rule	if $A_i \doteq C_i \in \mathcal{T}_u$, $(a : A_i, I, -) \in \mathcal{L}(x)$ and $(a : C_i, I \cup \{i\}, a : A_i) \notin \mathcal{L}(x)$ then $\mathcal{L}(x) := \mathcal{L}(x) \cup \{(a : C_i, I \cup \{i\}, a : A_i)\}$
$U_{\doteq}^-$-rule	if $A_i \doteq C_i \in \mathcal{T}_u$, $(a : \neg A_i, I, -) \in \mathcal{L}(x)$ and $(a : \neg C_i, I \cup \{i\}, a : \neg A_i) \notin \mathcal{L}(x)$, then $\mathcal{L}(x) := \mathcal{L}(x) \cup \{(a : \neg C_i, I \cup \{i\}, a : \neg A_i)\}$
$U_{\sqsubseteq}$-rule	if $A_i \sqsubseteq C_i \in \mathcal{T}_u$, $(a : A_i, I, -) \in \mathcal{L}(x)$ and $(a : C_i, I \cup \{i\}, a : A_i) \notin \mathcal{L}(x)$, then $\mathcal{L}(x) := \mathcal{L}(x) \cup \{(a : C_i, I \cup \{i\}, a : A_i)\}$
$\sqcap$-rule	if $(a : C_1 \sqcap C_2, I, -) \in \mathcal{L}(x)$, and $\{(a : C_1, I, a : C_1 \sqcap C_2), (a : C_2, I, a : C_1 \sqcap C_2)\} \not\subseteq \mathcal{L}(x)$, then $\mathcal{L}(x) := \mathcal{L}(x) \cup \{(a : C_1, I, a : C_1 \sqcap C_2), (a : C_2, I, a : C_1 \sqcap C_2)\}$
$\sqcup$-rule	if $(a : C_1 \sqcup C_2, I, -) \in \mathcal{L}(x)$, and $\{(a : C_1, I, a : C_1 \sqcup C_2), (a : C_2, I, a : C_1 \sqcup C_2)\} \cap \mathcal{L}(x) = \emptyset$, then create two $\sqcup$-successor y, z of x with: $\mathcal{L}(y) := \mathcal{L}(x) \cup \{(a : C_1, I, a : C_1 \sqcup C_2)\}$ $\mathcal{L}(z) := \mathcal{L}(x) \cup \{(a : C_2, I, a : C_1 \sqcup C_2)\}$
$\exists$-rule	if $(a : \exists R.C, I, -) \in \mathcal{L}(x)$, a is not blocked (see Section 3.4), and $\{(R(a, b), I, a : \exists R.C), (b : C, I, a : \exists R.C)\} \not\subseteq \mathcal{L}(x)$, where b is an individual name not occurring in $\mathcal{L}(x)$ then $\mathcal{L}(x) := \mathcal{L}(x) \cup \{(R(a, b), I, a : \exists R.C), (b : C, I, a : \exists R.C)\}$
$\forall$-rule	if $(a : \forall R.C, I, -) \in \mathcal{L}(a)$, and $(R(a, b), J, a : \exists R.D_i) \in \mathcal{L}(x)$ then $\mathcal{L}(x) := \mathcal{L}(x) \cup \{(b : C, I \cup J, a : \forall R.C)\}$
$\sqsubseteq$-rule	if $(C_i \sqsubseteq D_i) \in \mathcal{T}_g$, and there exists $(-: E, -, -) \in \mathcal{L}(x)$, $Sig(E) \cup Sig(C_i) \neq \emptyset$, a is not blocked, and $(a : \neg C_i \sqcup D_i, I \cup \{i\}, -) \notin \mathcal{L}(x)$, for every individual a in the node then $\mathcal{L}(x) := \mathcal{L}(x) \cup \{(a : \neg C_i \sqcup D_i, I \cup \{i\}, a : C)\}$

During the expansion, concept descriptions are assumed to be converted to negation normal form.[3] We now explain the expansion rules. The three rules ($U_{\doteq}^+$-rule, $U_{\doteq}^-$-rule and $U_{\sqsubseteq}$-rule) describe the *unfolding* procedure. Unfolding

---
[3] A concept description is in negation normal form when negations apply only to concept names, and not to compound terms.

a concept expression is to replace defined names by their definitions, so that it does not contain names defined in the terminology. These rules are used for optimisation (also called lazy unfolding) [5]. That means only unfolding concepts as required by the progress of the satisfiability testing algorithm. The $U_{\doteq}^{+}$-rule and $U_{\doteq}^{-}$-rule reflect the symmetry of the equality relation in the non-primitive definition $A \doteq C$, which is equivalent to $A \sqsubseteq C$ and $\neg A \sqsubseteq \neg C$. The $U_{\sqsubseteq}$-rule on the other hand reflects the asymmetry of the subsumption relation in the primitive definition $A \sqsubseteq C$.

Disjunctive concept elements $(a : C_1 \sqcup C_2, -, -) \in \mathcal{L}(x)$ result in *non-deterministic* expansion. We deal with this non-determinism by creating two $\sqcup$-successors y, z of x with: $\mathcal{L}(y) := \mathcal{L}(x) \cup \{(a : C_1, \cdots)\}$, and $\mathcal{L}(z) := \mathcal{L}(x) \cup \{(a : C_2, \cdots)\}$.

For any existential role restriction concept $(a : \exists R.C, I, -) \in \mathcal{L}(x)$, the algorithm introduces a new individual b as the role filler, and this individual must satisfy the constraints expressed by the restriction. Thus, b is an individual of C, and hence $(b : C, I, a : \exists R.C)$ and $(R(a,b), I, a : \exists R.C)$ are added to the label of the node. A universal role restriction concept $(a : \forall R.D, J, -) \in \mathcal{L}(x)$ interacts with already defined role relationships to impose new constraints on individuals. That is, if $(R(a,b), I, a : \exists R.C)$ exists in $\mathcal{L}(x)$, then b is also an individual of D; new concept elements $(b : D, I \cup J, a : \forall R.D)$ and $(b : C, I \cup J, a : \exists R.C)$ are added to the label.

If there exists a concept C in the signature of the left-hand side of a GCI axiom $(\alpha_i \in \mathcal{T}_g, \alpha_i$ is $C_i \sqsubseteq D_i)$, and there is an element $(a : C, I, -) \in \mathcal{L}(x)$, and the signature of C has common elements with $Sig(C_i)$ then we apply the $\sqsubseteq$-rule to α_i. The newly added element will be $(a : \neg C_i \sqcup D_i, I \cup \{i\}, a : C)$. With this technique we are able to trace which element in the tree invokes the application of expansion rules on GCI axioms, therefore we can trace how the GCI axioms cause the concept's unsatisfiability.

The algorithm repeatedly expands the tree by applying the rules in Table 2 as many times as possible until either any one of the fully expanded leaf nodes has no clash or none of the rules is applicable to any node of the tree. A node is fully expanded when none of the rules can be applied to it. $\mathbf{T}$ is fully expanded when all of its leaf nodes are fully expanded. A node x contains an obvious *clash* when, for some individual b and some concept C, $\{(b : C, -, -), (b : \neg C, -, -)\} \subseteq \mathcal{L}(x)$.

When a clash is found in a node, the classical tableaux algorithm [4] either backtracks and selects a different leaf node, or reports the clash and terminates, if no node remains to be expanded. The main difference is that our algorithm terminates when either (1) any one of the fully expanded leaf nodes is without a clash or (2) none of the rules is applicable. Since the rules are still applicable to a node even when a clash is found, there may be more than one clash in the node, and furthermore this clash may also occur in other nodes (repeated nodes). As a result, we can obtain all the clashes in the tree and eliminate the repeated clashes. If the input of the tableaux algorithm is a concept C and a terminology $\mathcal{T}$, we have the following property: C is *unsatisfiable* iff each path from the root to the leaf node in the tree contains at least one clash. This implies that an unsatisfiable concept becomes satisfiable if all the clashes in any one of the paths of the tree are resolved (i.e., a complete path from root to leaf). This is because whenever the non-deterministic ⊔-rule is applied, two new ⊔-successor nodes are created; this is the only way to create the leaf nodes. It is sufficient to resolve all clashes in either of the two branches created.

3.3 Sequences of a Clash

Figure 1 shows how the tableau algorithm is applied to Example 1 (shown in Section 1) to check for the satisfiability of A. The tree **T** contains a root node x whose label contains a clash because $\{(b : B, \{1,2\}, a : \forall R.B), (b : \neg B, \{1,2\}, a : \exists R.\neg B)\} \subseteq \mathcal{L}(x)$. According to Definition 1, we can obtain two sequences, Seq^+ and Seq^- (see Figure 2). Note that the union of the index sets of the first elements in the sequences of the clashes in the tree gives the set of axioms which cause A to be unsatisfiable. The above two sequences show that axiom α_1 and α_2 cause the unsatisfiability of A.

---

(1) Initialise the root node x with $\mathcal{L}(x) := \{(a : A, \emptyset, nil)\}$,

(2) Apply the $U_{\doteq}^+$-rule to $(a : A, \emptyset, nil)$,
it gives $\mathcal{L}(x) := \mathcal{L}(x) \cup \{(a : C \sqcap \forall R.B \sqcap D, \{1\}, a : A)\}$,

(3) Apply the ⊓-rule twice to $(a : C \sqcap \forall R.B \sqcap D, \{1\}, \cdots)$,
it gives $\mathcal{L}(x) := \mathcal{L}(x) \cup \{(a : C \sqcap \forall R.B, \{1\}, a : C \sqcap \forall R.B \sqcap D)$,
$(a : D, \{1\}, a : C \sqcap \forall R.B \sqcap D), (a : C, \{1\}, a : C \sqcap \forall R.B)$,
$(a : \forall R.B, \{1\}, a : C \sqcap \forall R.B)\}$

(4) Apply the $U_{\doteq}^+$-rule to $(a : C, \{1\}, \cdots)$, followed by applying the ⊓-rule,
it gives $\mathcal{L}(x) := \mathcal{L}(x) \cup \{(a : \exists R.\neg B \sqcap B, \{1,2\}, a : C)$,
$(a : \exists R.\neg B, \{1,2\}, a : \exists R.\neg B \sqcap B), (a : B, \{1,2\}, a : \exists R.\neg B \sqcap B)\}$,

(5) Apply the ∃-rule to $(a : \exists R.\neg B, \{1,2\}, \cdots)$,
it gives $\mathcal{L}(x) := \mathcal{L}(x) \cup \{(b : \neg B, \{1,2\}, a : \exists R.\neg B), (R(a,b), \{1,2\}, a : \exists R.\neg B)\}$

(6) Apply the ∀-rule to $(a : \forall R.B, \{1\}, \cdots)$,
it gives $\mathcal{L}(x) := \mathcal{L}(x) \cup \{(b : B, \{1,2\}, a : \forall R.B)\}$

Fig. 1. The application of expansion rules on A in Example 1

Definition 1 (Sequences of a Clash). *Given a clash in a tree, the sequences of a clash, Seq^+ and Seq^-, contain elements involved in the clash. The sequences are of the form $\langle(a_0 : C_0, I_0, a_1 : C_1), (a_1 : C_1, I_1, a_2 : C_2), \cdots, (a_{n-1} : C_{n-1}, I_n, a_n : C_n), (a_n : C_n, \emptyset, nil)\rangle$, where $I_{i-1} \subseteq I_i$ for each $i = 1, \cdots, n$. The first elements of Seq^+ and Seq^- are of the form $(a : C, I', a' : C')$ and $(a : \neg C, I'', a'' : C'')$ respectively. The last element of both sequences is the same.*

$\mathcal{L}(x) := \{(a : A, \emptyset, nil), (a : C \sqcap \forall R.B \sqcap D, \{1\}, a : A),$
$(a : C \sqcap \forall R.B, \{1\}, a : C \sqcap \forall R.B \sqcap D), (a : D, \{1\}, a : C \sqcap \forall R.B \sqcap D),$
$(a : C, \{1\}, a : C \sqcap \forall R.B), (a : \forall R.B, \{1\}, a : C \sqcap \forall R.B),$
$(a : \exists R.\neg B \sqcap B, \{1, 2\}, a : C), (a : \exists R.\neg B, \{1, 2\}, a : \exists R.\neg B \sqcap B),$
$\underline{(a : B, \{1, 2\}, a : \exists R.\neg B \sqcap B)}, (b : \neg B, \{1, 2\}, a : \exists R.\neg B),$
$(R(a, b), \{1, 2\}, a : \exists R.\neg B), (b : B, \{1, 2\}, a : \forall R.B)\}$

(4). Matches (2), does not exist in Seq^+ or Seq^-

$Seq^+ := \langle (b : B, \{1, 2\}, a : \forall R.B), (a : \forall R.B, \{1\}, a : C \sqcap \forall R.B),$
$(a : C \sqcap \forall R.B, \{1\}, a : C \sqcap \forall R.B \sqcap D), (a : C \sqcap \forall R.B \sqcap D, \{1\}, a : A),$
$(a : A, \emptyset, nil)\rangle,$

(2). Matches *(a:C, {1},...)*   (3). Matches (2), but exists in Seq^-

$Seq^- := \langle (b : \neg B, \{1, 2\}, a : \exists R.\neg B), \underline{(a : \exists R.\neg B, \{1, 2\}, a : \exists R.\neg B \sqcap B)},$
$\underline{(a : \exists R.\neg B \sqcap B, \{1, 2\}, a : C)}, \underline{(a : C, \{1\}, a : C \sqcap \forall R.B)},$
$(a : C \sqcap \forall R.B, \{1\}, a : a : C \sqcap \forall R.B \sqcap D), (a : C \sqcap \forall R.B \sqcap D, \{1\}, a : A),$
$(a : A, \emptyset, nil)\rangle$ (1). Remove *(a:C, {1},...)*

Fig. 2. The fully expanded tree for A in Example 1

Now that clashes in the tree have been found, we want to identify the axioms which could be removed to resolve the unsatisfiability. We can identify these by looking at the nodes in the tree which contain clashes. The example in Figure 3 (on the left) shows a tree with six clashes (nodes with clashes are shaded). We now describe how Reiter's Hitting Set algorithm [19] can be adapted to make a general procedure for identifying the sets of clashes to be resolved. Firstly, for each path from the root to a leaf of the tree, we gather the set of each of the nodes on that path which has a clash. In our example the following sets are found: $\{a, b, d\}, \{a, b\}, \{a, c, e\}, \{a, c, f\}$. Now, using these sets we apply the Hitting Set algorithm; the Hitting set Tree is shown in Figure 3 on the right-hand side. Now for each leaf node n we gather the set E_n of all edge labels on the path from the root to that node. The sets thus obtained from each leaf node are gathered into one large set S. This gives a set with 13 elements; some of these $E_n \in S$ are subsets of each other; we pick out the *minimal* sets; i.e., the sets $E_i \subset S$ for which there is no $E_j \in S$ such that $E_j \subset E_i$. In our example this gives $S = \{\{a\}, \{b, c\}, \{b, e, f\}, \{b, c, d\}\}$, as desired. The axioms involved in each clash from the above nodes are actually the same as the notion of minimal unsatisfiability preserving sub-TBoxes (MUPS) in [22], that is there are four sets of MUPS in the unsatisfiable concept above.

From each MUPS, we know which axioms cause the unsatisfiability. Furthermore, from the sequences of the clashes, we know which concepts within these axioms cause the unsatisfiability. We can assign a specific number to each MUPS, and annotate the problematic concepts in these axioms with a specific superscript number corresponding to the MUPS which it occurs in. Note that a concept component may be involved in more than one MUPS, therefore it may be annotated

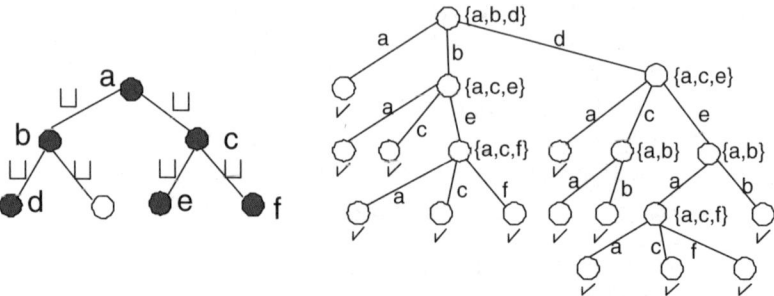

Fig. 3. Left-hand side: a fully expanded tree with six clashes; right-hand side: hitting set tree

with more than one number. We introduce the notion of arity of a concept C in an axiom α, denoted by $arity(\alpha, C)$, to count the number of times it appears in the clashes. This idea is similar to the core of MUPS in [22]. This means that removing a concept component with arity n can resolve n clashes. In order to illustrate the benefit of our fine-grained approach, we add the following axioms to Example 1:

$\alpha_4 \colon K \doteq C \sqcap \forall R.(P \sqcap F)$
$\alpha_5 \colon P \doteq \forall R.F \sqcap B$

In this case, concept K is also unsatisfiable due to the existence of a clash in a node of the tree for K. For simplicity, we do not show the sequences in the clash. We now annotate the concepts in the axioms which are involved in the two unsatisfiable concepts with superscript numbers as follows:

$\alpha_1 \colon A^1 \doteq C^1 \sqcap \forall R^1.B^1 \sqcap D$,
$\alpha_2 \colon C^{1,2} \doteq \exists R^{1,2}.(\neg B)^{1,2} \sqcap B$,
$\alpha_3 \colon G \doteq \forall R.(C \sqcap F)$
$\alpha_4 \colon K^2 \doteq C^2 \sqcap \forall R^2.(P^2 \sqcap F)$
$\alpha_5 \colon P^2 \doteq \forall R.F \sqcap B^2$

From the above, we can easily see which concepts in the axioms cause which concepts to be unsatisfiable. It is obvious that removing the concept $\exists R.\neg B$ in axiom α_2 can resolve two unsatisfiable concepts.

3.4 Refined Blocking

To deal with cyclic axioms, it is necessary to add cycle detection (often called *blocking*) to the preconditions of some of the expansion rules in order to guarantee termination [3,7]. We use a simple example to describe the necessity of blocking, by using the classical tableau algorithm:

Example 2. Given an ontology containing a single cyclic axiom, $\alpha_1 \colon A \doteq \exists R.A$, then testing the satisfiability of A leads to:

1. $\mathcal{L}(x) := \{(a_0 : A), (a_0 : \exists R.A)\}$
2. $\mathcal{L}(x_1) := \mathcal{L}(x) \cup \{R(a_0, a_1), (a_1 : A), (a_1 : \exists R.A)\}$
3. $\mathcal{L}(x_2) := \mathcal{L}(x_1) \cup \{R(a_1, a_2), (a_2 : A,), (a_2 : \exists R.A)\}$ $\cdots$

The application of the $U_{\doteq}^{+}$-rule leads to $(a_0 : \exists R.A)$ being added to $\mathcal{L}(x)$, and the application of the $\exists$-rule leads to the creation of a new individual a_1 with new elements $R(a_0, a_1), (a1 : A)$ added into $\mathcal{L}(x_1)$, the same expansion rules would be applied and the process would continue indefinitely. Since all individuals a_1, a_2, $\cdots$ receive the same concept assertions as a_0, we may say the algorithm has run into a cycle. Therefore, blocking is necessary to ensure termination. The general idea is to stop the expansion of a node whenever the same concept assertions recur in the node. Blocking imposes a condition on the $\exists$-rule: in the classical algorithm, an individual a is *blocked* by an individual b in a node label $\mathcal{L}(x)$ iff $\{D|(a : D) \in \mathcal{L}(x)\} \subseteq \{D'|(b : D') \in \mathcal{L}(x)\}$. In our example, that would mean a_1 in $\mathcal{L}(x_1)$ is blocked by a_0, because $\{A, \exists R.A\} \subseteq \{A, \exists R.A\}$ in the classical version. Intuitively, it can be seen that termination is now guaranteed because a finite terminology can only produce a finite number of different concept expressions and therefore a finite number of different labelling sets; all nodes must therefore eventually be blocked [9].

Our blocking approach is slightly different from the classical one. We define the refined blocking condition as follows: the application of the $\exists$-rule to an individual a is blocked by b iff $\{(D, I)|(a : D, I, -) \in \mathcal{L}(x)\} = \{(D', I')|(b : D', I', -) \in \mathcal{L}(x)\}$. Informally, the justification for this refinement is the following. If I is not equal to I', then we treat $(a : C, I, -)$ and $(a : C, I', -)$ as different elements; this is because the concept C in the two elements has been introduced from different axioms. Therefore, we still apply the rules to both $(a : C, I, -)$ and $(a : C, I', -)$ to expand the tree. As a result, in our approach, an individual a is blocked by b iff each of the elements in $\mathcal{L}(x)$ with individual a is exactly matched with one of the elements in $\mathcal{L}(x)$ with individual b, and vice versa; i.e. these matched elements have the same concept and index-set. In contrast, the classical tableau algorithm does not take the index-set of axioms into account when blocking is performed; the elements in the labels of nodes only have one parameter. The elements $(a : C, I, -)$ and $(a : C, I', -)$ will be presented as $(a : C)$ in the classical one, and therefore only one rule is applied to $(a : C)$ once.

Example 3. This example describes how the refined blocking works:
α_1: $A \sqsubseteq \neg C \sqcap D \sqcap E \sqcap F \sqcap \exists R.A$
α_2: $D \sqsubseteq C$
α_3: $E \sqsubseteq \forall R.C$
α_4: $F \sqsubseteq \forall R.\forall R.C$

We use Example 3 to illustrate why our refined blocking is necessary[4]. For simplicity, we do not show the third parameter of the elements in the node label. Figure 4 shows the fully expanded tree. In step 2, after applying the $\exists$-rule on $(a : \exists R.A, \{1\})$, we can see that, in $\mathcal{L}(x_1)$ in the classical algorithm,

---
[4] Note that despite the apparent complexity, this example is the simplest possible to illustrate the need for our refined blocking.

Step 1

$\mathcal{L}(x) := \{(a : A, \emptyset), (a : \neg C \sqcap D \sqcap E \sqcap F \sqcap \exists R.A, \{1\}), (a : \neg C, \{1\}),$
$(a : D, \{1\}), (a : E, \{1\})(a : F, \{1\}), (a : \exists R.A, \{1\}), (a : C, \{1, 2\}),$
$(a : \forall R.C, \{1, 3\}), (a : \forall R.\forall R.C, \{1, 4\})\}$ *Clash 1*

Step 2: Apply the $\exists$-rule on $(a : \exists R.A, \{1\})$ *Clash 2* (1)

$\mathcal{L}(x_1) := \mathcal{L}(x) \cup \{(b : A, \{1\}), (b : \forall R.C, \{1, 4\}), (b : C, \{1, 3\}),$
$(b : \neg C \sqcap D \sqcap E \sqcap F \sqcap \exists R.A, \{1\}), (b : \neg C, \{1\}), (b : D, \{1\}),$
$(b : E, \{1\}), (b : F, \{1\}), (b : \exists R.A, \{1\}), (b : C, \{1, 2\}),$
$(b : \forall R.\forall R.C, \{1, 4\}), (b : \forall R.C, \{1, 3\})\}$
(2)   *Clash 3*

Step 3: Apply the $\exists$-rule on $(b : \exists R.A, \{1\})$ *Clash 4*

$\mathcal{L}(x_2) := \mathcal{L}(x_1) \cup \{(c : A, \{1\}), (c : C, \{1, 4\}), (c : C, \{1, 3\}),$
$(c : \forall R.C, \{1, 4\}), (c : \neg C \sqcap D \sqcap E \sqcap F \sqcap \exists R.A, \{1\}), (c : \neg C, \{1\}),$
$(c : D, \{1\}), (c : E, \{1\}), (c : F, \{1\}), (c : \exists R.A, \{1\}), (c : C, \{1, 2\}),$
$(c : \forall R.\forall R.C, \{1, 4\}), (c : \forall R.C, \{1, 3\})\}$
(3)

Step 4: Apply the $\exists$-rule on $(c : \exists R.A, \{1\})$

$\mathcal{L}(x_3) := \mathcal{L}(x_2) \cup \{(d : A, \{1\}), (d : C, \{1, 4\}), (d : C, \{1, 3\}),$
$(d : \forall R.C, \{1, 4\}), (d : \neg C \sqcap D \sqcap E \sqcap F \sqcap \exists R.A, \{1\}), (d : \neg C, \{1\}),$
$(d : D, \{1\}), (d : E, \{1\}), (d : F, \{1\}), (d : \exists R.A, \{1\}), (d : C, \{1, 2\}),$
$(d : \forall R.\forall R.C, \{1, 4\}), (d : \forall R.C, \{1, 3\})\}$

Fig. 4. The fully expanded tree of Example 3

the set of concept elements with b is a subset of the set of concept elements with a, therefore, individual b is blocked by a. The $\exists$-rule cannot be applied on $(b : \exists R.A, \{1\})$, so the algorithm would terminate. Three clashes are found in $\mathcal{L}(x_1)$; axioms α_1, α_2 and α_3 are all involved in the clashes (cf. *Clash 1, 2, 3* in Figure 4). However α_4 would be missed out by the classical algorithm, although it also triggers a clash in our tree. The reason is that the set of concept elements with a is the same as the set of concept elements with b in the classical algorithm (i.e., $\{D|(a : D, -) \in \mathcal{L}(x_1)\} = \{D|(b : D, -) \in \mathcal{L}(x_1)\}$); $(b : C, \{1, 3\})$ is the same as $(b : C, \{1, 2\})$ (cf. **(1)** in Figure 4), and $(b : \forall R.C, \{1, 4\})$ is the same as $(b : \forall R.C, \{1, 3\})$ (cf. **(2)**). In our approach, these elements are different. Therefore we still apply the $\forall$-rule to $(b : \forall R.C, \{1, 4\})$ and add a new element $(c : C, \{1, 4\})$ into the node label, which is different from the existing elements $(c : C, \{1, 2\})$ and $(c : C, \{1, 3\})$ (cf. **(3)**). The newly added element from α_4 triggers another clash (cf. *Clash 4*). Next, we keep applying the $\exists$-rule to $(c : \exists R.A, \{1\})$ and create a new individual d. Finally, each of the elements in $\mathcal{L}(x_3)$ with individual d is exactly matched with one of the elements in $\mathcal{L}(x_3)$ with individual c, and vice versa; i.e. these matched elements have the same concept and index-set. The individual c is blocked by d, and then the application of the rules is terminated.

3.5 Complexity, Soundness and Completeness

The differences between our algorithm and the classical one are that (1) when a clash is detected, the classical algorithm either backtracks and selects a different node, or reports the clash and terminates if no more nodes remain to be expanded, whereas our algorithm will not do so; it only terminates when the tree is fully expanded or until blocking occurs, in order to find all possible clashes. Therefore, the complexity of our algorithm is the same as the classical one in the worst case [23], as both need to fully expand all nodes; (2) we add two extra parameters in each of the elements of a node label. The expansion rules do not depend on these two parameters, and hence they add only a constant amount to each expansion and do not affect the complexity and correctness of the original algorithm [4]; (3) our refined blocking condition is: the application of the $\exists$-rule to an individual a is blocked by b iff $\{(D, I) | (a : D, I, -) \in \mathcal{L}(x)\} = \{(D', I') | (b : D', I', -) \in \mathcal{L}(x)\}$. The number of elements with different concept descriptions that can be introduced in each fully expanded leaf node is finite. Also, for each of concept description C, there can be only a finite number of elements $(a : C, I_1, -)$, $(a : C, I_2, -), \cdots$, $(a : C, I_n, -)$ with n bounded by the number of axioms in the ontology. The algorithm is therefore guaranteed to terminate.

3.6 Removing Clashes

Given an unsatisfiable concept A in $\mathcal{T}$, we can obtain a fully expanded tree containing a node with at least one clash. For each clash, the sequences of the clash, Seq^+ and Seq^-, are obtained as in Definition 1. We can derive the following lemma:

Lemma 2. *Let the first elements of the sequences be $(a : C, I', -)$ and $(a : \neg C, I'', -)$, and let the last element of the sequences be $(b : A, \emptyset, nil)$. We know that the set of axioms $I := I' \cup I''$ causes A to be unsatisfiable. Let $\mathcal{D}$ be the set of all concepts appearing in the elements of the sequences: removing one of the concepts in $\mathcal{D}$ from one of the axioms in I is sufficient to resolve the clash.*

Proof. For any concept picked from $\mathcal{D}$, it must occur in the sequences and have an adjacent element which is before or after. For any two adjacent elements in a sequence, e_1 and e_2, there are only two possibilities:

- e_1 and e_2 are of the form $(a : E_1, -, a : E_2)$ and $(a : E_2, -, -)$ containing the same individual, this means the concept E_1 is a superconcept of E_2. If E_1 (or E_2) is removed, the subsumption relationship between E_2 and E_1 is removed. Therefore, the individual a no longer belongs to E_1 (or E_2), nor does it belong to any of the concepts in the elements preceding the occurrence of e_1 in the sequences. That means the concept of the first element in the

sequence is not subsumed by the removed concept either, hence the clash is resolved.
- e_1 and e_2 are of the form $(a : E_1, -, b : E_2)$ and $(b : E_2, -, -)$ containing different individuals, this means the concept E_1 participates in a role relationship with E_2. If E_1 or E_2 is removed, then the role relationship will be removed, therefore there will be no such individual a participating in the role, and all the concepts in the elements preceding the occurrence of e_1 will not be related to a, and hence the clash will be resolved. □

4 Impact of Removing Axioms

After the parts of the axioms causing the unsatisfiability of concept(s) are identified, the next step is to resolve the unsatisfiability. In this section, we discuss, with examples, the impact of removing axioms on an ontology.

The simplest way to resolve unsatisfiability is to remove parts of the problematic axioms or the whole axioms. However, in this case, it will be easy for ontology modellers to accidentally remove indirect or implicit entailments in the ontology. We use the following mad_cow[5] example to explain what we mean by the impact of removing axioms from an ontology:

Example 4. Given an ontology where Mad_Cow is unsatisfiable due to axioms $\alpha_1, \alpha_3, \alpha_4, \alpha_5$, the concepts and roles tagged with a star (*) are responsible for the unsatisfiability:

α_1: Mad_Cow* $\doteq$ ∃ eats*.((∃part_of*.Sheep*) ⊓ Brain) ⊓ Cow*
α_2: (∃part_of.Plant ⊔ Plant) ⊑ ¬ (∃part_of.Animal ⊔ Animal)
α_3: Cow* ⊑ Vegetarian*
α_4: Vegetarian* $\doteq$ ∀ eats.(¬ Animal) ⊓ Animal ⊓ ∀eats*.(¬∃part_of*.Animal*)
α_5: Sheep* ⊑ ∀ eats.Grass ⊓ Animal*
α_6: Grass ⊑ Plant
α_7: Giraffe ⊑ Vegetarian

When an axiom involved in the unsatisfiability of a concept is changed, we calculate the impact of removal on the ontology in three ways: (1) *the named concepts involved in the unsatisfiability*: These concepts might lose entailments which are not responsible for the unsatisfiability. To resolve Mad_Cow, one may claim that not all cows are vegetarians if there exist mad cows, therefore, α_3 is removed. However, the indirect assertion Mad_Cow ⊑ Animal ⊓ ∀eats.(¬ Animal) and Cow ⊑ Animal ⊓ ∀eats.(¬ Animal) will be lost, as we know the Animal ⊓ ∀eats.(¬ Animal) in α_4 is not responsible for Mad_Cow's unsatisfiability. Similarly, if α_4 is removed, the indirect assertion Vegetarian ⊑ Animal ⊓ ∀eats.(¬ Animal) and the above two assertions will be all lost. (2) *the satisfiable concepts irrelevant to the unsatisfiability*: Other named concepts irrelevant to the satisfiability might lose entailments introduced by the axiom to be changed. The entailments we consider in this case are indirectly asserted in the ontology before

---
[5] http://www.cs.man.ac.uk/~horrocks/OWL/Ontologies/mad_cows.owl

the change. If the user removes the problematic part ∀eats.(¬∃ part_of.Animal) from α_4, then all the subconcepts of Vegetarian will be affected. The indirect assertion all giraffes only eat something which is not part of an animal inherited from Vegetarian will be lost. Cow, which is involved in the unsatisfiability, is not considered here, as the assertion all cows only eat something which is not part of an animal will still make Mad_Cow unsatisfiable; (3) *the classification of the named concepts of the ontology*: The satisfiable named concepts might lose implicit subsumption relations due to the change of axioms. We run classification on the example, and find that Sheep is subsumed implicitly by Vegetarian due to axioms $\alpha_2, \alpha_4, \alpha_5, \alpha_6$. The change of α_4 might also remove the inferred subsumption between Sheep and Vegetarian.

We now deal with each of the above three cases.

4.1 Impact on Named Concepts Involved in the Unsatisfiability

We first describe how to calculate the impact of the removal of parts of axioms on the concepts involved in the unsatisfiability. In the following we use an example to explain how to find entailments, which are not responsible for the concept unsatisfiability in the ontology, by analysing the sequences of the clashes of an unsatisfiable concept.

Our idea is to search for any element which exists in the fully expanded tree but not in the sequences of the clashes. In Example 1, if C in axiom α_1 is going to be removed, then we have to calculate the lost entailments of A which are not responsible for A's unsatisfiability. Figure 2 shows the nodes and the sequences of the clash in A. We find that $(a : C, \{1\}, a : \forall R.B)$ exists in Seq^- (cf. 1 in Figure 2). We search for elements in the tree whose second concept assertion is $a : C$, but which do not exist in Seq^- or Seq^+. $(a : \exists R.\neg B \sqcap B, \{1, 2\}, a : C)$ matches $a : C$ but exists in Seq^- (cf. 2), so we keep searching for other elements whose second concept assertion is $a : \exists R.\neg B \sqcap B$. The matched elements are $(a : \exists R.\neg B, \{1, 2\}, a : \exists R.\neg B \sqcap B)$ which exists in Seq^- (cf. 3) and $(a : B, \{1, 2\}, a : \exists R.\neg B \sqcap B)$ (cf. 4) which does not exist in Seq^- or Seq^+, and has the same individual as $(a : A, \emptyset, nil)$. This means, B is a superconcept of A, and hence, the lost entailment is $A \sqsubseteq B$.

Assume that A is an unsatisfiable concept, and α_i is involved in its unsatisfiability, and there exists a clash in node x in the fully expanded tree. When a concept C in α_i is to be removed, we can calculate the lost entailments of A with the algorithm shown in Figure 5.

4.2 Impact on Satisfiable Concepts Irrelevant to the Unsatisfiability

We now describe how to calculate the impact on named concepts irrelevant to the unsatisfiability. Note that when a concept is unsatisfiable, it is trivially a subconcept of all satisfiable concepts and equivalent to all unsatisfiable concepts. If an axiom $C \sqsubseteq D$ is removed, any named concept in other axioms, which refers to C, will lose entailments introduced by this axiom. In general we lose $X \sqsubseteq Y$ where X is a subconcept of C and Y is a superconcept of D. Continuing the

Given: an unsatisfiable A, the sequences of Seq^+, Seq^- of a clash, the label of node x is $\mathcal{L}(x)$, and C is to be removed from α_i

1. let a be the individual of the last element of the Seq^+;
2. $setEle := \{\}$; $lostEnt := \{\}$;
3. $roleSeq := \langle\rangle$;
4. $ele := SearchSequence((-:C,-,-), Seq^+)$, where $ele = (a':C,-,-)$
        //search for the element in the sequence whose first concept is C
5. if (ele != null)   then $Seq := Seq^+$;
6. else $ele := SearchSequences((-:C,-,-), Seq^-)$, where $ele = (a':C,-,-)$
7. $Seq := Seq^-$;
8. $\mathcal{S} := SearchElement((-,-,a':C), \mathcal{L}(x), setEle)$
9. for each $\varepsilon \in \mathcal{S}$, where $\varepsilon = (a_1 : D_1, -, -)$
10.   if $(a = a_1)$, then $lostEnt := lostEnt \cup \{A \sqsubseteq D_1\}$;
11.   else $roleSeq := SearchRoleSeq((a':C,-,-), Seq, roleSeq, a_1)$;
12. $lostEnt := lostEnt \cup \{createSubsumption(A, roleSeq, D_1)\}$;
        //$createSubsumption$ creates a subsumption relationship for A,
        //e.g., if $roleSeq = \langle \forall R, \exists R \rangle$, then $A \sqsubseteq \forall R.(\exists R.D_1)$ is created.
13. return $lostEnt$;

14. subroutine: $SearchElement((-,-,a':C), \mathcal{L}(x), setEle)$
15. $\mathcal{S} := search((-,-,a':C), \mathcal{L}(x))$;
        //search for elements in $\mathcal{L}(x)$ whose second concept is C
16. for each $\varepsilon \in \mathcal{S}$, where $\varepsilon = (b : D_1, -, a' : C)$
17.   if ε exists in Seq^+ or Seq^-, then
18. $setEle := setEle \cup SearchElement((-,-,b:D_1), \mathcal{L}(x), setEle)$
19.   else $setEle := setEle \cup \{\varepsilon\}$;
20. end for
21. return $setEle$;

22. subroutine: $SearchRoleSeq((a':C,-,-), Seq, roleSeq, a_1)$
23. $\varepsilon := searchSuccessor((a':C,-,-), Seq)$, where $\varepsilon = (a':-,-,b:E)$, $a' \neq b$
        //search for the first element succeeding $(a':C,-,-)$
        //in the Seq with different individuals
24. if (ε = null), then
25. $\varepsilon := searchPredecessor((a':C,-,-), Seq)$, where $\varepsilon = (b:E,-,a':-)$, $a' \neq b$
        //search for the first element preceding $(a':C,-,-)$
        //in the Seq with different individuals
26. if E of the form $\forall R.-$, then
27. $roleSeq := roleSeq \cdot \langle \forall R \rangle$;   // $\cdot$ means to append an element to a sequence
28. else $roleSeq := roleSeq \cdot \langle \exists R \rangle$;
29. if $(a_1 = b)$, then   return $roleSeq$;
30. else   return $SearchRoleSeq((b:E,-,-), Seq, roleSeq, a_1)$;

Fig. 5. Algorithm for Finding Lost Entailments

mad_cow example, when the problematic part $\forall$ eats.($\neg\exists$ part_of.Animal) from α_4 is removed, all the subconcepts of Vegetarian which are not responsible for the unsatisfiability will be affected. It is obvious that the lost entailment of Giraffe is Giraffe $\sqsubseteq \forall$ eats.($\neg\exists$ part_of.Animal).

For those named concepts which refer to a concept to be removed not just via subsumption relations, the lost entailments cannot be as easily obtained as above. For the mad_cow example, if α_4 is changed to be Vegetarian $\doteq$ $\forall$eats.Plant $\sqcap$ Animal $\sqcap$ $\forall$eats.($\neg\exists$part_of.$\bot$), then we cannot say the lost entailment is Vegetarian $\sqsubseteq$ $\forall$eats.($\neg\exists$part_of.Animal), because the definition of Vegetarian still implies that it only eats part of anything, which includes $\neg$Animal.

The lost entailment of such concepts can be computed by calculating the difference between the original and modified concepts. To do this we adapt the notion of the "*difference*" operator between concepts which is defined in [24]. The difference between C and C' (1) contains enough information to yield the information in C if added to C', i.e., it contains all information from C which is missing in C', and (2) is maximally general, i.e., it does not contain any additional unnecessary information.

Definition 3 (Difference of Concepts). *Let C and C' be the original and modified concept expressions, the difference between C and C', which is a set of concepts, is defined as*

$$\textit{difference}(C, C') = \begin{cases} \max_{\sqsupseteq}\{E | E \doteq C \sqcup \neg C'\} & \textit{if } C \sqsubseteq C', \\ \max_{\sqsupseteq}\{E | E \doteq C' \sqcup \neg C\} & \textit{if } C' \sqsubseteq C \end{cases}$$

For Example 1, if concept $\exists R.\neg B$ in axiom α_2 is removed, then the modified axiom becomes $C \sqsubseteq B$. As α_3 refers to C, the lost entailment of G will be $\forall R.(\exists R.\neg B \sqcap B \sqcap F) \sqcup \neg \forall R.(B \sqcap F)$, i.e., $\forall R.(\exists R.\neg B) \sqcup \neg \forall R.(B \sqcap F)$. The disadvantage of this calculation is that the representation of lost entailments could be too complicated for human users to understand, the simplification of such representations is therefore necessary. Brandt et al. [6] introduced a syntax-oriented difference operator, but the algorithm only supports the difference between an $\mathcal{ALC}$- and an $\mathcal{ALE}$-concept description. As $\mathcal{ALE}$ does not support disjunction concepts, their difference operator is not applicable to our approach. In the future work, the approaches to updating of DLs [14,8] can be borrowed.

4.3 Impact on the Classification

Besides deciding the satisfiability of concept expressions, description logic reasoners are able to compute the classification of an ontology. Classification is the process of determining the subsumption relationship between any two named concepts in an ontology; e.g., for A and B, it determines whether $A \sqsubseteq B$ and/or $B \sqsubseteq A$. Recall that reasoners decide subsumption relationships by reducing the problem to a satisfiability test (i.e., $A \sqcap \neg B$ is unsatisfiable if $A \sqsubseteq B$ holds). Whenever an axiom is changed, the classification of the ontology might be affected. In this paper we aim to point out to the user which parts of the classification will be affected if a certain change is made to the ontology. If the classification of the entire ontology must be checked after each change, then it will involve n^2 subsumption tests for n named concepts; moreover, each subsumption test (checking for satisfiability in $\mathcal{ALC}$ w.r.t general inclusion axioms) is EXPTIME-complete [23]. It is impractical to run this classification test after each change made to the ontology. In this section, we will describe how we make use of the sequences of clashes (satisfiability test) to check if existing subsumption relations will be affected. If it is not affected, the subsumption test can be skipped.

Due to the monotonicity of the DLs we consider in this paper, removal of (part of) axioms cannot add new entailments, and will not change any previous non-subsumption relationships. Therefore, we only need to re-check if the removal of axioms will invalidate the previously found subsumption relationships. By building a tree with the application of the expansion rules on $A \sqcap \neg B$, we can obtain the sequences of the clashes. The elements in the sequences are the cause of the unsatisfiability, that is the subsumption relationship. With the sequences of clashes in the tree, we can analyse if a certain removal/change of (part of) an axiom will affect the current subsumption relation. Therefore, we are able to predict which subsumption relationships of named concepts will be affected, and skip the subsumption tests for the unaffected named concepts.

We check if a concept component of an axiom which is going to be removed will affect the previously found subsumption as follows:

Lemma 4. *Given a terminology T such that $T \vDash A \sqsubseteq B$, where A and B are named concepts, and a fully expanded tree $\mathbf{T}$ of $A \sqcap \neg B$, the sequences of clashes in the tree are obtained. Let I_u be the union of the index-set of the first element in all of the sequences. Assume that a concept component C in α_i is going to be removed, where $\alpha_i \in T$, the subsumption $A \sqsubseteq B$ is unaffected if either one of the following conditions hold:*

1. *$i \notin I_u$, α_i is not involved in the unsatisfiability,*
2. *$(-:C,I,-)$ and $(-:C',I,-)$ do not exist in any sequences of clashes where $i \in I$, $i \in I_u$ and C' is a negated form of C*

Proof. The sequences of the clashes in $\mathbf{T}$ contain the concept components and sets of axioms which are relevant to the subsumption.

1. If an axiom α_i going to be changed does not exist in the index-set of any sequence of the clashes, i.e., $i \notin I_u$, then α_i is not involved in the unsatisfiability, any change of α_i does not affect the subsumption.
2. If α_i is involved in the unsatisfiability (i.e., $i \in I_u$), but $(-:C,I,-)$ and $(-:C',I,-)$, where $i \in I$, do not appear in any sequences of clashes, then they are not responsible for the clashes in the tree, and therefore not responsible for the subsumption. Since B is negated for the satisfiability test $(A \sqcap \neg B)$, we need to check the negated form of C as well. □

We use the following example to illustrate how we make use of the sequences of clashes (satisfiability test between two named concepts) to detect if some change will affect a subsumption.

$\mathcal{L}(x) := \{(a : B \sqcap \neg A, \emptyset, nil), (a : B, \emptyset, a : B \sqcap \neg A), (a : \neg A, \emptyset, a : B \sqcap \neg A),$
$(a : E \sqcap F, \{2\}, a : B), \underline{(a : \neg D, \{1\}, a : \neg A)}, (a : E, \{2\}, a : E \sqcap F),$
$\underline{(a : F, \{2\}, a : E \sqcap F)}, \underline{(a : D, \{2, 3\}, a : E)}\}$ Clash

— to be removed, not exists in Seq^- or Seq^+

Clash:
$Seq^+ := \langle (a : D, \{2, 3\}, a : E), (a : E, \{2\}, a : E \sqcap F),$
$(a : E \sqcap F, \{2\}, a : B), (a : B, \emptyset, a : B \sqcap \neg A), (a : B \sqcap \neg A, \emptyset, nil) \rangle$

$Seq^- := \langle (a : \neg D, \{1\}, a : \neg A), (a : \neg A, \emptyset, a : B \sqcap \neg A), (a : B \sqcap \neg A, \emptyset, nil) \rangle$

Fig. 6. Subsumption Test on $B \sqsubseteq A$

Example 5. Given a terminology with the following axioms, we check if $B \sqsubseteq A$.

α_1: $A \doteq D$
α_2: $B \doteq E \sqcap F$
α_3: $E \sqsubseteq D$

As seen in Figure 6, $B \sqsubseteq A$ holds, because a clash exists in the label of the root node, and so $B \sqcap \neg A$ is unsatisfiable. Assume the concept component F in α_2 is to be removed, we know that $B \sqsubseteq A$ still holds, because $(a : F, \{2\}, -)$ does not exist in either of the sequences of the clash.

5 Harmful and Helpful Changes

In this section we study ways of changing problematic axioms to resolve unsatisfiability. It should be noted that improperly rewriting a problematic axiom might not resolve the unsatisfiability, and could introduce additional unsatisfiability. It is important to help ontology modellers to make changes in order not to introduce unintended contradictions. For this purpose, we define *harmful* and *helpful* changes. Harmful changes either fail to resolve the existing unsatisfiability or introduce additional unsatisfiability. Helpful changes resolve the problem without causing additional contradictions, and restore some lost entailments.

5.1 Harmful Changes

Given an unsatisfiable concept A in $\mathcal{T}$, assume a concept E on the right-hand side of a problematic axiom α_i is chosen to be replaced by some other concept. We can find the harmful concepts for the replacement of E by analysing the elements in the sequences of the clashes of concept A.

Definition 5 (Harmful Change). *A change which transforms $\mathcal{T}$ to $\mathcal{T}'$ is harmful with respect to an unsatisfiable concept A in $\mathcal{T}$, if one of the following conditions holds:*

- *$\mathcal{T}' \vDash A \sqsubseteq \bot$, where $\mathcal{T}'$ is the changed ontology;*
- *if some named concept A_i which is satisfiable in $\mathcal{T}$ is not satisfiable in $\mathcal{T}'$. That is, $\mathcal{T} \nvDash A_i \sqsubseteq \bot$ and $\mathcal{T}' \vDash A_i \sqsubseteq \bot$, for some A_i in $\mathcal{T}$.*

The following lemma identifies the changes which are harmful due to the fact that they fail to resolve the existing unsatisfiability. To identify other harmful changes (which introduce additional unsatisfiability unrelated to the original problem), the whole ontology may have to be rechecked.

Lemma 6. *Assume a concept C on the right-hand of axiom α_i is to be rewritten. Given two sequences of a clash, Seq^+ and Seq^-, involving C, if one of the elements, ε, in Seq^+, is of the form $(a : C, I, -)$ and $i \in I$, then*

1. *All the concepts in the elements in Seq^+ preceding $(a : C, I, -)$, which contain the same individual as ε, are harmful for replacing C;*
2. *The negation of all the concepts in elements in Seq^-, which contain the same individual as ε, are also harmful, because these replacements still keep the unsatisfiability.*

The lemma is analogous for the element ε in Seq^-.

Proof. Assume that a concept C in axiom α_i is to be rewritten, and two sequences of a clash, Seq^+ and Seq^-, involving C, are obtained from a node of the tree **T**. In a sequence, for every two adjacent elements, ε_1 and ε_2, which are of the form $(a : E_1, -, a : E_2)$ and $(a : E_2, -, -)$, containing the same individual, the concept E_1 is a superconcept of E_2. This extends inductively to all elements preceding ε_1, i.e., they are all superconcepts of E_2.

1. If an element ε in Seq^+, which is of the form $(a : C, I, -)$ and $i \in I$, then the concepts in all the elements, which are preceding ε and contain individual a, are harmful for replacing C. This is because they are superconcepts which are involved in the clash.
2. The elements in Seq^- lead to a negated concept, which results in a contradiction. Hence, the negation of all the concepts in elements in Seq^-, which contain the same individual a, are also harmful. □

In Example 1, if C in axiom α_1 is going to be replaced, we know that there exists an element $(a : C, \{1\}, a : C \sqcap \forall R.B)$ in Seq^- of the clash, then the harmful concepts for the replacements will be $\exists R.\neg B \sqcap B$, $\exists R.\neg B$, $\neg(\forall R.B)$, $\neg(C \sqcap \forall R.B)$, $\neg(C \sqcap \forall R.B \sqcap D)$, and $\neg A$. The first two items are from Seq^-, the rest are from negated elements in Seq^+.

5.2 Helpful Changes

If we know which concepts are harmful to replace a concept in a problematic axiom, then all the concepts which are not harmful are candidates for replacement. However, there are many possible candidates. Our aim is to find desirable concepts for replacement in order to minimise the impact of changes. To do this we introduce *helpful* changes which cover for the lost entailments due to the removal. When an axiom $A \sqsubseteq C$ in $\mathcal{T}$ is changed to be $A \sqsubseteq C'$ (where A is a named concept), this change is helpful if (1) C' can compensate for at least one lost entailment due to the removal of C, (2) the changes are not harmful, that means all concepts which are satisfiable in $\mathcal{T}$ are also satisfiable in the changed ontology. Note that we only change concepts in the right-hand side of axioms. We now formally define a helpful change.

Definition 7 (Helpful Change). *A helpful change is defined as the removal of an axiom followed by an addition. Assume that $\mathcal{T}$ is the original ontology and an axiom α in $\mathcal{T}$ involved in the unsatisfiability of concept A is going to be removed, resulting in intermediate ontology $\mathcal{T}_1$. A new axiom is then added to $\mathcal{T}_1$, resulting in the changed ontology $\mathcal{T}'$. The change is helpful with respect to A, if the following conditions hold:*

1. *if Ω is the set of lost entailments in going from $\mathcal{T}$ to $\mathcal{T}_1$ (i.e., due to the removal of α), such that $\forall \gamma \in \Omega$, $\mathcal{T} \vDash \gamma$, then there exists $\beta \in \Omega$, such that $\mathcal{T}_1 \nvDash \beta$ and $\mathcal{T}' \vDash \beta$;*
2. $\mathcal{T}' \nvDash A \sqsubseteq \bot$.

Lemma 8. *Assume C on the right-hand side of a problematic axiom (involved in the unsatisfiability of A) is going to be replaced by C', the change is helpful if C' is a superconcept of C and is not involved in the clash of A.*

Proof. It is obvious that any concept which is not involved in the clash is not harmful as a replacement for C. We now prove its superconcepts are helpful. Given that in an axiom $\alpha : E \sqsubseteq C$ in $\mathcal{T}$, concept C is going to be replaced by its superconcept C'. We divide the change into two steps:

1. Remove C from α, the changed ontology $\mathcal{T}_1 = \mathcal{T} \setminus \{E \sqsubseteq C\}$;
2. Add C' to α, the final ontology $\mathcal{T}' = \mathcal{T}_1 \cup \{E \sqsubseteq C'\}$.

As C' is a superconcept of C, $E \sqsubseteq C$ is removed in $\mathcal{T}_1$, so the indirect subsumption relationships of A with C's superconcepts are also lost, that means $\mathcal{T}_1 \nvDash E \sqsubseteq C'$, but obviously, $\mathcal{T}' \vDash E \sqsubseteq C'$. □

Lemma 9. *Given two sequences of a clash w.r.t the unsatisfiability of A obtained from a fully expanded tree $\mathbf{T}$, assume a concept C on the right-hand side of axiom α_i is to be rewritten. C' is helpful as a replacement for C, if the following conditions hold:*

1. *there exist two elements e and e' in $\mathbf{T}$, which are $(a : C, I, -)$ and $(a : C', I', -)$, and no element of the form $(a : C', I', -)$ exists in either of the two sequences;*
2. $I \subset I'$, *the index-set of the element with concept C is a proper subset of that of the element with concept C'.*

Proof. We have to prove that (1) C' is a superconcept of C, this is a sufficient condition to ensure that the first requirement for helpfulness is met; and (2) C' is not involved in the clash.

1. If elements e and e' in **T** contain the same individual, then they have a subsumption relationship (i.e., C is either a subconcept or superconcept of C'). Additionally, if the index-set of the element e is a proper subset of the index-set of the element e', then that means e' is added to $\mathcal{L}(x)$ after the addition of e (i.e., the addition of e' is triggered by e). Then we can confirm that C' is a superconcept of C.
2. If an element, which is of the form $(a : C', -, -)$, exists in **T**, but not in either of the two sequences, then C' is not involved in the clash. □

Continuing with Example 1, assume C in axiom α_1 is going to be replaced, there exists an element $(a : C, \{1\}, a : C \sqcap \forall R.B)$ in Seq^- of the clash (see Figure 2), we find that the two elements $(a : D, \{1\}, \cdots)$ and $(a : B, \{1, 2\}, \cdots)$ do not exist in either of the sequences of the clash. However, the former element does not fulfill condition (2) in Lemma 9, because the index set of $(a : C, \{1\}, \cdots)$ is not a proper subset of $(a : D, \{1\}, \cdots)$. Hence, the only helpful concept for the replacement is the concept of the latter element, B, because B is a superconcept of A, but D is not.

Overall, the helpful changes include the replacements of a concept by its superconcepts not involved in any clash (see Lemma 9), and the lost entailments irrelevant to the unsatisfiability of the ontology (see Section 4). These changes are suggested to the user to add back to the ontology in order to minimise the impact of changes.

6 Evaluation

To demonstrate the effectiveness of our proposed approach, we have built a prototype. The implementation extends the Pellet[6]1.3 reasoner to support our fine-grained approach. In this section we describe a usability evaluation to evaluate the benefits of our approach; the result is compared with existing debugging tools. Next, we present the performance evaluation of our prototype using a set of satisfiability tests and comparing it with an existing DL reasoner.

6.1 Usability Evaluation

We created a plugin in Protégé 3.2 for repairing ontologies, called 'RepairTab'. Figure 7 shows our plugin displaying the problematic axioms of mad_cow, which is an unsatisfiable concept from the Mad_Cow ontology[7]. As can be seen, the parts of axioms responsible for the unsatisfiability are highlighted. The parts of axioms or whole axioms can be removed by striking out (cf. (A) in Figure 7). If the user decides to remove vegetarian from the axiom cow ⊑ vegetarian, the lost entailments of this removal can be previewed. The harmful and helpful changes are also listed. The user can choose to add the helpful changes to the ontology to minimise the impact of the removal (cf. (B)).

---

[6] http://www.mindswap.org/2003/pellet/
[7] http://cohse.semanticweb.org/ontologies/people.owl

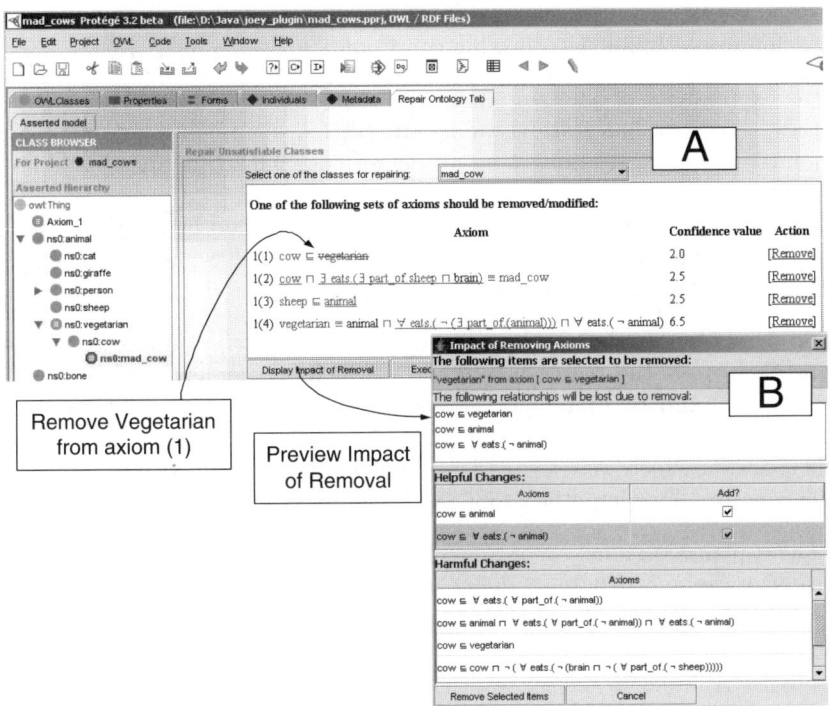

Fig. 7. (A) mad_cow is unsatisfiable. The problematic parts of the axioms are highlighted. (B) The lost entailments of the selected item can be previewed. The helpful and harmful changes are listed.

For the purpose of evaluation, we decided to compare RepairTab with OWLDebugger[8] and SWOOP[9]. OWLDebugger is another Protégé plugin, which provides explanations for unsatisfiable concepts. SWOOP is a stand-alone editor. We are interested in two main functionalities in SWOOP [12]: (1) explanations of unsatisfiability – it pinpoints the problematic axioms for unsatisfiable concepts, and is able to strike out irrelevant parts of axioms that do not contribute to the unsatisfiability; (2) ontology repair service – it displays the impact on ontologies due to the removal of axioms. When an axiom is removed, it shows the fixed and remaining unsatisfiable concepts, as well as the lost and retained entailments.

We conducted a usability-study with three ontologies and three groups of subjects. Fifteen subjects, who were postgraduate students in the Computing Science Department at the University of Aberdeen, were chosen for the evaluation. They had knowledge of OWL ontologies and Description Logics; they had experience of using both Protégé and SWOOP. None of the subjects had seen these ontologies before, and they were divided into three groups to debug

---

[8] http://www.co-ode.org/downloads/owldebugger/
[9] http://www.mindswap.org/2004/SWOOP/

the same set of ontologies using one of these tools. Ideally, ontologies in our evaluation would fulfill the following conditions:

1. the expressivity of ontologies is in $\mathcal{ALC}$;
2. they should be interestingly axiomatised, i.e., containing axioms like disjointness, role restrictions, concept definitions, and so on, and should not be simply taxonomies;
3. the domain of the ontologies can be easily understood by subjects.
4. they are available on the Web and contain unsatisfiable concepts which could be difficult for non-expert users to debug.

The Mad_Cow[10], Bad-food.owl[11] and University.owl[12] ontologies available on the Web meet the requirements and were chosen for evaluation. Both the Mad_Cow.owl and Bad-food.owl ontologies each contain one unsatisfiable concept. University.owl was simplified into $\mathcal{ALC}$ format, and it contains 12 unsatisfiable concepts which were sorted based on the number and size of the MUPSs of the concepts. Our hypotheses for this usability study were:

1. The explanation function of RepairTab, which highlights parts of the axioms causing the unsatisfiability, helps users resolve the unsatisfiability. This is a relative advantage of RepairTab when compared with OWLDebugger and SWOOP.
2. The subjects using RepairTab will take less time to understand the source of errors and resolve them, compared with OWLDebugger and SWOOP.
3. RepairTab's list of lost entailments helps subjects decide which change(s) should be made in order to minimise the impact on the ontologies.
4. RepairTab's list of helpful changes provides useful (as rated by subjects) suggestions for subjects to add axioms back to the ontologies in order to minimise the impact of the changes on the ontologies.
5. RepairTab's list of harmful changes provides useful (as rated by subjects) guidance for subjects about which changes should not be made in order to prevent more unsatisfiable concepts being created.

The usability study was conducted as follows. Each subject was given a tutorial on the debugger they would use. A detailed walkthrough of the relevant explanation and debugging functions was given using a sample ontology. Groups A, B and C were assigned to RepairTab, OWLDebugger and SWOOP respectively. Each group was to resolve all unsatisfiable concepts in the three ontologies using their respective tools.

The subjects in the three groups were asked to answer a survey. For each task, they were asked if they understood the cause of the unsatisfiable concepts, which axioms were changed, and how many changes were made etc. At the end of the session, they were also asked to rate the usefulness of the tool used on a 5 point scale where 5 is 'very useful' and 1 corresponds to 'useless'. For Group A, the

---

[10] http://www.cs.man.ac.uk/~horrocks/OWL/Ontologies/mad_cows.owl
[11] http://www.mindswap.org/dav/ontologies/commonsense/food/foodswap.owl
[12] http://www.mindswap.org/ontologies/debugging/university.owl

subjects were also asked how useful the lost entailments, helpful and harmful changes facilities were, and how many helpful changes they had selected to add back to the three ontologies. For Group C, the subjects were also asked about the usefulness of the explanation and repairing functionalities provided by SWOOP. In addition, we also asked the subjects for their comments on the tool used, and how it could be improved. The time taken by each subject for resolving the unsatisfiability in each ontology was recorded. The modified ontologies were also recorded for analysis by the experimenter.

6.2 Analysis of Results

Table 3 shows the results for the three tools used by the subjects. We took the average of the times for each group to complete the tasks. As some tools do not provide certain functionalities, those ratings are not included in the table. As can be seen from the Table 3, firstly, the explanation function (i.e. highlighting the problematic parts of axioms) of RepairTab was rated to be more useful than SWOOP and OWLDebugger in two examples, but less useful on the Bad-food.owl ontology compared with OWLDebugger. Secondly, the subjects in Group A took less time to resolve the unsatisfiability than Group B; Group C had similar performance with Group A. Therefore, we cannot verify the first and second hypothesis currently. Both the lost entailments and helpful changes were rated to be useful overall, the ratings were in agreement with the third and fourth hypotheses. However, the harmful changes are less useful relatively, therefore the final hypothesis was falsified. We now analyse their performance for each ontology.

Table 3. Results of Debugging ontologies (A = RepairTab, B = OWLDebugger, C = SWOOP)

	Mad_Cow			Bad-food			University		
Group	A	B	C	A	B	C	A	B	C
Average Time Taken (in mins)	5	8.8	6.9	6.4	6.8	6.0	10.2	16.3	11.5
No. of subjects who understood the errors	5/5	4/5	3/5	3/5	2/5	3/5	0/5	0/5	0/5
Rating of Explanation Function	5	4	2.6	3.5	4.5	3.5	5	4	2.6
Rating of Lost & Retained Entailments (SWOOP)	-	-	3	-	-	4	-	-	5
Rating of Fixed & Remaining Unsat. Concepts (SWOOP)	-	-	3	-	-	3	-	-	5
Rating of Lost Entailments (RepairTab)	5	-	-	4	-	-	5	-	-
Rating of Helpful Changes (RepairTab)	5	-	-	4	-	-	4	-	-
Rating of Harmful Changes (RepairTab)	4	-	-	2.5	-	-	2.5	-	-

For Mad_Cow.owl, more subjects using RepairTab understood the errors in Mad_cow.owl than those using OWLDebugger or SWOOP. It is suggested this is because the problematic axioms of mad_cow were highlighted by RepairTab, and so the subjects understood the error quickly. However, it is difficult to resolve the problem correctly. The subjects in Group A usually resolved the error by removing part of an axiom and then adding the helpful changes suggested by the plugin; the subjects in Group B had to explore changes to the definitions of concepts or add extra subconcepts for cow (e.g., to have Normal_Cow as a sibling of mad_cow), some also triggered additional unsatisfiable concepts. Two subjects in Group C failed to understand the cause of unsatisfiable mad_cow, because some irrelevant parts of axioms were not struck out, this led the subjects to think that the irrelevant parts were responsible for the unsatisfiability.

In the case of Bad-food.owl, we report two issues. Firstly, the times taken for this ontology were similar in all three tools; the subjects in Group B took relatively less time to debug this ontology than when they were debugging Mad_Cow.owl. Secondly, the explanation function of OWLDebugger was rated to be more useful than RepairTab or SWOOP. The following is our explanation for this observation. OWLDebugger explains the error was due to the disjoint axiom, when in fact all the axioms referring to this disjoint axiom are also causing the problem. As a result of OWLDebugger's recommendation most subjects immediately chose to remove this axiom without understanding the cause of the unsatisfiable concept; if they understood the precise reason they could instead have altered one component of an axiom referring to the disjoint axiom. Our plugin facilitates these fine-grained changes. However, it is not without its shortcomings: two subjects found it difficult to analyse the problematic axioms which were presented in the formal DL notation. This problem was pronounced with Bad-food.owl because the axioms are relatively complicated. Furthermore, the fine-grained approach was not applicable because all parts of the axioms are relevant to the unsatisfiability, and hence all were highlighted in red. This explanation given for this example is similar in SWOOP. As a result, the subjects using RepairTab or SWOOP found it difficult to understand the reason for the unsatisfiability and to decide which changes should be made.

For the University.owl, we report two issues. Firstly, the rating of usefulness of the explanation in RepairTab and OWLDebugger is higher than that of SWOOP. This is because, for the unsatisfiable concept Person, SWOOP strikes out the whole right-hand side of a problematic axiom; some subjects thought that the explanation was confusing. Secondly, the subjects using RepairTab and SWOOP took less time to complete the task than those using OWLDebugger. We suggest the following reasons: (1) RepairTab sorted the twelve unsatisfiable concepts in order of size of problematic axioms. The subjects were guided to debug the concept with the least problematic axioms first. SWOOP highlights the root and derived unsatisfiable concepts. When a concept was resolved, most of its subconcepts were resolved as well. However, the subjects in Group B had to explore each unsatisfiable concept one by one. (2) RepairTab and SWOOP provide previews of the impact of removal, but OWLDebugger does not. We noticed that two subjects in Group B removed the disjoint axioms which caused the problems. This removal causes many lost entailments, but the subjects did not realise this. On the other hand, the subjects in Group A or C were discouraged from this type of removal because they previewed the impact of removal. Three subjects in Group A also changed their minds after exploring the consequences of different modifications (i.e., after seeing many lost entailments or more helpful changes provided). Helpful changes were usually added back to the ontology. The subjects in Group C tried to remove some axioms and preview the impact of the removal on the ontology. Some subjects chose to remove axioms which caused fewer lost entailments and more retained entailments. However, there is no functionality to add the lost entailments back to the ontology in SWOOP. In some cases, the displayed lost entailment is exactly the same as the axiom just removed by the subjects. Therefore, in comparison, RepairTab is able to minimise the impact on the ontologies in the case of removing parts of axioms, by providing helpful changes facility.

Interestingly, we found that some subjects claimed they understood the reasons for the unsatisfiability, but they simply deleted disjoint axioms or subclass-of relationships, particularly in University.owl. Therefore, we classified these subjects as not understanding the errors. We believe this ontology, which contains one of the most common OWL modelling errors, is very difficult for the subjects. In the case of Person in University.owl, none of the subjects realised that FrenchUniversity $\doteq$ $\forall$ offerCourse.Frenchcourse, the domain of offersCourse is University, FrenchUniversity is a subclass of University, therefore, University is defined as equivalent to owl:Thing implicitly, then Person which is disjoint with owl:Thing is unsatisfiable. Two subjects using SWOOP did not realise that SWOOP displays the implicit axiom University $\doteq$ owl:Thing, they removed the domain or disjoint axiom to resolve the problem. However, when some subjects in Group A were exploring the removal of FrenchUniversity $\doteq$ $\forall$ offerCourse.Frenchcourse, they discovered that a helpful change FrenchUniversity $\sqsubseteq$ $\forall$ offerCourse.Frenchcourse could be added back to the ontology, and they decided to make this change.

6.3 Overall Comments and Summary

We learnt some useful lessons based on the results of the study and the comments given by the subjects.

Group A – RepairTab. The subjects using RepairTab appreciated that the problematic parts of axioms are highlighted, this helped them to analyse the cause of errors. For the impact of change, for those subjects who understood the problems but had no idea what changes should be made, the impact of removal and suggested changes were rated to be very useful. On the other hand, for those subjects who already had an idea what changes should be made, the suggestions of changes were less useful; for example, if a subject wants to make complex changes, such as changing role restrictions or creating new concepts; our plugin does not support these changes. Also, the list of harmful changes was rated as 3 on average. This is because the subjects who understood the causes of problems, already knew what changes should not be made.

The overall comments on our plugin were that it is useful for resolving inconsistencies, but that the presentation of problematic axioms could be more user friendly, such as using natural language. Two subjects thought the presentation of problematic axioms was too formal;they took longer to analyse the meaning of those axioms. For example, Protégé presents disjoint concepts in a 'Disjoints' table, but a disjoint axiom is presented in our plugin as '$C \sqsubseteq \neg D$'.

Group B – OWLDebugger. Most subjects thought the plugin was useful because it indicated which conditions contradict with each other; the clash information was also shown in quasi-natural language. Debugging steps were provided to suggest which concepts should be debugged. For example, subjects were pointed to debug CS_Student when the concept AIStudent was chosen to be debugged. However, sometimes it was not helpful because the explanation of the unsatisfiable concept was oversimplistic when the cause of the unsatisfiability was too complex to explain.

Group C – SWOOP. (i) *Explanation Function*: Two subjects thought the function was confusing, because in some cases, it does not strike out all of the irrelevant parts (mad_cow in Mad_Cow.owl is an example), sometimes, it strikes out the relevant parts of axioms. Person in University.owl is an example, in which the whole right-hand side of an axiom was struck out, this misled the subjects to think that the problematic axiom was not responsible for the unsatisfiability. This is because the implementation in the latest version of SWOOP 2.3 Beta 3 is incomplete with respect to the published algorithm [12]. Thus, this function only works in a few cases in our study.

(ii) *Repairing Function*: Most subjects thought the tool was useful because (1) it separates the root and derived unsatisfiable concepts, so that they can focus on only debugging the root ones; (2) it enables the user to try removing different axioms and preview the impact of removal before committing the change; (3) it displays the lost and retained entailments when axioms are removed. Additionally, in some cases, the tool provides (Why?) hyperlinks which explain why entailments are lost and retained. However, there is no explanation for the fixed and remaining unsatisfiable concepts.

However, two subjects thought that SWOOP's repair service is limited to the removal of the whole axioms, rather than changing certain parts of axioms. Removing whole axioms will unnecessarily cause additional information loss. For the Mad_Cow.owl example, one subject claimed the definition of mad_cow was modelled poorly. If the definition axiom of mad_cow is completely removed, then all information about mad_cow will be lost. This is not a desired change for the subject, though the ontology becomes satisfiable.

6.4 Performance Analysis

The non-determinism in the expansion rule (i.e., $\sqcup$-rule) results in poor performance of the tableau algorithm. Existing DL reasoners employ optimisation techniques. They have demonstrated that even with expressive DLs, highly optimised implementations can provide acceptable performance in realistic DL applications. For example, dependency directed backtracking is used to prune the search tree [9]. However, in our fine-grained approach, these techniques are no longer applicable, as we aim to detect all possible clashes by fully expanding the tree. This will adversely affect the performance of the algorithm especially if there is extensive non-determinism in the ontology. Considering that the number of unsatisfiable concepts is relatively small compared to the total number of concepts in realistic ontologies, we believe it is practical to first check the consistency of ontologies using optimised reasoners to find the unsatisfiable concepts, and then run the fine-grained algorithm on those unsatisfiable concepts. For example, Sweet-JPL.owl[13] contains 1537 concepts, and one concept is unsatisfiable. Hence, our algorithm is then only applied to the unsatisfiable concept, instead of the whole ontology.

In this subsection we report an evaluation with a number of realistic ontologies. RepairTab, a plugin for Protégé, was implemented in Java. The tests were performed on a PC (Intel Pentium IV with 2.4GHz and 1GB RAM) with Windows XP SP2 as operating system. Benchmarking with real-life ontologies is obviously a convincing way to evaluate the quality of our approach. However, there is only a limited number of realistic ontologies that are both represented in $\mathcal{ALC}$ and unsatisfiable. We therefore constructed simplified $\mathcal{ALC}$ versions for a number of ontologies downloaded from the Internet. We then removed, for example, numerical constraints, role hierarchies and instance information. As some ontologies are satisfiable, we randomly changed them such that each change on its own lead to unsatisfiable concepts. For example, we added disjointness statements among sibling concepts, and introduced some common ontology modelling errors enumerated by [18]. Figure 8 (left-hand side) shows the average runtime (in seconds) of the satisfiability test of a set of ontologies. The brackets of the ontology names indicate the number of unsatisfiable concept tested. The execution time of our extended algorithm is increased by 15% on average compared with that of Pellet, because our algorithm aims to detect all possible clashes given that it requires a fully expanded tableau tree, while many optimisations are disabled. In the cases of Transportation.owl and Economy.owl, the running time for checking the satisfiability of 20 and 30 concepts is less than 0.6 second. The result shows that the performance of our algorithm is feasible in realistic ontologies which do not contain a large number of unsatisfiable concepts.

We also were interested in the GALEN ontology[14], which models medical terms and procedures. It contains over 2700 classes and about 400 GCIs. As its DL expressivity is $\mathcal{SHf}$, we constructed a simplified $\mathcal{ALC}$ version of it. Figure 8 (right-hand side) shows the average runtime (in seconds) of from 1 to 1000 satisfiability tests. Note that there is a large number of GCIs in the GALEN ontology, the optimised reasoner is able to eliminate non-determinism by absorbing them into primitive concept introduction axioms whenever possible (CN $\sqsubseteq$ D, where CN is a named concept, D is a concept description). Although the execution time of RepairTab dramatically increases with the number of unsatisfiable concepts with the same reason as the above, *absorption* is still applicable to our revised algorithm, because it is algorithm independent. Absorption is used to preprocess the ontology before the tableau algorithm is applied. For example, given two

---
[13] http://www.mindswap.org/ontologies/debugging/buggy-sweet-jpl.owl
[14] http://www.cs.man.ac.uk/~horrocks/OWL/Ontologies/galen.owl

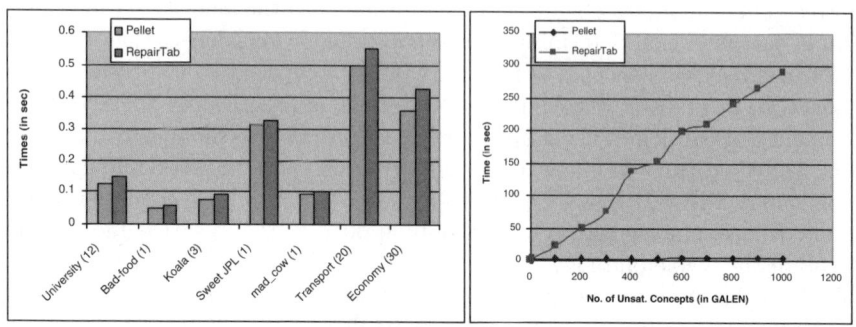

Fig. 8. Performance Test of Pellet and RepairTab

axioms (1) $\mathsf{CN} \sqsubseteq \forall R.\neg C \sqcap \neg D$, (2) $\forall R.\neg C \sqsubseteq \neg \mathsf{CN} \sqcup D$. Axiom (2) will be absorbed as $\mathsf{CN} \sqsubseteq D \sqcup \exists R.C$, and can then be merged with axiom (1), the resulting axiom is $\mathsf{CN} \sqsubseteq (\forall R.\neg C \sqcap \neg D) \sqcap (D \sqcup \neg \exists R.C)$. We then apply the fine-grained algorithm to trace which parts of the axiom cause the unsatisfiability. However, the algorithm modifies the original axioms; in this example, two axioms are modified into one axiom, we can only tag the parts of the resulting axioms (modified by the algorithm) relevant to the unsatisfiability, instead of the original asserted axioms. In future work, to improve usability, it might be necessary to explain the correlation between the originally asserted axioms and the axioms (modified by the tableau algorithm) in a way that is understandable to the user.

7 Related Work

Several methods have been developed in the literature to deal with unsatisfiable ontologies. In this section, we first review three existing approaches to analysing unsatisfiable ontologies, and then describe two related fine-grained approaches used in debugging ontologies. Finally, we discuss the related work on resolving unsatisfiable concepts in ontologies.

7.1 Analysing Unsatisfiable Ontologies

We now describe three approaches to analysing unsatisfiable ontologies. One approach is to find maximally satisfiable sub-ontologies by excluding problematic axioms [4,15]. Another approach is to find minimal unsatisfiable sub-ontologies by pinpointing possible problematic axioms [22,21,10,13]. Finally there is the heuristic approach to explaining unsatisfiability [26].

Baader et al. [4] investigate the problem of finding the maximally satisfiable subsets of ABox assertions. In their approach, each element in the nodes in a tree is labeled with a propositional formula which indicates the sources of axioms, whereas Meyer et al. [15] use an index-set associated with every element of the label of nodes in a tree. The index-set is used to exclude axioms involved in the unsatisfiability of concepts, so that maximally concept-satisfiable subontologies (so called MCSS) can be obtained.

Schlobach et al. [22,21] proposed to pinpoint the so called Minimal Unsatisfiability Preserving Sub-ontologies (MUPSs), which are sets of axioms responsible for an unsatisfiable concept. This is called *axiom pinpointing*. Roughly, a MUPS of a named concept contains only axioms that are necessary to preserve its unsatisfiability. They further exploit the minimal hitting-set algorithm described by Reiter [19] to calculate *diagnosis sets*, i.e minimal subsets of an ontology that need to be repaired/removed to make the ontology satisfiable.

Overall, the above approaches achieve the same result. A MCSS can be obtained by excluding the axioms in any one of the diagnosis sets. Moreover, they are only applicable to unfoldable terminologies $\mathcal{T}$; they simply remove problematic axioms from the ontology, and the support for rewriting the axioms is still limited.

Kalyanpur et al. [13,10] extended the axiom pinpointing technique (i.e., finding MUPS) to the more expressive description logic $\mathcal{SHOIN}$. They utilise a glass-box strategy for finding the first MUPS of an unsatisfiable concept. The description logic tableaux reasoner was modified to keep track the cause for the unsatisfiability of a concept, so that the minimal set of relevant axioms in the ontology that support the concept unsatisfiability was obtained. Their tool, SWOOP, also detects interdependencies between unsatisfiable concepts, in which root and derived unsatisfiable concepts are identified. The user can differentiate the root bugs from others which are caused by the root unsatisfiable concepts, and focus solely on the root concepts. This is a particularly effective approach to fixing a large set of derived unsatisfiable concepts. Then, they use a black-box approach, which is reasoner independent, to derive the remaining MUPSs from the first MUPS. Reiter's Hitting Set Tree (HST) algorithm [19] was adapted to find the remaining MUPSs [12]. The advantage of this approach is that it makes use of the optimisation techniques embedded in the reasoner. The disadvantage is that the complexity of generating the HST is exponential with the number of MUPSs. Their results showed the algorithm performed well in practice, because most of the satisfiability tests exhibited at most three or four MUPSs, with five to ten axioms each [11]. In comparison, RepairTab detects all MUPSs of an unsatisfiable concepts by fully expanding the tree. The disadvantage of our approach is that most optimisations are not applicable, however, its complexity is independent of the number of MUPSs.

Roctor et al [18] addressed some common problems of ontology users during the modelling of OWL ontologies. Based on these common errors, the authors developed a set of *heuristic rules* and incorporated them into a Protégé-OWL plugin. Their program is called OWLDebugger; it can detect commonly occurring error patterns in OWL ontologies. This alleviates the user from troubleshooting the unsatisfiable concepts. It helps users to track down the reasons for errors in OWL concepts. Quasi-natural language explanations for unsatisfiable OWL concepts are also generated. As the heuristic approach and pattern matching cannot determine the causes of the inconsistency in every case, the authors are still investigating how to extend and improve the set of heuristic rules. However, the process of resolving problems is left to the user who has to run the reasoner frequently to check if consistency has been achieved.

7.2 Fine-Grained Approaches

Schlobach et al. [22] apply syntactic generalisation techniques to highlight the exact position of a contradiction within the axioms of the TBox. This is called *concept pinpointing*. Concepts are diagnosed by successive generalisation of axioms until the most general form which is still unsatisfiable is achieved. The main difference with our work is that in [22] the concepts in axioms are generalised and only these generalised axioms are shown to the user. For example, $\alpha_1: A \sqsubseteq C \sqcap D \sqcap E$, $\alpha_2: C \sqsubseteq \neg D \sqcap F$, then the generalised axioms $A \sqsubseteq C \sqcap D$, and $C \sqsubseteq \neg D$ are shown. It can be an additional burden on the user to correlate between the generalised axioms and the originally asserted axioms. In the case of very complicated axioms, the user might find it difficult to know which generalised axioms correspond to which of the original asserted axioms. Compared to our approach, we use a tracing technique to pinpoint problematic parts of axioms, the asserted axioms are directly displayed and faulty parts are highlighted.

Kalyanpur et al. [12] also propose a fine-grained approach, which determines which parts of the asserted axioms are responsible for the unsatisfiability of concepts. Their idea is to rewrite the axioms in an ontology in a normal form and split up conjunctions in the normalised version, e.g., $A \sqsubseteq \exists R.(C \sqcap D)$ is rewritten as $A \sqsubseteq \exists R.E$, $E \sqsubseteq C$, $E \sqsubseteq D$ and $C \sqcap D \sqsubseteq E$. In comparison, we achieve the same results as their approach, but we identify the irrelevant parts of axioms by making use of the tableaux algorithm, instead of splitting the axioms.

7.3 Resolving Unsatisfiable Concepts

Few approaches have been proposed which address the strategies for resolving unsatisfiable concepts. Plessers et al. [17] propose a set of rules to rewrite axioms to resolve the detected inconsistencies. They weaken restrictions either by removing an axiom, replacing it with its superconcepts, or changing its cardinality restriction values.

On the other hand, in SWOOP[13], the rewriting axioms suggestions are provided, but these suggestions are limited to a small number of common errors patterns. Moreover, the common error patterns may only apply for those ontologies built by non-expert users, it is insufficient to cover other applications, such as ontology merging/integration. The lost information due to their suggestions for rewriting axioms is also not considered. For example, an intersection concept $C \sqcap D$ is suggested to be changed as $C \sqcup D$, the modified concept is more generic, and hence certain information is lost.

Furthermore, Kalyanpur et al. [13] analyse the impact on an ontology when a whole axiom is removed. Currently, they only consider the subsumption/ disjointness between two named concepts (i.e., $A \sqsubseteq B$) and an instantiation (i.e., $B(a)$) which will be lost due to axiom removal. The difference with our work is the following: (1) the lost entailments we consider in Section 4 which are not responsible for concepts' unsatisfiability can be added back to the ontology, whereas this feature is not available in their approach. (2) we calculate the lost entailments of named concepts when a part of an axiom or a whole axiom is removed; they only consider the impact when a whole axiom is removed. (3) we adapt the "difference" operator to calculate the lost entailment of a concept (see Section 4.2); their lost entailment is limited to subsumption/disjointness between two named concepts and instantiations. (Continuing our mad_cow example in Example 4, if α_4 is removed, their lost entailment is Cow $\sqsubseteq$ Animal.[15] See Section 4 to compare with our results).

8 Conclusion

In this paper we have proposed a fine-grained approach to rewriting problematic axioms in an ontology, by revising the classical tableaux algorithm. Our technique not only identifies the problematic axioms, but also captures which parts of the axioms are responsible for the unsatisfiability of concepts. Moreover, we present methods for finding harmful and helpful changes for concepts which are going to be replaced. With our approach, users are provided with support to help them to: (1) understand the reasons for the unsatisfiability of concepts, and (2) rewrite axioms in order to resolve the problems with minimal impact on the ontology. The results of our usability evaluation have demonstrated the applicability of our approach in practice. The plugin which we have developed, RepairTab, is very useful for ontology users who want to diagnose problematic axioms at a fine-grained level and achieve satisfiable ontologies. In future work, we plan to extend our algorithms to support more expressive Description Logics.

References

1. Baader, F., Calvanese, D., McGuinness, D.L., Nardi, D., Patel-Schneider, P.: The Description Logic Handbook: Theory, Implementation and Applications. Cambridge University Press, Cambridge (2003)
2. Baader, F., Nutt, W.: Basic description logics. The Description Logic Handbook: Therory, Implementation, and Applications
3. Baader, F., Buchheit, M., Hollunder, B.: Cardinality restrictions on concepts. Artif. Intell. 88(1-2), 195–213 (1996)
4. Baader, F., Hollunder, B.: Embedding defaults into terminological knowledge representation formalisms. J. Autom. Reasoning 14(1), 149–180 (1995)
5. Baader, F., Hollunder, B., Nebel, B., Profitlich, H.-J., Franconi, E.: An empirical analysis of optimization techniques for terminological representation systems or "making KRIS get a move on". In: International Conference on the Principles of Knowledge Representation and Reasoning, San Mateo, pp. 270–281. Morgan Kaufmann, San Francisco (1992)

---

[15] The result is obtained from the latest version of SWOOP 2.3 Beta3.

6. Brandt, S., Küsters, R., Turhan, A.-Y.: Approximation and difference in description logics. In: KR 2002. Proceedings of the Eighth International Conference on Principles of Knowledge Representation and Reasoning, pp. 203–214. Morgan Kaufmann, San Francisco (2002)
7. Buchheit, M., Donini, F.M., Schaerf, A.: Decidable reasoning in terminological knowledge representation systems. Journal of Artificial Intelligence Research 1, 109–138 (1993)
8. De Giacomo, G., Lenzerini, M., Poggi, A., Rosati, R.: On the update of description logic ontologies at the instance level. In: Proceedings of the 21st National Conference on Artificial Intelligence, pp. 1271–1276. AAAI Press, Stanford (2006)
9. Horrocks, I.: Optimising Tableaux Decision Procedures for Description Logics. PhD thesis, University of Manchester (1997)
10. Kalyanpur, A., Parsia, B., Grau, B.C., Sirin, E.: Justifications for entailments in expressive description logics. Technical report, University of Maryland (January 2006)
11. Kalyanpur, A.: Debugging and Repair of OWL Ontologies. PhD thesis, Dept. of Computer Science, University of Maryland (2006)
12. Kalyanpur, A., Parsia, B., Cuenca-Grau, B.: Beyond asserted axioms: Fine-grain justifications for OWL-DL entailments. In: DL 2006. International Workshop on Description Logics (June 2006)
13. Kalyanpur, A., Parsia, B., Sirin, E., Cuenca-Grau, B.: Repairing Unsatisfiable Concepts in OWL Ontologies. In: ESWC 2006. Proceedings of the Third European Semantic Web Conference (June 2006)
14. Liu, H., Lutz, C., Milicic, M., Wolter, F.: Updating description logic ABoxes. In: KR. Proceedings of International Conference of Principles of Knowledge Representation and Reasoning, pp. 46–56 (June 2006)
15. Meyer, T., Lee, K., Booth, R., Pan, J.Z.: Finding maximally satisfiable terminologies for the description logic ALC. In: AAAI 2006. Proceedings of the 21st National Conference on Artificial Intelligence (July 2006)
16. Nebel, B.: Reasoning and Revision in Hybrid Representation Systems. Springer, Heidelberg (1990)
17. Plessers, P., De Troyer, O.: Resolving inconsistencies in evolving ontologies. In: Sure, Y., Domingue, J. (eds.) ESWC 2006. LNCS, vol. 4011, pp. 200–214. Springer, Heidelberg (2006)
18. Rector, A., Drummond, N., Horridge, M., Rogers, J., Knublauch, H., Stevens, R., Wang, H., Wroe, C.: OWL Pizzas: Practical experience of teaching OWL-DL: Common errors & common patterns. In: Motta, E., Shadbolt, N.R., Stutt, A., Gibbins, N. (eds.) EKAW 2004. LNCS (LNAI), vol. 3257, pp. 63–81. Springer, Heidelberg (2004)
19. Reiter, R.: A theory of diagnosis from first principles. Artificial Intelligence 32(1), 57–95 (1987)
20. Schaerf, A.: Reasoning With Individuals in Concept Languages. Data and Knowledge Engineering 13(2), 141–176 (1994)
21. Schlobach, S., Huang, Z., Cornet, R.: Inconsistent ontology diagnosis: Evaluation. SEKT Deliverable 3.6.2, University of Karlsruhe (January 2006)
22. Schlobach, S., Cornet, R.: Non-standard reasoning services for the debugging of description logic terminologies. In: IJCAI 2003. 8th International Joint Conference on Artificial Intelligence, Morgan Kaufmann, San Francisco (2003)
23. Schmidt-Schauß, M., Smolka, G.: Attributive concept descriptions with complements. Artifical Intelligence 48(1), 1–26 (1991)

24. Teege, G.: Making the difference: A subtraction operation for description logics. In: KR 1994. 4th International Conference on Principles of Knowledge Representation and Reasoning, Morgan Kaufmann, San Francisco (1994)
25. Uschold, M., Gruninger, M.: Ontologies: Principles, Methods and Applications. The Knowledge Engineering Review (1996)
26. Wang, H., Horridge, M., Rector, A., Drummond, N., Seidenberg, J.: Debugging OWL-DL Ontologies: A heuristic approach. In: Gil, Y., Motta, E., Benjamins, V.R., Musen, M.A. (eds.) ISWC 2005. LNCS, vol. 3729, pp. 745–757. Springer, Heidelberg (2005)

Deploying Semantic Web Services-Based Applications in the e-Government Domain

Alessio Gugliotta[1], John Domingue[1], Liliana Cabral[1], Vlad Tanasescu[1], Stefania Galizia[1], Rob Davies[2], Leticia Gutierrez Villarias[2], Mary Rowlatt[2], Marc Richardson[3], and Sandra Stincic[3]

[1] Knowledge Media Institute, The Open University,
Walton Hall, Milton Keynes, MK7 6AA, UK
{a.gugliotta, j.b.domingue, l.s.cabral, v.tanasescu,
s.galizia}@open.ac.uk
[2] Essex County Council, County Hall,
Chelmsford, CM1 1LX, UK
{Leticia.gutierrez, maryr}@essexcc.gov.uk,
rob.davies@mdrpartners.com
[3] BT Exact
Adastral Park Martlesham, Ipswich IP5 3RE, UK
{marc.richardson, sandra.stincic}@bt.com

Abstract. Joining up services in e-Government usually implies governmental agencies acting in concert without a central control regime. This requires to the sharing scattered and heterogeneous data. Semantic Web Service (SWS) technology can help to integrate, mediate and reason between these datasets. However, since a few real-world applications have been developed, it is still unclear which are the actual benefits and issues of adopting such a technology in the e-Government domain. In this paper, we contribute to raising awareness of the potential benefits in the e-Government community by analyzing motivations, requirements and expected results, before proposing a reusable SWS-based framework. We demonstrate the application of this framework by showing how integration and interoperability emerge from this model through a cooperative and multi-viewpoint methodology. Finally, we illustrate added values and lessons learned by two compelling case studies: a change of circumstances notification system and a GIS-based emergency planning system, and describe key challenges which remain to be addressed.

Keywords: e-Government, Semantic Web Services, Case Study, GIS, Change of Circumstances.

1 Introduction

To a large extent, tiers of government – such as national, county, and district – operate autonomously, without central control of service provision. Additionally, they each have distinct viewpoints which may differ from that of general citizens. Therefore, integration and interoperability are significant requirements in the development of service-oriented applications in the e-Government domain.

Integration leads to "form a temporary or permanent larger unit of government entities for the purpose of merging processes and/or sharing information" [18]. In particular, this requires the assembly and transformation of processes needed to support specific user tasks into a single service with the corresponding back-office practices. As a result, interoperation among multiple government entities at different levels occurs "whenever independent or heterogeneous information systems - or their components - controlled by different jurisdictions/administrations or by external partners smoothly and effectively work together in a predefined and agreed upon fashion" [18].

Interoperability is a key issue in order to allow for data and information to be exchanged and processed seamlessly across governments. A working paper by the Commission of European Communities [6] emphasized its role in e-Government, not only as a technical issue concerned with linking up computer networks, but also as a fundamental requirement to share and re-use knowledge between networks, and re-organize administrative processes to better support the services themselves. Additionally in [7], the following three levels of interoperability were individuated:

I. *Technical*: concerning with the technical issues of linking up computer systems, the definition of open interfaces, data formats and protocols, including telecommunications;
II. *Semantic:* concerning with the exchange of information in an understandable way - whether within and between administrations, either locally or across countries and with the enterprise sector - by any other application not initially developed for this purpose.
III. *Organizational:* concerning with modelling business processes, aligning information architectures with organizational goals and enabling processes to co-operate, by rewriting rules for how governmental agencies work internally, interact with their customers, and use Information and Communication Technologies (ICT).

The semantic Web [3] can alleviate integration and interoperability issues by creating a universal medium for information exchange and by giving meaning (semantics) to contents on the Web, in a manner understandable by machines. The semantic Web moreover allows the development of easy to use applications and transparent access to services and data. In particular, Semantic Web Services (SWS) technology [31], [8] provides an infrastructure in which new services can be added, discovered and composed continually, and the organization processes automatically updated to reflect new forms of cooperation [16]. SWS combine the flexibility, reusability, and universal access that typically characterize Web services with the expressivity of semantic mark-up and reasoning, in order to make feasible the invocation, composition, mediation, and automatic execution of complex services with multiple paths of execution and levels of process nesting.

The adoption of SWS in e-Government therefore appears to be a natural development. However, demonstrating this to the e-Government community requires the achievement of several prerequisites: (a) creating compelling demonstrators and prototypes; (b) establishing visible standards; (c) developing stable and mature technology and products; (d) proving convincing business cases.

In our work, a close collaboration has been established with the *Essex County Council (ECC)* - a large local authority in South East England (UK) comprised of 13 boroughs and containing a population of 1.3M – to deploy real-world applications in the e-Government domain. During this collaboration, we developed, tested and refined a specific framework designed around an existing SWS broker: IRS-III [8]. In this paper, we report our experience by firstly introducing the devised approach and then focusing on the obtained results. The main contributions are to provide a proof of concept of the added values introduced by SWS in real-world application scenarios, propose a guide for the deployment of new e-Government applications, test the IRS-III approach with complex use cases and outline future research directions on the basis of the lessons learned.

The rest of the paper is structured as follows: Section 2 briefly introduces the technologies at the basis of our work: Web services, ontologies and SWS; in Section 3 we discuss the rationales that prompted our work by identifying motivations, requirements and expected results of matching two present-day research areas: SWS and e-Government; Section 4 and Section 5 provide an overview of IRS-III and our framework for creating SWS-based applications; Section 6 details and demonstrates our approach through two e-Government applications. On the basis of these two implementations, we summarize the lessons learned and point out the open challenges in Section 7. Finally, Section 8 describes the related work and Section 9 reports our conclusions.

2 Web Services, Ontologies, and Semantic Web Services

From an information technology viewpoint the two important features of *Web Services* are that: (a) they are accessible over the Internet using standard XML-based protocols and (b) the interface of a Web service encapsulates its actual implementation. The first feature gives Web services high availability whereas the second feature facilitates reusability and interoperability since interface descriptions are independent from software platforms.

From a business perspective one key feature is that Web services can be used to expose the business services – i.e. value-producing activities directly accessible by the customer - of an organization. For example, Google [13] has a Web service interface to its search engine and Amazon allows software developers to directly access their technology platform and product data [2]. The ability to couple business services to Web accessible software components will have profound effects on the nature of business and on the structure of participating organisations.

Three main technologies are currently used to implement Web services: SOAP [28], WSDL [36] and UDDI [33]. SOAP is an XML based, stateless, one-way message exchange paradigm for interacting with Web services. SOAP messages are transported over HTTP and are composed of two elements: a header and a body. WSDL is also an XML-based format and defines services as collections of network endpoints or ports. UDDI is a registry which allows clients to find Web services through descriptions of theirs entities, provided functionalities or via technically oriented aspects.

A key problem with the above technologies is that they are purely syntactic. They thus rely on human developers to understand the intended meaning of the descriptions and to carry out the activities related to Web service use.

The *semantic Web* [3] is an extension of the current Web where documents incorporate machine processable meaning. The overall semantic Web vision is that one day it will be possible to delegate non-trivial tasks, such as booking a holiday, to computer based agents able to locate and reason with relevant heterogeneous online resources. One of the key building blocks for the semantic Web is the notion of an ontology [14]. An *ontology* is an explicit formal shared conceptualization of a domain of discourse. More specifically, an ontology captures the main concepts and relations that a community shares over a particular domain. Within the context of the semantic Web, ontologies facilitate interoperability as the underlying meaning of terms within a Web document can be made explicit for computer based agents to support processing.

Semantic Web Services (SWS) research aims to automate the development of Web service based applications through the semantic Web technologies. By providing formal descriptions with well defined semantics, SWS facilitate the machine interpretation of Web service – functional and not functional - properties. The research agenda for SWS identifies a number of key areas of concern, namely:

- *Discovery:* finding the Web service which can fulfil a task. Discovery usually involves matching a formal task description against semantic descriptions of Web services.
- *Mediation*: we can not assume that the software components which we find are compatible. Mediation aims to overcome all incompatibilities involved. Typically this means mismatches at the level of data format, message protocol and underlying business processes.
- *Composition*: often no single service will be available to satisfy a request. In this case we need to be able to create a new service by composing existing components. Artificial Intelligence (AI) planning engines are typically used to compose Web service descriptions from high goals.

3 Motivations, Requirements, and Expected Results

In our work, we address the following two research questions: (a) how can semantic Web support interoperability and reuse of software components available on the Web? (b) How can SWS support e-Government? In the following, we detail these two perspectives by analyzing motivations, requirements, and expected results of moving from SWS to e-Government (Section 3.1) and from e-Government to SWS (Section 3.2), respectively.

3.1 From Semantic Web Services to e-Government

Currently, one of the main needs of SWS technology is the development of real-world applications that demonstrate its added (business) values. The next application-driven research challenge thus can be defined only through the feedback from practical prototypes and applications. The full potential application of SWS requires many more large-scale testing domains.

Since it is an enormous challenge to achieve interoperability and to address semantic differences related to the great variety of datasets and information technology solutions which should be networked, e-Government may be a very effective test-bed for evaluating SWS technology. E-Government moreover exhibits further significant characteristics which may indicate several research issues for SWS. For example, e-Government is characterized by top-down prescribed constraints in key areas (e.g. laws, legal requirements, policies in the use of services and access to data); limited central control; strong requirements to come to same decisions in similar situations; high requirements for non-functional properties such as security, privacy, and trust; wide information imbalances between stakeholders, as well as multiple and heterogeneous stakeholders involved in the same process.

3.2 From e-Government to Semantic Web Services

The ability to aggregate and reuse diverse information resources relevant to a given situation in a cost-effective way and to make this available as a basis for transparent interaction between community partner organizations and individual citizens is a key benefit that SWS technology can provide to e-Government. Specifically, SWS technology promises to:

a) *Provide added value joined up services:* allowing software agents to create interoperating services transparently to the users and hence automate integration, reasoning and mediation among heterogeneous data sources and processes available at distinct governmental levels.
b) *Enable formalization of government business processes in an unambiguous structure:* allowing the creation of a common understanding of processes and visualization of the knowledge involved. This could eventually lead to a reengineering of the governmental systems and simplification of processes.
c) *Reduce risk and cost*: (i) moving from "hard coding" services to reusable functionalities through, for example, utility computing of shared services (e.g. payment platforms, legal resources, etc.); (ii) keeping government organizations' autonomy in the description/management of their domains; (iii) increasing flexibility; enabling discovery of new or previously unknown services; (iv) aggregating services on the basis of user preferences; (v) providing better service to third-parties and customers; (vi) easily addressing the evolution and change of existing services and scenario.
d) *Provide better support to front line:* allowing one-stop, customer focused, and multiple viewpoint access to services and shared information.

The e-Government community (stakeholders, administrations, end-users, but also researchers) needs to perceive these benefits more clearly before it will adopt the technology. At present, Web services are being introduced as infrastructure (often experimental) in some areas of government and the broad awareness of need for semantic enrichment is increasing. However, since SWS are completely new – and are mainly visible to the academic and industrial research 'e-Government' sector - a measurable benefit to service and achievable cost savings, or "cashable benefits" will need to be established.

In absence of golden standards, demonstrating real-world applications is the important first step to accomplish this goal. Perhaps more importantly, this may provide a way to address existing barriers and perceptions, such as:

e) *Trust in automated data sharing*: governmental organizations are concerned about: (i) ownership, control and quality among service providers; (ii) security, data protection, confidentiality, and privacy issues.
f) *Patchy awareness of Web services*: stakeholders are often unclear about the distinction between Web services and general services available via Web.
g) *Up-front Infrastructure costs* (e.g. investment in Web Services): governmental organizations are reluctant to be the pioneers which take the initial financial 'hit' in implementing SWS, as with almost any new technology.
h) *Market development:* in terms of raising the awareness of potential SWS benefits in e-Government, increasing pilot applications, and promoting the availability of working SWS platforms.

4 IRS-III: A Broker-Based Approach for SWS

IRS-III [8] is a platform and broker for developing and executing SWS. By definition, a broker is an entity which mediates between two parties and IRS-III mediates between a service requester and one or more service providers. To achieve this, IRS-III adopts a semantic Web based approach and is thus founded on ontological descriptions. At the heart of IRS-III there is the SWS Library, where semantic descriptions of various aspects of Web services, reference Domain Ontologies and Knowledge bases (instances) are stored using OCML representation language [23]. Specific IRS-III components interpret such descriptions to discover and select the appropriate Web service, choreograph and ground to the Web service operations [9], orchestrate multiple Web services, and mediate semantic descriptions by running mediation rules or invoking mediation services [5]. Note that IRS-III supports grounding to standard Web services with a WSDL description, as well as stand-alone Java and Lisp code. Similarly, Web applications accessible as HTTP GET requests are handled internally by IRS-III.

4.1 The IRS-III Service Ontology

The IRS-III service ontology forms the epistemological basis for IRS-III and provides semantic links between the knowledge level components describing the capabilities of a service and the restrictions applied to its use. The IRS-III service ontology is based on the WSMO standard [37] which specifies the following main aspects:

- *Non-functional properties*: these properties are associated with every main component model and can range from information about the provider such as organisation, to information about the service such as category, cost and quality of service, to execution requirements such as scalability, security or robustness.
- *Ontologies*: provide the foundation for describing domains semantically. They are used by the three other WSMO components.

- *Goal-related information*: a goal description represents the user perspective of the required functional capabilities. It includes a description of the requested Web service capability.
- *Web service-related information:* a Web service interface represents the functional behavior of an existing deployed Web service. It includes a description of: (a) *Functional capabilities* which represent the provider perspective of what the service does in terms of assumptions, effects, pre-conditions and post-conditions. Capabilities are expressed by logical expressions that constrain the state or the type of inputs and outputs. (b) *Choreography* which specifies how to communicate with a Web service. (c) *Grounding* which is part of the Web service choreography and describes how the semantic declarations are associated with a syntactic specification such as WSDL. (d) *Orchestration* which specifies the decomposition of Web service capability in terms of the functionality of other Web services.
- *Mediators*: in WSMO, a mediator specifies which WSMO top elements are connected and which type of mismatches can be resolved between them. WSMO defined four kinds of mediators: *GG-mediator* which links different goals; *WG-mediator* which connects Web services with goals; *OO-mediator* which enables components to import heterogeneous ontologies; and *WW-mediator* which links Web services to Web services.

The WSMO conceptual model has been represented using OCML representation language [23] and extended in the following ways:

- *Explicit input and output role declaration*: IRS-III requires that goals and Web services have input and output roles, which include a name and a semantic type. The declared types are imported from domain ontologies. This makes the definition of goal and Web services easier when complex choreographies are not required.
- *Web services are linked to goals via WG-mediators:* if a WG-mediator associated with a Web service has a goal as a source, then this Web service is considered to solve that goal. An assumption expression can be introduced for further refining the applicability of the Web service.
- *GG-mediators provide data-flow between sub-goals* – in IRS-III, GG-mediators are used to link sub-goals within an orchestration and so they also provide dataflow between the sub-goals.
- *Web services can inherit from goals* - Web services which are linked to goals 'inherit' the goal's input and output roles. This means that input role declarations within a Web service are not mandatory and can be used to either add extra input roles or to change an input role type.
- *Client choreography* – the provider of a Web service must describe the choreography from the viewpoint of the client. This means IRS-III can interpret the choreography in order to communicate with the deployed Web service.
- *Mediation services are goals* – a mediator declares a goal as the mediation service which can simply be invoked. The required transformation is performed by the associated Web service.

- *IRS-III component goals* – the main components of IRS-III (e.g. the orchestration and choreography interpreters and the handlers for the different WSMO mediators) are implemented using internal goal, Web service and mediator descriptions. Additionally, a number of utility goals, for example a number of arithmetic and list primitives are incorporated.

4.2 The IRS-III Core Functionalities

A core design principle for IRS-III is to support capability-based selection and invocation of Web services. A client sends a request which captures a desired outcome or goal and, using the set of semantic Web service descriptions introduced in the previous section, IRS-III will:

F1. Discover potentially relevant Web services.
F2. Select the set of Web services which best fit the incoming request.
F3. Invoke the selected Web services whilst adhering to any data, control flow and Web service invocation constraints.
F4. Mediate any mismatches at the data, goal or process level.

In the following sub-sections, we highlight the main aspects associated with the aforementioned functionalities.

4.2.1 Discovery

As introduced in Section 4.1, IRS-III makes use of WG-mediators to link a goal to all Web services that can solve it. Figure 1 depicts the specific ontology concepts and relations involved in the IRS-III discovery and selection.

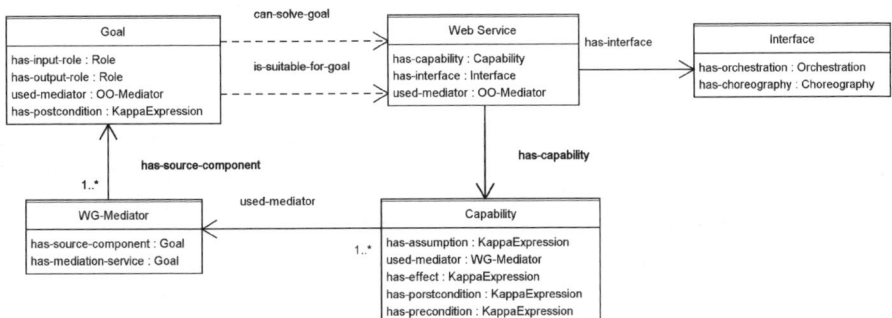

Fig. 1. The ontology concepts and relations involved in the IRS-III discovery

Given a goal, multiple WG-mediators can define such a goal as their source component. In turn, distinct capability descriptions can refer to a specific WG-mediator and thus link to a goal. Finally, each capability description is part of a unique Web service description.

On the basis the semantic descriptions above, a pool of Web services that potentially satisfy a given goal is identified by a backward chaining rule-based reasoning. In particular, the `can-solve-goal` relation is inferred at runtime during the goal achievement process. The listing below shows the OCML [23] definition of the `can-solve-goal` relation. The sufficient conditions of the definition (`:sufficient`) specify the clauses to be proved when inferring such a relation. The IRS-III interpreter will fire the clauses in the order in which these are listed, by finding any instance which makes true the specific clause. As a result, starting from a goal instance given in input (`?goal`), it is possible to identify: (i) all of the WG-mediators (`?mediator`) which use such a goal as source component[1]; (ii) the capabilities (`?capabilities`) which use the identified WG-mediators; (iii) the Web services (`?thing`) which define the identified capabilities.

```
(def-relation can-solve-goal (?goal ?thing)
    "Returns the web services which solve a goal.
    Uses the mediator to find the link"
    :sufficient (and (instance-of ?goal goal)
                    (= ?goal (the-slot-value ?mediator has-source-component))
                    (instance-of ?mediator WG-mediator)
                    (= ?mediator (the-slot-value ?capability used-mediator))
                    (instance-of ?capability capability)
                    (= ?capability (the-slot-value ?thing has-capability))
                    (instance-of ?thing web-service)))))
```

4.2.2 Selection

The selection process aims to identify the most appropriate Web services which satisfy a goal, starting from the results of the previous phase (`can-solve-goal` relation). On the basis of the current goal inputs, the IRS-III interpreter will test the applicability conditions of each discovered Web service.

The listing below shows the `suitable-web-service-goal` which is invoked to check if a Web service is satisfactory for a specific goal invocation[2].

```
Suitable-web-service-goal
Input Role
    has-goal goal "sexpr"
    has-actual-role-pairs list "sexpr"
    has-web-service web-service "sexpr"
    has-combined-oo-mediator-ontology ontology "sexpr"
Output Role
    is-suitable-web-service boolean "sexpr"
Post Condition
    (kappa (goal-inst)
        (== (has-role-value goal-inst is-suitable-web-service)
            (is-suitable-for-goal
                (instantiate (has-role-value goal-inst has-goal)
                            (has-role-value goal-inst has-actual-role-pairs))
                    web-service)))
```

`Suitable-web-service-goal` has four input roles which respectively represent: (a) the current goal; (b) the values for the current goal's input roles; (c) the Web service under consideration; and, (d) an ontology created specifically for the goal invocation. Note that for each input role, we specify the type of values permissible and a SOAP grounding (`sexpr` in the listing above) which is 'inherited' by Web services linked through a WG-mediator. Moreover, the ontology created in step (d)

---

[1] The `the-slot-value` function returns the value of a specific slot (e.g. `has-source-component`) of an instance (e.g. ?mediator).

[2] As mentioned earlier, IRS-III components themselves are modelled using WSMO descriptions.

combines the goal and Web service ontologies, making use of OO-mediators – both goal and Web service descriptions refer to OO-mediators (Figure 1) - to resolve any data mismatches (Section 4.2.4).

The output role (`is-suitable-web-service`) is a boolean value which is true if the Web service is suitable for the goal instance, false otherwise.

The post condition expresses the expected result as an OCML anonymous relation, called *kappa expression*. The latter takes as argument the `suitable-web-service-goal` itself and is satisfied if its clauses hold for the given argument. In the given example, the `is-suitable-for-goal` relation is used to state the relationship between the considered goal and the selected Web services.

To accomplish the `suitable-web-service-goal` introduced above and thus infer the `is-suitable-for-goal` relation, an internal IRS-III Web service is invoked. The latter exposes an OCML function which performs the following tasks: (i) retrieving the applicability conditions – currently the assumptions defined in the WSMO capability description – of a given Web service and (ii) testing the applicability conditions according to the input roles defined in the given goal instance. Checking the following OCML relation is the core of such a function.

```
(def-relation applicable-to-goal (?web-service ?goal)
  :iff-def (or (not (and (= ?capability
                             (the-slot-value ?web-service has-capability))
                         (instance-of ?capability capability)
                         (= ?exp (the-slot-value ?capability has-assumption))
                         (not (= ?exp :nothing))))
               (and (= ?capability
                       (the-slot-value ?web-service has-capability))
                    (instance-of ?capability capability)
                    (= ?exp (the-slot-value ?capability has-assumption))
                    (not (= ?exp :nothing))
                    (holds ?exp ?goal))))
```

Sufficient and necessary conditions of the definition above (`:iff-def`) specify the clauses to be proved. Similar to the `can-solve-goal` relation introduced in Section 4.2.1, the IRS-III interpreter will fire the clauses. The `or` expression of the definition introduces two main cases[3].

The first case manages the situation of Web services that do not define any assumption. We assume that Web services which do not define assumptions are applicable to the goal. In this way, for example, we can deal with general purpose Web services.

The second case manages the situation of Web services that define assumptions. The `?exp` variable captures the stated assumption which is expressed as a *kappa expression* (e.g. the goal post condition defined above). The `holds` function invokes the IRS-III interpreter to test the retrieved kappa expression, using the current goal instance `?goal` as given parameter. If the kappa expression is satisfied, the Web service is applicable to the goal.

Note that several Web services can be selected. The current IRS-III policy is invoking the first Web service of the list, since a ranking mechanism is not defined.

---

[3] As in Prolog, depth-first search with chronological backtracking is used in OCML to control the proof process.

However, future work concerns improving current IRS-III selection with trust-based mechanisms [12].

4.2.3 Invocation, Choreography and Orchestration

According to the WSMO model, the IRS-III interface provides information on how the functionality of the deployed Web services is achieved, and, as stated in Section 4.1, the main interface components are orchestration and choreography. The semantic descriptions of the interface model are interpreted by IRS-III when the latter identified the Web service to satisfy a goal. According to such descriptions, specific actions are performed.

The overall view is that Web service execution consists of a number of discrete steps, and, at any given point, the next action performed within an interface execution will depend upon the current state. IRS-III performs its interface abstract model through the tuple ⟨E, S, C, T⟩, where: E is a finite set of events; S is the (possibly infinite) set of states; C is the (possibly infinite) set of conditions; T represents the (possibly infinite) set of transitions rules.

The *events* represent actions performed during the interface execution. The subset of events from E which can occur in choreography and orchestration differs. Specifically, $E = Ec \cup Eo$: where Ec is the set of choreography events; and Eo is the set of orchestration events. In more detail, Ec = *{obtain, present, provide, receive, obtain-initiative, present-initiative}* [9]. Every choreography event maps to an operation during the conversation viewed from the IRS-III perspective. Similarly, the set of possible orchestration events are Eo = *{invoke-goal, invoke-mediator, find-mediator, evaluate-logical-expression, return-output}*.

Given a transition step Ti, a **state** $s_i \in S$ is a non-empty set of ontologies that define a state signature over which transition rules are executed. Optional mediators are used to solve ontology or data mismatches (Section 4.2.4). The parameterized *choreography state* is a set of instances, concerning message exchange patterns and the choreography execution. Every state includes a constant subset, which identifies the Web service host, port, and location, which is invariant whenever the same Web service is invoked, and the event instantiation $e \in Ec$, dependent on the event which occurred at step Ti. The *orchestration states* characterize the phases of the workflow process during goal decomposition. Given a transition step Ti, an orchestration state contains a description of the triggering-event, the control flow step identifier, and the result - the output of the achieved sub-goal.

A **condition** $c \in C$ (also called guard) depicts a situation occurring during interface execution. Every constraint within the condition has to be verified before the next event is triggered.

The **transition rules** express changes of state by modifying a set of instances within the signature ontology. In particular, a transition rule, $t \in T$, updates the state after the occurrence of an event, $e \in E$, and consists of a function, $t : \left(S, 2^C\right) \underset{E}{\to} S$, that associates a couple $(s, \{c_1, .., c_n\})$ to s', where s and $s' \in S$, and every $c_i \in C$ $(1 \le i \le n)$. *Choreography transition rules* are defined with the following two specific restrictions: (a) '*If* rules do not chain and are of the form "*If* condition **then Fire** Event"; and (b) conditions are mutually exclusive so only one rule can fire at a time. These rules represent the interaction between IRS-III and the Web service and are applied when executing the choreography. *Orchestration transition rules* provide a workflow model based on the following set of control flow constructs: *sequence, conditional, loop, fork, join.* These rules describe the model of a composed Web service. The distinguishing characteristic of this model is that the basic unit within composition is a goal. Further, dataflow and the resolution of mismatches between goals are supported by mediators.

4.2.4 Mediation

The overall design goal for IRS-III is to act as a semantic broker between a client application and deployed Web services available at large on the internet. This brokering activity can be seen as mediation itself, which in IRS-III is further broken down into goal, process and data mediation [5]. *Goal Mediation* takes places during F2, and the types of mismatches that can occur are: the input types of a goal are different from the input types of the target Web service; and Web services have more inputs than the goal. A WG-mediator is mainly involved in this mediation. *Process Mediation* takes places during F3 – specifically, during orchestration - and the types of mismatches which can occur are: output types of a sub-goal are different from the input types of the target sub-goal; output values of a sub-goal are in a different order from the inputs of the target sub-goal; and, the output of a sub-goal has to be split or concatenated into the inputs of the target sub-goals. A GG-mediator is mainly involved in this mediation. *Data Mediations* is used by both goal and process mediation to map data across domain ontologies. An OO-mediator is mainly involved in this mediation.

In IRS-III, a mediator declares a source component, a target component and either a mediation service or mapping rules to solve mismatches between the two.

The *mediation service* is just another goal that can be accomplished by published Web services. For example (Figure 2), a mediation service of a WG-mediator (or GG-mediator) transforms input values coming from the source goal into an input value used by the target Web service (or Goal). The mediation goal is invoked and then accomplished when the respective mediator is considered by the IRS-III interpreter.

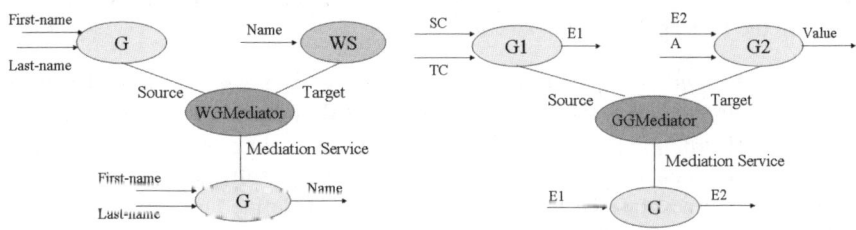

Fig. 2. Use of mediation services for WG and GG mediators

Mapping rules are used between two ontologies, source and target components (Figure 3). They represent backward chaining rules, based on three OCML main mapping primitives: Maps-to, a relation created internally for every mapped instance; Def-concept-mapping, generates the mappings specified with the maps-to relation between two ontological concepts; Def-relation-mapping, generates a mapping between two relations using a rule definition within an ontology. Since OCML represents concept attributes as relations, this primitive can be used to map between input and output descriptions.

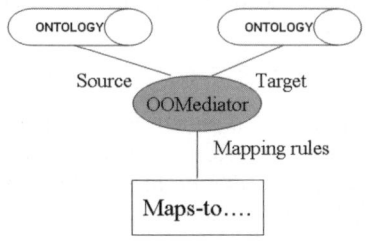

Fig. 3. Use of mapping rules for OO-mediator

5 Creating Semantic Web Services Based Applications

In this section, we describe the general infrastructure and the methodology adopted to deploy our e-Government applications. Since government legacy systems are often isolated - i.e. not interconnected and/or use distinct technological solutions - our approach firstly enables the data and functionalities provided by existing legacy systems of the involved governmental partners to be exposed as Web services. The latter are then semantically annotated and published following the IRS-III approach (Section 4). The generic application architecture presented in Section 5.1 reflects and explains this double stage process. The setting up of a domain-specific application is driven by a cooperative and multi-viewpoint methodology refined during our work, and here described in Section 5.2.

5.1 Generic Application Architecture

The proposed generic application architecture is depicted in Figure 4. From the bottom up the four application layers are:

- *Legacy System layer:* consists of the existing data sources and IT systems available from each of the organizations involved in the integrated application.
- *Service Abstraction layer:* exposes (micro-) functionalities of the legacy systems as Web Services, abstracting from the hardware and software platforms. At this level we address thus the level I of interoperability defined by [7] and introduced in Section 1. Web Services are distributed and stored within the multiple organizational infrastructures that expose the functionality. Existing Enterprise Application Integration (EAI) software can be used to facilitate the creation of required Web Services. For example, for standard databases the necessary functionalities of Web Services can simply be implemented as SQL query functions. Further services available on the Web - and not related to the involved legacy systems - can be integrated to perform supporting functionalities (e.g. mediation services).

- *Semantic Web Service layer*: this layer is implemented by IRS-III which provides the functionalities F1 – F4 described in Section 4.2. At this level we address thus the levels II and III of interoperability defined by [7] and introduced in Section 1. To set up an application, a set of application-specific SWS descriptions has to be provided: goals, mediators, and Web services, all supported by the relevant ontologies (see Section 5.2). These descriptions are centrally stored within the SWS Library of IRS-III (Section 4.1). Note that we distinguish two main sets of SWS descriptions: *basic SWS* (bottom of the layer) that simply wrap the Web Services to achieve simple goals; and *complex SWS* (top of the layer) that require a composition of basic or complex SWS to achieve complex goals.
- *Presentation layer:* consist of a Web application accessible through a standard Web browser. The goals defined within the SWS layer are reflected in the structure of the interface and can be invoked either through the IRS-III API or as an HTTP GET request. The goal requests are filled with data provided by the user and sent to the Semantic Web Service layer. We should emphasise that the presentation layer may be comprised of a set of Web applications to support distinct user communities. In this case, each community would be represented by a set of goals supported by community related ontologies.

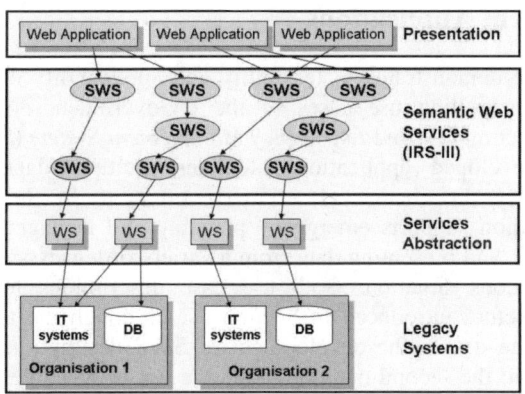

Fig. 4. The generic architecture used to create IRS-III-based e-Government applications

5.2 Development Methodology

In order to successfully create applications from SWS as depicted in Figure 4 four key activities need to be carried out as follows:

1. *Requirements capture:* the requirements for the overall application are captured using standard software engineering methodologies and tools. We do not advocate any particular requirements capture method but envisage that the resulting documents describe the stakeholders, the main users, roles, and goals, any potential providers for Web services, and any requirements on the deployed infrastructure and interfaces.
2. *Goal description*: using the requirements documents above relevant goals are identified and semantically described in IRS-III. During this process any required

supporting domain ontologies will either be created from scratch or existing ontologies will be re-used.
3. *Web service description*: descriptions of relevant Web services are created within the IRS. Again, any domain ontologies required to support the Web service descriptions are either defined or re-used as necessary.
4. *Mediator description*: mismatches between the ontologies used, and mismatches within and between the formal goal and Web service descriptions are identified and appropriate mediators created.

All of the above steps are carried out by the SWS application developer. The first two steps are user/client centric and therefore involve discussions with the relevant client stakeholders and domain experts, whereas step 3 will require dialogue with the Web service providers and domain experts. Steps 2 and 3 are mostly independent and in the future we expect libraries of goals and Web services to become generally available to support reuse. Steps 2, 3 and 4 are supported by means of IRS-III clients that provide a set of tools for defining, editing and managing a library of semantic descriptions, as well as for grounding the descriptions to services. As a result, we obtain a semi-automatic knowledge acquisition process for the development of our applications.

6 e-Government Applications

In this section, we demonstrate the feasibility and applicability of our approach by describing two compelling use cases in the e-Government domain: *Change of Circumstances* (Section 6.1) and *Emergency Management System* (Section 6.2). In the first one, the developed application integrates multiple datasets in order to automatically notify the change of a citizen situation. In the second one, the developed application supports emergency planning and management personnel by retrieving, filtering, and presenting data from a variety of legacy systems to deal with a specified hazardous situation. Both use case descriptions follow the generic application architecture introduced in Section 5.1, although the technical emphasis varies: the first one details the development of SWS descriptions for setting up a specific application; the second one highlights the use of SWS descriptions within a specific application.

6.1 Change of Circumstances

The application has been developed to solve a specific use case problem at Essex County Council (ECC). Whenever the circumstances in which a given citizen lives change, he/she might be eligible for a set of services and benefits provided by ECC and other governmental agencies together with public service providers. An example of such a change of circumstances is, if an elderly, partly disabled woman moves in together her daughter. This changes the circumstances of both, the mother and the daughter. For instance, the mother might no longer receive a "meals on wheels" service, whereas the daughter might get financial supporting for caring her mother. Starting from existing legacy systems, the aim is to provide integrated functionalities, such as: change patient details within multiple legacy systems, change patient pending equipment orders, list of all services for a patient, stop providing service to patient and assess equipment to patient.

6.1.1 Legacy System Layer

Generally, even very simple process in a change of circumstances requires the interaction of many different government agencies. Each agency has different legacy systems in place to keep track of citizen records, provided services, third-party service providers, etc. In our prototype, the following two data sources provided by two different departments (at two distinct governmental levels) were considered:

- *Citizen Assessment (Community Care Department of the ECC)*: this relates to information about citizens registered in ECC for assessment of services and benefits (e.g. meals on wheels; someone goes and cleans the house; someone goes and stays with the patient, etc). This information is stored in the SWIFT database.
- *Order Equipment (Housing department of the Chelmsford District Council)*: this relates to information about equipment (e.g. stair lift, wheel chair, crutch, etc) which is provided to citizens registered in Essex. This information is stored in the ELMS database.

Both SWIFT and ELMS are relational databases that are independently developed and use different data formats to store the same information - e.g. they both hold personal details of the patients. Our prototype accesses two testing databases that exactly replicate the schemata of the two real systems and contain dummy data of the same quality – i.e. both databases contain records with errors, duplicates, inconsistent records. As a result, the two databases used in the prototype mimic the behavior and properties of the real systems.

Figure 5 depicts the database schema of the ELMS system.

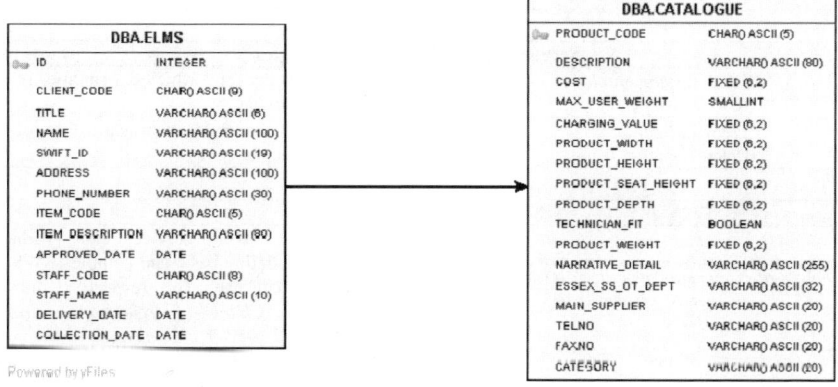

Fig. 5. The database schema of the ELMS system

Specific SQL queries provide for each of the tables of the two databases CRUD style functionalities; for instance functionalities for creating, reading, updating and deleting records.

6.1.2 Service Abstraction Layer

On top of the two legacy systems, we developed a set of Web services that perform the SQL queries introduced in the previous section and the basic operations introduced above. We created 8 Web services from the SWIFT database and 19 Web services from the ELMS database. The Web services were deployed and stored into the SAP Exchange Infrastructure (SAP XI) [27]. Moreover, we developed some Web services - implemented in a mixture of Common Lisp and OCML [23] – to support application-specific operations (e.g. merging results of distinct database queries).

6.1.3 Semantic Web Service Layer

To provide the SWS descriptions (Section 5.1) and the required supporting domain ontologies - steps 2, 3, and 4 of our development methodology (Section 5.2) - we devised two teams composed of SWS developers and domain experts. Each team worked on a distinct domain: Citizen Assessment and Order Equipment. The following tables summarise the resulting ontologies.

User Oriented Domain Ontologies	
e-Government-upper-level-ontology (Citizen Assessment Team, Order Equipment Team)	It is an upper ontology for representing commonly accepted concepts, such as organization, person, citizen, etc. It has been used as the starting point for developing domain-specific user-oriented ontologies
Change-of-circumstances-citizen-ontology (Citizen Assessment Team)	It extends the concepts introduced in the e-Government upper level ontology by introducing domain-specific concepts, such as address, assessment, health problem and benefit.
Change-of-circumstances-equipment-ontology (Order Equipment Team)	It extends the concepts introduced in the e-Government upper level ontology by introducing domain-specific concepts, such as order, care-item, equipment and supplier.

Service Oriented Domain Ontologies	
SWIFT-service-ontology (Citizen Assessment Team)	It mainly represents concepts which map entities of the SWIFT database schema.
ELMS-service-ontology (Order Equipment Team)	It mainly represents concepts which map entities of the ELMS database schema.

SWS Description Ontologies	
Change-of-circumstances-citizen-basic-SWS (Citizen Assessment Team)	It contains goal, Web service and mediator descriptions which define basic and complex SWS on top of SWIFT database. The respective domain ontologies are: *Change-of-circumstances-citizen-ontology* and *SWIFT-service-ontology*
Change-of-circumstances-equipment-basic-SWS (Order Equipment Team)	It contains goal, Web service and mediator descriptions which define basic and complex SWS on top of ELMS. The respective domain ontologies are: *Change-of-circumstances-equipment-ontology* and *ELMS-service-ontology*
Change-of-circumstances-citizen-complex-SWS (Citizen Assessment Team)	It contains goal, Web service and mediator descriptions which define complex SWS, integrating functionalities of both domains. These descriptions refer to the *Change-of-circumstances-citizen-ontology* as domain ontology and make use of *Citizen Assessment* and *Order Equipment* basic SWS.

Figure 6 shows the graphical representation of the dependencies (i.e. "inheritance") among ontologies: WSMO is the top ontology; *white boxes* represent the domain ontologies (user and service oriented); *gray boxes* represent the ontologies containing SWS descriptions. It is important to note the absence of dependencies that cross the two different domains. Only the bottom ontology (Change-of-circumstances-citizen-complex-SWS) crosses the two domains; this ontology defines appropriate mediators to deal with mismatching.

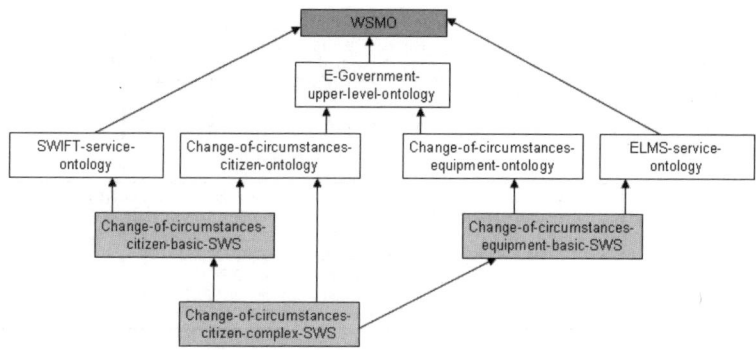

Fig. 6. The ontologies of the Change of Circumstances scenario

To illustrate the development process, we first consider a SWS description of the Order Equipment domain: Find Item ELMS by Impairment and Weight. The latter is a complex operation which is decomposed into three basic operations: two queries of the ELMS database and intersecting the two obtained outputs (Figure 7).

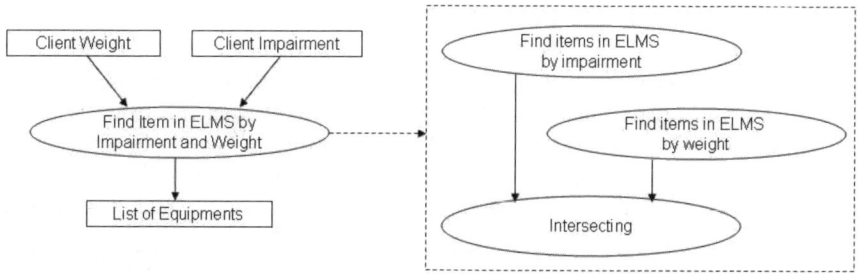

Fig. 7. The Find Item ELMS by Impairment and Weight functionality

Each ellipse in Figure 7 represents a goal which has to be accomplished by simple or integrated functionalities. Specifically, the three goals on the right are accomplished by functionalities provided by Web services available at the service abstraction layer. Such goals have to be automatically orchestrated to accomplish the main goal on the left. Figure 8 depicts, as example, the IRS-III browser interface for describing the main goal above and the resulted OCML code [23]. The goal defines two inputs (`has-input-role`) and one output (`has-output-role`). The inputs (weight and impairment) are classes of the `Change-of-circumstances-equipment-ontology`. The output is a list of equipments (`item-list`). Every equipment description in the list is an instance of the `catalogue-data` class of the `ELMS-service-ontology`.

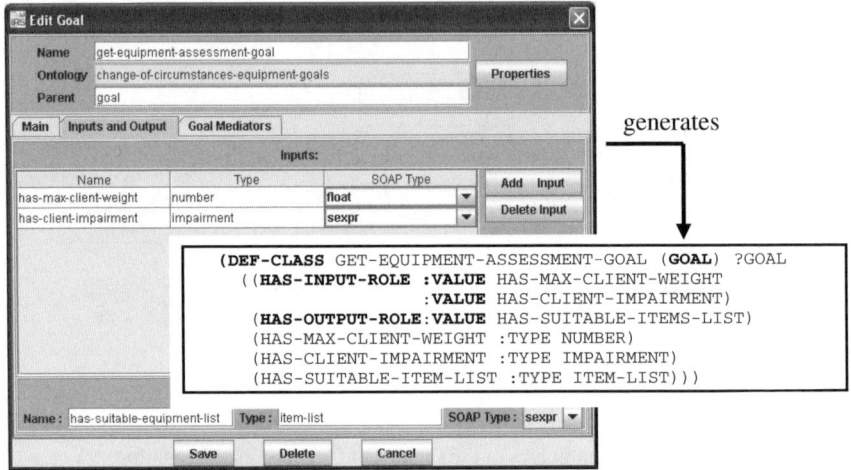

Fig. 8. Snapshot of the IRS-III editor and the generated OCML code

Such a class maps the respective ELMS database schema (Figure 5). At runtime – when the goal is invoked to be accomplished - the instances of the input classes are selected through the user interface of the application, while the instances of the `catalogue-data` class are created on-the-fly - i.e. lifted from the syntactic to the semantic level - from the results of Web service invocations.

For each goal, the respective Web service and mediator descriptions have been created. Figure 9 below represents the `Find Item ELMS by Impairment and Weight` functionality introduced in Figure 7 in terms of goal, mediator and Web service descriptions. The Web service that accomplishes the main goal (`Get-equipment-assessment-goal`) defines the orchestration as the sequence of three sub-goals. In our approach the orchestration is defined at the semantic level as follows:

```
(DEF-CLASS GET-EQUIPMENT-ASSESSMENT-WEB-SERVICE-INTERFACE-ORCHESTRATION
    ((HAS-BODY
      :VALUE ((ORCH-SEQUENCE
                FIND-ITEMS-MATCHING-WEIGHT-GOAL
                FIND-ITEMS-MATHCING-IMPAIRMENT-GOAL
                LIST-INTERSECTION-GOAL)
               (ORCH-RETURN (ORCH-GET-GOAL-VALUE LIST-INTERSECTION-GOAL))))))
```

Each sub-goal, invoked through the orchestration, is accomplished by the respective Web service. Conversely to the main Web service, these Web services ground to syntactic Web services - at the service abstraction layer - and they thus define choreography, as follows:

```
(DEF-CLASS FIND-ITEMS-MATCHING-WEIGHT-WEB-SERVICE-INTERFACE-CHOREOGRAPHY
    (CHOREOGRAPHY)
    ((HAS-GROUNDING
        :VALUE (GROUNDED-TO-WSDL ONLY-OPERATION
                ("c:/CatalogueEntryByWeightInterfaceOut.wsdl"
                "CatalogueEntryByWeightInterfaceOut"
                "CatalogueEntryByWeightInterfaceOut"
                "http://sap.com/research/dip/wp9/elmdb"
                "SAP"
                ((has-client-weight "CatalogueEntryByWeightRequest-Type"))
                "CatalogueEntryResponseType")))
    (HAS-GUARDED-TRANSITIONS :VALUE
        ((RULE1
            (INIT-CHOREOGRAPHY)
            THEN
                (SEND-MESSAGE 'ONLY-OPERATION))))
```

Moreover, Figure 9 outlines the linking roles of WG and GG mediators in our approach: a goal to the Web services that may accomplish it; two sub-goals within an orchestration. More detailed descriptions about the use of WG and GG mediators, during discovery, selection and mediation phases, are presented in the next use case.

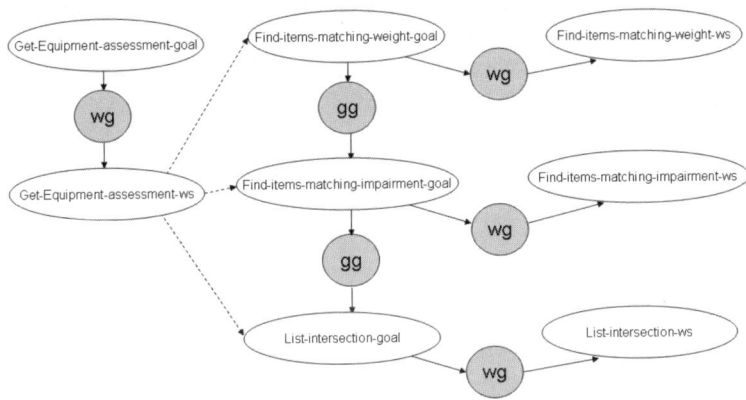

Fig. 9. Structure of the SWS descriptions created for the Find Item ELMS by Impairment and Weight functionality

The resulting Find Item ELMS by Impairment and Weight SWS description accomplishes the requested functionality (goal) by integrating services of the same legacy system. Note that each legacy system is an autonomous entity within the given scenario and the provided Web services abstract from the underlying technology. Therefore, we would not have any central control on the involved parties and detailed information about the respective technologies. For example, we could not require a new SQL query of the ELMS database that can simply implement the Find Item ELMS by Impairment and Weight functionality.

The effectiveness of a SWS-base approach becomes clearer when integrating services from multiple distributed autonomous entities. In this case, we need to deal with the distinct viewpoints of each involved party. To prove this aspect in the current scenario, we consider a further complex SWS description: Assess Equipment to

Patient. The latter is part of the Change-of-circumstances-citizen-complex-SWS ontology and integrates functionalities of both domains. It is decomposed into two complex operations (Figure 10).

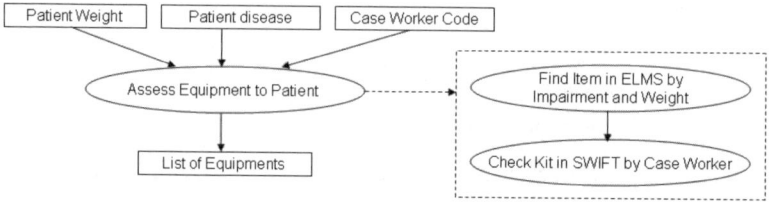

Fig. 10. The cross-domain Assess Equipment to Patient functionality

The first operation is the aforementioned Find Item ELMS by Impairment and Weight. The second operation filters the equipments retrieved in the first operation by checking if the current case worker – an employee of the Community Care Department – is entitle to provide the equipments to the user. The following listing shows the goal and orchestration definitions of the Assess Equipment to Patient functionality.

```
(DEF-CLASS ASSESS-EQUIPMENT-TO-PATIENT-GOAL (GOAL) ?GOAL
    ((HAS-INPUT-ROLE :VALUE HAS-CITIZEN-WEIGHT
                    :VALUE HAS-CITIZEN-DISEASE
                    :VALUE HAS-CASE-WORKER-CODE)
    (HAS-OUTPUT-ROLE:VALUE HAS-SUITABLE-ITEMS-LIST)
    (HAS-CITIZEN-WEIGHT  :TYPE NUMBER)
    (HAS-CITIZEN-DISEASE :TYPE DISEASE)
    (HAS-CASE-WORKER-CODE :TYPE NUMBER)
    (HAS-SUITABLE-ITEM-LIST :TYPE ITEM-LIST)))
(DEF-CLASS ASSESS-EQUIPMENT-TO-PATIENT-WEB-SERVICE-INTERFACE-ORCHESTRATION
    ((HAS-BODY
      :VALUE ((ORCH-SEQUENCE
                GET-EQUIPMENT-ASSESSMENT-GOAL
                CHECK-EQUIPMENT-CASE-WORKER-GOAL)
              (ORCH-RETURN (ORCH-GET-GOAL-VALUE CHECK-EQUIPMENT-CASE-WORKER-GOAL))))))
```

As in the previous SWS description, the new functionality has been created by simply stating the sequence of goals to accomplish into an orchestration description. Note that the first goal of the orchestration is the goal depicted in Figure 8. Conversely to the previous SWS description, however, the first goal of the sequence refers to the Order Equipment domain ontologies, while the second one - as well as the main goal – refers to the Citizen Assessment domain ontologies. Particularly, the inputs of the main goal refer to citizen and disease classes, while the inputs of the first goal refer to client and impairment classes, respectively. Moreover, the first goal adopts the ELMS catalogue-data in the output list of equipments, while the second and main goals use the SWIFT care-item in the respective list of equipments. To map between the two domains and thus solve the mismatches, we make use of OO-mediators. As described in Section 4.2, OO-mediators are linked to the goal through the used-mediator relation and define mapping rules to solve data mismatching. The mapping rules are valuated when the goal is invoked. The listing below shows as excerpt of the mapping rules for the `catalogue-data` and `care-item` classes.

```
(def-concept-mapping catalogue-data care-item)

(def-relation-mapping catalogue-care-max-weight-mapping
    ((has-max-citizen-weight ?care-item ?value)
     if
     (maps-to ?care-item ?catalogue-data)
     (has-max-user-weight ?catalogue-data ?value)))
```

The example above makes use of the primitives introduced in Section 4.2.4. More specifically, the definitions above link the `has-max-user-weight` slot of class `catalogue-data` in the source ontology to the `has-max-citizen-weight` slot of class `care-item` in the target ontology. The `def-concept-mapping` construct associates each instance of the `catalogue-data` class to a newly created instance of the `care-item` class and link them by generating instances of the relation `maps-to` internally. The `def-relation-mapping` construct uses the generated `maps-to` relation within a rule which asserts the value of the mapped catalogue max user weight to the value of the care item max citizen weight.

As a result, we easily defined and reused SWS descriptions to implement an integrated functionality, abstracting from the underlying legacy systems, keeping the autonomy of involved parties and covering multiple heterogeneous domains. If new systems need to be integrated, we simply introduce the appropriate SWS descriptions and mediation facilities - when mismatches occur - likewise we have done in the second example of the present use case. Conversely, standard database techniques would necessitate that the different parties harmonise their database schemas or agree upon a unifying schema. The addition of a single new system would require a new consensus to be agreed upon.

Further benefits of our approach are highlighted in the next use case.

6.1.4 Presentation Layer

The application is a service oriented portal for the employees of the Community Care department at ECC. Employees assist citizens to notify their changes of circumstances, and the system delivers the change to the different agencies involved in the process. In this way, citizens only have to inform the public administration once about their changes. The user interface uses the Java API of IRS-III to invoke the defined goals. The user selects the action to perform from a list of available goals. After the user has entered the required data, he/she triggers the execution of a goal and IRS-III performs the appropriate Web service - in the case of get equipment assessment, the three basic Web services are performed.

6.2 Emergency Management System

In an emergency situation, multiple agencies need to collaborate, sharing data and information about actions to be performed. However, many emergency relevant resources are not available on the network and interactions among agencies or emergency corps usually occur on a personal/phone/fax basis. The resulting interaction is therefore limited in scope and slower in response time, contrary to the nature of the need for information access in an emergency situation.

Emergency relevant data is often spatial-related. *Spatial-Related Data (SRD)* is traditionally managed with the help of *Geographical Information Systems (GIS)*, which allow access to different layers of SRD such as highways, transportation, postal addresses index, land use, etc. GIS support decision making by facilitating the integration, storage, querying, analysis, modeling, reporting, and mapping of this data. Following several interviews with SRD holders in ECC, it was decided to focus the scenario on a real past emergency situation: a snowstorm which affected the M11 motorway on 31st January 2003.

6.2.1 Legacy Systems Layer

The Emergency Management System (EMS) aggregates data and functionalities from three different sources:

- *Meteorological Office*: is a national UK organization which provides environmental resources, such as weather forecast, snow and pollution data.
- *ViewEssex*: is a collaboration between ECC and British Telecommunications (BT) which has created a single corporate spatial data warehouse. As can be expected ViewEssex contains a wide range of data including data for roads, administrative boundaries, buildings and Ordnance survey maps, as well as environmental and social care data.
- *BuddySpace:* is an Instant Messaging client facilitating lightweight communication, collaboration, and presence management [10] built on top of the instant messaging protocol Jabber[4]. The BuddySpace client can be accessed on standard PCs, as well as on PDAs and mobile phones which in an emergency situation may be the only hardware device available.

6.2.2 Service Abstraction Layer

We distinguish between two classes of services: *data* and *smart*. The former refer to the three data sources introduced above, and they are exposed by means of standard Web services:

- *Meteorological services:* provide weather information - e.g. snowfall level - over a given rectangular spatial area.
- *ViewEssex services*: return detailed information on specific types of rest centre. For example, `getHospitals` is a Web service that returns a list of relevant hospitals within a given circular area.
- *BuddySpace services*: allow presence information on online users to be accessed.

Smart services represent specific emergency planning reasoning and operations on the data provided by the data services. They are implemented in a mixture of Common Lisp and OCML [23] and make use of the EMS ontologies. In particular, we created a number of services that filter the data retrieved from ViewEssex according to emergency-specific requirements: e.g. rest centres with heating system, hotels with at least 40 beds, easy accessible hospital, etc. The used criteria were gained from our discussions with emergency officers of ECC.

---

[4] Jabber. http://www.jabber.org/

6.2.3 Semantic Web Service Layer

The following tables summarise the ontologies reflecting the client and provider domains to support SWS descriptions.

Service Oriented Domain Ontologies	
Meteorology Domain Ontology	It contains the concepts used to semantically describe the services attached to the data sources of the Met-Office domain, such as snow and rain.
Emergency Planning Domain Ontology	It contains the concepts used to semantically describe the services attached to the data sources of the ViewEssex domain, such as hospitals and supermarkets.
Jabber Domain Ontology	It contains the concepts used to semantically describe the services attached to the data sources of the Jabber domain, such as session and preferences.

As in the previous use case, we introduced *lifting operations* to get the information provided by Web services up to the semantic level. These lisp functions automatically extract data from SOAP/XML messages and create instances of the domain ontologies. The mapping information between syntactic data types and ontological classes is defined at design time by developers.

User Oriented Domain Ontologies	
GUI Ontology	It contains GUI and user-oriented concepts. It maps the ontology elements which will be displayed to the elements of the particular user interface which is used. Note that although the choice of the resulting syntactic format depends of the chosen lowering operation, concepts from the GUI ontology are used in order to achieve this transformation in a suitable way.
Archetypes Ontology	It is a minimal ontological commitment ontology aiming to provide a cognitively meaningful insight into the nature of a specialized object; for example, by conveying the cognitive ("naïve") feeling that for example an hospital, as a "container" of people and provider of "shelter" can be assimilated to the more universal concept of "house". The latter can be considered as an *archetypal* concept, i.e. based on image schemata and therefore supposed to convey meaning immediately. It is moreover assumed that any client, whilst maybe lacking the specific representation for a specific basic level concept, knows its archetypal representation.
Spatial Ontology	It describes geographical concepts of location, such as coordinates, points, polygonal areas and fields. It also allows describing spatial objects as entities with a location and a set of attributes.
Context Ontology	It allows describing *context n-uples* which represent a particular situation. In the emergency planning application, context n-uples have up to four components, the use case, the user role, the location, and the type of object. Contexts are linked with (WSMO-) goals; i.e. if this type of user accesses this type of object around this particular location, these particular goals will be presented. Contexts also help to inform goals, e.g. if a goal provides information about petrol stations in an area, the location part of the context is used to define this area, and input from the user is therefore not needed.

The purpose of the GUI, Archetypes and Spatial ontologies is the aggregation of different data sources on, respectively, a representation, a cognitive and a spatial level. Therefore we can group them under the appellation *aggregation* ontologies. They allow the different data sources to be handled and presented in a similar way. Inversely to the lifting operations, *lowering operations* transform instances of aggregation ontologies into syntactic documents to be used by the server and client applications. This step is usually fully automated since aggregation ontologies are, by definition, quite stable and unique.

SWS Description Ontologies	
Met-Office SWS	It contains goal, Web service and mediator descriptions which define SWS on top of the Met Office database.
Emergency Planning SWS	It contains goal, Web service and mediator descriptions which define SWS on top of the ViewEssex GIS system.
BuddySpace SWS	It contains goal, Web service and mediator descriptions which define SWS on top of the BuddySpace instant messaging system.

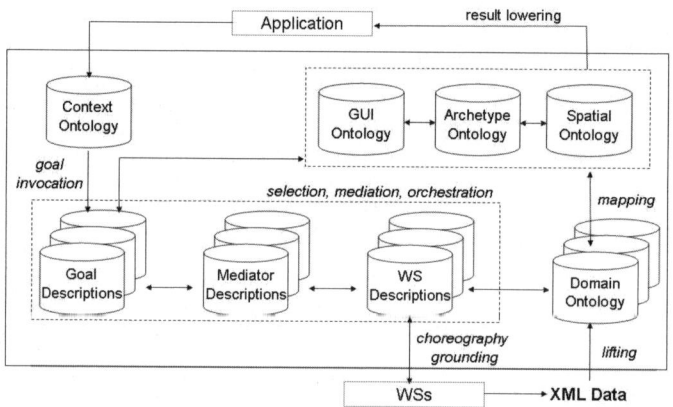

Fig. 11. The use of semantics within the Semantic Web Service Layer

Figure 11 outlines how the ontologies and SWS descriptions stored within the SWS library of IRS-III link the user interface (Application) to the Met Office, ECC Emergency Planning, and BuddySpace Web services (WSs). Starting from the application, counterclockwise, the *italics* words in the picture represent the main operations performed within IRS-III. The Web service descriptions make use of domain ontologies - Meteorology, ViewEssex and Jabber – whilst the goal encodings rely on the GUI, archetypes and spatial ontologies. Mismatches are resolved by mediation services linked to WG and GG mediators.

Figure 12 shows an example of the created SWS descriptions: Get-Polygon-GIS-data-with-Filter-Goal represents a request for available shelters within a given area. The user specifies a polygon area and the shelter type (e.g. hospitals, inns, hotels). The results obtained by querying ViewEssex need to be filtered in order to return shelters correlated to emergency-specific requirements only. The problems to be solved in this example include: (i) *discovering* and *selecting* the appropriate ViewEssex Web service; (ii) *meditating* the difference in area representations (polygon vs. circular) between the user goal and available Web services; (iii) *composing* the retrieve and filter data operations.

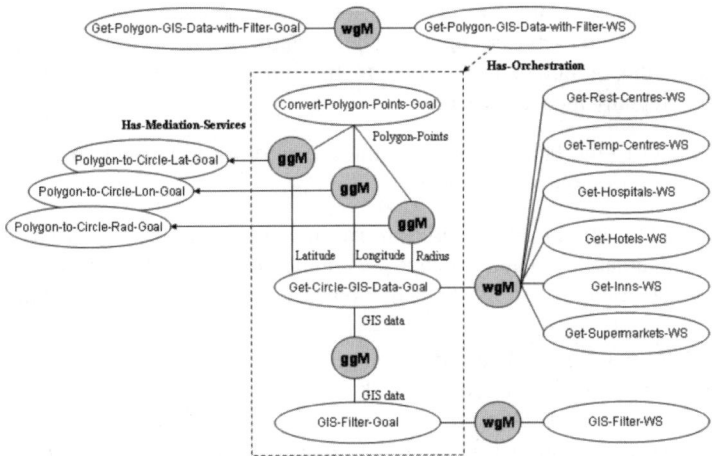

Fig. 12. A portion of WSMO descriptions for the EMS prototype

We outline below how the SWS representations in Figure 12 address these problems.

- *Web service discovery and selection:* when the `Get-Circle-GIS-Data-Goal` is invoked, IRS-III discovers all of Web services that can solve it by means of the WG-mediator (Section 4.2.1). Each semantic description of ViewEssex Web service defines the Web service capability - i.e. the class of shelter provided by the Web service. The listing below reports an example of kappa expression defining a capability assumption:

```
(DEF-CLASS GET-ECC-HOSPITALS-WEB-SERVICE-CAPABILITY (CAPABILITY) ?CAPABILITY
   ((USED-MEDIATOR :VALUE GET-GIS-DATA-MEDIATOR)
    (HAS-ASSUMPTION:VALUE
       (KAPPA(?WEB-SERVICE)
          (= (WSMO-ROLE-VALUE ?WEB-SERVICE'HAS-SPATIAL-OBJECT-QUERY)
             'HOSPITALSQUERY)))))
```

If the Web service provides the class of shelters defined in one of the inputs of the goal, IRS-III selects it (Section 4.2.2). In the example above, the Web service is selected if the request class of shelters is hospital ('hospitalquery).

- *Area mediation and orchestration:* the `Get-Polygon-GIS-data-with-Filter-Goal` is associated with a unique Web service that orchestrates three sub-goals in sequence. The first one gets the list of polygon points from the input; the second one is the `Get-Circle-GIS-Data-Goal` described above; the third one invokes the smart service which filters the list of shelter data. The first and second sub-goals are linked by three GG-mediators which return the centre, in the form of latitude and longitude, and the radius of the smallest circle that circumscribes the given polygon. To accomplish this, we created three mediation services represented by three distinct goals: `Polygon-to-Circle-Lat-Goal`, `Polygon-to-Circle-Lon-Goal`, and `Polygon-to-Circle-Rad-Goal`. Each mediation service is performed by a specific Web service, exposing a Lisp function (the respective WG-mediator and Web service ovals were omitted to avoid cluttering the diagram). The results of the mediation services and the class of shelter required are the inputs to the second sub-goal. A unique GG-mediator connects the output of the second to the input of the third sub-goal, without introducing any mediation service.

Additionally to the benefits of our approach introduced in Section 6.1.3, this use case highlighted the following aspects:

- We created complex SWS descriptions on top of three distinct kinds of legacy system: database, GIS and instance messaging. The use of Web services allows us to abstract from the underlying technologies and ease thus their integration.
- A given goal – e.g. `Get-Circle-GIS-Data-Goal` – might be achieved by several Web services. The most appropriate one is selected on the basis of the specific situation. The effective workflow – i.e. the actual sequence of service invocations – is known at run-time only. In existing Web service-based approaches the functionalities are mapped at design-time, when the actual context is not known.
- The use of WG and GG mediators allows goal and process mediation and thus a smoothly crossing among services of distinct domains in the same workflow. The most appropriate mediation service is selected at run-time, according to the specific situation.
- If new Web services will be available – for instance providing data from further GIS - new Web Service descriptions can be simply introduced and linked to the `Get-Circle-GIS-Goal` by the proper mediators - or reusing the existing one, if semantic mismatches do not exist - without affecting the current structure. In the same way, new filter services - e.g. more efficient ones - may be introduced.

6.2.4 Presentation Layer

The Emergency Management System (EMS) prototype is in effect a decision support system, which assists the end-user – currently the Emergency Planning Officer (EPO) – in assembling information related to a certain type of event, more quickly and accurately. The application's user interface is based on Web standards. XHTML and CSS are used for presentation, while JavaScript (i.e. EcmaScript) is used to handle user interaction together with AJAX techniques to communicate with IRS-III. One of the main components of the interface is a map, which uses the Google Maps API [13] to display polygons and objects (custom images) at specific coordinates and zoom level. Each time an object is displayed by a user at a particular location, a function of the context ontology provides the goals which need to be displayed and what inputs are implicit. A screencast with an example of end-user interactions as well as a live version are available online[5], to be used preferably with the Firefox Web browser.

---

[5] http://irs-test.open.ac.uk/sgis-dev/

Deploying Semantic Web Services-Based Applications in the e-Government Domain 123

7 Lessons Learned

On the basis of challenges encountered - and the ways in which they were overcome - we now summarize the lessons learned in terms of: identifying the suitable scenario, following the adequate development process, verifying the advantages of SWS over other technologies and outlining the open challenges.

7.1 The Scenario

The first challenge is the identification of the proper scenario; i.e. a scenario where SWS technology can provide substantial benefits. On the basis of our experience, we can outline the following main features:

- The scenario is a distributed and heterogeneous environment with a lack of centralized control, which provides a large amount of alternative – i.e. providing different functionalities in distinct situations - and competitive - i.e. providing the same functionalities in the same situation – services.
- The services used in the scenario are connected to external environments and access to common data/resources already available on the Web.
- The scenario involves multiple stakeholders - clients and service providers - that need to collaborate. They represent the heterogeneous viewpoints/domains to describe.
- The scenario is not static, but subject to changes and evolutions. The dynamism may involve the viewpoint descriptions – e.g. government policies, citizen needs, agencies' participation – or the service descriptions - e.g. changes in the service business process, or new services provided by existing or new partners.

In our work, we preliminary identified a lot of promising service-oriented application fields, such as e-Procurement, school admissions, libraries, health, GIS applications (e.g. emergency planning), change of circumstance, child care/children's services, youth services, adult social care, benefits and revenues, and criminal justice initiatives. On the basis of existing legacy systems, services and datasets, resources, stakeholders' requirements and needs within ECC, we refined the list reported above and chose the use cases described in Section 6.

7.2 The Development Process

According to the features of the suitable scenario outlined in the previous section, we expect that, during the development process, new requirements may arise or some domain aspects may be better comprehended, new services need to be developed or integrated in order to cover existing lacks, and new datasets may be available in order to improve the existing information space. These aspects are common in almost every scenario, but they are particularly true when dealing with distributed and heterogeneous sources. Therefore, we aimed to design a *pragmatic* - in order to quickly lead to a working outcome – as well as *flexible* - in order to easily respond to possible changes or improvements and meet the multiple actors' viewpoints – development process. The prototyping approach is a commonly used methodology to mach such requirements. Moreover, the semantic approach generally helps to address flexibility, since the changes mainly concern the semantic descriptions only - e.g. ontologies and SWS descriptions of the Semantic Web Service layer - and not the overall architecture of the system. The challenge was to identify an appropriate prototyping methodology which takes advantage of the decoupled nature of SWS descriptions (WSMO approach). As a result, we tailored a *SWS-oriented prototyping development process* composed of the following three straightforward phases: requirements capture, SWS description, evaluation (Figure 13).

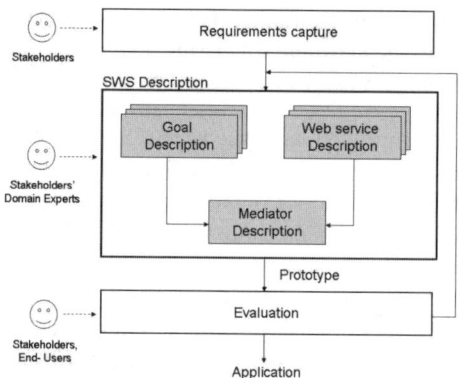

Fig. 13. Main steps of the devised prototyping process

The first phase represents the step 1 of the methodology presented in Section 5.2. The second phase focuses on the semantic descriptions, and encloses the required flexibility of the process. This phase is decomposed into several activities that deal with the knowledge acquisition and representation of the multiple domains and actors' viewpoints of the application context. Each activity can be independently iterated whenever an improvement or change only involves the respective domain/viewpoint. This phase represents the steps 2, 3 and 4 of the methodology presented in Section 5.2. The last phase introduces the prototyping iterations of the whole application development process. The prototype has been shown to stakeholders (clients and service providers) and end-users. Prototype improvements and changes have been mainly based on their feedback. Finally, it is important to note that:

- Along the whole development process, we keep a constant contact with the stakeholders and users. In the first phase, we mainly interview stakeholders' manager and technical people. Then, we cooperate with domain experts (i.e. organization employees). Finally, we consult again the stakeholders and involve the end-users. In this way, we can address the barriers e) and f) identified in Section 3.2.
- The structure of the second phase leads to a sound approach that separately focuses on each of the involved actors – i.e. their viewpoints and specific languages/terminology/skills - keeps organizations' autonomy in the description of their domain and allows the cooperative development of the application.
- The proposed methodology is not an e-Government specific formula.

7.3 The Verified Added Values

The deployed applications highlighted advantages of adopting SWS over other technologies. In this section, we summarise the comparison with existing Web services-based and ontology-based approaches. Other technologies (e.g. standard database technologies), indeed, do not provide the adequate abstraction over heterogeneous and autonomous legacy systems (Section 6.1.3).

- *SWS vs. Web Services.* By using Web Services, data and functionalities can be shared with anyone through the Internet. As introduced in Section 2, the supplied services are autonomous and platform-independent computational elements. The syntactic definitions used in these specifications allow fast composition and good results in term of application performance. However, they do not completely describe the capability of a service and cannot be understood by software programs. A human developer is required to interpret the meaning of inputs, outputs and applicable constraints, as well as the context in which services can be used. Moreover, Web Services lack in flexibility: for instance, if a new Web Service is deployed, the application developers need to re-model several syntax descriptions – introducing a cost - in order to integrate it.

  On the other hand, the SWS approach is able to model the background knowledge of a context together to the requested and provided capabilities, and it hence addresses *automatic reasoning* and *reuse* (Section 6.1.3). As a result, service invocation, discovery, composition and mediation are *automated* by adopting the best available solutions for a specific request and increasing the *flexibility, scalability,* and *maintainability* of an application. Moreover, the execution sequence of a complex SWS (Sections 6.1.3 and 6.1.3) is not hard-coded, and it is dynamically created by using a goal-based invocation: several Web Services may be associated with a goal, and only the best one will be discovered and invoked at runtime only (late binding); if a new service will be available, the developers simply will describe and then link it to an existing goal; if a service will change, only the specific semantic description will be affected, and not the whole process (Section 6.2.3).

- *SWS vs. other ontology-based approaches.* Creating and managing ontologies is a bottleneck: understanding a domain, acquiring and representing knowledge, populating with instances and evolving ontologies are big tasks for the application developers. In complex domain such as e-Government, centralized ontologies would require an unrealistic development effort with no guarantee of satisfactory results. Moreover, government agencies deal with huge datasets (e.g. demographic, GIS, etc.) that cannot easily transposed to ontology's instances. However, in the context of semantic-based applications, such a cost cannot be deleted, but it may be contained.

  SWS technology makes knowledge capture and maintenance process simpler and more efficient (Section 6.1.3). (a) The only knowledge which must be modeled is related to the exposed functionality of the Web service. This means describing the concepts used by the Web service only, such as inputs and output. Moreover, the instances of a concept are not defined a priori, but they are created at runtime – i.e. lifted after the execution of the Web service. This minimalist approach makes easy the management of ontologies – i.e. evolution and maintenance. (b) The knowledge capturing process is distributed among all of the stakeholders: each partner describes – and it is responsible for – its particular domain. In this way, the several viewpoints can be independently and concurrently described by the proper knowledge holders. Partners can also reuse their own existing ontologies. As a result, we obtain a model that reflects the e-Government structure and addresses the required lack of central control.

Moreover, a WSMO based approach addresses *interoperability* among very heterogeneous knowledge sources and *mediation* among several viewpoints (users, multiple providers, etc.). WSMO mediators are mappings that solve existing mismatches and do not affect service descriptions. In our applications, we have gathered the following mediation requirements and solutions:

- *Data mediation*: organizations have their own databases and hence different data formats for the same concept. Lifting at the semantic level these distinct data formats, the resulting instances can be mapped by means of either mediation services (Section 6.2.3) or mapping rules (Section 6.1.3).
- *Goal mediation*: Multiple Web services can be linked to the same goal via mediators. In principle, goal and web service descriptions are provided by distinct organizations, and a mediation service is used to solve the existing mismatches (Section 6.2.3).
- *Process mediation*: organizational processes behave in different ways according to their own set of operational procedures, requirements and constraints. Added value functionalities can be provided by composing several goal descriptions. Mediation between two goals in sequence may be necessary to solve exiting mismatches (Section 6.2.3).

7.4 Open Challenges

Since we are adopting a young technology and e-Government is a very complex domain, we are aware that not all of the existing issues are completely addressed. The main remaining challenges identified are:

- *SWS infrastructure*. SWS technology is an ongoing research, and some of its main features - e.g. mediation, orchestration, non functional properties based discovery - are still under development. However, in order to respond to the needs of real-world applications, IRS-III already introduced some solutions. During the development of the presented applications, we continually improved and tested selection, choreography, orchestration and mediations of IRS-III. However, further use cases will highlight unconsidered aspects and allow us to improve IRS-III performances. Moreover, the choice of a specific SWS approach involves the adoption of its defined features; for instance, IRS-III uses client instead of service choreography, goal-based orchestration instead of goal and web service composition, etc. However, in a wide domain such as e-Government, some features may be adequate in a context but not in others, and several partners may adopt distinct approaches. The openness of IRS-III aims to address the interoperability of multiple SWS approaches.

- *Commercialization.* The transition of the currently available systems into a stable and robust infrastructure is one of the major challenges that need to be solved, before a SWS-based solution can be deployed into a productive environment. However, the prototyping development (Section 7.2) of carefully targeted applications, with clear objectives stated, can lead to real-world operational systems.
- *Organizational and social aspects.* The employees of governmental agencies usually perform their tasks well established procedures; the inappropriately-handled introduction of new processes or applications may lead to the reluctance of use them. Active participation of stakeholders and end-users in the design and development processes allows developers to deploy applications that respect current procedures and, at the same time, ease the work of staff, leading to improved acceptance. As described in Section 7.2, our approach follows this idea; however, more detailed investigations on the approach/methodology to follow and social implications could be performed.
- *Privacy, Security, and Trust.* As stated in Section 3.2, these are fundamental requirements in e-Government. At the syntax level, efficient solutions for addressing privacy and security issues already exist (e.g. SSL protocol and virtual private networks for protecting the communications, firewalls and digital certificates for avoiding malicious accesses and protecting data), or there is relevant ongoing research (e.g. enriching Web Services description with digital certificates and signatures). In the Change of Circumstances application, where citizen information had to be protected, we based on the security and privacy solutions provided by the adopted EAI system [27].

    The semantic level should extend the syntactic solutions by ontologically describing security and privacy policies of accessing data and processes. Moreover, trust-based discovery of SWS would be a crucial issue, in order to avoid invocation of malicious or unreliable services, for which there are no defined standards by which SWS may expose their policies and trust features. Most of existing approaches inherit methodologies from the peer-to-peer networks [21], [24]. Trust evaluation algorithms for SWS consider security issues, such as confidentiality, authorization, authentication, as rating statements [17],[19],[20],[21], or more generically Quality of Service performance properties [35], such as precision and accuracy of data, timeliness in executing a task, and security. The key to enabling a trust-based selection for SWS lies in a common ontological representation, where Web service and client perform their trust guarantees and requirements. In [12], we propose our trust managing approach based on IRS-III. Essentially, all participants can expose their trust guarantees and requirements by specifying trust policies. Since this work is still in progress, we do not apply it to the presented use cases.
- *Ease of use of SWS technology in e-Government.* The full integration between e-Government and SWS is not an easy task. The following further requirements should be considered. (a) Government agencies usually do not directly use the SWS infrastructure to represent knowledge internally. For instance, organizations will likely adopt their own workflow paradigm to describe their processes [1]. (b) Organization processes involve interactions with non-software agents, such as citizens, employees, managers, and politicians; thereby, component services

cannot in general be executed in a single-response step, and may require to following an interaction protocol with humans that involves multiple sequential, conditional and iterative steps. For instance, a service may require a negotiation between the citizen and the provider. In our approach, the management of such an interaction is embedded in the Presentation layer, because IRS-III supports one-shot goal invocation only.

In order to address these issues, we argue that a more complex semantic layer – i.e. an *explicit e-Government framework* - needs to be modelled. In [15], we identify and model three knowledge levels: *Constraints*, describing the context that bounds the creation and evolution of services: legislations, policies, and strategies influencing the development and management of an e-Government service-supply scenario; *Configuration*, describing the context in which services are supplied: requirements, resources, actor's role, business processes, and transactions of an e-Government service-supply scenario; *Service delivery*, adopting SWS technology as the base for the description, discovery, composition, mediation, and execution of (Web) services.

- *Standardization*. Currently, there are not reference standards for (semantic) service oriented applications in e-Government. The e-Government community is still debating on the approach to follow between, as a broadly described option, standardization versus integration - i.e. focusing on interoperation among several existing approaches. We believe that our approach is open to both solutions and our results may contribute to the investigation of possible standards.

8 Related Work

In the last years, several projects applied SWS technology in the e-Government domain, but only a few of them show reusability and composability in real usage scenarios. The *OntoGov* project [25] develops a platform that will facilitate the consistent composition, reconfiguration and evolution of e-Government services. It focuses more on the service life cycle than the interoperability and integration issues. Services are described by means of a "meta ontology" that extends OWL-S [26] by introducing WSMO [36] features. *Terregov* [32] is a project at an early stage of development. It aims to address the issue of interoperability of e-Government services. Its architecture is composed by a framework and intelligent agents that will offer configuration and reconfiguration of service workflows by selecting competing Web Services on the basis of their performance, and composing dynamic workflows based on semantic descriptions. In order to represent e-Government processes, it adopts OWL-S for describing the behaviors of Web Services, and BPEL [4] workflow description language for their orchestration. *WebSenior* [22] uses ontologies to automatically generate Web Services customized to senior citizen's needs and government program laws and regulations. Differently to both OntoGov and Terregov, WebSenior proposes a solution to a specific real usage scenario. This highlights the practical applicability of its approach, but limits the reusability and flexibility.

No one of the mentioned approaches adopts mediation mechanisms to overcome data and process mismatches: they only propose centralized ontologies for representing the entire domain and thereby addressing interoperability.

Further efforts on investigating multiple aspects of the application of semantic technologies in the e-Government domain are under way: BRITE [11] aims to enable interoperations in a transnational scenario among institutions that concert the registration of businesses in the European Union; FIT [29] will develop, test, and validate a self-adaptive citizen-oriented e-government framework; SAKE [30] will develop a holistic framework - and the supporting tools – that will be sufficiently flexible to adapt changing, diverse environment, and needs; and SemanticGov [34] will provide a WSMO-based infrastructure for Pan-European e-Government services. Since all of these projects started in 2006, they are still in their initial phase.

9 Summary and Future Work

In our work, we successfully established a close collaboration with a large local authority in UK in order to define a reusable SWS-based framework for deploying real-world applications in the e-Government domain. The aim is to dealing with complex scenarios, by easily interconnecting heterogeneous domains and allowing governmental agencies to cooperate and consume shared data in an easy way and without a centralized control. SWS technology promises to address interoperability and integration issues, and automate the development of service-oriented applications through semantic Web technologies (Section 2).

The analysis of motivations, requirements, and expected results of matching SWS and e-Government research areas (Section 3) provided us the aspects to stress first in the design of our framework and then in the development of compelling use cases.

To provide semantics and step towards the creation of added value services, we adopted IRS-III, an existing SWS broker (Section 4). In our work, we enclosed IRS-III into a 4-layers generic application architecture (Section 5.1) and devised a development methodology (Section 5.2) to propose a reusable framework for deploying SWS-based applications. The layering of the architecture proved to be very useful: (a) the development of ontologies and SWS descriptions could be decoupled from the implementation of the user interface and the deployment of Web Services; (b) using Web Services on top legacy systems, we abstracted from the technical details of involved legacy systems. The proposed methodology allowed the easy development of agile and flexible applications based on the idea of reuse. For instance, the methodology involves the ontological decoupling of the client's context from the providers' one. This led us to lower the cost of application deployment by introducing cooperative development and creating small ontologies focused on the specific service functionalities.

Following our approach, we deployed two e-Government applications (Section 6): Change of Circumstances and Emergency Management System. In this way, we (a) tested the reusability and adaptability of our approach to different e-Government contexts, (b) proved how our framework addresses interoperability and integration issues, and (c) stressed all of the aspects associated with the development of SWS-based applications: e.g. knowledge acquisition, discovery, composition, and mediation. Note that the development of the second application got benefits from the lessons learned in the development of the first one. In particular, we reduced the time of capturing requirements and describing SWS and obtained more qualitative results.

On the basis of these considerations and the results obtained from the two applications introduced above, we reported the main lessons learned (Section 7). We outlined a general scenario where SWS technology can provide substantial benefits; detailed our prototyping development process and highlighted the active role of stakeholders and end-users; summarized the verified added values of SWS over other technologies; and pointed out the open challenges that will drive our future work.

The analysis of related work (Section 8) showed that the application of SWS in e-Government is a really interesting topic, but a few projects provide real-world applications yet. Since e-Government community claims for creating compelling prototypes, establishing visible standards, stable and mature technologies, and convincing business cases, we believe that our work may contribute to raising awareness of the potential benefits of SWS in e-Government. Perhaps more importantly, the lessons learned may be also used to (a) guide the efforts of new e-Government applications/projects; (b) influence the e-Government standards environment and the e-Government strategic environment so as to encourage take up of SWS technologies.

Acknowledgments. This work is supported by the DIP (Data, Information and Process Integration with Semantic Web Services) project. DIP (FP6 – 507483) is an Integrated Project funded under the European Union's IST programme.

References

[1] der Aalst, W.V., ter Hofstede, A., Weske, M.: Business process management: a survey. In: BPM 2003. LNCS, vol. 2678, pp. 1–12. Springer, Heidelberg (2003)
[2] Amazon: Amazon web services (2006), http://www.amazon.com/gp/browse.html/104-6906496-9857523?%5Fencoding=UTF8&node=3435361/
[3] Berners-Lee, T., Hendler, J., Lassila, O.: The Semantic Web. Scientific American 284(4), 34–43 (2001)
[4] BPEL4WS Consortium: Business process execution language for web services (2004), http://www.ibm.com/developerworks/library/ws-bpel
[5] Cabral, L., Domingue, J.: Mediation of Semantic Web Services in IRS-III. In: Proceeding of the Workshop on Mediation in Semantic Web Services in conjunction with the 3rd International Conference on Service Oriented Computing, Amsterdam, The Netherlands (2005)
[6] Commission of the European Communities: The Role of e-Government for Europe's Future. Commission Staff Working Paper COM 567, 26.9 (2003)
[7] Commission of the European Communities: Linking up Europe: the Importance of Interoperability for e-Government Services. Commission Staff Working Paper SEC, 801 (2003)
[8] Cabral, L., Domingue, J., Galizia, S., Gugliotta, A., Norton, B., Tanasescu, V., Pedrinaci, C.: IRS-III: A Broker for Semantic Web Services based Applications. In: Cruz, I., Decker, S., Allemang, D., Preist, C., Schwabe, D., Mika, P., Uschold, M., Aroyo, L. (eds.) ISWC 2006. LNCS, vol. 4273, Springer, Heidelberg (2006)
[9] Domingue, J., Galizia, S., Cabral, L.: Choreography in IRS-III- Coping with Heterogeneous Interaction Patterns in Web Services. In: Gil, Y., Motta, E., Benjamins, V.R., Musen, M.A. (eds.) ISWC 2005. LNCS, vol. 3729, pp. 171–185. Springer, Heidelberg (2005)

[10] Eisenstadt, M., Komzak, J., Dzbor, M.: Instant messaging + maps = powerful collaboration tools for distance learning. In: Proceedings of TelEduc 2003, Havana, Cuba (2003)
[11] van Elst, L., Klein, B., Maus, H., Schoning, H., Tommasi, A., Zavattari, C., Favaro, J., Giannella, V.: Business Register Interoperability throughout Europe: The BRITE Project. In: AAAI Spring Symposium Semantic Web meets eGovernment, AAAI Press, Stanford (2006)
[12] Galizia, S.: WSTO: A Classification-Based Ontology for Managing Trust in Semantic Web Services. In: Proceedings of 3th International Semantic Web Conference, Budva, Montenegro (2006)
[13] Google: Google Web APIs (2005), http://www.google.com/apis/index.html
[14] Gruber, T.R.: A Translation Approach to Portable Ontology Specifications. Knowledge Acquisition 5(2) (1993)
[15] Gugliotta, A., Cabral, L., Domingue, J.: Knowledge Modeling for Integrating e-Government Applications and Semantic Web Services. In: AAAI Spring Symposium Semantic Web meets eGovernment, AAAI Press, Stanford (2006)
[16] Gugliotta, A., Cabral, L., Domingue, J., Roberto, V.: A semantic web service-based architecture for the interoperability of e-Government services. In: Proceeding of the International Workshop on Web Information Systems Modeling, Sydney, Australia (2005)
[17] Kagal, L., Paoucci, M., Srinivasan, N., Denker, G., Finin, T., Sycara, K.: Authorization and privacy for Semantic Web Services. In: Proceeding of AAAI 2004 Spring Symposium on Semantic Web Services, Stanford University (2004)
[18] Klischewski, R., Scholl, H.J.: Information Quality as a Common Ground for Key Players in e-Government Integration and Interoperability. In: Proceedings of the 39th Hawaii International Conference on System Sciences, Hyatt Regency Kauai, Hawaii (2006)
[19] Kolovski, V., Parsia, B., Katz, Y., Hendler, J.: Representing Web Service Policies in OWL-DL. In: Proceedings of 4th International Semantic Web Conference, Galway, Ireland (2005)
[20] Mani, A., Nagarajan, A.: Understanding quality of service for Web Services: Improving the performance of your Web Services -IBM-report (2002), http://www-128.ibm.com/developerworks/library/ws-quality.html
[21] Maximilien, E.M., Singh, M.P.: Toward Autonomic Web Services Trust and Selection. In: ICSOC 2004. Proceedings of 2nd International Conference on Service Oriented Computing, New York (2004)
[22] Medjahed, B., Bouguettaya, A.: Customized Delivery of E-Government Web Services. Web Services, IEEE Intelligent Systems 20(6) (2005)
[23] Motta, E.: An Overview of the OCML Modelling Language. In: Proceedings of the 8th Workshop on Knowledge Engineering Methods and Languages (1998)
[24] Olmedilla, D., Lara, R., Polleres, A., Lausen, H.: Trust Negotiation for Semantic Web Services. In: Proceedings of 1st International Workshop on Semantic Web Services and Web Process Composition in conjunction with the 2004 IEEE International Conference on Web Services, San Diego, California, USA (2004)
[25] OntoGov: Ontogov project (2004), http://www.ontogov.com
[26] OWL-S Coalition: OWL-S 1.1 release (2004), http://www.daml.org/services/owl-s/1.1/
[27] SAP: SAP exchange infrastructure: The integration solution for process-centric collaboration, http://www.sap.com/xi
[28] SOAP: SOAP Version 1.2 Part 0: Primer (2003), http://www.w3.org/TR/soap12-part0/

[29] Stojanovic, N., Stojanovic, L., Hinkelmann, K., Mentzas, G., Abecker, A.: Fostering self-adaptative e-Government services improvement using semantic technologies. In: AAAI Spring Symposium Semantic Web meets eGovernment, AAAI Press, Stanford (2006)
[30] Stojanovic, N., Mentzas, G., Apostolou, D.: Semantic-enbled Agile Knowledge-based e-government. In: AAAI Spring Symposium Semantic Web meets eGovernment, AAAI Press, Stanford (2006)
[31] Sycara, K., Paoulucci, M., Ankolekar, A., Srinivasan, N.: Automated discovery, interaction and composition of semantic web services. Journal of Web Semantic 1(1) (2003)
[32] TerreGov: Terregov project (2004), http://www.terregov.eupm.net/my spip/index.php
[33] UDDI: UDDI Spec Technical Committee Specification v. 3.0 (2003), http://uddi.org/pubs/uddi-v3.0.1-20031014.htm
[34] Vitvar, T., Kerrigan, M., van Overeem, A., Peristeras, V., Tarabanis, K.: Infrastructure for the Semantic Pan-European E-Government Services. In: AAAI Spring Symposium Semantic Web meets eGovernment, AAAI Press, Stanford (2006)
[35] Vu, L., Hauswirth, M.H., Aberer, K.: QoS-based Service Selection and Ranking with Trust and Reputation Management. Technical Report IC2005029, Swiss Federal Institute of Technology at Lausanne (EPFL), Switzerland (2005)
[36] WSDL: Web Services Description Language (WSDL) 1.1 (2001), http://www.w3.org/TR/2001/NOTE-wsdl-20010315
[37] WSMO Working Group, D2v1.0: Web Service Modeling Ontology (WSMO). WSMO Working Draft (2004), http://www.wsmo.org/2004/d2/v1.0/

Linking Data to Ontologies

Antonella Poggi[1], Domenico Lembo[1], Diego Calvanese[2],
Giuseppe De Giacomo[1], Maurizio Lenzerini[1], and Riccardo Rosati[1]

[1] Dipartimento di Informatica e Sistemistica, Università di Roma "La Sapienza",
Via Salaria 113, 00198 Roma, Italy
{poggi,degiacomo,lembo,lenzerini,rosati}@dis.uniroma1.it
[2] Faculty of Computer Science, Free University of Bozen-Bolzano,
Piazza Domenicani 3, I-39100 Bolzano, Italy
calvanese@inf.unibz.it

Abstract. Many organizations nowadays face the problem of accessing existing data sources by means of flexible mechanisms that are both powerful and efficient. Ontologies are widely considered as a suitable formal tool for sophisticated data access. The ontology expresses the domain of interest of the information system at a high level of abstraction, and the relationship between data at the sources and instances of concepts and roles in the ontology is expressed by means of mappings. In this paper we present a solution to the problem of designing effective systems for ontology-based data access. Our solution is based on three main ingredients. First, we present a new ontology language, based on Description Logics, that is particularly suited to reason with large amounts of instances. The second ingredient is a novel mapping language that is able to deal with the so-called impedance mismatch problem, i.e., the problem arising from the difference between the basic elements managed by the sources, namely data, and the elements managed by the ontology, namely objects. The third ingredient is the query answering method, that combines reasoning at the level of the ontology with specific mechanisms for both taking into account the mappings and efficiently accessing the data at the sources.

1 Introduction

In several areas, such as Enterprise Application Integration, Data Integration [19], and the Semantic Web [13], ontologies are considered as the ideal formal tool to provide a shared conceptualization of the domain of interest. In particular, in many of the above areas, ontologies are advocated for realizing what we can call *ontology-based data access*, that can be explained as follows: we have a set of pre-existing data sources forming the data layer of our information system, and we want to build a service on top of this layer, aiming at presenting a conceptual view of data to the clients of the information system. Specifically, the conceptual view is expressed in terms of an ontology, that will represent the unique access point for the interaction between the clients and the system, and the data sources are independent from the ontology. In other words, our aim is to link to the ontology a collection of data that exist autonomously, and have not been necessarily structured with the purpose of storing the ontology instances.

Therefore, in ontology-based data access, the ontology describes the domain of interest at a high level of abstraction, so as to abstract away from how data sources are maintained in the data layer of the system itself. It follows that the conceptual view and the data sources are both at different abstraction levels, and expressed in terms of different formalisms. For example, while logical languages are nowadays used to specify the ontology, the data sources are usually expressed in terms of the relational data model.

Taking into account these differences, the specific issues arising from the interaction between the ontology and the data sources can be briefly summarized as follows:

1. Ontologies exhibit to the client a conceptual view of the domain of interest, and allow for expressing at the intensional level complex kinds of semantic conditions over such domain. One of the main challenges in this respect is to single out ontology languages that provide an acceptable compromise between expressive power and computational complexity of reasoning over both the ontology and the underlying sources storing data about the domain.
2. The amount of data stored at the sources can be very large. Therefore, one needs to resort to a technology that is able to efficiently access very large quantities of data. Nowadays, relational database technology is the best (if not the only) one that fulfills such a requirement. Hence, in our context, we are interested in determining how much one can push the expressive power of the formalism used for expressing the conceptual layer, while still maintaining the ability to answer queries by relying on a relational DBMS to access data at the sources.
3. Since we assume that the data sources exist in the information system independently of the conceptual layer, the whole system will be based on specific mechanisms for mapping the data at the sources to the elements of the ontology. So, in ontology-based data access, the mapping is the formal tool by which we determine how to link data to the ontology, i.e., how to reconstruct the semantics of data stored in the sources in terms of the ontology.
4. In general, there is a mismatch between the way in which data is (and can be) represented in a relational database, and the way in which the corresponding information is rendered in an ontology. Specifically, while the database of a data source stores data, instances of concepts in an ontology are objects, each one denoted by an object identifier, not to be confused with a data value. Such a problem is known as *impedance mismatch*. The language used to specify the mappings between the data and the ontology should provide specific mechanisms for addressing the impedance mismatch problem.
5. The main reason to build an ontology-based data access system is to provide high-level services to the clients of the information system. The most important service is query answering. Clients express their queries in terms of the conceptual view (the ontology), and the system should reason about the ontology and the mapping and should translate the request into suitable queries posed to the sources.

Recent research in the area of ontology languages for the Semantic Web has addressed several important aspects regarding the issues mentioned above.

As for issue 1, an effort has been undertaken to understand which language would be best suited for representing ontologies in a setting where an ontology is used for accessing large quantities of data [7,26,17]. This work has shown that most of the languages proposed so far are not really suited for this task. Indeed, the most significant fragments of OWL [14][1] that have been proposed by the W3C (namely, OWL-DL and OWL-Lite) are actually coNP-hard in data complexity [10,7], i.e., when complexity is measured with respect to the size of the data layer only, which is indeed the dominant parameter in this context [31]. This means that, in practice, computations over large amounts of data are prohibitively costly. A way to overcome such a problem is to impose restrictions on the ontology language, so as to guarantee that reasoning remains computationally tractable with respect to data complexity. Possible restrictions that guarantee polynomial reasoning have been studied and proposed in the context of description logics, such as Horn-$\mathcal{SHIQ}$ [17], $\mathcal{EL}^{++}$ [3], and DLP [12]. Among such fragments, of particular interest are those belonging to the *DL-Lite* family [6,7]. These logics allow for answering complex queries (namely, conjunctive queries, i.e., SQL select-project-join queries, and unions of conjunctive queries) in LOGSPACE with respect to data complexity. More importantly, after a preprocessing phase which is independent of the data, they allow for delegating query processing to the relational DBMS managing the data layer.

Hence, by adopting a technology based on logics of the *DL-Lite* family, we also aim at a solution to issue 2 above. Specifically, according to [7] there are two maximal languages in the *DL-Lite* family that allow for delegating query processing to a DBMS. The first one, called *DL-Lite$_\mathcal{F}$* in [7], allows for specifying the main modeling features of conceptual models, including cyclic assertions, ISA on concepts, inverses on roles, domain and range of roles, mandatory participation to roles, and functional restrictions on roles. The second one, called *DL-Lite$_\mathcal{R}$*, is able to fully capture (the DL fragment of) RDFS, and has in addition the ability of specifying mandatory participation to roles and disjointness between concepts and roles. The language obtained by unrestrictedly merging the features of *DL-Lite$_\mathcal{F}$* and *DL-Lite$_\mathcal{R}$*, while quite interesting in general, is not in LOGSPACE with respect to data complexity anymore [7], and hence looses the most interesting computational feature for ontology-based data access. Hence, to obtain a language whose expressive power goes beyond that of *DL-Lite$_\mathcal{F}$* or *DL-Lite$_\mathcal{R}$* and that is still useful, we need to restrict how the features of both languages are merged and can interact.

Regarding issues 3 and 4, i.e., the impedance mismatch between data items in the data layer and objects at the conceptual level, we observe that such a problem has received only little attention in the Semantic Web community. Some of the issues that need to be addressed when putting into correspondence a relational data source with an ontology, arise also in the context of ontology integration and alignment, which is the topic of several recent research works. These works study

---

[1] http://www.w3.org/TR/owl-features/

formalisms for specifying the correspondences between elements (concepts, relations, individuals) in different ontologies, ranging from simple correspondences between atomic elements, to complex languages allowing for expressing complex mappings. We now briefly discuss the most significant of such proposals found in the literature.

C-OWL and DDLs (Distributed Description Logics) [30] are extensions of OWL and DLs with so-called *bridge rules*, expressing simple forms of semantic relations between concepts, roles, and individuals. At the semantic level, the sets of objects in two ontologies are disjoint, but objects are related to each other by means of *domain relations*, which model simple translation functions between the domains. Reasoning in C-OWL is based on tableaux techniques. MAFRA [23] is a system that allows one to extract mappings from ontologies, and to use them for the transformation of data between ontologies. It does so by providing a so-called *Semantic Bridge Ontology*, whose instantiation provides the ontology mapping, and which can also be used as input for data transformations. The Ontology Mapping Language [29] of the Ontology Management Working Group (OMWG)[2] is an ontology alignment language that is independent of the language in which the two ontologies to be aligned are expressed. The alignment between two ontologies is represented through a set of mapping rules that specify a correspondence between various entities, such as concepts, relations, and instances. Several concept and relation constructors are offered to construct complex expressions to be used in mappings.

While the above proposals deal with the alignment between ontologies, none of them addresses properly the problem of establishing sound mechanisms for linking existing data to the instances of the concepts and the roles in the ontology. This issue is studied in [11,5], where specific mapping languages are proposed for linking data to ontologies. Such approaches, however, do not deal with the problem of the *impedance mismatch* between objects and values, which needs to be addressed by defining suitable mechanisms for *mapping* the data values to the objects in the ontology, and specifying how object identifiers can be built starting from data values. Instead, such a problem has already been considered in databases, and specifically in the context of declarative approaches to data integration. For example, in [9], a mechanism is proposed for annotating the mappings from the data to a global schema (which plays the role of an ontology). Such annotations, together with specific conversion and matching predicates, specify which attributes should be used to identify objects at the conceptual level, and how data coming from different data sources should be joined. We also mention the work done in deductive object-oriented databases on query languages with invention of objects [15,16]. Such objects are created starting from values specified in the body of a query, by applying suitable (Skolem) functions.

We argue that the results of the above mentioned papers, although interesting from several points of view, do not provide a clear and comprehensive solution to the problem of designing effective and efficient tools for ontology-based data

---

[2] http://www.omwg.org/

access. The goal of this paper is to present one such solution. Specifically, we present three contributions towards this end:

- We propose a new logic of the *DL-Lite* family. By looking at the interaction between the distinguishing features of $DL\text{-}Lite_\mathcal{F}$ and $DL\text{-}Lite_\mathcal{R}$, we have been able to single out an extension of both logics that is still LOGSPACE with respect to data complexity, and allows for delegating the "data dependent part" of the query answering process to the relational DBMS managing the data layer. In devising this logic, called $DL\text{-}Lite_\mathcal{A}$, we take seriously the distinction between objects and values (a distinction that is typically blurred in description logics), and introduce, besides concepts and roles, also attributes, which describe properties of concepts represented by values rather than objects.
- We illustrate a specific language for expressing mappings between data at the sources and instances of concepts and roles in the ontology. The mapping language has been designed in such a way to provide a solution to the impedance mismatch problem. Indeed, with respect to previous proposals of mapping languages, the distinguishing feature of our proposal is the possibility to create new object identifiers by making use of values retrieved from the database. We have borrowed this idea from the work mentioned above on query languages with invention of objects [15,16]. With respect to these works, our approach looks technically simpler, since the mapping mechanism used to create object terms does not allow for recursion. However, we have to deal with the complex constructs presented in the ontology, which significantly complicates matters.
- Our mapping mechanism also deals with the fact that the data sources and the ontology $\mathcal{O}_m$ are based on different semantical assumptions. Indeed, the semantics of data sources follows the so-called "closed world assumption" [28], which intuitively sanctions that every fact that is not explicitly stored in the database is false. On the contrary, the semantics of the ontology is open, in the sense that nothing is assumed about the facts that do not appear explicitely in the ABox.
- We devise a novel query answering method, which is able to fully take into account both the ontology and the mappings from the data layer to the ontology itself. The method extends the ones already presented in [7] for the two sub-logics $DL\text{-}Lite_\mathcal{F}$ and $DL\text{-}Lite_\mathcal{R}$. Similar to these, it works by first *expanding* the query according to the constraints in the ontology. In this case, however, the expanded query is not directly used to compute the result. Rather, the expanded query is the input of a novel step, called *unfolding*, that, taking into account the mappings, translates the expanded query in terms of the relations at the sources. The unfolded query is then evaluated at the sources, and the result is processed so as to conform to the concepts and roles in the ontology. The unfolding step relies on techniques from partial evaluation [21], and the whole query answering method runs in LOGSPACE in data complexity, i.e., the complexity measured with respect to the size of source data.

The rest of the paper is organized as follows. In Section 2 we present the description logic we deal with, namely $DL\text{-}Lite_\mathcal{A}$. In Section 3 we present the framework for linking external data sources to an ontology expressed in $DL\text{-}Lite_\mathcal{A}$. In Section 4 we provide an overview the query answering method, and in Sections 5 and 6 we provide the technical details of such method. Finally, Section 7 concludes the paper.

2 The Description Logic $DL\text{-}Lite_\mathcal{A}$

Description Logics (DLs) [4] are logics that represent the domain of interest in terms of *concepts*, denoting sets of objects, and *roles*, denoting binary relations between (instances of) concepts. Complex concept and role expressions are constructed starting from a set of atomic concepts and roles by applying suitable constructs. Different DLs allow for different constructs. A DL ontology is constituted by a TBox and an ABox, where the first component specifies general properties of concepts and roles, whereas the second component specifies the instances of concepts and roles.

The study of the trade-off between expressive power and computational complexity of reasoning has been traditionally one of the most important issues in DLs. Recent research has shown that OWL, the W3C Web Ontology Language for the Semantic Web[3], if not restricted, is not suited as a formalism for representing ontologies with large amounts of instance assertions in the ABox [7,26,17], since reasoning in such a logic is inherently exponential (coNP-hard) with respect data complexity, i.e., with respect to the size of the ABox.

On the contrary, the *DL-Lite* family [6,7,8] is a family of DLs specifically tailored to capture basic ontology languages, conceptual data models (e.g., Entity-Relationship [1]), and object-oriented formalisms (e.g., basic UML class diagrams[4]) while keeping the complexity of reasoning low. In particular, ontology satisfiability, instance checking, and answering conjunctive queries in these logics can all be done in LOGSPACE with respect to data complexity.

In this section, we present a new logic of the *DL-Lite* family, called $DL\text{-}Lite_\mathcal{A}$. Such a DL is novel with respect to the other DLs of the *DL-Lite* family, in that it takes seriously the distinction between objects and values, and therefore distinguishes:

- concepts from value-domains – while a concept is abstraction for a set of objects, a value-domain, also known as concrete domain [22], denotes a set of (data) values,
- attributes from roles – while a role denotes a binary relation between objects, a (concept) attribute denotes a binary relation between objects and values.

We notice that the distinction between objects and values, although present in OWL, is typically blurred in many DLs. In the following, we first illustrate

---
[3] http://www.w3.org/TR/owl-features/
[4] http://www.omg.org/uml/

the mechanisms provided by $DL\text{-}Lite_\mathcal{A}$ for building expressions, and then we describe how expressions are used to specify ontologies, and which is the form of queries allowed in our logic. Finally, we conclude the section by describing relevant reasoning tasks over $DL\text{-}Lite_\mathcal{A}$ ontologies.

2.1 $DL\text{-}Lite_\mathcal{A}$ Expressions

Like in any other logics, $DL\text{-}Lite_\mathcal{A}$ expressions are built over an alphabet. In our case, the alphabet comprises symbols for atomic concepts, value-domains, atomic roles, atomic attributes, and constants.

The value-domains that we consider in $DL\text{-}Lite_\mathcal{A}$ are those corresponding to the data types adopted by the Resource Description Framework (RDF)[5]. Intuitively, these types represent sets of values that are pairwise disjoint. In the following, we denote such value-domains by $T_1, \ldots, T_n$.

Furthermore, we denote with Γ the alphabet for constants, which we assume partitioned into two sets, namely, Γ_V (the set of constant symbols for values), and Γ_O (the set of constant symbols for objects). In turn, Γ_V is partitioned into n sets $\Gamma_{V_1}, \ldots, \Gamma_{V_n}$, where each Γ_{V_i} is the set of constants for the values in the value-domain T_i.

In providing the specification of our logics, we use the following notation:

- A denotes an *atomic concept*, B a *basic concept*, C a *general concept*, and $\top_C$ denotes the *universal concept*. An atomic concept is a concept denoted by a name. Basic and general concepts are concept expressions whose syntax is given at point 1 below.
- E denotes a basic value-domain, i.e., the range of an attribute, F a *value-domain expression*, and $\top_D$ the *universal value-domain*. The syntax of value-domain expressions is given at point 2 below.
- P denotes an *atomic role*, Q a *basic role*, and R a *general role*. An atomic role is simply a role denoted by a name. Basic and general roles are role expressions whose syntax is given at point 3 below.
- U_C denotes an *atomic attribute* (or simply attribute), and V_C a *general attribute*. An atomic attribute is an attribute denoted by a name, whereas a general attribute is a concept expression whose syntax is given at point 4 below.

Given an attribute U_C, we call the *domain* of U_C, denoted by $\delta(U_C)$, the set of objects that U_C relates to values, and we call *range* of U_C, denoted by $\rho(U_C)$, the set of values that U_C relates to objects. Note that the domain $\delta(U_C)$ of an attribute U_C is a concept, whereas the range $\rho(U_C)$ of U_C is a value-domain.

We are now ready to define $DL\text{-}Lite_\mathcal{A}$ expressions.

1. Concept expressions:

$$B ::= A \mid \exists Q \mid \delta(U_C)$$
$$C ::= \top_C \mid B \mid \neg B \mid \exists Q.C$$

---

[5] http://www.w3.org/RDF/

2. Value-domain expressions:

$$E ::= \rho(U_C)$$
$$F ::= \top_D \mid T_1 \mid \cdots \mid T_n$$

3. Role expressions:

$$Q ::= P \mid P^-$$
$$R ::= Q \mid \neg Q$$

4. Attribute expressions:

$$V_C ::= U_C \mid \neg U_C$$

The meaning of every $DL\text{-}Lite_\mathcal{A}$ expression is sanctioned by the semantics. Following the classical approach in DLs, the semantics of $DL\text{-}Lite_\mathcal{A}$ is given in terms of first-order logic interpretations. All such intepretations agree on the semantics assigned to each value-domain T_i and to each constant in Γ_V. In particular, each T_i is interpreted as the set $val(T_i)$ of values of the corresponding RDF data type, and each $c_i \in \Gamma_V$ is interpreted as one specific value, denoted $val(c_i)$, in $val(T_i)$. Note that, for $i \neq j$, it holds that $val(T_i) \cap val(T_j) = \emptyset$.

Based on the above observations, we can now define the notion of interpretation in $DL\text{-}Lite_\mathcal{A}$. An *interpretation* is a pair $I = (\Delta^I, \cdot^I)$, where

- Δ^I is the interpretation domain, that is the disjoint union of two non-empty sets: Δ_O^I, called the *domain of objects*, and Δ_V^I, called the *domain of values*. In turn, Δ_V^I is the union of $val(T_1), \ldots, val(T_n)$.
- $\cdot^I$ is the *interpretation function*, i.e., a function that assigns an element of Δ^I to each constant in Γ, a subset of Δ^I to each concept and value-domain, and a subset of $\Delta^I \times \Delta^I$ to each role and attribute, in such a way that
  - for each $a \in \Gamma_V$, $a^I = val(a)$,
  - for each $a \in \Gamma_O$, $a^I \in \Delta_O^I$,
  - for each $a, b \in \Gamma$, $a \neq b$ implies $a^I \neq b^I$,
  - for each T_i, $T_i^I = val(T_i)$,
  - the following conditions are satisfied:

$$\top_C^I = \Delta_O^I \qquad (\rho(U_C))^I = \{\, v \mid \exists o.\,(o,v) \in U_C^I \,\}$$
$$\top_D^I = \Delta_V^I \qquad (\delta(U_C))^I = \{\, o \mid \exists o.\,(o,v) \in U_C^I \,\}$$
$$A^I \subseteq \Delta_O^I \qquad (P^-)^I = \{\, (o,o') \mid (o',o) \in P^I \,\}$$
$$P^I \subseteq \Delta_O^I \times \Delta_O^I \qquad (\exists Q)^I = \{\, o \mid \exists o'.\,(o,o') \in Q^I \,\}$$
$$U_C^I \subseteq \Delta_O^I \times \Delta_V^I \qquad (\exists Q.C)^I = \{\, o \mid \exists o'.\,(o,o') \in Q^I \wedge o' \in C^I \,\}$$
$$(\neg U_C)^I = (\Delta_O^I \times \Delta_V^I) \setminus U_C^I \qquad (\neg B)^I = \Delta_O^I \setminus B^I$$
$$(\neg Q)^I = (\Delta_O^I \times \Delta_O^I) \setminus Q^I$$

Note that the above definition implies that different constants are interpreted differently in the domain, i.e., $DL\text{-}Lite_\mathcal{A}$ adopts the so-called unique name assumption.

2.2 $DL\text{-}Lite_\mathcal{A}$ Ontologies

As usual when expressing ontologies in DLs, a $DL\text{-}Lite_\mathcal{A}$ ontology $\mathcal{O} = \langle \mathcal{T}, \mathcal{A} \rangle$ represents the domain of discourse in terms of two components: the TBox $\mathcal{T}$, representing the intensional knowledge, and the ABox $\mathcal{A}$, representing the extensional knowledge. $DL\text{-}Lite_\mathcal{A}$ TBoxes and ABoxes are defined as follows. $DL\text{-}Lite_\mathcal{A}$ *intensional assertions* are assertions of the form:

$$
\begin{array}{lll}
B \sqsubseteq C & \text{(concept inclusion assertion)} \\
Q \sqsubseteq R & \text{(role inclusion assertion)} \\
E \sqsubseteq F & \text{(value-domain inclusion assertion)} \\
U_C \sqsubseteq V_C & \text{(attribute inclusion assertion)} \\
(\text{funct } Q) & \text{(role functionality assertion)} \\
(\text{funct } U_C) & \text{(attribute functionality assertion)}
\end{array}
$$

A concept (respectively, value-domain, role, and attribute) inclusion assertion expresses that a basic concept B (respectively, basic value-domain E, basic role Q, and atomic attribute U_C) is subsumed by a general concept C (respectively, value-domain F, role R, attribute V_C). A role functionality assertion expresses the (global) functionality of a role. In the case where $Q = P$, the functionality constraint is imposed on an atomic role, while in the case where $Q = P^-$, it is imposed on the inverse of an atomic role. Analogously, an attribute functionality assertion expresses the (global) functionality of an atomic attribute. Concept (respectively, value-domain, and role) inclusions of the form $B_1 \sqsubseteq \neg B_2$ (respectively, $E_1 \sqsubseteq \neg E_2$, $Q_1 \sqsubseteq \neg Q_2$) are called *negative inclusion assertions*.

Then, $DL\text{-}Lite_\mathcal{A}$ TBoxes are finite sets of $DL\text{-}Lite_\mathcal{A}$ intensional assertions where suitable limitations in the combination of such assertions are imposed. To precisely describe such limitations, we first introduce some preliminary notions. An atomic attribute U_C (respectively, a basic role Q) is called an *identifying property in a TBox* $\mathcal{T}$, if $\mathcal{T}$ contains a functionality assertion (funct U_C) (respectively, (funct Q)). Let X be an atomic attribute or a basic role. We say that X *appears positively* (respectively, *negatively*) in the right-hand side of an inclusion assertion α if α has the form $Y \sqsubseteq X$ (respectively, $Y \sqsubseteq \neg X$). Also, an atomic attribute or a basic role is called *primitive in a TBox* $\mathcal{T}$, if it does not appear positively in the right-hand side of an inclusion assertion of $\mathcal{T}$, and it does not appear in an expression of the form $\exists Q.C$ in $\mathcal{T}$. Then,

> a $DL\text{-}Lite_\mathcal{A}$ TBox is a finite set $\mathcal{T}$ of $DL\text{-}Lite_\mathcal{A}$ intensional assertions satisfying the condition that every identifying property in $\mathcal{T}$ is primitive in $\mathcal{T}$.

Roughly speaking, in a $DL\text{-}Lite_\mathcal{A}$ TBox, *identifying properties cannot be specialized*, i.e., they cannot appear positively in the right-hand side of inclusion assertions.

We now specify the semantics of a TBox $\mathcal{T}$, again in terms of interpretations. An interpretation I satisfies

- a concept (respectively, value-domain, role, attribute) inclusion assertion $B \sqsubseteq C$ (respectively, $E \sqsubseteq F$, $Q \sqsubseteq R$, $U_C \sqsubseteq V_C$), if

$$B^I \subseteq C^I \quad \text{(respectively, } E^I \subseteq F^I, Q^I \subseteq R^I, U_C^I \subseteq V_C^I\text{)}$$

- a role functionality assertion (funct Q), if for each $o_1, o_2, o_3 \in \Delta_O^I$

$$(o_1, o_2) \in Q^I \text{ and } (o_1, o_3) \in Q^I \text{ implies } o_2 = o_3$$

- an attribute functionality assertion (funct U_C), if for each $o \in \Delta_O^I$ and $v_1, v_2 \in \Delta_V^I$

$$(o, v_1) \in U_C^I \text{ and } (o, v_2) \in U_C^I \text{ implies } v_1 = v_2.$$

I is a *model* of a *DL-Lite$_\mathcal{A}$* TBox $\mathcal{T}$, or, equivalently, I *satisfies* $\mathcal{T}$, written $I \models \mathcal{T}$, if and only if I satisfies all intensional assertions in $\mathcal{T}$.

We next illustrate an example of a *DL-Lite$_\mathcal{A}$* TBox. In all the examples of this paper, we write concept names in *lowercase*, role names in *UPPERCASE*, attribute names in sans serif font, and domain names in typewriter font.

Example 1. Let $\mathcal{T}$ be the TBox containing the following assertions:

$tempEmp \sqsubseteq employee$	(1)	$project \sqsubseteq \delta(\mathsf{ProjName})$	(9)
$manager \sqsubseteq employee$	(2)	(funct $\mathsf{ProjName}$)	(10)
$employee \sqsubseteq person$	(3)	$\rho(\mathsf{ProjName}) \sqsubseteq \mathtt{xsd{:}string}$	(11)
$employee \sqsubseteq \exists WORKS\text{-}FOR$	(4)	$tempEmp \sqsubseteq \delta(\mathsf{until})$	(12)
$\exists WORKS\text{-}FOR^- \sqsubseteq project$	(5)	$\delta(\mathsf{until}) \sqsubseteq \exists WORKS\text{-}FOR$	(13)
$person \sqsubseteq \delta(\mathsf{PersName})$	(6)	(funct until)	(14)
(funct $\mathsf{PersName}$)	(7)	$\rho(\mathsf{until}) \sqsubseteq \mathtt{xsd{:}date}$	(15)
$\rho(\mathsf{PersName}) \sqsubseteq \mathtt{xsd{:}string}$	(8)	$manager \sqsubseteq \neg\delta(\mathsf{until})$	(16)

The above TBox $\mathcal{T}$ models information about employees and projects they work for. Specifically, the assertions in $\mathcal{T}$ state the following. Managers and temporary employees are two kinds of employees (2, 1), and employees are persons (3). Each employee works for at least one project (4, 5), whereas each person and each project has a unique name (6, 7, 9, 10). Both person names and project names are strings (8, 11), whereas the attribute until associates objects with dates (14, 15). In particular, any temporary employee has an associated date (which indicates the expiration date of her/his contract) (12), and everyone having a value for attribute until participates in the role $WORKS\text{-}FOR$ (13). Finally, $\mathcal{T}$ specifies that a manager does not have any value for the attribute until (16), meaning that a manager has a permanent position, Note that this implies that no employee is simultaneously a temporary employee and a manager. □

We now specify the form of *DL-Lite$_\mathcal{A}$* ABoxes. A *DL-Lite$_\mathcal{A}$* ABox is a finite set of assertions, called *membership assertions*, of the form:

$$A(a), \quad P(a, b), \quad U_C(a, b)$$

where a and b are constants in the alphabet Γ.

As for the semantics of a $DL\text{-}Lite_\mathcal{A}$ ABox $\mathcal{A}$, we now specify when an interpretation $I = (\Delta^I, \cdot^I)$ satisfies a membership assertion α in $\mathcal{A}$, written $I \models \alpha$. I satisfies:

- $A(a)$ if $a^I \in A^I$;
- $P(a,b)$ if $(a^I, b^I) \in P^I$;
- $U_C(a,b)$ if $(a^I, b^I) \in U_C^I$.

I is *model of* $\mathcal{A}$, or, equivalently, I *satisfies* $\mathcal{A}$, written $I \models \mathcal{A}$, if I satisfies all the membership assertions in $\mathcal{A}$.

We next illustrate an example of a $DL\text{-}Lite_\mathcal{A}$ ABox. In the example, we use the **bold face** font for constants in Γ_O, and the *slanted* font for constants in Γ_V.

Example 2. Consider the following ABox $\mathcal{A}$:

$tempEmp(\mathbf{Palm})$	(17)
$\text{until}(\mathbf{Palm}, \textit{25-09-05})$	(18)
$\text{ProjName}(\mathbf{DIS\text{-}1212}, \textit{QuOnto})$	(19)
$manager(\mathbf{White})$	(20)
$WORKS\text{-}FOR(\mathbf{White}, \mathbf{FP6\text{-}7603})$	(21)
$\text{ProjName}(\mathbf{FP6\text{-}7603}, \textit{Tones})$	(22)

The ABox assertions in $\mathcal{A}$ state that the object (identified by the constant) **Palm** denotes a temporary employee who works until the date *25-09-05*. Moreover, **DIS-1212** and **FP6-7603** are projects whose names are respectively *QuOnto* and *Tones*. Finally, the object **White** is a manager. □

Now that we have introduced $DL\text{-}Lite_\mathcal{A}$ TBoxes and ABoxes, we are able to define the semantics of a $DL\text{-}Lite_\mathcal{A}$ ontology, which is given in terms of interpretations which satisfy both the TBox and the ABox of the ontology. More formally, an interpretation $I = (\Delta^I, \cdot^I)$ is *model of a $DL\text{-}Lite_\mathcal{A}$ ontology $\mathcal{O} = \langle \mathcal{T}, \mathcal{A} \rangle$*, or, equivalently, I *satisfies* $\mathcal{O}$, written $I \models \mathcal{O}$, if both $I \models \mathcal{T}$ and $I \models \mathcal{A}$. We say that $\mathcal{O}$ is *satisfiable* if it has at least one model.

Example 3. Let $\mathcal{O} = \langle \mathcal{T}, \mathcal{A} \rangle$ be the $DL\text{-}Lite_\mathcal{A}$ ontology whose TBox $\mathcal{T}$ is the one of Example 1, and whose ABox $\mathcal{A}$ is the one of Example 2. The first observation is that $\mathcal{O}$ is satisfiable. Furthermore, it is easy to see that every model $I = (\Delta^I, \cdot^I)$ of $\mathcal{A}$ satisfies the following conditions:

$$\mathbf{Palm}^I \in tempEmp^I$$
$$(\mathbf{Palm}^I, \textit{25-09-05}^I) \in \text{until}^I$$
$$(\mathbf{DIS\text{-}1212}^I, \textit{QuOnto}^I) \in \text{ProjName}^I$$
$$\mathbf{White}^I \in manager^I$$
$$(\mathbf{White}^I, \mathbf{FP6\text{-}7603}^I) \in WORKS\text{-}FOR^I$$
$$(\mathbf{FP6\text{-}7603}^I, \textit{Tones}^I) \in \text{ProjName}^I.$$

Furthermore, the following are necessary conditions for I to be a model of the TBox $\mathcal{T}$ (we indicate in parenthesis the reference to the relevant axiom of $\mathcal{T}$):

$\mathbf{Palm}^I \in \mathit{employee}^I$, to satisfy inclusion assertion (1)
$\mathbf{White}^I \in \mathit{employee}^I$, to satisfy inclusion assertion (2)
$\mathbf{Palm}^I \in \mathit{person}^I$, to satisfy inclusion assertion (3)
$\mathbf{White}^I \in \mathit{person}^I$, to satisfy inclusion assertion (3)
$\mathbf{Palm}^I \in \exists \mathit{WORKS\text{-}FOR}^I$, to satisfy inclusion assertion (4)
$\mathbf{FP6\text{-}7603}^I \in \mathit{project}^I$, to satisfy inclusion assertion (5)
$\mathbf{Palm}^I \in (\delta(\mathsf{PersName}))^I$, to satisfy inclusion assertion (6)
$\mathbf{White}^I \in (\delta(\mathsf{PersName}))^I$, to satisfy inclusion assertion (6)

Notice that, in order for an interpretation I to satisfy the condition specified in the fifth row above, there must be an object $o \in \Delta_O^I$ such that $(\mathbf{Palm}^I, o) \in \mathit{WORKS\text{-}FOR}^I$. According to the inclusion assertion (5), such an object o must also belong to $\mathit{project}^I$ (indeed, in our ontology, every employee works for at least one project). Similarly, the last two rows above derive from the property that every person must have a name (inclusion (6)).

We note that, besides satisfying the conditions discussed above, an interpretation I' may also add other elements to the interpretation of concepts, attributes, and roles specified by I. For instance, the interpretation I' which adds to I the tuple

$$(\mathbf{White}^{I'}, \mathbf{DIS\text{-}1212}^{I'}) \in \mathit{WORKS\text{-}FOR}^{I'}$$

is still a model of the ontology.

Note, finally, that there exists no model of $\mathcal{O}$ such that **White** is interpreted as a temporary employee, since, according to (20), **White** is a manager and, as observed in Example 1, the sets of managers and temporary employees are disjoint. □

The above example clearly shows the difference between a database and an ontology. From a database point of view the ontology $\mathcal{O}$ discussed in the example might seem incorrect: for example, while the TBOx $\mathcal{T}$ sanctions that every person has a name, there is no explicit name for **White** (who is a person, because he has been asserted to be a manager, and every manager is a person) in the ABox $\mathcal{A}$. However, the ontology is not incorrect: the axiom stating that every person has a name simply specifies that in every model of $\mathcal{O}$ there will be a name for **White**, even if such a name is not known.

2.3 Queries over *DL-Lite$_\mathcal{A}$* Ontologies

We are interested in expressing queries over ontologies expressed in *DL-Lite$_\mathcal{A}$*, and similarly to the case of relational databases, the basic query class that we consider is the class of conjunctive queries.

A *conjunctive query* (CQ) q over a *DL-Lite$_\mathcal{A}$* ontology is an expression of the form

$$q(\boldsymbol{x}) \leftarrow \mathit{conj}(\boldsymbol{x}, \boldsymbol{y})$$

where x is a tuple of distinct variables, the so-called *distinguished variables*, y is a tuple of distinct existentially quantified variables (not occurring in x), called the *non-distinguished* variables, and $conj(x, y)$ is a *conjunction* of atoms of the form $A(x)$, $P(x,y)$, $D(x)$, $U_C(x,y)$, $x = y$, where:

- A, P, D, and U_C are respectively an atomic concept, an atomic role, an atomic value-domain, and an atomic attribute in $\mathcal{O}$,
- x, y are either variables in x or in y, or constants in Γ.

We say that $q(x)$ is the *head* of the query whereas $conj(x, y)$ is the *body*. Moreover, the *arity* of q is the arity of x.

We will also refer to the notion of *conjunctive query with inequalities* (CQI), that is simply a conjunctive query in which atoms of the $x \neq y$ (called inequalities) may appear. Finally, a *union of conjunctive queries* (UCQ) is a query of the form:

$$Q(x) \leftarrow conj_1(x, y_i) \cup \cdots \cup conj_n(x, y_n).$$

Unions of conjunctive queries with inequalities are obvious extensions of unions of conjunctive queries. In the following, we use the Datalog notation for unions of conjunctive queries. In this notation a union of conjuctive queries is written in the form

$$Q(x) \leftarrow conj_1(x, y_1)$$
$$\ldots\ldots\ldots$$
$$Q(x) \leftarrow conj_n(x, y_n)$$

Given an interpretation $I = (\Delta^I, \cdot^I)$, the query $Q(x) \leftarrow \varphi(x, y)$ (either a conjunctive query or a union of conjunctive queries) is interpreted in I as the set of tuples $o_x \in \Delta^I \times \cdots \times \Delta^I$ such that there exists $o_y \in \Delta^I \times \cdots \times \Delta^I$ such that if we assign to the tuple of variables (x, y) the tuple (o_x, o_y), then the formula φ is true in I [1].

Example 4. Let $\mathcal{O}$ be the ontology introduced in Example 3. Consider the following query asking for all employees:

$$q_1(x) \leftarrow employee(x).$$

If I is the model described in Example 3, we have that:

$$q_1^I = \{(\mathbf{White}^I), (\mathbf{Palm}^I)\}.$$

Note that we would obtain an analogous result by considering the model I' introduced in Example 3. Suppose now that we ask for project workers, together with the name of the project s/he works in:

$$q_2(x, y) \leftarrow \textit{WORKS-FOR}(x, z), \mathsf{ProjName}(z, y).$$

Then we have the following (we assume that, according to I, p is the project for which $\mathbf{Palm}^I$ works):

- $q_2^I = \{(\mathbf{White}^I, \mathit{Tones}^I), (\mathbf{Palm}^I, p)\}$;

- $q_2^{I'} = \{(\mathbf{White}^{I'}, Tones^{I'}), (\mathbf{White}^{I'}, QuOnto^{I'})\}.$ □

Let us now describe what it means to answer a query over a $DL\text{-}Lite_\mathcal{A}$ ontology. Let $\mathcal{O}$ be a $DL\text{-}Lite_\mathcal{A}$ ontology, Q a UCQ over $\mathcal{O}$, and $\boldsymbol{t}$ a tuple of elements of Γ. We say that $\boldsymbol{t}$ is a *certain answer* to q over $\mathcal{O}$, written $\boldsymbol{t} \in ans(Q, \mathcal{O})$, if for every model I of $\mathcal{O}$, we have that $\boldsymbol{t}^I \in Q^I$. Answering a query Q posed to an ontology $\mathcal{O}$ means exactly to compute the certain answers.

Example 5. Consider again the ontology introduced in Example 3, and queries q_1, q_2 of Example 4. One can easily verify that the set of certain answers to q_1 is $\{\mathbf{White}, \mathbf{Palm}\}$, whereas the set of certain answers to q_2 is $\{(\mathbf{White}, QuOnto)\}$.

2.4 Reasoning over $DL\text{-}Lite_\mathcal{A}$ Ontologies

Our logic $DL\text{-}Lite_\mathcal{A}$ is equipped with traditional DL reasoning services, such as concept and role subsumption, ontology satisfiability and instance checking. Notably, it can be shown (cf. [8]), that all these services can be reduced to satisfiability and query answering. In the following, we therefore briefly discuss satisfiability and query answering for $DL\text{-}Lite_\mathcal{A}$ ontologies, and present some important properties of such services. The technical results mentioned in this subsection are easy extensions of analogous results presented in [8,6,27].

Before discussing the main properties of our reasoning method, we observe that we assume that the ABox of a $DL\text{-}Lite_\mathcal{A}$ ontology is represented by a relational database. More precisely, if $\mathcal{O} = \langle \mathcal{T}, \mathcal{A} \rangle$ is a $DL\text{-}Lite_\mathcal{A}$ ontology, then we represent $\mathcal{A}$ in terms of the relational database $db(\mathcal{A})$, defined as follows:

- $db(\mathcal{A})$ contains one unary relation T_A for every atomic concept A appearing in $\mathcal{T}$. Such relation has the tuple t in $db(\mathcal{A})$ if and only if the assertion $A(t)$ is in $\mathcal{A}$.
- $db(\mathcal{A})$ contains one binary relation T_P for every atomic role P appearing in $\mathcal{T}$. Such relation has the tuple t in $db(\mathcal{A})$ if and only if the assertion $P(t)$ is in $\mathcal{A}$.
- $db(\mathcal{A})$ contains one binary relation T_U for every atomic attribute U appearing in $\mathcal{T}$. Such relation has the tuple t in $db(\mathcal{A})$ if and only if the assertion $U(t)$ is in $\mathcal{A}$.

One notable property of $DL\text{-}Lite_\mathcal{A}$ is that, by virtue of the careful definition of the expressive power of the logic, reasoning over the ontology $\mathcal{O} = \langle \mathcal{T}, \mathcal{A} \rangle$ can be reduced to answering suitable queries over $db(\mathcal{A})$.

As for satisfiability, i.e., the problem of checking whether $\mathcal{O} = \langle \mathcal{T}, \mathcal{A} \rangle$ is satisfiable, it can be shown [8,27] that such a reasoning task can be reduced to the task of evaluating a suitable query, called $\mathsf{Violates}(\mathcal{T})$. Intuitively, $\mathsf{Violates}(\mathcal{T})$ is a first-ored query that asks for all constants in $\mathcal{A}$ violating either:

- explicit constraints corresponding to the functionality and disjointness assertions in $\mathcal{T}$, or
- implicit constraints, following from the semantics of $\mathcal{T}$, namely constraints imposing that every concept is disjoint from every domain, and that, for every pair T_i, T_j of *value–domains*, T_i and T_j are disjoint.

We denote with $\mathsf{ViolatesDB}(\mathcal{T})$ the function that transforms the query $\mathsf{Violates}(\mathcal{T})$ by changing every predicate X in $\mathsf{Violates}(\mathcal{T})$ into T_X. Therefore, the query $\mathsf{ViolatesDB}(\mathcal{T})$ is equivalent to $\mathsf{Violates}(\mathcal{T})$, but is expressed over $db(\mathcal{A})$. Also, it is immediate to verify that $\mathsf{ViolatesDB}(\mathcal{T})$ can be expressed in SQL.

The correctness of this reduction is sanctioned by the results of [8,6,27], summarized here by the following theorem.

Theorem 1. *The DL-Lite$_\mathcal{A}$ ontology $\mathcal{O} = \langle \mathcal{T}, \mathcal{A} \rangle$ is satisfiable if and only if the result of evaluating $\mathsf{Violates}(\mathcal{T})$ over $\mathcal{O}_m$ is the empty set, if and only if the result of evaluating $\mathsf{ViolatesDB}(\mathcal{T})$ over $db(\mathcal{A})$ is the empty set.*

Example 6. Consider the ontology introduced in Example 3. Then, $\mathsf{Violates}(\mathcal{T})$ is a union of conjunctive queries including the following disjuncts (corresponding to explicit constraints):

$$Q^s(x) \leftarrow manager(x), until(x,y)$$
$$Q^s(x) \leftarrow \mathsf{PersName}(x,y_1), \mathsf{PersName}(x,y_2), y_1 \neq y_2$$
$$Q^s(x) \leftarrow \mathsf{ProjName}(x,y_1), \mathsf{ProjName}(x,y_2), y_1 \neq y_2$$
$$Q^s(x) \leftarrow until(x,y_1), until(x,y_2), y_1 \neq y_2$$

□

As for query answering, it can be shown that computing the certain answers of a query with respect to a satisfiable DL-Lite$_\mathcal{A}$ ontology $\mathcal{O} = \langle \mathcal{T}, \mathcal{A} \rangle$ can be reduced, through a process called *perfect reformulation*, to the evaluation over $db(\mathcal{A})$ of a suitable union of conjunctive queries. The crucial task of perfect reformulation is carried out by the function $\mathsf{PerfectRef}$. Informally, $\mathsf{PerfectRef}$ takes as input a UCQ Q over $\mathcal{O}_m$ and the TBox $\mathcal{T}$, and reformulates Q into a new query Q', which is still a UCQ and has the following property: the answers to Q' with respect to $\langle \emptyset, \mathcal{A} \rangle$ coincide with the certain answers to Q with respect to $\langle \mathcal{T}, \mathcal{A} \rangle$. Thus, all the knowledge represented by the TBox $\mathcal{T}$ that is relevant for computing the certain answers of the query Q is compiled into $\mathsf{PerfectRef}(Q, \mathcal{T})$.

We denote with $\mathsf{PerfectRefDB}(Q, \mathcal{T})$ the function that transforms the query $\mathsf{PerfectRef}(Q, \mathcal{T})$ by changing every predicate X in $\mathsf{PerfectRef}(Q, \mathcal{T})$ into T_X. Therefore, the query $\mathsf{PerfectRefDB}(Q, \mathcal{T})$ is equivalent to $\mathsf{PerfectRef}(Q, \mathcal{T})$, but is expressed over $db(\mathcal{A})$. Also, it is immediate to verify that $\mathsf{PerfectRefDB}(Q, \mathcal{T})$ can be expressed in SQL.

From the results of [8,6,27], we have the following:

Theorem 2. *If $\mathcal{O} = \langle \mathcal{T}, \mathcal{A} \rangle$ is a satisfiable DL-Lite$_\mathcal{A}$ ontology, and Q is a union of conjunctive queries over $\mathcal{O}$, then $\mathbf{t} \in ans(Q, \mathcal{O})$ if and only if $\mathbf{t} \in ans(\mathsf{PerfectRef}(Q, \mathcal{T}), \langle \emptyset, \mathcal{A} \rangle)$, if and only if $\mathbf{t}$ is in the result of evaluating $\mathsf{PerfectRefDB}(Q, \mathcal{T})$ over $db(\mathcal{A})$.*

Example 7. Consider again the ontology $\mathcal{O}$ of Example 3 and the query q asking for all workers, i.e., those objects which participate to the *WORKS-FOR* role:

$$q(x) \leftarrow \textit{WORKS-FOR}(x,y).$$

It can be shown that PerfectRef($q, \mathcal{T}$) is the following query Q^p (that is a UCQ):

$$Q^p(x) \leftarrow \textit{WORKS-FOR}(x, y)$$
$$Q^p(x) \leftarrow \textsf{until}(x, y)$$
$$Q^p(x) \leftarrow tempEmp(x)$$
$$Q^p(x) \leftarrow employee(x)$$
$$Q^p(x) \leftarrow manager(x).$$

By virtue of the above theorem, the result of evaluating Q^p over $db(\mathcal{A})$ coincides with the set of certain answers to q over $\mathcal{O}$. Roughly speaking, in order to return all workers, Q^p looks in those concepts, relations, and attributes, whose extensions in $db(\mathcal{A})$ provide objects that are workers, according to the knowledge specified by $\mathcal{T}$. In our case, the answer to the query is {**White, Palm**}. □

We finally point out that, from the properties discussed above, namely that both ontology satisfiability and query answering are reducible to first-order query evaluation over a suitable relational database, it follows that, after the reformulation process, the task of computing the certain answers to a query can be delegated to a standard relational DBMS [7]. In turn, this implies that all reasoning tasks in *DL-Lite$_\mathcal{A}$* can be done in LOGSPACE with respect to data complexity [8,27].

3   Linking Relational Data to *DL-Lite$_\mathcal{A}$* Ontologies

The discussion presented in the previous section on *DL-Lite$_\mathcal{A}$* ontologies assumed a relational representation for the ABox assertions. This is a reasonable assumption only in those cases where the ontology is managed by an ad-hoc system, and is built from scratch for the specific application.

We argue that this is not a typical scenario in current applications (e.g., in Enterprise Application Integration). As we said in the introduction, we believe that one of the most interesting real-world usages of ontologies is what we call "ontology-based data access". Ontology-based data access is the problem of accessing a set of existing data sources by means of a conceptual representation expressed in terms of an ontology. In such a scenario, the TBox of the ontology provides a shared, uniform, abstract view of the intensional level of the application domain, whereas the information about the extensional level (the instances of the ontology) reside in the data sources that are developed independently of the conceptual layer, and are managed by traditional technologies (such as the relational database technology). In other words, the ABox of the ontology does not exist as an independent syntactic object. Rather, the instances of concepts and roles in the ontology are simply an abstract and virtual representation of some real data stored in existing data sources. Therefore, the problem arises of establishing sound mechanisms for linking existing data to the instances of the concepts and the roles in the ontology.

In this section we present the basic idea for our solution to this problem, by presenting a mapping mechanism that enables a designer to link existing data sources to an ontology expressed in *DL-Lite$_\mathcal{A}$*, and by illustrating a formal framework capturing the notion of $DL\text{-}Lite_\mathcal{A}$ ontology with mappings. In the following, we assume that the data sources are expressed in terms of the relational data model. In other words, all the technical development presented in the rest of this section assumes that the set of sources to be linked to the ontology is one relational database. Note that this is a realistic assumption, since many data federation tools are now available that are able to wrap a set of heterogeneous sources and present them as a single relational database.

Before delving into the details of the method, a preliminary discussion on the notorious *impedance mismatch problem* between values (data) and objects is in order [24]. When mapping relational data sources to ontologies, one should take into account that sources store values, whereas instances of concepts are objects, where each object should be denoted by an ad hoc identifier (e.g., a constant in logic), not to be confused with any data item. For example, if a data source stores data about persons, it is likely that values for social security numbers, names, etc. will appear in the sources. However, at the conceptual level, the ontology will represent persons in terms of a concept, and instances of such concepts will be denoted by object constants.

One could argue that data sources might, in some cases, store directly object identifiers. However, in order to use such object identifiers at the conceptual level, one should make sure that such identifiers have been chosen on the basis of an "agreement" among the sources on the form used to represent objects. This is something occurring very rarely in practice. For all the above reasons, in $DL\text{-}Lite_\mathcal{A}$, we take a radical approach. To face the impedance mismatch problem, and to tackle the possible lack of an a-priori agreement on identification mechanisms at the sources, we keep data values appearing in the sources separate from object identifiers at the conceptual level. In particular, we consider object identifiers formed by (logic) terms built out from data values stored at the sources. The way by which these terms will be defined starting from the data at the sources will be specified through suitable mapping assertions, to be described later in this section. Note that this idea traces back to the work done in deductive object-oriented databases [15].

To realize this idea from a technical point of view, we specialize the alphabets of object constants in a particular way, that we now describe in detail.

We remind the reader that Γ_V is the alphabet of value constants in $DL\text{-}Lite_\mathcal{A}$. We assume that data appearing at the sources are denoted by constants in Γ_V[6], and we introduce a new alphabet Λ of function symbols in $DL\text{-}Lite_\mathcal{A}$, where each function symbol has an associated arity, specifying the number of arguments it accepts. On the basis of Γ_V and Λ, we inductively define the set $\tau(\Lambda, \Gamma_V)$ of all *terms* of the form $f(d_1, \ldots, d_n)$ such that

- $f \in \Lambda$,
- the arity of f is $n > 0$, and
- $d_1, \ldots, d_n \in \Gamma_V$.

---

[6] We could also introduce suitable conversion functions in order to translate values stored at the sources into value constants in Γ_V, but, for the sake of simplicity, we do not deal with this aspect here.

We finally sanction that the set Γ_O of symbols used in *DL-Lite$_A$* for denoting objects actually coincides with $\tau(\Lambda, \Gamma_V)$. In other words, we use the terms built out of Γ_V using the function symbols in Λ for denoting the instances of concepts in *DL-Lite$_A$* ontologies.

All the notions defined for our logics remain unchanged. In particular, an interpretation $I = (\Delta^I, \cdot^I)$ still assigns a different element of Δ^I to every element of Γ, and, given that Γ_O coincides with $\tau(\Lambda, \Gamma_V)$, this implies that different terms in $\tau(\Lambda, \Gamma_V)$ are interpreted as different objects in Δ_O^I, i.e., we enforce the unique name assumption on terms. Formally, this means that I is such that:

- for each $a \in \Gamma_V$: $a^I \in \Delta_V^I$,
- for each $a \in \Gamma_O$, i.e., for each $a \in \tau(\Lambda, \Gamma_V)$: $a^I \in \Delta_O^I$,
- for each $a, b \in \Gamma$, $a \neq b$ implies $a^I \neq b^I$.

The syntax and the semantics of a *DL-Lite$_A$* TBox, ABox and UCQ, introduced in the previous section, do not need to be modified. In particular, from the point of view of the semantics of queries, the notion of certain answers is exactly the same as the one presented in Section 2.4.

We can now turn our attention to the problem of specifying mapping assertions linking the data at the sources to the objects in the ontology. In the following, we make the following assumptions:

- As we said before, we assume that the data sources are wrapped into a relational database $\mathcal{DB}$ (constituted by the relational schema, and the extensions of the relations), so that we can query such data by using SQL, and that all value constants stored in $\mathcal{DB}$ belong to Γ_V.
- As mentioned in the introduction, the database $\mathcal{DB}$ is independent from the ontology; in other words, our aim is to link to the ontology a collection of data that exist autonomously, and have not been necessarily structured with the purpose of storing the ontology instances.
- $ans(\varphi, \mathcal{DB})$ denotes the set of tuples (of the arity of φ) of value constants returned as the result of the evaluation of the SQL query φ over the database $\mathcal{DB}$.

With these assumptions in place, to actually realize the link between the data and the ontology, we adapt principles and techniques from the literature on data integration [19]. In particular, we use the notion of *mappings* as described below.

A *DL-Lite$_A$ ontology with mappings* is characterized by a triple $\mathcal{O}_m = \langle \mathcal{T}, \mathcal{M}, \mathcal{DB} \rangle$ such that:

- $\mathcal{T}$ is a *DL-Lite$_A$* TBox;
- $\mathcal{DB}$ is a relational database;
- $\mathcal{M}$ is a set of *mapping assertions*, partitioned into two sets, $\mathcal{M}_t$ and $\mathcal{M}_a$, where:
  - $\mathcal{M}_t$ is a set of so-called *typing mapping assertions*, each one of the form

$$\Phi \leadsto T_i$$

where Φ is a query of arity 1 over $\mathcal{DB}$ denoting the projection of one relation over one of its columns, and T_i is one of the $DL\text{-}Lite_{\mathcal{A}}$ data types;
- $\mathcal{M}_a$ is a set of *data-to-object mapping assertions* (or simply mapping assertions), each one of the form

$$\Phi \rightsquigarrow \Psi$$

where Φ is an arbitrary SQL query of arity $n > 0$ over $\mathcal{DB}$, Ψ is a conjunctive query over $\mathcal{T}$ of arity $n' > 0$ without non-distinguished variables, that possibly involves *variable terms*. A variable term is a term of the same form as the object terms introduced above, with the difference that variables appear as argument of the function. In other words, a variable term has the form $f(z)$, where f is a function symbol in Λ of arity m, and z denotes an m-tuple of variables.

We briefly comment on the assertions in $\mathcal{M}$ as defined above. Typing mapping assertions are used to assign appropriate types to constants in the relations of $\mathcal{DB}$. Basically, these assertions are used for interpreting the values stored in the database in terms of the types used in the ontology, and their usefulness is evident in all cases where the types in the data sources do not directly correspond to the types used in the ontology. Data-to-object mapping assertions, on the other hand, are used to map data in the database to instances of concepts, roles, and attributes in the ontology.

We next give an example of $DL\text{-}Lite_{\mathcal{A}}$ ontology with mappings.

Example 8. Let $\mathcal{DB}$ be the database constituted by a set of relations with the following signature:

$$D_1[\text{SSN}:\textbf{STRING},\text{PROJ}:\textbf{STRING},\text{ D}:\textbf{DATE}],$$
$$D_2[\text{SSN}:\textbf{STRING},\text{NAME}:\textbf{STRING}],$$
$$D_3[\text{CODE}:\textbf{STRING},\text{NAME}:\textbf{STRING}],$$
$$D_4[\text{CODE}:\textbf{STRING},\text{SSN}:\textbf{STRING}]$$

We assume that, from the analysis of the above data sources, the following meaning of the above relations has been derived. Relation D_1 stores tuples (s, p, d), where s and p are strings and d is a date, such that s is the social security number of a temporary employee, p is the name of the project s/he works for (different projects have different names), and d is the ending date of the employment. Relation D_2 stores tuples (s, n) of strings consisting of the social security number s of an employee and her/his name n. Relation D_3 stores tuples (c, n) of strings consisting of the code c of a manager and her/his name n. Finally, relation D_4 relates managers' code with their social security number.

A possible extension for the above relations is given by the following sets of tuples:

$$D_1 = \{(20903,\ Tones,\ 25\text{-}09\text{-}05)\}$$
$$D_2 = \{(20903,\ Rossi),\ (55577,\ White)\}$$
$$D_3 = \{(X11,\ White),\ (X12,\ Black)\}$$
$$D_4 = \{(X11,\ 29767)\}$$

Now, let $\Lambda = \{\mathbf{pers}, \mathbf{proj}, \mathbf{mgr}\}$ be a set of function symbols, where **pers**, **proj** and **mgr** are function symbols of arity 1. Consider the $DL\text{-}Lite_{\mathcal{A}}$ ontology with mappings $\mathcal{O}_m = \langle \mathcal{T}, \mathcal{M}, \mathcal{DB} \rangle$ such that $\mathcal{T}$ is the TBox of Example 1, and $\mathcal{M} = \mathcal{M}_t \cup \mathcal{M}_a$, where $\mathcal{M}_t$ is as follows:

$$
\begin{aligned}
M_{t_1} &: \text{SELECT SSN FROM } D_1 \rightsquigarrow \text{xsd:string} \\
M_{t_2} &: \text{SELECT SSN FROM } D_2 \rightsquigarrow \text{xsd:string} \\
M_{t_3} &: \text{SELECT CODE FROM } D_3 \rightsquigarrow \text{xsd:string} \\
M_{t_4} &: \text{SELECT CODE FROM } D_4 \rightsquigarrow \text{xsd:string} \\
M_{t_5} &: \text{SELECT PROJ FROM } D_1 \rightsquigarrow \text{xsd:string} \\
M_{t_6} &: \text{SELECT NAME FROM } D_2 \rightsquigarrow \text{xsd:string} \\
M_{t_7} &: \text{SELECT NAME FROM } D_3 \rightsquigarrow \text{xsd:string} \\
M_{t_8} &: \text{SELECT SSN FROM } D_4 \rightsquigarrow \text{xsd:string} \\
M_{t_9} &: \text{SELECT D FROM } D_1 \rightsquigarrow \text{xsd:date}
\end{aligned}
$$

and $\mathcal{M}_a$ is as follows:

M_{m_1} : SELECT SSN,PROJ,D FROM D_1 $\rightsquigarrow$ $tempEmp(\mathbf{pers}(\text{SSN}))$, $WORKS\text{-}FOR(\mathbf{pers}(\text{SSN}), \mathbf{proj}(\text{PROJ}))$, $ProjName(\mathbf{proj}(\text{PROJ}), \text{PROJ})$, $until(\mathbf{pers}(\text{SSN}), \text{D})$

M_{m_2} : SELECT SSN,NAME FROM D_2 $\rightsquigarrow$ $employee(\mathbf{pers}(\text{SSN}))$, $PersName(\mathbf{pers}(\text{SSN}), \text{NAME})$

M_{m_3} : SELECT SSN, NAME FROM D_3, D_4 WHERE D_3.CODE=D_4.CODE $\rightsquigarrow$ $manager(\mathbf{pers}(\text{SSN}))$, $PersName(\mathbf{pers}(\text{SSN}), \text{NAME})$

M_{m_4} : SELECT CODE, NAME FROM D_3 WHERE CODE NOT IN (SELECT CODE FROM D_4) $\rightsquigarrow$ $manager(\mathbf{mgr}(\text{CODE}))$, $PersName(\mathbf{mgr}(\text{CODE}), \text{NAME})$

We briefly comment on the data-to-ontology mapping assertions in $\mathcal{M}_a$. M_{m_1} maps every tuple (s, p, d) in D_1 to a temporary employee $\mathbf{pers}(s)$ with name p, working until d for project $\mathbf{proj}(p)$. M_{m_2} maps every tuple (s, n) in D_2 to an employee $\mathbf{pers}(s)$ with name n. M_{m_3} and M_{m_4} tell us how to map data in D_3 and D_4 to managers and their name in the ontology. Note that, if D_4 provides the social security number s of a manager whose code is in D_3, then we use the social security number to form the corresponding object term, i.e., the object term has the form $\mathbf{pers}(s)$. If D_4 does not provide such information, then we use an object term of the form $\mathbf{mgr}(c)$ to denote the corresponding instance of the concept *manager*. □

In order to define the semantics of a $DL\text{-}Lite_{\mathcal{A}}$ ontology with mappings, we need to define when an interpretation *satisfies an assertion in* $\mathcal{M}$ *with respect to a database* $\mathcal{DB}$. To this end, we make use of the notion of ground instance of a formula. Let $\Psi(\boldsymbol{x})$ be a formula over a $DL\text{-}Lite_{\mathcal{A}}$ TBox with n distinguished variables $\boldsymbol{x}$, and let $\boldsymbol{v}$ be a tuple of value constants of arity n. Then the ground instance $\Psi[\boldsymbol{x}/\boldsymbol{v}]$ of $\Psi(\boldsymbol{x})$ is the formula obtained by substituting every occurrence of x_i with v_i (for $i \in \{1,..,n\}$) in $\Psi(\boldsymbol{x})$. We are now ready to define when an interpretation satisfies a mapping assertion:

- Let m_t be an assertion in $\mathcal{M}_t$ of the form $\Phi \rightsquigarrow T_i$. We say that the interpretation I satisfies m_t with respect to a database $\mathcal{DB}$, if for every $v \in ans(\Phi, \mathcal{DB})$, we have that $v \in val(T_i)$.
- Let m_a be an assertion in $\mathcal{M}_a$ of the form

$$\Phi(\boldsymbol{x}) \rightsquigarrow \Psi(\boldsymbol{t}, \boldsymbol{y})$$

where $\boldsymbol{x}$ and $\boldsymbol{y}$ are variables, $\boldsymbol{y} \subseteq \boldsymbol{x}$ and $\boldsymbol{t}$ are variable terms of the form $f(\boldsymbol{z})$, $f \in \Lambda$ and $\boldsymbol{z} \subseteq \boldsymbol{x}$.
We say that I satisfies m_a with respect to a database $\mathcal{DB}$, if for every tuple of values $\boldsymbol{v}$ such that $\boldsymbol{v} \in ans(\Phi, \mathcal{DB})$, and for each ground atom X in $\Psi[\boldsymbol{x}/\boldsymbol{v}]$, we have that:
  - if X has the form $A(s)$, then $s^I \in A^I$;
  - if X has the form $D(s)$, then $s^I \in D^I$;
  - if X has the form $P(s_1, s_2)$, then $(s_1^I, s_2^I) \in P^I$;
  - if X has the form $U_C(s_1, s_2)$, then $(s_1^I, s_2^I) \in U_C^I$.

Finally, we say that an interpretation $I = (\Delta^I, \cdot^I)$ is a *model* of $\mathcal{O}_m = \langle \mathcal{T}, \mathcal{M}, \mathcal{DB} \rangle$ if:

- I is a model of $\mathcal{T}$;
- I satisfies $\mathcal{M}$ with respect to $\mathcal{DB}$, i.e., satisfies every assertion in $\mathcal{M}$ with respect to $\mathcal{DB}$.

We denote as $Mod(\mathcal{O}_m)$ the set of models of $\mathcal{O}_m$, and we say that a *DL-Lite$_\mathcal{A}$* ontology with mappings $\mathcal{O}_m$ is satisfiable if $Mod(\mathcal{O}_m) \neq \emptyset$.

Example 9. One can easily verify that the ontology with mappings $\mathcal{O}_m$ of Example 8 is satisfiable. □

Note that, as we said in the introduction, the mapping mechanism described above nicely deals with the fact that the database $\mathcal{DB}$ and the ontology $\mathcal{O}_m$ are based on different semantical assumptions. Indeed, the semantics of $\mathcal{DB}$ follows the so-called "closed world assumption" [28], which intuitively sanctions that every fact that is not explicitly stored in the database is false. On the contrary, the semantics of $\mathcal{O}_m$ is open, in the sense that nothing is assumed about the facts that do not appear explicitly in the ABox. In a mapping assertion of the form $\Phi \rightsquigarrow \Psi$, the closed semantics of $\mathcal{DB}$ is taken into account by the fact that Φ is evaluated as a standard relational query over the database $\mathcal{DB}$, while the open semantics of $\mathcal{O}_m$ is reflected by the fact that mappings assertions are interpreted as "material implication" in logic. It is well known that a material implication of the form $\Phi \rightsquigarrow \Psi$ imposes that every tuple of Φ contribute to the answers to Ψ, leaving open the possibility of additional tuples satisfying Ψ.

Let Q denote a UCQ expressed in terms of the TBox $\mathcal{T}$ of $\mathcal{O}_m$. We call *certain answers to Q posed over $\mathcal{O}_m$* the set of n-tuples of terms in Γ, denoted $Q^{\mathcal{O}_m}$, that is defined as follows:

$$Q^{\mathcal{O}_m} = \{\boldsymbol{t} \mid \boldsymbol{t}^I \in Q^I, \forall I \in Mod(\mathcal{O}_m)\}$$

Clearly, given an ontology with mappings and a query Q posed in terms of $\mathcal{T}$, query answering is the problem of computing the certain answers to Q.

4 Overview of the Reasoning Method

Our goal in the next sections is to illustrate a method for both checking satisfiability, and query answering in *DL-Lite$_\mathcal{A}$* ontologies with mappings. In this section, we present an overview of our reasoning method, by concentrating in particular on the task of query answering.

The simplest way to tackle reasoning over a *DL-Lite$_\mathcal{A}$* ontology with mappings is to use the mappings to produce an actual ABox, and then reasoning on the ontology constituted by the ABox and the original TBox, applying the techniques described in Section 2.4. We call such approach "bottom-up". However, such a bottom-up approach requires to actually build the ABox starting from the data at the sources, thus somehow duplicating the information already present in the data sources. To avoid such redundancy, we propose an alternative approach, called "top-down", which essentially keeps the ABox virtual.

We sketch out the main ideas of both approaches below. As we said before, we refer in particular to query answering, but similar considerations hold for satisfiability checking too. Before delving into the discussion, we define the notions of *split version of an ontology* and of *virtual ABox*, which will be useful in the sequel.

4.1 Splitting the Mapping

Let $\mathcal{O}_m = \langle \mathcal{T}, \mathcal{M}, \mathcal{DB} \rangle$ be a *DL-Lite$_\mathcal{A}$* ontology with mappings as defined in the previous section. We show how to compute the *split version* of $\mathcal{O}_m$, that is characterized by a particularly "friendly form". Specifically, we denote as $\mathsf{Split}(\mathcal{O}_m) = \langle \mathcal{T}, \mathcal{M}', \mathcal{DB} \rangle$ a new ontology with mappings that is obtained from $\mathcal{O}_m$, by constructing $\mathcal{M}'$ as follows:

1. all typing assertions in $\mathcal{M}$ are also in $\mathcal{M}'$;
2. for each mapping assertion $\Phi \rightsquigarrow \Psi \in \mathcal{M}$, and for each atom $X \in \Psi$, the mapping assertion $\Phi' \rightsquigarrow X$ is in $\mathcal{M}'$, where Φ' is the projection of Φ over the variables occurring in X.

Example 10. Consider the ontology with mappings $\mathcal{O}_m = \langle \mathcal{T}, \mathcal{M}, \mathcal{DB} \rangle$ of Example 8. By splitting the mappings as described above, we obtain the ontology $\mathsf{Split}(\mathcal{O}_m) = \langle \mathcal{T}, \mathcal{M}', \mathcal{DB} \rangle$ such that $\mathcal{M}'$ contains all typing assertions in $\mathcal{M}$ and contains furthermore the following split mapping assertions:

$M_{m_{11}}$: SELECT SSN　　　　　　　$\leadsto$　$tempEmp(\mathbf{pers}(\text{SSN}))$
　　　　　FROM D_1
$M_{m_{12}}$: SELECT SSN, PROJ　　　　$\leadsto$　$WORKS\text{-}FOR(\mathbf{pers}(\text{SSN}), \mathbf{proj}(\text{PROJ}))$
　　　　　FROM D_1
$M_{m_{13}}$: SELECT PROJ　　　　　　$\leadsto$　$ProjName(\mathbf{proj}(\text{PROJ}), \text{PROJ})$
　　　　　FROM D_1
$M_{m_{14}}$: SELECT SSN,D　　　　　　$\leadsto$　$until(\mathbf{pers}(\text{SSN}), \text{D})$
　　　　　FROM D_1
$M_{m_{21}}$: SELECT SSN　　　　　　　$\leadsto$　$employee(\mathbf{pers}(\text{SSN}))$
　　　　　FROM D_2
$M_{m_{22}}$: SELECT SSN,NAME　　　　$\leadsto$　$PersName(\mathbf{pers}(\text{SSN}), \text{NAME})$
　　　　　FROM D_2
$M_{m_{31}}$: SELECT SSN　　　　　　　$\leadsto$　$manager(\mathbf{pers}(\text{SSN}))$
　　　　　FROM D_3, D_4
　　　　　WHERE D_3.CODE=D_4.CODE
$M_{m_{32}}$: SELECT SSN, NAME　　　　$\leadsto$　$PersName(\mathbf{pers}(\text{SSN}), \text{NAME})$
　　　　　FROM D_3, D_4
　　　　　WHERE D_3.CODE=D_4.CODE
$M_{m_{41}}$: SELECT CODE　　　　　　$\leadsto$　$manager(\mathbf{mgr}(\text{CODE}))$
　　　　　FROM D_3
　　　　　WHERE CODE NOT IN
　　　　　　(SELECT CODE FROM D_4)
$M_{m_{42}}$: SELECT CODE, NAME　　　$\leadsto$　$PersName(\mathbf{mgr}(\text{CODE}), \text{NAME})$
　　　　　FROM D_3
　　　　　WHERE CODE NOT IN
　　　　　　(SELECT CODE FROM D_4)

□

The relationship between an ontology with mappings and its split version is characterized by the following theorem.

Proposition 1. *Let $\mathcal{O}_m = \langle \mathcal{T}, \mathcal{M}, \mathcal{DB} \rangle$ be a DL-Lite$_\mathcal{A}$ ontology with mappings. Then, we have that:*
$$Mod(\mathsf{Split}(\mathcal{O}_m)) = Mod(\mathcal{O}_m).$$

Proof. The result follows straightforwardly from the syntax and the semantics of the mappings. □

The theorem essentially tells us that every ontology with mappings is logically equivalent to the corresponding split version. Therefore, given any arbitrary DL-Lite$_\mathcal{A}$ ontology with mappings, we can always reduce it to its split version. Moreover, such a reduction has PTIME complexity in the size of the mappings and does not depend on the size of the data. This allows for assuming, from now on, to deal only with split versions of DL-Lite$_\mathcal{A}$ ontologies with mappings.

4.2 Virtual ABox

In this subsection we introduce the notion of virtual ABox. Intuitively, given a DL-Lite$_\mathcal{A}$ ontology with mappings $\mathcal{O}_m = \langle \mathcal{T}, \mathcal{M}, \mathcal{DB} \rangle$, the virtual ABox corresponding to $\mathcal{O}_m$ is the ABox whose assertions are computed by "applying" the mapping assertions starting from the data in $\mathcal{DB}$. Note that in our method we do not explicitly build the virtual ABox. However, this notion will be used in the technical development presented in the sequel of the paper.

Definition 1. Let $\mathcal{O}_m = \langle \mathcal{T}, \mathcal{M}, \mathcal{DB} \rangle$ be a DL-Lite$_\mathcal{A}$ ontology with mappings, and let M be a mapping assertion in $\mathcal{M}$ of the form $M = \Phi \rightsquigarrow X$. We call virtual ABox generated by M from $\mathcal{DB}$ the following set of assertions:

$$\mathcal{A}(M, \mathcal{DB}) = \{X[\boldsymbol{x}/\boldsymbol{v}] \mid \boldsymbol{v} \in ans(\Phi, \mathcal{DB})\},$$

where $\boldsymbol{v}$ and Φ are of arity n, and, as we said before, $X[\boldsymbol{x}/\boldsymbol{v}]$ denotes the ground atom obtained from $X(\boldsymbol{x})$ by substituting the n-tuple of variables $\boldsymbol{x}$ with the n-tuple of constants $\boldsymbol{v} \in \Gamma_V^n$. Moreover, the virtual ABox for $\mathcal{O}_m$, denoted $\mathcal{A}(\mathcal{M}, \mathcal{DB})$, is the set of assertions

$$\mathcal{A}(\mathcal{M}, \mathcal{DB}) = \{\mathcal{A}(M, \mathcal{DB}) \mid M \in \mathcal{M}\}.$$

Notice that $\mathcal{A}(\mathcal{M}, \mathcal{DB})$ is an ABox over the constants $\Gamma = \Gamma_V \cup \tau(\Lambda, \Gamma)$, as shown by the following example.

Example 11. Let $\mathsf{Split}(\mathcal{O}_m)$ be the DL-Lite$_\mathcal{A}$ ontology with split mappings of Example 10. Consider in particular the mappings $M_{m_{21}}$, $M_{m_{22}}$. Suppose we have $D_2 = \{(20903, \text{Rossi}), (55577, \text{White})\}$ in the database $\mathcal{DB}$. Then, the sets of assertions $\mathcal{A}(M_{m_{21}}, \mathcal{DB})$, $\mathcal{A}(M_{m_{22}}, \mathcal{DB})$ are as follows:

$\mathcal{A}(M_{m_{21}}, \mathcal{DB}) = \{employee(\mathbf{pers}(20903)), employee(\mathbf{pers}(55577))\}$
$\mathcal{A}(M_{m_{22}}, \mathcal{DB}) = \{\mathsf{PersName}(\mathbf{pers}(20903), \text{Rossi}), \mathsf{PersName}(\mathbf{pers}(55577), \text{White})\}$

□

By proceeding in the same way for each mapping assertion in $\mathcal{M}$, we can easily obtain the whole virtual ABox for $\mathcal{O}_m$.

Virtual ABoxes allow for expressing the semantics of DL-Lite$_\mathcal{A}$ ontologies with mappings in terms of the semantics of DL-Lite$_\mathcal{A}$ ontologies as follows:

Proposition 2. *If $\mathcal{O}_m = \langle \mathcal{T}, \mathcal{M}, \mathcal{DB} \rangle$ is a DL-Lite$_\mathcal{A}$ ontology with mappings, then*

$$Mod(\mathcal{O}_m) = Mod(\langle \mathcal{T}, \mathcal{A}(\mathcal{M}, \mathcal{DB}) \rangle).$$

Proof. Trivial, from the definition. □

Now that we have introduced virtual ABoxes, we discuss in more detail both the bottom-up and the top-down approach.

4.3 A Bottom-Up Approach

The proposition above suggests an obvious, and "naive", bottom-up algorithm to answer queries over a satisfiable DL-Lite$_\mathcal{A}$ ontology $\mathcal{O}_m = \langle \mathcal{T}, \mathcal{M}, \mathcal{DB} \rangle$ with mappings, which we describe next. First, we materialize the virtual ABox for $\mathcal{O}_m$, i.e., we compute $\mathcal{A}(\mathcal{M}, \mathcal{DB})$. Second, we apply to the $DL\text{-}Lite_\mathcal{A}$ ontology $\mathcal{O} = \langle \mathcal{T}, \mathcal{A}(\mathcal{M}, \mathcal{DB}) \rangle$, the algorithms for query answering, briefly described in Section 2.4.

Unfortunately, this approach has the following drawbacks. First, the time complexity of the proposed algorithm is PTIME in the size of the database, since the generation of the virtual ABox is by itself a PTIME process. Second, since the database is independent of the ontology, it may happen that, during the lifetime of the ontology with mappings, the data it contains are modified. This would clearly require to set up a mechanism for keeping the virtual ABox up-to-date with respect to the database evolution, similarly to what happens in data warehousing. Thus, next, we propose a different approach (called "top-down"), which uses an algorithm that avoids materializing the virtual ABox, but, rather, takes into account the mapping specification *on-the-fly*, during reasoning. In this way, we can both keep the computational complexity of the algorithm low, which turns out to be the same of the query answering algorithm for ontologies without mappings (i.e., in LOGSPACE), and avoid any further procedure for data refreshment.

4.4 A Top-Down Approach

While the bottom-up approach described in the previous subsection is only of theoretical interest, we now present an overview of our top-down approach to query answering.

Let $\mathcal{O}_m = \langle \mathcal{T}, \mathcal{M}, \mathcal{DB} \rangle$ be a $DL\text{-}Lite_\mathcal{A}$ ontology with split mappings, and let Q be a UCQ over $\mathcal{O}_m$. According to the top-down approach, query answering is constituted by three steps, called reformulation, unfolding, and evaluation, respectively.

- **Reformulation.** In this step, we compute the perfect reformulation $Q' = \mathsf{PerfectRef}(Q, \mathcal{T})$ of the original query Q, according to what we said in Section 2.4. Q' is a first-order logic query satisfying the following property: the certain answers to Q with respect to $\mathcal{O}_m$ coincide with the set of tuples computed by evaluating Q' over $db(\mathcal{A}(\mathcal{M}, \mathcal{DB}))^7$, i.e., the database representing $\mathcal{A}(\mathcal{M}, \mathcal{DB})$.
- **Unfolding.** Instead of materializing $\mathcal{A}(\mathcal{M}, \mathcal{DB})$ and evaluating Q' over $\mathcal{A}(\mathcal{M}, \mathcal{DB})$ (as in the bottom-up approach), we "unfold" Q' according to $\mathcal{M}$, i.e., we compute a new query Q'', which is an SQL over the source relations. As we will show in Section 6, this computation is done by using logic programming techniques, and allows us to get rid of $\mathcal{M}$, in the sense that the set of tuples computed by evaluating Q'' over the sources coincides with the set of tuples computed by evaluating Q' over $db(\mathcal{A}(\mathcal{M}, \mathcal{DB}))$.

---

[7] The function db is defined in Section 2.

- **Evaluation.** The evaluation step consists simply in delegating the evaluation of Q'' over the database $\mathcal{DB}$ to the DBMS managing such database.

Example 12. Consider the ontology $\mathsf{Split}(\mathcal{O}_m)$ of Example 10, and assume it is satisfiable. The mapping assertions in $\mathcal{M}'$ of $\mathsf{Split}(\mathcal{O}_m)$ can be encoded in the following portion of a logic program (see Section 6):

$$\begin{aligned}
tempEmp(\mathbf{pers}(s)) &\leftarrow Aux_{11}(s) \\
\textit{WORKS-FOR}(\mathbf{pers}(s), \mathbf{proj}(p)) &\leftarrow Aux_{12}(s, p) \\
\mathsf{ProjName}(\mathbf{proj}(p), p) &\leftarrow Aux_{13}(p) \\
until(\mathbf{pers}(s), d) &\leftarrow Aux_{14}(s, d) \\
employee(\mathbf{pers}(s)) &\leftarrow Aux_{21}(s) \\
\mathsf{PersName}(\mathbf{pers}(s), n) &\leftarrow Aux_{22}(s, n) \\
manager(\mathbf{pers}(s)) &\leftarrow Aux_{31}(s) \\
\mathsf{PersName}(\mathbf{pers}(s), n) &\leftarrow Aux_{32}(s, n) \\
manager(\mathbf{mgr}(c)) &\leftarrow Aux_{41}(c) \\
\mathsf{PersName}(\mathbf{mgr}(c), n) &\leftarrow Aux_{42}(c, n)
\end{aligned}$$

where Aux_{ij} is a suitable predicate denoting the result of the evaluation over $\mathcal{DB}$ of the query $\Phi_{m_{ij}}$ in the left-hand side of the mapping $M_{m_{ij}}$ (note that for different Aux_{ih} and Aux_{ik}, we may have $\Phi_{m_{ih}}$ equal to $\Phi_{m_{ik}}$). Now, let

$$q(x) \leftarrow \textit{WORKS-FOR}(x, y)$$

be the query discussed in Example 7. As we saw in Section 2, its reformulation $Q' = \mathsf{PerfectRef}(q, \mathcal{T})$ is:

$$\begin{aligned}
Q'(x) &\leftarrow \textit{WORKS-FOR}(x, y) \\
Q'(x) &\leftarrow until(x, y) \\
Q'(x) &\leftarrow tempEmp(x) \\
Q'(x) &\leftarrow employee(x) \\
Q'(x) &\leftarrow manager(x)
\end{aligned}$$

In order to compute the unfolding of Q', we unify each of its atoms in all possible ways with the left-hand side of the mapping assertions in $\mathcal{M}'$, and we obtain the following *partial evaluation* of Q':

$$\begin{aligned}
q(\mathbf{pers}(s)) &\leftarrow Aux_{12}(s, p) \\
q(\mathbf{pers}(s)) &\leftarrow Aux_{14}(s, d) \\
q(\mathbf{pers}(s)) &\leftarrow Aux_{11}(s) \\
q(\mathbf{pers}(s)) &\leftarrow Aux_{21}(s) \\
q(\mathbf{pers}(s)) &\leftarrow Aux_{31}(s, n) \\
q(\mathbf{mgr}(c)) &\leftarrow Aux_{41}(c, n)
\end{aligned}$$

From the above formulation, it is now possible to derive the corresponding SQL query Q'' that can be directly issued over the database $\mathcal{DB}$:

```
SELECT CONCAT(CONCAT('pers (',SSN),')')
FROM D₁
UNION
SELECT CONCAT(CONCAT('pers (',SSN),')')
FROM D₂
UNION
SELECT CONCAT(CONCAT('pers (',SSN),')')
FROM D₃,D₄
WHERE D₃.CODE=D₄.CODE
UNION
SELECT CONCAT(CONCAT('mgr (',CODE),')')
FROM D₃
WHERE CODE NOT IN (SELECT CODE FROM D₄)
```
□

In the next two sections we delve into the details of our top-down method for reasoning about ontologies with mappings. In particular, in Section 5 we deal with the unfolding step, whereas in Section 6 we present the complete algorithms for both satisfiablity checking and query answering, and we discuss their formal properties. In both sections, we assume to deal only with ontologies with split mappings.

5 Dealing with Mappings

As we saw in the previous section, the unfolding step is one of the ingredients of our top-down method for reasoning about ontologies with mappings. The goal of this section is to illustrate the technique we use to perform such a step.

Suppose we are given a *DL-Lite$_\mathcal{A}$* ontology with split mappings $\mathcal{O}_m = \langle \mathcal{T}, \mathcal{M}, \mathcal{DB} \rangle$ and an UCQ Q over $\mathcal{O}_m$. The purpose of "unfolding" Q according to $\mathcal{M}$, is to compute a new query Q' satisfying the following properties:

1. Q' is a query (in particular, an SQL query) over the source relations,
2. the set of tuples computed by evaluating Q' over the data sources coincides with the set of tuples computed by evaluating Q over $db(\mathcal{A}(\mathcal{M}, \mathcal{DB}))$.

From the above specification, it is clear that the unfolding step is crucial for avoiding materializing the virtual ABox.

The method we use for carrying out the unfolding step is based on logic programming notions [20]. The reason why we resort to logic programming is that mapping assertions are indeed similar to (simple forms of) rules of a logic program. The connection between data integration mappings and logic programming has already been noticed in several papers (see, for example, [25]). Our case, however, differs from those addressed in such papers, for two main reasons:

- while most of the above works use Datalog rules for modeling mappings, our mapping assertions contain functional terms, and therefore they go beyond Datalog;

– we do not want to use the rules for directly accessing data. Instead, we aim at using the rules for coming up with the right queries to ship to the data sources. In this sense, we use the rules only "partially".

The fact that we use the rules only partially is the reason why we will make use of the notion of "partial evaluation" of a logic program. This notion, together with more general notions of logic programming, is introduced in the next subsection.

5.1 Relevant Notions from Logic Programming

We briefly recall some basic notions from logic programming [20], upon which we build our unfolding technique. In particular, we exploit some crucial results on the partial evaluation [18] of logic programs given in [21], which we briefly recall below.

Definition 2. *A definite program clause is an expression of the form*

$$A \leftarrow W$$

where A is an atom, and W is a conjunction of atoms $A_1, \ldots, A_n$. The left-hand side of a clause is called its head, *whereas its right-hand side is called its* body. *Either the body or the head of the clause may be empty. When the body is empty, the clause is called* fact *(and the $\leftarrow$ symbol is in general omitted). When the head is empty, the clause is called a* definite goal. *A definite program is a finite set of definite program clauses.*

Notice that $A \leftarrow W$ has a first-order logic reading, which is represented by the following sentence:

$$\forall x_1, \cdots, \forall x_s (A \vee \neg W).$$

where $x_1, \ldots, x_s$ are all the variables occurring in W and A. This reading explains why a logic program clause is also called a rule.

From now on, when we talk about programs, program clauses and goals, we implicitly mean definite programs, definite program clauses and definite goals, respectively.

A well-known property of logic programs is that every definite program $\mathcal{P}$ has a *minimal model*, which is the intersection $M_\mathcal{P}$ of all Herbrand models for $\mathcal{P}$ [20]. Intuitively, the minimal model of $\mathcal{P}$ is the set of all positive ground facts (i.e., atomic formulae without variables) that are true in all the models of $\mathcal{P}$. We say that an atomic formula (or atom) containing no variable is *true* in a logic program $\mathcal{P}$ if it is true in the minimal model of $\mathcal{P}$.

Logic program clauses are used to derive formulae from other formulae. The notion of derivation is formalized by the following definition.

Definition 3. *If G is a goal of the form $\leftarrow A_1, \cdots, A_m, \cdots, A_k$, and C is a program clause $A \leftarrow B_1, \cdots, B_q$, then G' is derived from G and C through* the selected atom A_m using the most general unifier[8] (mgu) θ if the following conditions hold:

- θ is an mgu of A_m and A, and
- G' is the goal

$$\leftarrow (A_1, \ldots, A_{m-1}, B_1, \ldots, B_q, A_{m+1}, \ldots, A_k)\theta$$

where $(A_1, \cdots, A_n)\theta = A_1\theta, \cdots, A_n\theta$, and $A\theta$ is the atom obtained from A applying the substitution θ.

Next we define the notion of resultant. We actually present a simplified definition of this notion, which is sufficient for our purpose.

Definition 4. *A resultant is an expression of the form*

$$Q_1 \leftarrow Q_2$$

where Q_1 is a conjunction of atoms, and Q_2 (called the body of the resultant) is either absent or a conjunction of atoms.

The possible derivations of a goal using a program are represented by a special tree, called SLD-tree, which is defined next.

Definition 5. *(SLD-Tree [21]) Let $\mathcal{P}$ be a program and let G' be a goal with body G. Then, an SLD-Tree of $\mathcal{P} \cup \{G'\}$ is a tree satisfying the following conditions:*

- *each node is a resultant,*
- *the root node is $G_0\theta_0 \leftarrow G_0$, where $G_0 = G$, and θ_0 is the empty substitution,*
- *let $G\theta_0 \cdots \theta_i \leftarrow G_i$[9] be a node N at depth $i \geq 0$ such that G_i has the form $A_1, \ldots, A_m, \ldots, A_k$, and suppose that A_m is the atom selected in G_i. Then, for each program clause C of the form $A \leftarrow B_1, \cdots, B_q$ in $\mathcal{P}$ such that A_m and A are unifiable with mgu θ_{i+1}, the node N has a child*

$$G\theta_0\theta_1 \cdots \theta_{i+1} \leftarrow G_{i+1},$$

where the goal $\leftarrow G_{i+1}$ is derived from the goal $\leftarrow G_i$ and C through A_m using θ_{i+1}, i.e., G_{i+1} has the form $(A_1, \ldots, B_1, \ldots, B_q, \ldots, A_k)\theta_{i+1}$,
- *a node which is a resultant with an empty body has no children.*

We say that a branch of an SLD-tree is failing if it ends in a node such that the selected atom does not unify with the head of any program clause. Moreover, we say that an SLD-Tree is complete if all its non-failing branches end in the empty clause. An SLD-tree that is not complete is called partial.

Finally, given a node $Q\theta_0, \ldots, \theta_i \leftarrow Q_i$ at depth i, we say that the derivation of Q_i has length i with computed answer θ, where θ is the restriction of $\theta_0, \cdots, \theta_i$ to the variables in the goal G'.

---

[8] A unifier of two expressions is a substitution of their variables that makes such expressions equal. A most general unifer is a unifier with a minimal number of substitutions.
[9] The expression $\theta_1\theta_2 \cdots \theta_n$ denotes the composition of the substitutions $\theta_1, \ldots, \theta_n$.

Finally, we recall the definition of *partial evaluation* (PE for short) from [21]. The definition actually refers to two kinds of PE: the *PE of an atom in a program*, and the *PE of a program with respect to an atom*. Intuitively, to obtain a PE of an atom A in $\mathcal{P}$, one considers an SLD-tree T for $\mathcal{P} \cup \{\leftarrow A\}$, and chooses a *cut* in T. The PE of $\mathcal{P}$ with respect to A is defined as the union of the resultants that occur in the cut and do not fail in T.

Definition 6. *Let $\mathcal{P}$ be a program, A an atom, and T an SLD-tree for $\mathcal{P} \cup \{\leftarrow A\}$. Then,*

- *any set of nodes such that each non-failing branch of T contains exactly one of them is a PE of A in $\mathcal{P}$;*
- *the logic program obtained from $\mathcal{P}$ by replacing the set of clauses in $\mathcal{P}$ whose head contains A with a PE of A in $\mathcal{P}$ is a PE of $\mathcal{P}$ with respect to A.*

Note that, by definition, a PE of A in $\mathcal{P}$ is a set of resultant, while the PE of $\mathcal{P}$ with respect to A is a logic program.

Also, a well-known property of PE is that a program $\mathcal{P}$ and any PE of $\mathcal{P}$ with respect to any atom are procedurally equivalent, i.e., the minimal model of $\mathcal{P}$ and the minimal model of any PE of $\mathcal{P}$ with respect to any atom coincide.

5.2 The Unfolding Step

We are now ready to look into unfolding step for reasoning in $DL\text{-}Lite_{\mathcal{A}}$ ontologies with mappings. In particular, the goal is to define a function UnfoldDB, that, intuitively, takes as input a $DL\text{-}Lite_{\mathcal{A}}$ ontology with mappings $\mathcal{O}_m = \langle \mathcal{T}, \mathcal{M}, \mathcal{DB} \rangle$, and a UCQ (possibly with inequalities) Q over $\mathcal{O}_m$, and returns a set of resultants describing

1. the queries to issue to $\mathcal{DB}$, and
2. the substitution to apply to the result in order to obtain the answer to Q.

In order to use logic programming based techniques for unfolding, we express the UCQ Q and the relevant information about $\mathcal{M}$ and $\mathcal{DB}$ in terms of a logic program, called the *program for Q and $\mathcal{O}_m$*.

In all this subsection, unless otherwise stated, we consider $\mathcal{O}_m = \langle \mathcal{T}, \mathcal{M}, \mathcal{DB} \rangle$ to be a $DL\text{-}Lite_{\mathcal{A}}$ ontology with mappings, and Q to be a union of conjunctive queries over $\mathcal{O}_m$, possibly including inequalities.

Definition 7. *The program for Q and $\mathcal{O}_m$, denoted $\mathcal{P}(Q, \mathcal{M}, \mathcal{DB})$, is the logic program formed as follows:*[10]

1. *for each conjunctive query $(q(\boldsymbol{x}) \leftarrow Q') \in Q$, $\mathcal{P}(Q, \mathcal{M}, \mathcal{DB})$ contains the clause*

$$q(\boldsymbol{x}) \leftarrow \sigma(Q')$$

where $\sigma(\alpha)$ denotes the query obtained by replacing each $x \neq y$ in the body of α with the atom $Distinct(x, y)$, where $Distinct$ is an auxiliary binary predicate;

---
[10] We assume that the alphabet of $\mathcal{T}$ does not contain the predicate $Distinct$, and, for any i, does not contain the predicate Aux_i.

2. *for each mapping assertion* $m_k \in \mathcal{M}$ *of the form* $\Phi_k(\boldsymbol{x}) \leadsto p_k(\boldsymbol{t})$, $\mathcal{P}(Q, \mathcal{M}, \mathcal{DB})$ *contains the clause*

$$p_k(\boldsymbol{t}) \leftarrow Aux_k(\boldsymbol{x})$$

where Aux_k *is an auxiliary predicate associated to* m_k, *whose arity is the same as* Φ_k;

3. *for each* Φ_k *appearing in the left-hand side of a mapping assertion in* $\mathcal{M}$, *for each* $\boldsymbol{t} \in ans(\Phi_k, \mathcal{DB})$, $\mathcal{P}(Q, \mathcal{M}, \mathcal{DB})$ *contains the fact* $Aux_k(\boldsymbol{t})$;

4. *let* $\Gamma_{\mathcal{DB}}$ *be the set of all values appearing in* $\mathcal{DB}$; *then for each pair* t_1, t_2 *of distinct terms in* $\tau(\Lambda, \Gamma_{\mathcal{DB}}) \cup \Gamma_{\mathcal{DB}}$, $\mathcal{P}(Q, \mathcal{M}, \mathcal{DB})$ *contains the fact* $Distinct(t_1, t_2)$.

Intuitively, item (1) in the definition is used to represent the query Q in the logic program $\mathcal{P}(Q, \mathcal{M}, \mathcal{DB})$, with the proviso that all inequalities are expressed in terms of the predicate $Distinct$. Item (2) introduces one auxiliary predicates Aux_i for each Φ_i appearing in the left-hand side of the mapping assertion in $m_i \in \mathcal{M}$, and item (3) states that the extension of $Aux_i(\boldsymbol{x})$ coincides with $ans(\Phi_i, \mathcal{DB})$. Finally, item (4) is used to enforce the unique name assumption in $\mathcal{P}(Q, \mathcal{M}, \mathcal{DB})$.

The following two lemmas state formally the relationship between $\mathcal{P}(Q, \mathcal{M}, \mathcal{DB})$, $\mathcal{O}_m$ and Q. They essentially show that $\mathcal{P}(Q, \mathcal{M}, \mathcal{DB})$ is a faithful representation in logic programming of both $\mathcal{O}_m$ and Q.

Lemma 1. $\mathcal{A}(\mathcal{M}, \mathcal{DB})$ *coincides with the projection over the alphabet of* $\mathcal{T}$ *of the minimal model of* $\mathcal{P}(Q, \mathcal{M}, \mathcal{DB})$.

Proof. We first show that, for each tuple $\boldsymbol{t}$ of terms, if $X(\boldsymbol{t}) \in \mathcal{A}(\mathcal{M}, \mathcal{DB})$, then $X(\boldsymbol{t})$ is true in the minimal model $M_\mathcal{P}$ of $\mathcal{P}(Q, \mathcal{M}, \mathcal{DB})$. Consider a tuple $\boldsymbol{t}$ such that $X(\boldsymbol{t}) \in \mathcal{A}(\mathcal{M}, \mathcal{DB})$. Thus, by construction of $\mathcal{A}(\mathcal{M}, \mathcal{DB})$ we have that there exists a mapping $\Phi_k(\boldsymbol{x}) \leadsto X(\alpha)$ in $\mathcal{M}$, a tuple $\boldsymbol{t}'$ of values in $\Gamma_{\mathcal{DB}}$, and a substitution θ such that $\boldsymbol{t}' \in ans(\Phi_k, \mathcal{DB})$ and $\boldsymbol{t} = \alpha\theta$. But then, since $\boldsymbol{t}' \in ans(\Phi_k, \mathcal{DB})$, we have that $Aux_k(\boldsymbol{t}') \in \mathcal{P}(Q, \mathcal{M}, \mathcal{DB})$. Moreover, since $\Phi_k(\boldsymbol{x}) \leadsto X(\alpha)$ is a mapping in $\mathcal{M}$, we have that $X(\alpha) \leftarrow Aux_k(\boldsymbol{x}) \in \mathcal{P}(Q, \mathcal{M}, \mathcal{DB})$. Thus, θ is an mgu of $Aux_k(\boldsymbol{x})$ and $Aux_k(\boldsymbol{t}')$. Therefore, it is possible to derive $X(\boldsymbol{t})$ from $Aux_k(\boldsymbol{t}')$ and $X(\alpha) \leftarrow Aux_k(\boldsymbol{x})$ by using θ, and, by a well-known property of logic programming, $X(\boldsymbol{t})$ is true in $M_\mathcal{P}$.

Conversely, let $X(\boldsymbol{t})$ be true in the minimal model $M_\mathcal{P}$ of $\mathcal{P}(Q, \mathcal{M}, \mathcal{DB})$. By following a similar line of reasoning as above, it can be easily shown that $X(\boldsymbol{t}) \in \mathcal{A}(\mathcal{M}, \mathcal{DB})$. □

Lemma 2. *For each tuple* $\boldsymbol{t} \in \tau(\Gamma_V, \Lambda) \cup \Gamma_V$, *we have that*

$\boldsymbol{t} \in ans(Q, db(\mathcal{A}(\mathcal{M}, \mathcal{DB})))$ *if and only if* $\mathcal{P}(Q, \mathcal{M}, \mathcal{DB}) \cup \{\leftarrow q(\boldsymbol{t})\}$ *is unsatisfiable.*

Proof. The result follows directly from the previous lemma and the construction of $\mathcal{P}(Q, \mathcal{M}, \mathcal{DB})$. □

We now illustrate how to compute a specific PE of the program $\mathcal{P}(Q, \mathcal{M}, \mathcal{DB})$ (where Q has the form $q(\boldsymbol{x}) \leftarrow \beta$) with respect to $q(\boldsymbol{x})$, denoted $\mathcal{PE}(Q, \mathcal{M}, \mathcal{DB})$. Such a PE is crucial for our development.

We first define the function SLD-Derive($\mathcal{P}(Q, \mathcal{M}, \mathcal{DB})$) that takes as input $\mathcal{P}(Q, \mathcal{M}, \mathcal{DB})$, and returns a set S of resultants constituting a PE of $q(\boldsymbol{x})$ in $\mathcal{P}(Q, \mathcal{M}, \mathcal{DB})$, by constructs an SLD-Tree T for $\mathcal{P}(Q, \mathcal{M}, \mathcal{DB}) \cup \{\leftarrow q(\boldsymbol{x})\}$ as follows:

- it starts by selecting the atom $q(\boldsymbol{x})$,
- it continues by selecting the atoms whose predicates belong to the alphabet of $\mathcal{T}$, as long as possible;
- it stops the construction of a branch when no atom with predicate in the alphabet of $\mathcal{T}$ can be selected.

Note that the above definition implies that SLD-Derive($\mathcal{P}(Q, \mathcal{M}, \mathcal{DB})$) returns the set S of resultants obtained by cutting T only at nodes whose body contains only atoms with predicate Aux_i or $Distinct$.

Second, we use SLD-Derive($\mathcal{P}(Q, \mathcal{M}, \mathcal{DB})$) to define $\mathcal{PE}(Q, \mathcal{M}, \mathcal{DB})$, a specific PE of $\mathcal{P}(Q, \mathcal{M}, \mathcal{DB})$ with respect to $q(\boldsymbol{x})$. $\mathcal{PE}(Q, \mathcal{M}, \mathcal{DB})$ is obtained simply by dropping the clauses for q in $\mathcal{P}(Q, \mathcal{M}, \mathcal{DB})$, and replacing them by $S = $ SLD-Derive($\mathcal{P}(Q, \mathcal{M}, \mathcal{DB})$).

Obviously, since $\mathcal{PE}(Q, \mathcal{M}, \mathcal{DB})$ is a PE of $\mathcal{P}$, the two programs are procedurally equivalent, i.e., for every atom A, A is true in $\mathcal{PE}(Q, \mathcal{M}, \mathcal{DB})$ if and only if A is true in $\mathcal{P}(Q, \mathcal{M}, \mathcal{DB})$.

Let Q a UCQ of the form $q(\boldsymbol{x}) \leftarrow \beta$. We now define the function $spread_{\mathcal{O}_m}$ that takes as imput a resultant $q(\boldsymbol{x})\theta \leftarrow Q'$ in $\mathcal{PE}(Q, \mathcal{M}, \mathcal{DB})$, and returns an extended form of resultant $q(\boldsymbol{x})\theta \leftarrow Q''$ such that Q'' is a first-order query over $\mathcal{DB}$, which is obtained from Q' by proceeding as follows. At the beginning, Q'' has an empty body. Then, for each atom A in Q',

- if $A = Aux_k(\boldsymbol{x})$, it adds to Q' the query $\Phi_k(\boldsymbol{x})$; note that, by hypothesis, $\Phi_k(\boldsymbol{x})$ is an arbitrary first-order query with distinguished variables $\boldsymbol{x}$, that can be evaluated over $\mathcal{DB}$;
- if $A = Distinct(x_1, x_2)$, where x_1, x_2 have resp. the form $f_1(\boldsymbol{y}_1)$ and $f_2(\boldsymbol{y}_2)$, then:
  - if $f_1 \neq f_2$, then it does nothing,
  - otherwise, it adds to Q' the following conjunct:

$$\bigvee_{i \in \{1, \ldots, w\}} y_{1_i} \neq y_{2_i},$$

where w is the arity of f_1.

Note that in this case we obtain a disjunction of variables, which, again, can be obviously evaluated over a set of data sources $\mathcal{DB}$.

The next lemma establishes the relationship between the answers to the program $\mathcal{PE}(Q, \mathcal{M}, \mathcal{DB})$, and the tuples that are answers in the queries over the data sources that are present in the mapping assertions. It essentially sayss that every answer to the program $\mathcal{PE}(Q, \mathcal{M}, \mathcal{DB})$ is "generated" by tuples in the data sources.

This lemma and the next theorems make use of a new notion, that we now introduce. We say that an atom $q(t)$ is *obtained from* $q(x)$ *and* θ *through* t' if $q(x)\theta = q(t)$, and all constants used in θ appear in t'. For example, $q(f(2,3), 4)$ is obtained from $q(x_1, x_2)$ and the substitution $\{x_1/f(2,3), x_2/4\}$ through the tuple $(2, 3, 4)$.

Lemma 3. *Let Q be a UCQ of the form $q(x) \leftarrow \beta$. For each tuple $t \in \tau(\Gamma_V, \Lambda) \cup \Gamma_V$, $q(t)$ is true in $\mathcal{PE}(Q, \mathcal{M}, \mathcal{DB})$ if and only if there is a resultant $q(x)\theta \leftarrow Q'$ in $\mathcal{PE}(Q, \mathcal{M}, \mathcal{DB})$ and a tuple t' in Γ_V such that $q(x)\theta = q(t)$, $q(t)$ is obtained from $q(x)$ and θ through t', $spread_{\mathcal{O}_m}(q(x)\theta \leftarrow Q') = (q(x)\theta \leftarrow Q'')$, and $t' \in ans(Q'', \mathcal{DB})$.*

Proof. The if-direction is easy to prove. For the only-if-direction, if $q(t)$ is true in $\mathcal{PE}(Q, \mathcal{M}, \mathcal{DB})$, $q(t)$ can be derived using a resultant in $\mathcal{PE}(Q, \mathcal{M}, \mathcal{DB})$. Let $q(x)\theta \leftarrow Q'$ be such a resultant in $\mathcal{PE}(Q, \mathcal{M}, \mathcal{DB})$, and let Q' have the form $A_1(x_1), \cdots, A_n(x_n)$. By construction, $A_i(x_i)$ is either

- $Aux_{k_i}(x_i)$, or
- $Distinct(x_i)$, where $x_i = (x_{i_1}, x_{i_2})$.

Suppose that A_i has predicate Aux_{k_i} for each $i \leq j$ whereas it has predicate $Distinct$ for $j < i \leq n$. By construction, $spread_{\mathcal{O}_m}(q(x)\theta \leftarrow Q') = (q(x)\theta \leftarrow Q'')$, with Q'' of the form:

$$\{x, \cdots y_{i_{1_1}}, y_{i_{2_1}}, \cdots y_{i_{1_{w_i}}}, y_{i_{2_{w_i}}} \cdots \\ \mid \Phi_{k_1}(x_1), \cdots, \Phi_{k_j}(x_j), (\bigvee_{i \leq n} (\bigvee_{h \in \{1,\ldots,w_i\}} y_{i_{1_h}} \neq y_{i_{2_h}}))\}$$

where $(\bigvee_{h \in \{1,\ldots,w_i\}} y_{i_{1_h}} \neq y_{i_{2_h}})$ occurs together with the corresponding distinguished variables $y_{i_{1_h}}, y_{i_{2_h}}$ if there is an atom $Distinct(x_{i_1}, x_{i_2})$ in q such that $x_{i_1} = f(y_{i_1}), x_{i_2} = f(y_{i_2})$ where f has arity w_i.

Now, let t be a tuple in $\tau(\Gamma_V, \Lambda) \cup \Gamma_V$. We show next that if $q(t)$ is true in $\mathcal{PE}(Q, \mathcal{M}, \mathcal{DB})$, then there is a tuple t' in Γ_V such that $q(x)\theta = Q(t)$, $q(t)$ is obtained from $q(x)$ and θ through t', and $t' \in ans(Q'', \mathcal{DB})$. Suppose that $q(t)$ is true in $\mathcal{PE}(Q, \mathcal{M}, \mathcal{DB})$. Then there exists θ^q such that $q(t) = (A_1(x_1), \cdots, A_n(x_n))\theta^q$ is true in $\mathcal{PE}(Q, \mathcal{M}, \mathcal{DB})$. This implies that there exist n facts F_i in $\mathcal{PE}(Q, \mathcal{M}, \mathcal{DB})$ such that $F_i = A_i \theta^q$ is true in $\mathcal{PE}(Q, \mathcal{M}, \mathcal{DB})$ for each $i = 1, \cdots, n$. But then, by construction:

- if $i \leq j$, then F_i has the form $Aux_{k_i}(t_i)$, which by construction means that $t_i \in ans(\Phi_{k_i}, \mathcal{DB})$;
- otherwise, F_i has the form $Distinct(t_i)$, where $t_i = (t_{i1}, t_{i2})$ and t_{i1}, t_{i2} are such that $t_{i1} \neq t_{i2}$.

By the above observations, one can easily verify that $t' \in ans(Q'', \mathcal{DB})$. Indeed, for $i \leq j$ we have trivially that $\Phi_{k_i}(t'_i)$ is true, whereas for $j < i \leq k$, we have that if $f_1 = f_2$, then $v_{i_1} \neq v_{i_2}$. Thus, since $q(x)\theta^q$ belongs to $\mathcal{PE}(Q, \mathcal{M}, \mathcal{DB})$, then $q(t)$ is obtained from $q(x)$ and θ^p through t', and we have proved the claim. □

Before presenting the function UnfoldDB, we need to make a further observation. The program $\mathcal{P}(Q, \mathcal{M}, \mathcal{DB})$, being a faithful representation of Q and $\mathcal{O}_m$, contains also the facts regarding the predicates Aux_i and $Distinct$. Since we use partial evaluation techniques for computing the queries to issue to the data sources, we are interested in the program obtained from $\mathcal{P}(Q, \mathcal{M}, \mathcal{DB})$ by ignoring such facts. Formally, we define $\mathcal{P}(Q, \mathcal{M})$ to be the program obtained from $\mathcal{P}(Q, \mathcal{M}, \mathcal{DB})$ by eliminating all facts $Aux_k(t)$ and $Distinct(t)$. Notice that while $\mathcal{P}(Q, \mathcal{M}, \mathcal{DB})$ depends on the $\mathcal{DB}$, $\mathcal{P}(Q, \mathcal{M})$ does not. The next theorem shows that the programs $\mathcal{P}(Q, \mathcal{M}, \mathcal{DB})$ and $\mathcal{P}(Q, \mathcal{M})$ are equivalent with respect to partial evaluation.

Lemma 4. *SLD-Derive($\mathcal{P}(Q, \mathcal{M}, \mathcal{DB})$) = SLD-Derive($\mathcal{P}(Q, \mathcal{M})$).*

Proof. The proof follows from the observation that SLD-Derive($\mathcal{P}(Q, \mathcal{M}, \mathcal{DB})$) constructs an SLD-Tree for $\mathcal{P}(Q, \mathcal{M}, \mathcal{DB}) \cup \{\leftarrow q(\boldsymbol{x})\}$ by selecting only the atoms in the alphabet of $\mathcal{T}$, and that $\mathcal{P}(Q, \mathcal{M}, \mathcal{DB})$ and $\mathcal{P}(Q, \mathcal{M})$ coincide in the clauses containing atoms in the alphabet of $\mathcal{T}$. □

Now we are finally able to come back to the definition of UnfoldDB. As usual in this subsection, $\mathcal{O}_m = \langle \mathcal{T}, \mathcal{M}, \mathcal{DB} \rangle$ is an ontology with mappings, and Q a union of conjunctive queries (possibly with inequalities) over $\mathcal{O}_m$. We define UnfoldDB($Q, \mathcal{O}_m$) as the function that takes as input Q and $\mathcal{O}_m$, and returns a set S' of resultants by proceeding as shown in Fig. 1.

Algorithm UnfoldDB($Q, \mathcal{O}_m$)
Input: $DL\text{-}Lite_\mathcal{A}$ ontology with mappings $\mathcal{O}_m = \langle \mathcal{T}, \mathcal{M}, \mathcal{DB} \rangle$
    UCQ (possibly with inequalities) Q over $\mathcal{O}_m$
Output: set of resultants S'
    build the program $\mathcal{P}(Q, \mathcal{M})$;
    compute the set of resultants $S = $ SLD-Derive($\mathcal{P}(Q, \mathcal{M})$);
    for each $ans\theta \leftarrow q \in S$ **do**
        $S' \leftarrow spread_{\mathcal{O}_m}(ans\theta \leftarrow q)$;
    return S'

Fig. 1. The Algorithm UnfoldDB

The next theorem shows the correctness of UnfoldDB, i.e., termination, soundeness and completeness.

Theorem 3. *For every UCQ Q of the form $q(\boldsymbol{x}) \leftarrow \beta$ and for every $\mathcal{O}_m$, UnfoldDB($Q, \mathcal{O}_m$) terminates, and for each tuple of constants $\boldsymbol{t}$ in $\tau(\Gamma_V, \Lambda) \cup \Gamma_V$ we have that:*

   $\boldsymbol{t} \in ans(Q, db(\mathcal{A}(\mathcal{M}, \mathcal{DB})))$ *if and only if*
       $\exists (q(\boldsymbol{x})\theta \leftarrow Q'') \in $ UnfoldDB($Q, \mathcal{O}_m$) *such that* $q(\boldsymbol{x})\theta = q(\boldsymbol{t})$,
       $q(\boldsymbol{t})$ *is obtained from $q(\boldsymbol{x})$ and θ through $\boldsymbol{t}'$, and $\boldsymbol{t}' \in ans(Q'', \mathcal{DB})$.*

Proof. Termination of UnfoldDB is immediate. Soundness and completeness can be directly proved by using the lemmas presented in this section. □

Note that the algorithm UnfoldDB described in Fig. 1 returns a set of resultants, called S'. This form of the algorithm was instrumental for proving the correctness of our method. However, from a practical point of view, the best choice is to translate these set of resultants into a suitable SQL query that can be issued on the data sources. Indeed, this is exactly what our current implementation does. In particular, in the implementation, the final **for each** loop in the algorithm is replaced by a step that, starting from S, builds an SLQ query that, once evaluated over the data sources, computes directly the answers of the original query Q. For the sake of space, we do not describe such a step here. We only note that the kind of SQL queries obtained with this method can be seen by looking at example 12 in Section 4.

We end this section by observing that UnfoldDB allows for completely forgetting about the mappings during query evaluation, by compiling them directly in the queries to be posed over the underlying database. Next we show that this crucial property allows for devising reasoning procedures that exploit, on one hand, the results on reasoning over $DL\text{-}Lite_{\mathcal{A}}$ ontologies, and, on the other hand, the ability of the underlying database of answering arbitrary first-order queries.

6 Reasoning over $DL\text{-}Lite_{\mathcal{A}}$ Ontologies with Mappings

Now that we have described the unfolding step, we are ready to illustrate the complete algorithms for both satisfiablity checking and query answering, and to discuss their formal properties. We deal with satisfiability checking first, and then we address query answering.

Both algorithms make use of several functions that were introduced in the previous sections, and that we recall here. In what follows, we refer to a $DL\text{-}Lite_{\mathcal{A}}$ ontology $\mathcal{O}_m = \langle \mathcal{T}, \mathcal{M}, \mathcal{DB} \rangle$ with split mappings.

- The boolean function Violates takes as input the TBox $\mathcal{T}$, and computes a first-order query over $\mathcal{O}_m$ that intuitively looks for violations of functionality and disjointness assertions specified in the TBox $\mathcal{T}$.
- The function PerfectRef takes as input a UCQ Q over $\mathcal{O}_m$ and the TBox $\mathcal{T}$, and reformulates Q into a new query Q', which is still a UCQ and has the following property: answering Q' with respect to $\langle \emptyset, \mathcal{M}, \mathcal{DB} \rangle$ is the same as answering Q with respect to $\langle \mathcal{T}, \mathcal{M}, \mathcal{DB} \rangle$.
- The function UnfoldDB is the one discussed in Section 5.

6.1 Satisfiability Checking

In Fig. 2 we present the Algorithm Sat that checks the satisfiability of a $DL\text{-}Lite_{\mathcal{A}}$ ontology with mappings. More precisely, $\mathsf{Sat}(\mathcal{O}_m)$ issues the call $\mathsf{Violates}(\mathcal{T})$ to compute the query Q^s, asking, for each functionality assertion in $\mathcal{T}$ and each negative inclusion assertion in $cln(\mathcal{T})$, whether $db(\mathcal{A}(\mathcal{M}, \mathcal{DB}))$ violates the assertion. Then, by calling $\mathsf{UnfoldDB}(Q^s, \mathcal{O}_m)$, that allows for "compiling" the knowledge represented by the mapping assertions, $\mathsf{Sat}(\mathcal{O}_m)$ computes the set of resultants S' as discussed in the previous section. After extracting from S' the union of queries Q', $\mathsf{Sat}(\mathcal{O}_m)$ evaluates Q' over $\mathcal{DB}$, and returns *true*, if and only if $ans(Q', \mathcal{DB}) = \mathit{false}$.

Algorithm Sat
Input: *DL-Lite$_\mathcal{A}$* ontology with mappings $\mathcal{O}_m = \langle \mathcal{T}, \mathcal{M}, \mathcal{DB} \rangle$
Output: *true* or *false*
$\quad Q^s \leftarrow \mathsf{Violates}(\mathcal{T})$;
$\quad S' \leftarrow \mathsf{UnfoldDB}(Q^s, \mathcal{O}_m)$;
$\quad Q' \leftarrow \mathit{false}$;
$\quad$ **for each** $ans\theta \leftarrow q' \in S'$ **do**
$\quad\quad Q' \leftarrow Q' \cup \{q'\}$;
$\quad$ **return** $\mathbf{not}(ans(Q', \mathcal{DB}))$

Fig. 2. The Algorithm Sat

We next show the correctness of Algorithm Sat.

Theorem 4. *Let $\mathcal{O}_m = \langle \mathcal{T}, \mathcal{M}, \mathcal{DB} \rangle$ be a DL-Lite$_\mathcal{A}$ ontology with mappings. Then, $\mathsf{Sat}(\mathcal{O}_m)$ terminates, $\mathcal{O}_m$ is satisfiable if and only if $\mathsf{Sat}(\mathcal{O}_m) = \mathit{true}$.*

Proof. The termination of the algorithm follows from the termination of UnfoldDB.

Concerning the soundness and the completeness of the algorithm, by Proposition 2, we have that $\mathcal{O}_m$ is satisfiable if and only if $\mathcal{O} = \langle \mathcal{T}, db(\mathcal{A}(\mathcal{M}, \mathcal{DB})) \rangle$ is unsatisfiable. Moreover, as discussed in Section 2.4, we have that $\mathcal{O} = \langle \mathcal{T}, db(\mathcal{A}(\mathcal{M}, \mathcal{DB})) \rangle$ is unsatisfiable if and only if $ans(Q^s, db(\mathcal{A}(\mathcal{M}, \mathcal{DB}))) = \mathit{true}$ where $Q^s = \mathsf{Violates}(\mathcal{T})$. Thus, in order to prove the theorem, it suffices to prove that:

$$(*) ans(Q^s, db(\mathcal{A}(\mathcal{M}, \mathcal{DB}))) = \mathit{true} \text{ if and only if } ans(Q', \mathcal{DB}) = \mathit{true},$$

where Q' is such that $Q' = \bigcup_{ans\theta \leftarrow q' \in S'} q'$ and $S' = \mathsf{UnfoldDB}(Q^s, \mathcal{O}_m)$.

Clearly, this concludes the proof, since $(*)$ follows straightforwardly from the correctness of UnfoldDB. □

6.2 Query Answering

In Fig. 3 we present the algorithm Answer to answer UCQs posed over a *DL-Lite$_\mathcal{A}$* ontology with mappings. Informally, the algorithm takes as input a *DL-Lite$_\mathcal{A}$* ontology $\mathcal{O}_m$ with mappings and a UCQ Q over $\mathcal{O}_m$. If the ontology is not satisfiable, then it returns the set of all possible tuples of elements in $\Gamma_0 \cup \Gamma_\mathcal{V}$ denoted $AllTup(Q, \mathcal{O}_m)$, whose arity is the one of the query Q. Otherwise, it computes the perfect reformulation Q^p of Q, and then unfold Q^p by calling $\mathsf{UnfoldDB}(Q^p, \mathcal{O}_m)$ to compute the set of resultants S'. Then, for each resultant

Algorithm Answer
Input: *DL-Lite$_\mathcal{A}$* ontology with mappings $\mathcal{O}_m = \langle \mathcal{T}, \mathcal{M}, \mathcal{DB} \rangle$,
  UCQ Q over $\mathcal{O}_m$
Output: set of tuples R^s
  if $\mathcal{O}_m$ is not satisfiable
  then return *AllTup*$(Q, \mathcal{O}_m)$
  else
    $Q^p \leftarrow \bigcup_{q_i \in Q}$ PerfectRef$(q_i, \mathcal{T})$;
    $S' \leftarrow$ UnfoldDB$(Q^p, \mathcal{O}_m)$;
    $R^s \leftarrow \emptyset$;
    for each $ans\theta \leftarrow q' \in S'$ **do**
      $R^s \leftarrow R^s \cup ans(q', \mathcal{DB})\theta$;
    return R^s

Fig. 3. Algorithm Answer$(Q, \mathcal{O}_m)$

Q' in S', it extracts the conjunctive query in its body, evaluates it over $\mathcal{DB}$ and further processes the answers according to the substitution occurring in the head of Q'.

We next show the correctness of Algorithm Answer.

Theorem 5. *Let $\mathcal{O}_m = \langle \mathcal{T}, \mathcal{M}, \mathcal{DB} \rangle$ be a DL-Lite$_\mathcal{A}$ ontology with mappings, and Q a union of conjunctive queries over $\mathcal{O}_m$. Then, Answer$(Q, \mathcal{O}_m)$ terminates. Moreover, let R^s be the set of tuples returned by Answer$(Q, \mathcal{O}_m)$, and let $\mathbf{t}$ be a tuple of elements in $\Gamma_0 \cup \Gamma_V$. Then, $\mathbf{t} \in ans(Q, \mathcal{O}_m)$ if and only if $\mathbf{t} \in R^s$.*

Proof. The termination of the algorithm follows from the termination of the Algorithm PerfectRef and the function UnfoldDB.

Concerning the soundness and completeness of the Algorithm Answer, by Proposition 2, we have that: $Mod(\mathcal{O}_m) = Mod(\mathcal{O})$, where $\mathcal{O} = \langle \mathcal{T}, db(\mathcal{A}(\mathcal{M}, \mathcal{DB})) \rangle$. Moreover, given a union of conjunctive queries Q, as discussed in Section 2.4, we have that $ans(Q, \mathcal{O}) = ans(Q^p, db(\mathcal{A}(\mathcal{M}, \mathcal{DB})))$, where $(Q^p) =$ PerfectRef(Q). Then, since by definition, we have that:

- $ans(Q, \mathcal{O}) = \{\mathbf{t} \mid \mathbf{t}^I \in Q^I, I \in Mod(\mathcal{O})\}$, and
- $Q^{\mathcal{O}_m} = \{\mathbf{t} \mid \mathbf{t}^I \in Q^I, I \in Mod(\mathcal{O}_m)\}$,

it is easy to see that:

$$ans(Q, \mathcal{O}_m) = ans(Q^p, db(\mathcal{A}(\mathcal{M}, \mathcal{DB}))).$$

On the other hand, by construction, we have that:

$$R^s = \{\mathbf{t}'\theta \mid \mathbf{t}' \in ans(q', \mathcal{DB}), ans\theta \leftarrow q' \in S'\}$$

where S' is such that $S' =$ UnfoldDB$(Q^p, \mathcal{O}_m)$. Then, clearly, by the correctness of UnfoldDB, we obtain the claim. □

Note that the algorithm Answer reconstructs the result starting from the results obtained by evaluating the SQL queries q' over the database $\mathcal{DB}$. However, from a practical point of view, we can simply delegate such a reconstruction step to the SQL engine. Indeed, this is exactly what our current implementation does. In particular, in the implementation, the final **for each** loop in the algorithm is replaced by a step that, starting from S', builds an SQL query that, once evaluated over the data sources, computes directly the answers of the original query Q.

6.3 Computational Complexity

We first study the complexity of UnfoldDB. Note that, in this section, we assume that the mappings in $\mathcal{M}$ involve SQL queries over the underlying database $\mathcal{DB}$, and such SQL queries belong to the class of first-order logic queries. So, queries in the left-hand side of our mapping assertions, are LOGSPACE with respect to the size of the data in $\mathcal{DB}$.[11]

Lemma 5. *Let $\mathcal{O}_m = \langle \mathcal{T}, \mathcal{M}, \mathcal{DB} \rangle$ be a DL-Lite$_\mathcal{A}$ ontology with mappings, and Q a UCQ over $\mathcal{O}_m$. The function UnfoldDB$(Q, \mathcal{O}_m)$ runs in exponential time with respect to the size of Q, and in polynomial time with respect to the size of $\mathcal{M}$.*

Proof. Let Q be a UCQ, and let n be the total number of atoms in the body of all q's in Q. Moreover, let m be the number of mappings and let m_n be the maximum size of the body of mappings. The result follows immediately by considering the cost of each of the three steps of UnfoldDB$(Q, \mathcal{O}_m)$:

1. The construction of $\mathcal{P}(Q, \mathcal{M})$ is clearly polynomial in n and m.
2. The computation of SLD-Derive$(\mathcal{P}(Q, \mathcal{M}))$ builds first a tree of depth at most n such that each of its nodes has at most m children, and, second, it processes all the leaves of the tree to obtain the set S of resultants. By construction, this set has size $\mathcal{O}_m(m^n)$. Clearly, the overall computation has complexity $\mathcal{O}_m(m^n)$.
3. Finally, the application of the function $spread_{\mathcal{O}_m}$ to each element in S has complexity $\mathcal{O}_m(m^n \cdot m_n)$. □

Based on the above property, we are able to establish the complexity of checking the satisfiability of a *DL-Lite$_\mathcal{A}$* ontology with mappings and the complexity of answering UCQ over it.

Theorem 6. *Given a DL-Lite$_\mathcal{A}$ ontology with mappings $\mathcal{O}_m = \langle \mathcal{T}, \mathcal{M}, \mathcal{DB} \rangle$, Sat$(\mathcal{O}_m)$ runs LOGSPACE in the size of $\mathcal{DB}$ (data complexity). Moreover, it runs in polynomial time in the size of $\mathcal{M}$, and in polynomial time in the size of $\mathcal{T}$.*

---

[11] The assumption of dealing with SQL queries that are first-order logic queries allows for using the most common SQL constructs (except for few of them, e.g., the "groupby" construct). Obviously, our approach works also for arbitrary SQL queries. In such a case, the complexity of the overall approach is the complexity of evaluating such queries over the underlying database.

Proof. The claim is a consequence of the results discussed in Section 2.4, i.e., the fact that $\mathcal{O}_m$ is satisfiable if and only if $ans($Violates$(\mathcal{T}), db(\mathcal{A}(\mathcal{M}, \mathcal{DB})))$:

1. Violates$(\mathcal{T})$ returns a union of queries Q^s over $db(\mathcal{A}(\mathcal{M}, \mathcal{D}))$ whose size is polynomial in the size of $\mathcal{T}$;
2. each query Q contains two atoms and thus, by Lemma 5, the application of UnfoldDB to each Q is polynomial in the size of the mapping $\mathcal{M}$ and constant in the size of the data sources;
3. the evaluation of a union of SQL queries over a database can be computed in LOGSPACE with respect to the size of the database (since we assume that the SQL queries belong to the class of first-order logic queries). □

Theorem 7. *Given a DL-Lite$_\mathcal{A}$ ontology with mappings $\mathcal{O}_m$, and a UCQ Q over $\mathcal{O}_m$, Answer$(Q, \mathcal{O}_m)$ runs in* LOGSPACE *in the size of $\mathcal{DB}$ (data complexity). Moreover, it runs in polynomial time in the size of $\mathcal{M}$, in exponential time in the size of Q, and in polynomial time in the size of $\mathcal{T}$.*

Proof. The claim is a consequence of the results discussed in Section 2.4, i.e., the fact that $ans(Q, \mathcal{O}_m) = ans($PerfectRef$(Q, \mathcal{T}), db(\mathcal{A}(\mathcal{M}, \mathcal{DB})))$:

1. the maximum number of atoms in the body of a conjunctive query generated by the Algorithm PerfectRef is equal to the length of the initial query Q;
2. by Lemma 5, the algorithm PerfectRef $(Q, \mathcal{T})$ runs in time polynomial in the size of $\mathcal{T}$;
3. by Lemma 5, the cost of applying UnfoldDB to each conjunctive query in the union generated by PerfectRef has cost exponential in the size of the conjunctive query and polynomial in the size of $\mathcal{M}$; which implies that the query to be evaluated over the data sources can be computed in time exponential in the size of Q, polynomial in the size of $\mathcal{M}$ and constant in the size of $\mathcal{DB}$ (data complexity);
4. the evaluation of a union of SQL queries over a database can be computed in LOGSPACE with respect to the size of the database. □

7 Conclusions

We have studied the issue of ontology-based data access, under the fundamental assumption of keeping the data sources and the conceptual layer of an information system separate and independent. The solution provided in this paper is based on the adoption of the *DL-Lite$_\mathcal{A}$* description logic, which distinguishes between objects and values, and allows for connectingto external databases via suitable mappings. Notably, such a description logic admits advanced forms of reasoning, including satisfiability and query answering (with incomplete information), that are LOGSPACE in the size of the data at the sources. Even more significant from a practical point of view, *DL-Lite$_\mathcal{A}$* allows for reformulating such forms of reasoning in terms of the evaluation of suitable SQL queries issued over over the sources, while taking into account and solving the impedance mismatch between data and objects.

We are currently implementing our solution on top of the QuOnto system[12] [2], a tool for reasoning over ontologies of the *DL-Lite* family. QuOnto was originally based on *DL-Lite$_\mathcal{F}$*, a DL that does not distinguish between data and objects. By enhancing QuOnto with the ability of reasoning both over *DL-Lite$_\mathcal{A}$* ontologies and mappings, we have obtained a complete system for ontology-based data access.

While the possibility of reducing reasoning to query evaluation over the sources can only be achieved with description logics that are specifically tailored for this, such as *DL-Lite$_\mathcal{A}$*, we believe that the ideas presented in this paper on how to map a data layer to a conceptual layer and how to solve the impedance mismatch problem are of general value and can be applied to virtually all ontology formalisms.

References

1. Abiteboul, S., Hull, R., Vianu, V.: Foundations of Databases. Addison Wesley Publ. Co, Reading (1995)
2. Acciarri, A., Calvanese, D., De Giacomo, G., Lembo, D., Lenzerini, M., Palmieri, M., Rosati, R.: QuOnto: QUerying ONTOlogies. In: AAAI 2005. Proc. of the 20th Nat. Conf. on Artificial Intelligence, pp. 1670–1671 (2005)
3. Baader, F., Brandt, S., Lutz, C.: Pushing the $\mathcal{EL}$ envelope. In: IJCAI 2005. Proc. of the 19th Int. Joint Conf. on Artificial Intelligence, pp. 364–369 (2005)
4. Baader, F., Calvanese, D., McGuinness, D., Nardi, D., Patel-Schneider, P.F. (eds.): The Description Logic Handbook: Theory, Implementation and Applications. Cambridge University Press, Cambridge (2003)
5. Barrasa, J., Corcho, O., Gomez-Perez, A.: R2O, an extensible and semantically based database-to-ontology mapping language. In: WebDB 2004. Proc. of the 7th Int. Workshop on the Web and Databases (2004)
6. Calvanese, D., De Giacomo, G., Lembo, D., Lenzerini, M., Rosati, R.: DL-Lite: Tractable description logics for ontologies. In: AAAI 2005. Proc. of the 20th Nat. Conf. on Artificial Intelligence, pp. 602–607 (2005)
7. Calvanese, D., De Giacomo, G., Lembo, D., Lenzerini, M., Rosati, R.: Data complexity of query answering in description logics. In: KR 2006. Proc. of the 10th Int. Conf. on the Principles of Knowledge Representation and Reasoning, pp. 260–270 (2006)
8. Calvanese, D., De Giacomo, G., Lembo, D., Lenzerini, M., Rosati, R.: Tractable reasoning and efficient query answering in description logics: The DL-Lite family. J. of Automated Reasoning (to appear, 2007)
9. Calvanese, D., De Giacomo, G., Lenzerini, M., Nardi, D., Rosati, R.: Data integration in data warehousing. Int. J. of Cooperative Information Systems 10(3), 237–271 (2001)
10. Donini, F.M., Lenzerini, M., Nardi, D., Schaerf, A.: Deduction in concept languages: From subsumption to instance checking. J. of Logic and Computation 4(4), 423–452 (1994)
11. Goasdoue, F., Lattes, V., Rousset, M.-C.: The use of CARIN language and algorithms for information integration: The Picsel system. Int. J. of Cooperative Information Systems 9(4), 383–401 (2000)

---

[12] http://www.dis.uniroma1.it/~quonto/

12. Grosof, B.N., Horrocks, I., Volz, R., Decker, S.: Description logic programs: Combining logic programs with description logic. In: WWW 2003. Proc. of the 12th Int. World Wide Web Conf, pp. 48–57 (2003)
13. Heflin, J., Hendler, J.: A portrait of the Semantic Web in action. IEEE Intelligent Systems 16(2), 54–59 (2001)
14. Horrocks, I., Patel-Schneider, P.F., van Harmelen, F.: From $\mathcal{SHIQ}$ and RDF to OWL: The making of a web ontology language. J. of Web Semantics 1(1), 7–26 (2003)
15. Hull, R.: A survey of theoretical research on typed complex database objects. In: Paredaens, J. (ed.) Databases, pp. 193–256. Academic Press, London (1988)
16. Hull, R., Yoshikawa, M.: ILOG: Declarative creation and manipulation of object identifiers. In: VLDB 1990. Proc. of the 16th Int. Conf. on Very Large Data Bases, pp. 455–468 (1990)
17. Hustadt, U., Motik, B., Sattler, U.: Data complexity of reasoning in very expressive description logics. In: IJCAI 2005. Proc. of the 19th Int. Joint Conf. on Artificial Intelligence, pp. 466–471 (2005)
18. Komorowski, H.J.: A specification of an abstract Prolog machine and its application to partial evaluation. Technical Report LSST 69, Linköping University (1981)
19. Lenzerini, M.: Data integration: A theoretical perspective. In: PODS 2002. Proc. of the 21st ACM SIGACT SIGMOD SIGART Symp. on Principles of Database Systems, pp. 233–246 (2002)
20. Lloyd, J.W.: Foundations of Logic Programming, 2nd edn. Springer, Heidelberg (1987)
21. Lloyd, J.W., Shepherdson, J.C.: Partial evaluation in logic programming. J. of Logic Programming 11, 217–242 (1991)
22. Lutz, C.: Description logics with concrete domains: A survey. In: Balbiani, P., Suzuki, N.-Y., Wolter, F., Zakharyaschev, M. (eds.) Advances in Modal Logics, vol. 4, King's College Publications (2003)
23. Mädche, A., Motik, B., Silva, N., Volz, R.: MAFRA – a mapping framework for distributed ontologies. In: Gómez-Pérez, A., Benjamins, V.R. (eds.) EKAW 2002. LNCS (LNAI), vol. 2473, pp. 235–250. Springer, Heidelberg (2002)
24. Meseguer, J., Qian, X.: A logical semantics for object-oriented databases. In: Proc. of the ACM SIGMOD Int. Conf. on Management of Data, pp. 89–98 (1993)
25. Minker, J.: A logic-based approach to data integration. Theory and Practice of Logic Programming 2(3), 293–321 (2002)
26. Ortiz, M.M., Calvanese, D., Eiter, T.: Characterizing data complexity for conjunctive query answering in expressive description logics. In: AAAI 2006. Proc. of the 21st Nat. Conf. on Artificial Intelligence (2006)
27. Poggi, A.: Structured and Semi-Structured Data Integration. PhD thesis, Dipartimento di Informatica e Sistemistica, Università di Roma La Sapienza (2006)
28. Reiter, R.: On closed world data bases. In: Gallaire, H., Minker, J. (eds.) Logic and Databases, pp. 119–140. Plenum Publ. Co, New York (1978)
29. Scharffe, F., de Bruijn, J.: A language to specify mappings between ontologies. In: SITIS 2005. Proc. of the 1st Int. Conf. on Signal-Image Technology and Internet-Based Systems, pp. 267–271 (2005)
30. Serafini, L., Tamilin, A.: DRAGO: Distributed reasoning architecture for the Semantic Web. In: Gómez-Pérez, A., Euzenat, J. (eds.) ESWC 2005. LNCS, vol. 3532, pp. 361–376. Springer, Heidelberg (2005)
31. Vardi, M.Y.: The complexity of relational query languages. In: STOC 1982. Proc. of the 14th ACM SIGACT Symp. on Theory of Computing, pp. 137–146 (1982)

Context Representation in Domain Ontologies and Its Use for Semantic Integration of Data

Guy Pierra

Laboratory of Applied Computer Science (LISI)
National Engineering School for Mechanics and Aerotechnics (ENSMA), Poitiers
86960 Futuroscope Cedex - France
pierra@ensma.fr

Abstract. The goal of this paper is to identify various aspects of context-awareness needed to facilitate semantics integration of data, and to discuss how this knowledge may be represented within ontologies. We first present a taxonomy of ontologies and we show how various kinds of ontologies may cooperate. Then, we compare ontologies and conceptual models. We claim that their main difference is the consensual nature of ontologies when conceptual models are specifically designed for one particular target system. Reaching consensus, in turn, needs specific models of which context dependency has been represented and minimized. We identify five principles for making ontologies less contextual than models and suitable for data integration and we show, as an example, how these principles have been implemented in the PLIB ontology model developed for industrial data integration. Finally, we suggest a road map for switching from conventional databases to ontology-based databases without waiting until standard ontologies are available in every domains.

1 Introduction

A number of computer science problems, including heterogeneous database integration, natural language processing, intelligent document retrieval would benefit from the capability to model the absolute meaning of things of a domain, independently of any particular use of them. In the structured-data universe, information is represented as data. Indeed, many studies have been performed to integrate heterogeneous and autonomous databases [8], in particular using domain ontologies [33]. Distributed architecture models have been developed, where mediators [34] provide uniform access to heterogeneous data sources. Mediators export integrated schemas that reconcile data both at the structural (schematic heterogeneity) and at the meaning level (semantic heterogeneity). If large progresses have been made to automate schema integration at the structural level, using in particular new model management techniques [3], the major challenge remains the automation of semantic integration of several heterogeneous schemas. Such an automation would need enabling programs to identify unambiguously:

– those data having exactly the same semantic meaning,
– those data that are similar and may be converted in or compared with each others by given processes, and
– those data having no semantic commonality.

In the above list, data may be either atomic or structured data like tuple or entity instance. On the Internet, data is not the only means for representing information, another one is largely used, namely documents. Large progresses were achieved by search engines to retrieve over the Internet the most relevant documents with respect to a user query expressed as a sentence of words. Unfortunately, if semantic of both the query and target documents are not made computer-sensible, it is impossible to retrieve documents dealing with the query subject without using exactly the same words (e.g., worker instead of employee, size instead of length or convertible instead of car). Here again some kinds of computer interpretable representation of word meaning is needed:

– in a first step to improve search engine in order to retrieve which documents are semantically relevant for a topic defined by a set of words, even when the same words are not used, and
– in a second step, to retrieve which documents might provide answer to a user query.

Both kinds of information integration requiring explicit representation of meaning, these last ten years a lot of work has been done to develop domain ontology models[1] intended to capture the a priori nature of reality of some Universe of Discourse (UoD), as independently as possible from any particular use of this reality. Once defined, such representations may then be used to reconcile various information sources addressing this UoD at the meaning level.

The word ontology is now extensively used in a number of computer science domains, including e.g., knowledge management, natural language processing, database, object oriented modeling. If there seems to be some consensus on what an ontology structure should be - categories (classes), properties, logical relationships - the focus of the various approaches is so different that the same word seems to represent quite different realities, and that ontologies developed, e.g., for natural language processing seems to be nearly useless for e.g., database integration, and conversely.

The goal of this paper is twofold. The first goal is to investigate the concept of an ontology in a structured-data integration perspective. We claim that the major difference between ontologies and conceptual models is the existence of a consensus that founds ontologies as a shared meaning, and that consensus, in turn, needs representation of the modeling context. As an example, it is easy to reach consensus on the fact that the *resistance* is an essential property of a *resistor*. But the *resistance* depends upon the *temperature* where the *resistance* is measured, and it is nearly impossible to reach consensus on the *temperature*

---

[1] In this paper, we only consider domain ontologies, and not upper-level generic ontologies. Thus, for short, ontology means domain ontology.

where the *resistance* should be measured since this temperature depends upon the resistor target usage. To include in the ontology model a mechanism allowing to represent with each *resistance* value the *temperature* where it was evaluated (value-evaluation context awareness) enables consensus since it allows each user category to select its own *resistance* measuring process while making explicit commonality and differences. Thus, we propose five principles allowing to make ontologies much more generic through context representation, and thus more suitable for heterogeneous data integration. The second goal is to show how these principles have been implemented in the ontology model we have developed over the last 15 years. Discussed within an international standardization project (see Annex A), the PLIB ontology model (officially ISO 13584), was initially developed for giving meaning to technical data and for providing for automatic integration of heterogeneous engineering data sources. The overview of PLIB presented in this paper allows both to illustrate the context representation principles that we propose, and to show some typical uses of this ontology model.

The content of this paper is as follows. In the next section, we discuss the various kinds of ontologies needed for representing semantics. We distinguish between document-oriented linguistic ontology (LO) and information-modeling-oriented conceptual ontology (CO). In section 3, we investigate the differences between ontologies and models, and we propose mechanisms to represent both modeling and value context within an ontology. In section 4, we outline how PLIB ontologies are specified (and exchanged) thanks to an executable specification defined in the EXPRESS data specification language, and we present how context-awareness mechanisms are represented in the PLIB ontology model. In section 5, we present a formal model of PLIB ontologies, including the mapping capabilities to external ontologies, and we outline how such ontologies may be used to integrate various heterogeneous data bases. We suggest, in section 6, a road map for switching from conventional databases to ontology-based databases. A discussion of related work regarding context representation, ontology models and data integration is presented in section 7. Conclusion is presented in section 8. Some standards being quoted in the paper, Annex A outlines the standardization activities around PLIB.

2 Concept Ontologies and Linguistic Ontologies

Since the term ontology was borrowed from philosophy and introduced in the computer science vocabulary, many definitions have been offered. The most commonly cited definition is one by T. Gruber "An ontology is an explicit specification of a conceptualization", therefore "shared ontologies" provide for "knowledge sharing" [15]. In all the ontology models, such a conceptualization consists of three parts :

- *primitive items* of the ontology (where items are either classes or properties) are those items "for which we are not able to give a complete axiomatic

definition; we must rely on textual documentation and a background of knowledge shared with the reader" [15],
- *defined items* are those items for which the ontology provides a complete axiomatic definition by means of necessary and sufficient conditions, and
- *logical relationships* (or *inference rules*) provide for reasoning over ontology items, and for supporting some problem-solving activities over the ontology domain.

The agreed definition and structure description leave open what may be considered as the major criteria for classifying ontologies and ontology models: whether their area of interest consists of beings (what does exist in the world) or of words (how beings are apprehended and reflected in a particular natural language).

We call linguistic ontologies (LO) those ontologies whose goal is to represent the meaning of the words used in a particular UoD in a particular language. We call concept ontology (CO) those ontologies whose goal is to represent the categories of objects and object properties that are used to apprehend some part of the world. These two kinds of ontologies address quite different problems and should have quite different contents.

LOs [9] are document-oriented. The typical problem they address may be termed as follows:
"find all documents relevant to a query expressed as a set of words possibly connected by logical operators like AND, OR and NOT, even if these documents do not contain these words".

Since natural languages contain a number of different words for reflecting identical or similar meanings, LOs are large in nature. They include a number of *conservative definitions*, i.e., defined items that only introduce terminology and do not add any knowledge about the world [15]. They are language-specific and they use a number of linguistic relationships such that *synonym, hypernym, hyponym, overlap, covering, disjoint* to capture in a semi-formal way meaning relations [33]. Such relationships being not formally grounded, inference could only provide some help to a user supposed to be involved in some computer-aided search process. Development of LOs may be done through a semi-automatic process where significant words are automatically extracted from a document collection and then validated and structured by experts.

COs, for instance the measure ontology [15], are information-modeling-oriented. The typical problem they address may be termed as follows:
"decide whether two instances belong to the same class and whether two properties have identical meaning or may be converted into each other".

To be able to represent all the beings existing in some part of the world, COs need only to describe those primitive concepts that cannot be derived from other concepts. Like technical vocabulary where one and only one word should always be used for the same meaning, COs may be restricted to primitive concepts. Such primitive COs, that we call *canonical conceptual ontologies* (CCOs), are compact in nature. To reduce again the number of concepts that need to be represented, COs may also be property-oriented. This means that in place of introducing a number of different concepts such that "10-HP-engine","20-HP-engine","25-HP-engine", they introduce only two concepts that may express the same meaning: one class (engine) and one integer-valued property (power in HP). Indeed, only those classes that cannot be represented by restriction of an existing class by means of property values need to belong to a property-oriented CCO. The focus being on primitive concepts, and understanding such concepts being based on reader background knowledge, an extensive information model has to be used to describe both textually and formally each primitive concept. COs are multilingual because most concepts are language-independent. Even though a collection of documents in one particular language of which significant words are automatically extracted may be used as a starting point for defining a CO of some domain, development of a CO is mainly manual. Finally, if the relationships involved in a CO are formally defined, and if two data sources reference the same CO, semantic integration of these data sources may be done automatically [2].

Table 1. Typical characteristics of LO and CO

	LO	CO
Tokens	Word	Concept
Token identification	Word	Id
Token definition	Sentence	Model
Ontology Size	Extensive	Minimal
Relations	Formal + Linguistic	Formal
Content	Primitive Items	Primitive Items (CCO)
	+ Conservative Definitions	+ Conservative Definitions (NCCO)
Focus	Class-oriented	Property-oriented
Development	Automatic/Semi-automatic	Semi-automatic/Manual
Ontology usage	Computer-aided tasks	Task automation

When the goal of a CO is to define a common language for data exchange or data integration, CCOs are well suited. For data integration, the use of CCOs assumes that each source or agent is in charge of converting its own vocabulary onto the shared CCO. It is the approach followed by the PLIB ontology model developed to support exchange of industrial data. In PLIB ontologies, equivalences between ontology concepts are not represented within the PLIB ontology but as an external mapping between ontologies, called ontology articulations (see section 5.2). Example 1 presents an informal description of a small CCO that represents some categories of industrial components[2].

Example 1. A circular bearing is a mechanical component used to connect and to transmit load between two cylindrical shapes having the same axis but different diameters and rotational movements. Characteristic properties include *width*, *inner diameter* and *outer diameter*. But a crucial property, called *life-time*, is

---
[2] Such an ontology is formally defined in ISO 23768 using the PLIB ontology model.

the length of the time period where the bearing will behave correctly. The value of this property depends upon the number of revolutions done by the bearing, and of the load it must support. Mathematically, the bearing *life-time* is a function of the *velocity* (i.e. rotational speed), the *radical load* and the *axial load*. At the class level, *circular bearings* may be *circular ball bearings* (there are also other kinds of bearings, not modeled within this small ontology, having, e.g., needles or rollers). The *ball diameter* is a property that should be defined at the level of *circular ball bearing* where it is meaningful. Figure 1 presents the main properties of a *circular ball bearing*.

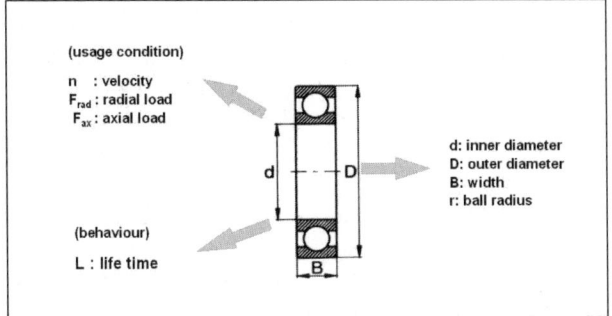

Fig. 1. Characterization of a bearing

Equivalence of concepts may also be represented within a CO. This may be done for instance using either formal class relationships like set-oriented operations (union, intersection and difference) and class restrictions (by property values), as it is done in OWL [20], or property value deduction, as it is done by F-logic rules, or property value algebraic derivation function, like in the EXPRESS language [30]. For example, the *thickness* of the bearing may be defined as (*outer diameter* − *inner diameter*)/2. Such COs, that we call *non-canonical conceptual ontologies* (NCCO), allow to integrate in the same ontology different conceptualizations and the articulations between them. NCCOs are in particular largely used in artificial intelligence. They allow to make inference over concept equivalence, but they often encounter scaling problems for processing large data sets.

Table 1 emphasizes the main differences between COs and LOs. But, in fact, LO, NCCO and CCO are complementary, and, in a number of ontology-based applications, all three kinds of constructs are needed over the same domain. It is the case, for instance, when a domain ontology is built using natural language processing (NLP) tools that extract terms from a document corpus. This set of terms is progressively structured by domain experts into a LO that contains both formal relationships, such that subsumption and class-property links, and linguistic relationships such that homonymy or synonymy. In this ontology, entries are still words of a particular language. From this LO, a NCCO may be extracted under expert supervision. In this ontology, entries become identifiers, and relationships are based on a clear mathematical semantics. Finally, a CCO may be chosen from the NCCO and all non-canonical concepts are formally defined in terms of canonical concepts. Note that this process is quite similar to the one defined in [24]. Similarly, all three kinds of constructs are also needed when one wants indexing a set of documents by means of concepts of a CO, either CCO or NCCO. If the starting ontology is a CCO, a NCCO needs first to be defined to address all the concepts usual in the CCO domain, even when some of them might be represented by some other ones. Then, a LO must be developed on top of this NCCO. This LO must include all the language-specific terms, and term patterns, that may be considered as representing each particular concept or particular property. Then, these terms may be used for indexing a set of documents, either automatically or under expert supervision. These two possible approaches for building domain ontology suggest a layered view of domain ontologies [18] in which CCOs, NCCOs and LOs may cooperate. In this view, a kernel CCO defines all the UoD semantics. We call this layer the *characterization layer*. Thanks to this CCO, any object belonging to the UoD may be characterized by class belonging and property-value pairs, thus providing a canonical language for information exchange. At the second layer, that we call *integration layer*, a NCCO extends this conceptual vocabulary by means of conservative definitions to encompass all concepts broadly used in the domain. Using the ontology defined according to this layer, several data sources addressing the same domain but based on different CCOs may be integrated, and inference may be performed. At the third layer, that we call *discourse layer*, a LO provides a multilingual natural language interface for person-system and person-person communication. Figure 1 show the resulting onion-shaped model that we call the Characterization-Integration-Discourse CID model of domain ontology.

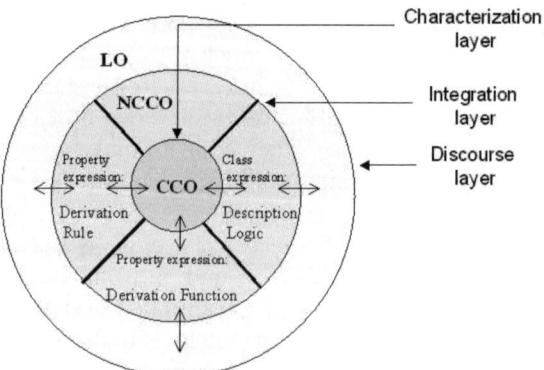

Fig. 2. The CID layered model of domain ontologies

Example 2. A CCO for characterizing (to some extent) persons might define the class *person* with two properties: *gender* and *age*. If one wants to cover more broadly the same domain, the two classes *man* and *woman* need to be introduced in a NCCO. *Man* for instance being defined as a *person* whose *gender=* male. Migrating to LO would need, beside the terms used as labels for the NCCO and that are formally grounded on this NCCO, other terms such that *children, boy, girl, oldster* that could not be formally defined.

Data integration being mainly concerned with CO, in the next section we discuss the differences between CO and conceptual models.

3 Concept Ontologies Versus Model

In the previous section we have discussed the differences between the various kinds of domain ontologies and we have proposed a model representing how they may fit and cooperate altogether. In this section we propose to clarify the differences between domain ontologies and conceptual models. Indeed, a conceptual model may be considered as an "explicit specification of a conceptualization". Therefore, as noticed by Guarino and Welty [16], conceptual models are sometimes denoted as ontologies. But we perfectly know that conceptual modeling leaves open the semantic heterogeneity problem. Thus, it is worthwhile investigating the difference between a shared ontology and a model if we want to use ontology as a tool for semantic integration of data.

An old definition from Minsky [22] would introduce the discussion: "To an observer B, an object A* is a model of an object A to the extent that B can use A* to answer questions that interest him about A". This definition emphasizes the ternary character of a model relationship: it depends on the object (A) and the observer (B), but it depends also on which questions the observer is interested about A. In other terms, in which context the model was built. In data engineering, we are in line with this definition when we teach that a conceptual model shall be built within a precise context. The key point here is that when one designs an application system, the context of the modeling activity is defined by the target system goals and environment. The functions that two systems must perform are never exactly the same. Thus models are always slightly different, enough to make instance data incompatible.

This shows that usual conceptual models can hardly fit several needs. If one wants to build shared ontologies, i.e., ontologies that reflect the information requirements of several application contexts, not only the conceptualization approach must be different from usual modeling activity directed toward a specific target system, but also the conceptualization formalism must have specific capabilities to allow specification of generic models. These generic models must be either context-independent or at least context explicit to fit the needs of various application contexts.

Importance of context representation for semantic integration of heterogeneous database was already underlined by researchers in multidatabase systems. Kashyap et al. [19] proposed an explicit representation of the modeling context at the schema definition level. For instance, what is the meaning of the "width" property when we try to use it with a "car engine" without knowing in the context of which class and with which precise meaning this property was described?

The property becomes clear when we know that it was defined in a *packaging perspective* for any *material object* as the *width of the virtual box* where it might be packaged.

But even if a property definition is clearly understood, property value may also be context dependent, such context-sensitivity was studied in particular by [31], [14]. These authors proposed to represent context at the extensional level, i.e., at the level of data values and object instances. For instance, what means the temperature of a particular city if we do not know when this temperature was measured, and in which unit? What means the life time of a bearing if we do not know which load it supports and what would be its rotational speed?

In fact most of the causes of semantic conflicts in data integration result from implicit context, either in schema definition or in value evaluation. They may be solved if both the *modeling context* and the *value context* are made explicit. Goh [14] identified three main causes for semantic heterogeneity:

1. *naming conflicts* occur when naming schemas of information differ significantly. A frequent phenomenon is the presence of homonyms and synonyms. We claim that naming conflicts may be avoided if data base schemas refer explicitly for all the shared concepts they represent to identifiers of a shared conceptual ontology, and if this shared ontology makes explicit the context of each definition. *Driving license id* is unambiguous if it is defined in the context of a *French car drivers* class, it becomes ambiguous (and may have several values) in a context of a *person*.
2. *scaling conflicts* occur when different reference systems are used to measure the value of some properties. Examples are different currencies. Scaling conflict may be avoided, either by associating explicitly at the schema level a computer-interpretable representation of the unit that shall be used for any value of a property, or by associating explicitly with each value its own unit.
3. *confounding conflicts* occur when information items seem to have the same meaning, but differ in reality, e.g., due to different temporal contexts. We claim that confounding conflicts may be avoided by investigating whether a value is an intrinsic and permanent property of some instance, or it depends on some evaluation context, and, in the latter case, by associating this value with its context. For instance the *driving license id* of a person depends on the *country* where the license was issued, its *weight* depends on the *date* where it was recorded, but its *birth date* is not context dependent (once the scaling conflicts is solved as above).

Moreover, most causes of schematic conflicts, and in particular schema isomorphism conflicts which means that semantically similar entities have a different number of attributes [19] also result from context sensitivity. It is not so difficult to identify, to describe and to reach consensus in some community on all the major properties which are rigid [16], i.e. which necessarily hold for all instances of a class. For instance, each *customer* has a *birth date*, each *mechanical component* has a *weight*, and each *town* has a (current) *number of inhabitants*. But it is impossible to agree on those rigid properties that should be represented for each class in a database. Thus, ontological description of a class should describe all its rigid properties (at least within some rather broad context common to all data sources that might exist in some target community) in order to reduce context-dependency in the class description. Then, each schema may restrict this general description to its design context by selecting those ontology-defined properties that are relevant to the problem at hand and are thus represented in the database. For instance, the *weight* or *birth date* of a *person* are seldom used in a customer database. So, when several schemas refer to a same ontology by means explicit mappings [2], these mappings allow to identify automatically which ontology-defined properties are semantically equivalent in several data sources, which properties are represented in some data sources without being represented in some others, and, possibly, which properties if any are not defined in the common ontology.

This discussion allows to define five principles that should be followed by ontology models to provide for automatic integration of several data sources. It also suggests five mechanisms that may be proposed for satisfying each principle.

- *Definition context representation.* At the schema level the modeling context in which each class or property is defined should be explicitly represented and minimized.
  Proposed mechanism: to represent its definition context, each property should be defined in the context of a class that defines its domain of application. To minimize its context-sensitivity, each class should define all its rigid properties, at least in some very broad context common to all the target data sources.
- *Point of view representation.* The perspective adopted by the modeling team when the ontology is designed and agreed upon in some community should be explicitly represented.
  Proposed mechanism: if several perspectives are needed over the ontology target domain, an ontology of perspectives should be defined or referenced. Then, each needed perspective should correspond to a specific domain ontology. Different perspectives over the same real world object should be represented either by an instance aggregate, one instance per perspective-specific ontology, or by multi-instantiation.
- *Locality of interpretation context.* Importation of resources from one ontology into another one should be possible while controlling the impact of the former over the interpretation of the latter.
  Proposed mechanism: importation on a class per class basis, and, for a class, on a property per property basis should be feasible. Domains of both ontologies should be separated.
- *Value context representation.* At the value level, the local context in which each value is evaluated should be explicit.
  Proposed mechanism: when the property value of some ontology class instance depends upon some evaluation context, this evaluation context should

be modeled by properties defined over this evaluation context, and the former property should be modeled as a function over the latter properties.
– *Value scaling representation* When the same property magnitude may be represented by different values depending upon some scaling process, scale should be explicitly represented, either at the ontology level, or at the instance level.
Proposed mechanism: When property value represents a physical (resp. a financial) amount, represent or reference in a computer-sensible way the physical unit (resp. the currency unit) used for scaling the value.

We present in the next section how these mechanisms have been implemented and may be represented in the PLIB ontology model.

4 PLIB: A Context-Explicit Ontology for Data Integration

Initiated in the early 90's the goal of the PLIB project was to develop an approach and standard models for exchanging and integrating automatically engineering component databases [26]. To allow such an automatic integration, an ontology-based approach has been developed. An ontology model (known as the PLIB ontology model) has been defined[3] and each PLIB-based data source is supposed to contain at least three parts: (1) an *ontology*, (2) a *database schema*, and (3) *instance data* represented according to the schema that references the ontology. Because one cannot assume that complete shared ontologies will ever exist, each database must have its own local ontology. But, to make automatic integration feasible, each particular local ontology may also contain (4) a *mapping* onto pre-existing shared ontology(ies) (e.g., standard ontologies) through semantic relationships. In particular, a specific subsumption relationship called *case-of* was defined to allow a local ontology to reference a shared ontology and to import properties without needing to duplicate class or property definitions. Development of standard ontologies is encouraged. Several such ontologies already exist or are in progress (see Annex A).

The role of a PLIB ontology is twofold. First it is intended to support user query over integrated component databases. Such queries need to be supported at various levels of abstraction (a *screw*, a *machine screw*, an *hexagon machine screw*, an *ISO 1014-compliant hexagon machine screw*). Thus, subsumption is a key feature of any PLIB ontology. Second, it provides for automatic integration.

We first present in this section a formalization of PLIB ontologies. 4.1 gives a short overview of the EXPRESS data specification language, and 4.2 presents, through two simplified schemas, the global architecture of the formal PLIB specification. Then, clauses 4.3 to 4.7 present the main mechanisms used to make context explicit in PLIB ontologies. Finally, clause 4.8 discusses the relationships between ontologies and schema in databases.

---
[3] ISO 13584-42:1998. Industrial Automation Systems and Integration, Parts Library, Methodology For Structuring Part Families. H. U. Wiedmer and G. Pierra, Eds. ISO, Geneva, 1998.

4.1 Specification of the PLIB Ontology Model: EXPRESS

The PLIB ontology model is defined in EXPRESS, a standard data specification language initially developed in ISO [30] to represent product models in the engineering field. The major advantage of this language is the integration of schema definition, constraint specification and instance representation capabilities in a common formalism with common semantics. This integration avoids the use of several models and languages like e.g., UML, OCL and XMI.

A specification in EXPRESS is represented by a set of schemas that may refer to each other. Each schema contains two parts. The first part is a set of entities that are structured in an object oriented approach supporting multiple inheritance. The second part is a procedural part that contains procedures and functions. These procedures and functions are used for restricting the allowed interpretation of the schemas by describing constraints on data. They are also used to specify how the value of a property of some entity may be computed from values of some other properties (derivation functions).

Each entity is described by a set of properties called attributes. Each attribute has a range (where it takes its values) defining a data type. It can be either a simple type (like integer, string ...), an entity type (meaning that the attribute establishes a relationship with another entity), a union of type (like integer OR string) or a collection over any data type (collections may be list, set, bag and array that are hard encoded in EXPRESS).

Syntactically one writes:

```
SCHEMA Foo1;
TYPE number_or_string = SELECT (REAL, STRING);END_TYTPE;
                              ENTITY b;
ENTITY a;                       att_1:number_or_string;
 att_a:OPTIONAL INTEGER;        att_2:LIST [0:?] OF STRING;
INVERSE                         att_3:a;
 att_i:                         DERIVE
   SET [0:2] OF b FOR att_3;    att_4:BOOLEAN
END_ENTITY;                         := EXISTS(SELF.att_3.att_a);
                              END_ENTITY;
END_SCHEMA;
```

Informally, the entity b has three attributes: a value that may be either a real or a string, a list of any number of strings and a pointer to another entity a. Entity a has only one integer attribute that may have no value (lack of value is represented by a particular symbol). Attribute att_i is an inverse attribute of entity a, corresponding to the inverse link defined by attribute att_3 in entity b. At most, two instances of b may reference an instance of a. Attribute att_4 is a derived attribute of entity b computed by the predefined EXPRESS function EXISTS. This function evaluates to *true* if its parameter has a value. In the case of entity b, this parameter is the optional att_a attribute of the instance of entity a referenced by the current instance (optional keyword SELF) of entity b. As usual, EXPRESS uses the dot notation to access attributes of an entity.

Semantically, an entity has a model. In the EXPRESS community, the model is named a physical file. The model consists of a set of entity instances with explicit instance identity. The attribute values are either literal values of the EXPRESS simple or structured built-in types or they are references to other entity instances. Instead of entering into deep semantic details, we give below an example of a model (physical file) which can be associated to the previous entity definitions. Note that an EXPRESS schema is an executable specification. EXPRESS compilers are able to generate both storage structures for managing EXPRESS models, checking constraints over these data or computing derivation functions and programs able to read and write physical files for which a standard syntax has been defined.

Let us consider a particular instance of the entity b, where att_1 evaluates to 4.0, att_2 is the list ('hello', 'bye') and att_3 points the particular instance of the entity a whose att_a attribute evaluates to 3. Then, the model (physical file) associated to these particular instances of the entities A and B is described by (derived and inverse attributes are not represented as they may be computed):

```
# 1=A(3);
# 2=B(4.0, ('hello','bye'), #1);
```

It is possible to limit the allowed population (elements) of the models to those instances that satisfy some stated constraints. EXPRESS uses first order logic which is completely processable since the set of instances (physical file) is finite. Constraints are introduced thanks to the WHERE clause of EXPRESS that provides for instance invariant, and thanks to the global RULE clause that provides for model invariant.

Let us assume that the allowed values for att_a in a are [1..10] and that exactly two instances of entity a shall have an attribute value equals to 1. We may write (QUERY is a built-in iterator on class, and SIZEOF a built-in function that returns the size of a collection):

```
ENTITY a;
   att_A:OPTIONAL INTEGER;
WHERE
   WR1: correct_range (SELF.att_A);   -- WR1 is the constraint label
END_ENTITY;
RULE Card FOR a;
   WHERE SIZEOF(QUERY(inst <* a|inst.att_a=1)) = 2; END_RULE;
FUNCTION correct_range (val: integer): Boolean;
   BEGIN RETURN ((val>=1) AND (val<=10));END_FUNCTION;
```

All value domains and operators are extended with the INDETERMINATE ('?') value to process optional attributes, and EXPRESS uses a tree-valued logic (TRUE, UNKNOWN, FALSE) to return values of predicates that cannot be assigned a Boolean result. Assignment, sequence and control structures (if statements, loops and recursion) can be used in the function bodies. These features give powerful expression possibilities to the language. Indeed, one gets the same expression possibility as other recursive specification languages. Derivations and constraints are the only places where functions may occur. They provide the two high level abstraction mechanisms identified as necessary in data driven active databases. Therefore, it is possible to specify formally a large class of problems. Moreover, derivations and constraints are inherited. These features define a set inclusion semantics to the EXPRESS inheritance mechanism.

4.2 PLIB Syntax and Semantics

To provide for easy integration of several ontologies, PLIB uses a meta-modeling approach for representing both ontologies, and ontology-based representation of domain objects. These two schemas are connected by formal constraints to ensure that instances of ontology classes fit with class descriptions. The partial schema below outlines the global structure of the PLIB ontology (meta) model (the data_type entity, not detailed, allows to specify the data type of a property).

```
SCHEMA PLIB_ontology;
TYPE class_id=STRING;END_TYPE; TYPE prop_id=STRING;END_TYPE;
TYPE class_ref=SELECT (class, class_id);END_TYPE;
TYPE prop_ref=SELECT (property, prop_id);END_TYPE;
ENTITY property;
 code:STRING; version:STRING; name:STRING; domain:class_ref;
 range:data_type; value_context:SET [0:?] OF prop_ref;
DERIVE
 prop_id:STRING:= compute_class_id(domain)+'.'+code +'-'+version;
END_ENTITY;
ENTITY class;
 id:class_id;  name:STRING;  superclass:OPTIONAL class_ref;
 case_of:SET [0:?] OF class_ref;
 imported_properties:SET [0:?] OF prop_ref;
 new_applicable_properties:SET [0:?] OF prop_ref;
DERIVE
 known_applicable_properties
    :SET [0:?] OF prop_ref := compute_applic (SELF);
WHERE
 WR1: is_acyclic([SELF], SELF.superclass);
 WR2: correct_importation(SELF.imported_properties, SELF.case_of);
 WR3: correct_applicability(SELF.new_applicable_properties, SELF);
END_ENTITY;
```

Properties and classes are identified by universal identifiers (UId) (*prop_id* and *class_id*), but references between them are done either by these identifiers, or by instance references to allow exchanging partial ontologies or referencing external ontologies. A property is defined in the context of the higher class (*domain*) where it is meaningful, even if it is not applicable (semi-rigid [16]) to some of its subclasses. Its UId concatenates the identifier of this class (user-defined function *compute_class_id*), its *code* and its *version*. If the value of a property depends upon some evaluation context (see 4.6), parameters that characterize this context are specified (*value_context*). A class has at most one superclass. It selects among all the inherited (semi-rigid) properties, those that become applicable, (rigid [16]), i.e., essential for all its instances (*new_applicable_properties*). Moreover, it may also establish subsumption links with other preexisting classes (*case-of*), for instance from standard ontologies, of which it imports any number of properties (*imported_properties*).

The rules that govern the semantics of such a specification are formally defined by means of user-defined functions. As examples, *is_acyclic* asserts that subclass/superclass relationships do not include loops, *correct_importation* asserts that only properties defined for the classes referenced by means of *case_of* are imported from these classes and *correct_applicability* asserts that the current class is (possibly by inheritance) in the domain of all the properties it selects as applicable by *new_applicable_properties*). The final set of applicable properties of a class (that gathers inherited applicable properties, new applicable properties and imported properties) is also formally specified by means of a function (*known_applicable_properties*). When the specification is run over some model (physical file), if some classes are only referenced by their *class_ids* but are not available in the model, the assertions do not fail. They return an UNKNOWN result as allowed by the EXPRESS language.

Let us consider the class of *ball bearing* presented in Fig.2. Let us assume that it is a subclass of a predefined *bearing* class whose *class_id* attributes equals 'XX.bearing-1' and where all Fig.2 properties, but *ball radius*, are already defined as applicable. Then, the model (physical file) allowing to extend this predefined ontology by a new *ball bearing* class associated with a new *ball radius* applicable property would be as follows (*measure_type*, not detailed here, allows to represent a subtype of *data_type* that is a real number associated with a measure unit, and '()' represents the empty set):

```
# 1=PROPERTY('b_radius','1','ball radius','XX.ball_bear-1,#10);
#10= MEASURE_TYPE(...);
# 2=CLASS('XX.ball_bear-1','ball bearing','XX.bearing-1',(),(),(#1));
```

Ontologies being represented as instances of the PLIB ontology schema, another schema, called the PLIB instance schema, has been developed for representing domain objects (e.g., a particular ball bearing) as ontology individuals. Such individuals, called ontology-based data, may be exchanged together or without the domain ontologies to which they correspond. The partial schema below outlines the structure of the PLIB instance schema (the REFERENCE clause imports all the definitions from a referenced schema):

```
SCHEMA PLIB_instance;
REFERENCE FROM PLIB_ontology;
TYPE primitive_value=SELECT (integer, string, instance); END_TYPE;
ENTITY property_value;
 property:prop_ref; value:primitive_value;
WHERE WR1: correct_type(SELF.property, SELF.value);
```

```
END_ENTITY;
ENTITY instance;
 class:class_ref; properties:LIST [0:?] OF property_value;
WHERE WR1: correct_properties(SELF.class, SELF.properties);
END_ENTITY;
```

When ontology and ontology-based data are gathered in the same model (i.e., physical file or database), thanks to the constraints specification capabilities of the EXPRESS language, constraints over the instance schema allow to assert that each ontology individuals complies with its ontological definition in the following sense. The user-defined *correct_type* function ensures that the value of each property belongs to the range defined for this property at the ontology level. The user-defined *correct_properties* function ensures that an instance of an ontology class may only be described by properties that are applicable to this class, and that if the evaluation context of a property depends upon some other properties, any value of the former is associated with values of the latter. Note that the database schema of a class consists of the union of all its applicable properties that are associated with values for at least one of its instances.

Let us consider an instance of the *ball bearing* class presented in Fig.2 that is only described by its *ball radius* property that evaluates to 3.0 (in the unit specified for this property in the ontology, e.g., millimeter). Then, the model (physical file) allowing to represent this particular bearing would be as follows :

```
# 1=PROPERTY_VALUE('XX.ball_bear-1.b_radius-1',3.0);
# 2=INSTANCE('XX.ball_bear-1',(#1));
```

Thus, both PLIB ontologies and PLIB ontology-based data may be modeled, exchanged and checked for consistency by automatic tools generated from the two EXPRESS schemas. Note that only simplified versions of these schemas were presented above. We describe informally in the next sections, the various mechanisms used to make context explicit in PLIB ontologies.

4.3 Global Structuring of the Definition Context and Point of View Representation

The role of ontologies being to capture the essence of beings, PLIB supports a distinction between:

- those properties that are rigid [16] for a class, i.e., that are *essential* for any instance of a class (i.e., that must hold or have a value): all these properties are associated with a particular class
- those properties that may or not hold or exist according to the role in which an entity is involved.

Each category of real world objects is represented by one or more ontology classes. One particular class, point of view-independent, contains all the rigid properties. If needed, point of view-specific classes gather those additional properties that correspond to a particular point of view over objects of the real world class.

For instance having a *birth date* is an essential property for any *person*: such a birth date may be unknown in some context, but, if it does not exist, the person does not exist. Contrariwise, having a *salary* is not an essential property. It exists only if the *person* is an employee of some organization and it corresponds to a *working status* point of view. For a mechanical part, having a *mass* is a rigid property, having a *price* is not. The *price* only exists if the part is sold on the market, and the price depends on the market (e.g., wholesaler or retail sale, quantity of order, discounted customer). It corresponds to the *marketing* point of view.

Of course, in a database schema, a *person* may have a *salary*, and a *part* may have a *price* and a *supplier*, but this is based on some implicit context assumptions that shall be explicit at the ontological level.

In fact, a PLIB ontology consists of three categories of classes of which only the first one was presented in clause 4.2.

- *definition classes* (modeled by the *class* entity in clause 4.2) capture the *beings* of the area of interest, together with all their rigid properties.
- *functional model classes* represent the additional properties that result from a particular role or point of view [27]. A functional model class exists only when associated with a definition class. Each instance of a functional model class is a view of an instance of a definition class. This relationship is termed *is-view-of*.
- *Point of view classes* capture the modeling context of (i.e., the point of view corresponding to) each particular functional model class: each functional model class shall reference a point of view class as its modeling context.

For instance, the definition class of a person should contain properties such that *birth date, gender, current name, first name*. An *employee* functional model class should contain properties like: *date of first employment, status, salary*. A *working status* point of view class allows to define the context of the functional model class. It may also contains for instance the *date of recording*, and the *employer id* attribute.

The definition class of a particular subclass of *mechanical* part, e.g., *screw* should contain properties like *threaded length, total length, threaded diameter, material*. The *screw procurement* functional model class should contain properties such that *price, quantity of order*. The *marketing* point of view class specifies the context of the screw procurement. It contains properties such that *date, kind of market* (e.g., wholesale, retail sale, negotiated), *supplier*.

4.4 Representation of the Local Definition Context

As noted in [19] a property cannot be understood if we don't know in which context it was defined: the same property names and informal definitions may be used with quite different meanings in different context. Thus, to define unambiguously classes and properties of an ontology, a basic modeling principle is that:

- a property cannot be defined without defining, in the mean time, its field of application by means of the class where it is meaningful; this class constitutes its definitions context;
- a class cannot be defined without defining, in the mean time, the properties that are essential for its instances.

Following this principle, a PLIB ontology includes two aspects:

- a classification tree where classes and properties are identified and connected;
- a set of meta-attributes that describe successively each class and each property.

Defined through a set of formal relationships, the first aspect allows to formally retrict the allowed interpretations of an ontology. Described through a number of human-readable pieces of information, the second part allows to make understandable the real world semantics of the conceptualization represented by the ontology.

Property definitions are formulated in the context of the higher class where they are meaningful (attribute *domain* in 4.2), even if they don't apply to all its subclasses (in PLIB jargon they are said to be *visible* for this class, and all its subclasses). Then, class definitions specify which properties are *applicable*, i.e., essential for every instance of this class (attribute *new_applicable_properties* and *imported_properties* in 4.2). Finally, when instances are represented within some model (physical file) or some database schema, only a subset of all the applicable properties may be used to describe them (such properties are said to be *provided*). For any class C the following holds:

$$provided(C) \subset applicable(C) \subset visible(C)$$

This formula shows, at the property level, the difference between an ontology and a schema: various schemas, designed by various database administrators, may represent for the same ontology class C various subsets of *applicable(C)*. During an integration process, and thanks to the UId of each ontology concept, it will be obvious which properties are the same and which are not.

Concerning the classes to be defined, PLIB is property-oriented: all what can be described meaningfully by properties is defined by properties. A class shall only be introduced in an ontology when it constitutes the domain of a new property, i.e., the property would be meaningless for the superclass of this new class, but it is meaningful for the new class and all its subclass. Thus reference ontologies are in general rather flat. For example, the *internal diameter* property is meaningless for a *mechanical component* whatever its definition. It becomes meaningful if one introduces a new subclass of mechanical components that models *circular bearings*.

But these formal relationships between classes ands properties are not sufficient for unambiguous definitions. Indeed, a PLIB ontology mainly consisting of primitive items, i.e., items whose definition "must rely on textual documentation and a background of knowledge shared with the reader to convey meanings" [15], the PLIB ontology model includes an extensive number of (meta) attributes used for representing the real world conceptualization and for connecting the ontology constructs to the background knowledge of the ontology user. In clause 4.2 only the *name* (meta) attribute was presented, in fact these (meta) attributes include: names and synonymous names, symbols, definitions with notes and remarks, pictures and drawings, references to document.

4.5 Locality of Ontology Interpretation Context

When a particular domain ontology is developed, it is often the case that (1) its domain overlaps the target domains of some other ontology, and (2) the perspective adopted in these various ontologies is, at least, partially different. For example, a travel ontology needs the capability to capture the concept of a *plane*. Let's assume that a plane ontology exists. If such an ontology has been developed to provide a suitable vocabulary for exchanging information between airplane manufacturers and airline companies, the ontological definition of a plane might contain such properties as *frequency of maintenance operation*, *guaranty duration*, and a number of technical properties which are useless in the context of the travel ontology. If the capability to use the basic *plane* properties in another ontology requires to integrate all the *plane* properties, more all the *plane* subclasses, probably the travel ontology designers would prefer to define their own *plane* concept. Indeed, the plane ontology might contain a number of technical details not understandable by the travel ontology designers, thus, they would not be able to understand the global conceptualization resulting from the global merging.

For addressing this issue, the PLIB ontology model introduces the *case-of* subsumption relationship. This relationship affects only one class of the referenced ontology from which it imports some selected properties, and the interpretation domains of both ontologies remains different.

Note that this importation is compatible with the local definition context representation discussed in 4.4: the referencing class being subsumed by the referenced one, the former is included in the domain of the latter. This mechanism allows to provide a view of a local ontology in terms of a global one, and, if the local classes is also defined as a restriction of the referenced classes, to migrate instances from the global context to the local one.

4.6 Representation of the Local Value Context

In a number of cases, the value of an instance property changes when its evaluation context changes. This means that the range of such properties is not a value set, it is a function set. Let C be the set of all instances of a class, P be a property whose domain includes C, D be the range of values of P, $EVAL_{C,P}$ be the set of all the states of the context where values of property P may be evaluated for any instance of C, P_1, ..., P_n be the set of properties allowing to characterize the states of $EVAL_{C,P}$, and D_1, ..., D_n their ranges of values.

- A *characteristic property* (*characteristic* for short) is a property that defines a function over C:
$$P : C \to D.$$
- A *context parameter* is a property that defines a function over $EVAL_{C,P}$:
$$P_i : EVAL_{C,P} \to D_i.$$
- A *context dependent property* is a property whose value is a function of the context:
$$P : C \to (EVAL_{C,P} \to D).$$

Table 2 shows various examples of characteristics and context dependent properties.

Table 2. Representing value context

Entity	Person	Ball bearing	Plane
characteristic	birth date	inner diameter	plane type
context-dependent property	hair color	life time	cheapest fare
context parameter	date	load, speed	customer age

In the PLIB ontology model, the signature of the function corresponding to a context dependent property is defined by the *value_context* attribute (see 4.2), and context parameters must be explicitly defined within the ontology. Two means are provided for specifying the function itself:

- either, as suggested in [31], it is discretized at the instance level as one or several sets of property-value pairs, each set defining the particular value of the context dependent property for a particular evaluation context state, defined by context parameter values;
- or, when the dependency may be expressed by an algebraic function that is the same for all instances and all interpretations, the function itself may be represented at the ontology level as an instance of an expression meta-model[4].

Moreover, on the database site, a database administrator may implement the function as a database-defined function, allowing a user to query the database by means of context parameters and context-dependant property values.

Of course, the ontology designer may decide to freeze all the context parameter values within a property definition, like: *hair color when birth; life time for 100 Pascal radial load and 6000 RPM; cheapest fare when 65 years old*. But, if the whole evaluation context is not specified within a property definition, this property shall be represented as a context-dependent property. In this case, the

---
[4] This expression meta-model is defined in ISO13584-20.

context parameters of which its value depends shall be explicitly modeled at the ontology level, together with the dependency relationships.

Note that representing instances is a question of schema and not of ontology. As discussed in Sciore et al. [31], all the context-parameter/value pairs that characterize a context dependent property value shall be represented by some means: at the property value level, at the instance level if the same context has been used for all the instance properties, or even at the level of the whole database if properties of all instances were evaluated in the same context. Anyway, the PLIB ontology model includes axioms that ensure that context-dependant values cannot exist in a model without their evaluation context.

4.7 Representation of Value Scaling

To provide for automatic value conversion and integration, units and currencies must be formally modeled. But they may be represented either at the ontology definition level, or at the value level. In a PLIB ontology, default units have to be represented at the ontology property definition level, together with alternative units. The default unit may be overridden by an alternative unit at the value level by associating each value with its own unit. The unit model allows to represent both dimensional exponents for a physical quantity, and all kinds of measure unit: either SI unit (e.g., millimeter), derived (e.g., m/s), or conversion-based unit (e.g., inch).

4.8 From Ontology to Schema

Provided that property inheritance and referential integrity is ensured, any subset of classes of a CCO, each one associated with any subset of its applicable properties, defines a database schema. We call *ontology-based database* (OBDB)[28] a database (1) that explicitly represents an ontology, (2) whose schema refers to the ontology for each of its represented class and property. In such a database, each data may be interpreted in a consistent way using the meaning defined for the corresponding ontology entry. Note that an OBDB is not required to populate either all the classes of its ontology or all the properties defined for a given class. Moreover, provided that the link from data to ontology is preserved, the schema structure is not required to preserve the ontology structure. Inheritance composition and view-of relationship may be "flattened". This means that values representing:

- properties of a definition class instance,
- properties of a part of this instance, and
- properties of a functional model class instance that is view-of the definition class instance

may all appear as values in the same database relation. This shows the diversity of the various schemas that may be built just from the same ontology while preserving semantic integration capabilities.

5 Formal Definition of PLIB Ontologies

In section 4 we have outlined, through partial schemas, how PLIB ontologies and ontology-based data were specified and exchanged using an executable data specification language. We also detailed informally the various mechanisms used for making context explicit in PLIB ontologies. In this section, we present a formal model of PLIB ontology semantics independent of any syntax (note that an XML syntax, called OntoML, is currently under ballot within ISO as an alternative for exchanging PLIB ontologies). This model covers globally the PLIB specification. Its only restriction is to focus on ontologies that consists of definition classes (no functional model class or point of view class as the use of these construct is not widespread). A PLIB ontology may be defined separately as a single ontology, but it may also be mapped onto one (or several) standard ontologies. These two models are presented respectively in 5.1 and in 5.2. Clause 5.3 outlines how a shared ontology and various mapped ontologies may be used to integrate heterogeneous data bases. To illustrate the various aspects of the formal definitions, example 3 represents formally the ontology described in example 1.

5.1 Single PLIB Ontology

Formally, a single PLIB ontology may be defined as a 8-tuple :
$$O = <C, P, U, IsA, PropCont, ClassCont, ValCont, ValScale>,$$
where:

- C is the set of classes used to describe the concepts of a given domain;
- P is the set of properties used to describe the instances of C; P is partitioned into P_{val} (characteristics properties), P_{fonc} (context dependent properties) and P_{cont} (context parameters);
- U is the set of units of measure, including currencies, used to describe the values of the properties of a given domain that define a measure;
- $IsA : C \to C$ is a partial function[5] that associates to a class its smallest subsumer[6]; IsA implies inheritance of both visible properties (as visible) and of applicable properties (as applicable);
- $PropCont : P \to C$ associates to each property the higher class where it is meaningful;
- $ClassCont : C \to 2^P$ associates to each class all the properties that are applicable to every instances of this class (rigid properties);
- $ValCont : P_{fonc} \to 2^{P_{cont}}$ associates to each context dependent property the context parameters of which its value depends;
- $ValScale : P \to U \times 2^U$ is a partial function that associates to each property that defines a measure the default unit used to represent its values, and, possibly, the other units that may be used to override the default unit.

---

[5] IsA is assumed to define a single subsumption hierarchy.
[6] C_1 subsumes C_2 iff $\forall x \in C_2 \Rightarrow x \in C_1$.

Example 3. Definition of the circular bearing ontology presented in example 1 is as follows.

- $C = \{circular\ bearing,\ circular\ ball\ bearing\}$;
- $P_{val}=\{inner\ diameter,\ outer\ diameter,\ width,\ ball\ radius\}$, $P_{cont} = \{velocity,\ radial\ load,\ axial\ load\}$, $P_{fonc} = \{life\ time\}$;
- $U = \{millimeter,\ meter,\ revolutions\ per\ minute,\ newton,\ hour\ \}$;
- $IsA(circular\ ball\ bearing) = circular\ bearing$, $IsA(circular\ bearing) = \emptyset$;
- $PropCont(inner\ diameter\ |\ outer\ diameter\ |\ width\ |\ velocity\ |\ radial\ load\ |\ axial\ |\ life\ time) = circular\ bearing$, $PropCont(\ ball\ radius\ ) = circular\ ball\ bearing$;
- $ClassCont(circular\ bearing) = \{inner\ diameter,\ outerdiameter,\ width,\ velocity,\ radial\ load,\ axial\ load,\ life\ time\}$, $ClassCont(circular\ ball\ bearing) = \{ball\ diameter\}$;
- $ValCont(life\ time) = \{velocity,\ radial\ load,\ axial\ load\}$;
- $ValScale(inner\ diameter\ |\ outer\ diameter\ |\ width\ |\ ball\ radius\ ) = (millimeter,\ \{meter\})$, $ValScale(radial\ load\ |\ axial\ load\ ) = (newton\ ,\ \{\})$, $ValScale\ (velocity) = (revolutions\ per\ minute,\ \{\})$, $ValScale(life\ time) = (hour,\ \{\})$;

Example 4. Let's assume that, using some bearing ontology, a user queries the life-time of a circular bearing whose part identification property equals XYZ when its velocity is 1500 rpm and it supports a radial load of 6000 N. Using the OntoML PLIB syntax, a system answer would be as follows (all class and property UIds come from a bearing ontology standardized as ISO 23768, the codes of class and properties have been changed to reflect their meaning, all concepts are in version 1, and *condition* is the OntoML tag for context parameters):

```
<item class-ref="ISO23768#CIRCULAR_BALL_BEARING#1">
        <property-value property-ref="ISO23768#PART_IDENTIFICATION#1">
                <val:string-value >XYZ</val:string-value>
        </property-value>
        <property-value property-ref="ISO23768#LIFE_TIME#1">
                <val:real-value>20000</val:real-value>
                <val:condition>
                        <val:element property-ref="ISO23768#VELOCITY#1">
                                <val:real-value>1500</val:real-value>
                        </val:element>
                        <val:element property-ref="ISO23768#RADIAL_LOAD#1">
                                <val:real-value>6000</val:real-value>
                        </val:element>
                </val:condition>
        </property-value>
</item>
```

Four axioms are defined on this formal PLIB model. If we define recursively the visible properties as[7]:
$$visible(c) = visible(IsA(c)) \bigcup PropCont^{-1}(c),$$
then the following axioms shall hold :

---

[7] To simplify notation, we extend all functions f by $f(\emptyset) = \emptyset$.

1. *IsA* defines a single sumsumption hierarchy: the graph G whose vertex are classes and whose edges are the *IsA* relationships is a forest, i.e., a disjoint union of trees. G is defined by:
   $G = \{C, \{(c_1, c_2)\} | c_1 \in C \wedge c_1 \in Dom(IsA) \wedge c_2 \in IsA(c_1)\}$
2. *IsA* implies inheritance of applicable properties:
   $ClassCont(c) \supseteq ClassCont(IsA(c))$
3. A context-dependent properties must not be defined in a class that does not belong to the domain of the context parameters of which it depends:
   $\forall c \in C, p \in P_{fonc} \;\; p \in ClassCont(c) \Rightarrow ValCont(p) \subset ClassCont(c)$

Moreover, for stand-alone ontologies, one more axiom applies: only meaningful properties (i.e., visible properties) may become applicable :

(4a) $ClassCont(c) - ClassCont(IsA(c)) \subset visible(c)$

5.2 Mapped PLIB Ontology

A major focus of PLIB ontologies being heterogeneous data source integration, PLIB does not assume that all data sources use the same ontology. Each data source may build its own local ontology without any external reference. It may also build it based upon one or several existing ontologies (e.g., standard ones). A class of a local ontology may be described as subsumed by one or several other class(es) defined in other ontologies by the *case-of* relationship. Through this relationship the subsumed class may import properties (their UIds and definitions are preserved, as presented in 4.2). But it may also map properties that are defined in the referenced class(es) (the properties are different but they are semantically equivalent) . A class of a local ontology may also define properties that are neither imported nor mapped.

A PLIB ontology O_m that includes mapping onto one (or several) other ontologies may be formally defined as a pair: $O_m = <O, M>$, where : $O = < C, P, U, IsA, PropCont, ClassCont, ValCont, ValScale >$ is an ontology, and $M = \{m_i\}$, is a mapping defined as a set of mapping objects.

Each mapping object has four attributes: $m = <domain, range, import, map>$

- *domain* $\in C$ defines the class that is mapped onto an external class by a *case-of* relationship;
- *range* $\in UId \subset \{string\}$ is the universal identifier of the external class onto which the *m.domain* class is mapped;
- *import* $\in 2^P$ is a set of properties visible or applicable in the *m.range* class that are imported in $ClassCont(m.domain)$;
- *map* $\subset \{(p, id) \mid p \in P \wedge id \in UId \subset \{string\}\}$ defines the mapping of properties defined in the *m.domain* class with equivalent properties visible or applicable in the *m.range* class. The latter are identified by their UIds.

Note that each mapping object defines a subsumption relationship between the *m.range* and *m.domain* classes. Nevertheless, the *m.range* class does not belong to C. The interpretation domain of the referencing ontology remains different from the one of the referenced ontology. Note also that when properties are imported, they belong to P.

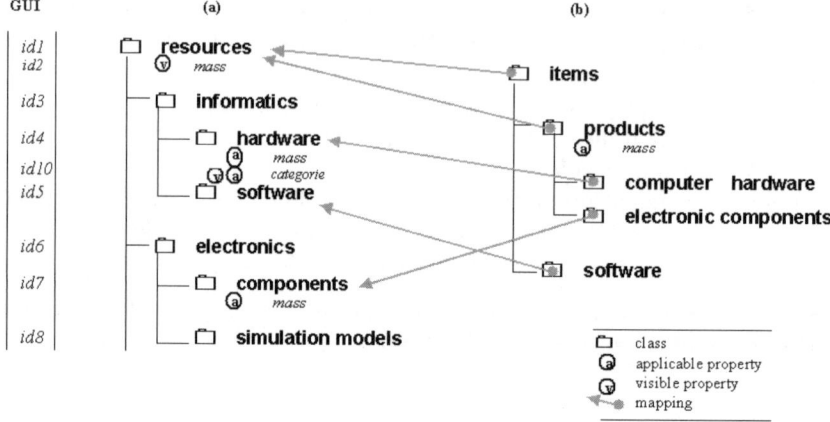

Fig. 3. An example of a reference ontology (a) and of an user defined ontology (b)

Example 5. Figure 2 (a) presents a single ontology. Class hierarchy is represented by indentation. $P = \{mass\}$. The *mass* properties applies to *hardware* and *components*, but not to *software* and *simulation models*. *mass* is visible at the level of *resources* : $PropCont(mass) = resources$, with a definition s. t. "the physical mass of a resource that is a material object". It becomes applicable in *hardware* and *components*: $ClassCont\ (hardware) = \{mass\}$; $ClassCont\ (component) = \{mass\}$

Example 6. Figure 2 (b) presents a (user-defined) ontology mapped on a reference ontology (a). $C = \{items, products, computer\ hardware, electronic\ components, software\}$ and $P = \{mass\}$. $M = m1, m2, m3, m4$ with $m_1 = (item, id1, (), ())$; $m_2 = (products, id1, (id2), ())$; $m_3 = (computer\ hardware, id4, (), ())$; $m_4 = (electronic\ components, id7, (), ())$. We note that no properties are mapped, they are all imported.

All the axioms for single ontologies hold. The specific axiom (4a) becomes (4b and 4c) that state that imported properties belongs to the set of applicable properties of the importing class (and of its subclasses), and that the other new applicable properties of the importing class shall belongs to its visible properties.
(4b) $\forall m \in M, ClassCont(m.domain) \supset m.import$,
(4c) $\forall m \in M, LetM(m) = \{m_i \in M \mid m_i.domain = m.domain\}$

$$(ClassCont(m.domain) - ClassCont(IsA^{-1}(m.domain))) - \bigcup_{m_i \in M(m)} m_i.import)$$
$$\subset visible(m.domain)$$

As shown by Figure 2, the structure of a (user) ontology may be quite different from the one of a standard ontology it references. Nevertheless, a system storing the user ontology $<O, M>$ may automatically answer queries against a standard ontology onto which O is mapped. It may also migrate instance data from its local user ontology to the standard ontology.

Note that the above mapping only allows to query local ontologies through one, or a set of standard ontologies of which the former are case-of, and to return the answer as standard ontology individuals. A typical application is the case where component provider data sources are based on ontologies defined as specialization, through case-of, of a standard ontology. The customer formulates its query in terms of the standard ontology. The answers is also returned in terms of the standard ontology, whatever local ontology is used by the provider. Nevertheless, this approach does not allow:

- to know the precise definition of the provider product; for example if additional properties were defined by the provider, value of these properties cannot be returned in the answer;
- to store automatically the returned data in the customer database when the customer has also created its own local ontology by specialization from the same standard ontology, as I recommend it in 6.

Concerning the first problem, if the customer needs this precise information, the provider may return the answer not as a projection onto the standard ontology, but in the native terms of the provider ontology together with the relevant specialization of the standard ontology defined locally. Then, these two pieces of information may be integrated automatically within a customer ontology-based database providing fine grain access to provider-defined specialization. This approach, called ExtendOnto, was proposed in [2]. Note that such an approach may be followed both with PLIB ontologies, using one of the PLIB exchange format, and with C-OWL [4] ontology, using OWL syntax.

Example 7. Let's assume that in Figure 2, 2a is the standard ontology and 2b is the provider ontology, and that a customer wants to retrieve those *hardware* products whose mass is less that 10^4 .

The provider answer may consist of two parts:

1. the *computer hardware* class definition together with all its applicable properties and its subsumption relationship with the standard *hardware* class;
2. the set of instances of the *computer hardware* class that correspond to the customer request.

Concerning the capability for a customer to map a set of standard-ontology-defined instances onto its own locally defined specialization of the standard ontology, this can be done by adding to each mapping object m a fifth attribute called $filter$ that is a predicate over the subsuming class instances:

$filter : (class\text{-}of(m.range))^I \longrightarrow Boolean.$[8]

The meaning of such a filter is that all instances of the subsuming class for which the predicate holds are members of the subsumed class:
$\forall x \in (class\text{-}of(m.range))^I, m.filter(x) \Longrightarrow x \in m.domain.$

---

[8] We note class-of the function that associates to a class identifier the corresponding class. As usual, we note $(.)^I$ the interpretation function.

Example 8. Let's now assume that, in Figure 2, 2a is the standard ontology and 2b is the customer ontology. The customer has retrieved those *hardware* products whose *mass* is less that 10^4, and the value of the *category* property of these *hardware* products. If, in the mapping m of his/her *computer hardware* class onto the standard *hardware* class, the following filter was added :
$m.filter = (category = "computer")$,
then all the returned *hardware* instances whose *category* values are *"computer"* are automatically recorded as a *computer hardware* instances. Other *hardware* instances are not recorded in the customer database.

5.3 Automatic Integration of Data Sources through a Priori Ontology Mapping

In the domains where it has been feasible (possibly using the context representation mechanisms defined in this paper) to define a consensual domain ontology, this ontology may be used to allow automatic integration of ontology-based data sources in the following sense:

– Let's assume that there exist some consensual ontology O over the domain that is common to all the sources;
– Let's also assume that each local source S_i is associated with a local ontology O_i and that each class C_{ij} of S_i that is in the domain modeled by O is mapped by a subsumption relationship (e.g. *case-of*), either directly or indirectly (through inheritance within O_i), onto its smallest subsuming class C_j in O (*smallest subsuming class reference requirement: SSCRR*) [2]
– Then, each local source, whatever its local ontology, may answer queries stated in terms of O.

Note that this automated integration technique leaves a lot of schematic autonomy to each data source. It only assumes that each database administrator wants to make its data available in terms of a standard domain ontology. Thus, each administrator is required to describe *a priori* a mapping between its own local ontology and the consensual ontology by means of a subsumption relationship ensuring the SSCRR assumption, and to import or to map properties having a common meaning. This *a priori* approach, different from most existing approaches where ontology mapping is done at integration time [23], seems to suit quite well the needs of a number of Web applications, including in particular B2B e-commerce. This approach is discussed in more details in [2].

6 A Road Map for Implementing Ontology-Based Databases in Manufacturing Enterprises

Currently, most of manufacturing enterprises still record their component information in conventional component databases where the various components are all described by the same set of relational attributes, one of them encoding in a long string (often called "designation") all the engineering properties (Fig. 3).

Such a representation has two major drawbacks. At the cost level, conventional component databases promote the increase in the number of similar components. Indeed, when a designer is searching for a component, there are very few chances that the best existing candidate be retrieved using string matching. As a result, new components are created again and again, increasing dramatically the cost of company products. At the quality level, few engineering properties may be encoded in a single string. Therefore, components are often selected only from force of habit without checking for each particular design whether all the engineering requirements of the problem at hand are really fulfilled by the selected component.

'SCREW-ISO1014-L10-D5-GRADa'

Fig. 4. Engineering information encoding in usual component database

Improving this situation requires migrating from conventional component database to engineering database where each class of components is defined by its own engineering properties. Taking into account that standard ontologies are emerging in more and more industrial domains, a major issue is to decide whether the corporate engineering database should use a private ontology or one (or a set of) standard ontology.

The direct use of standard ontologies may seems attractive, but it would have several drawbacks.

- A number of domains being not yet addressed, it would need to wait, but the market is not waiting.
- Even if the enterprise industrial sector is addressed, the relevant standard ontology probably does not contain all the classes and properties needed. And it surely contains a number of classes which are useless.
- Standards are rather stable. Nevertheless each standard is to be updated from time to time. Remaining in line with a standard ontology might request to change the corporate database schema when it is no longer in line with updated standards.

Contrariwise, developing its own corporate ontology would have a number of advantages.

- It is possible immediately, whatever the particular industrial sector is.
- Provided that there exist some mechanisms allowing to control impact of standard ontology evolution onto corporate ontology evolution, it would allow to gather standard definitions and local definitions. The corporate ontology may borrow class definitions and import standardized properties from standard ontologies, while adding company-specific classes and properties.
- It would ensure that each company remains free to upgrade its own ontology when and how it is needed, either by importing new standard properties or by creating new proprietary elements.

Note that both PLIB, through case-of, and OWL, through C-OWL [4] offer suitable mechanisms for controlling impact of standard ontology evolutions over local ontologies.

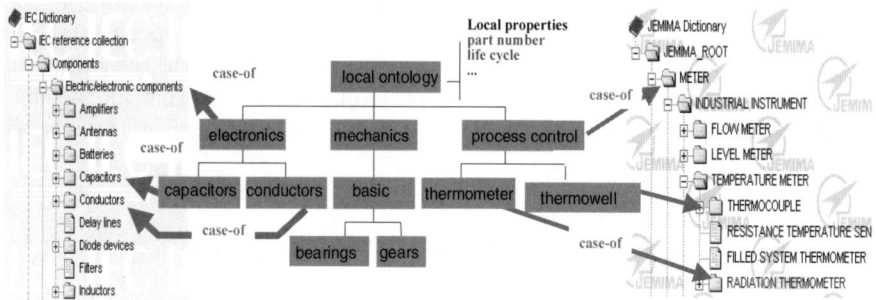

Fig. 5. Defining corporate ontology from standard ontologies (IEC 61360-4:1998 and ISO 13584-501:2006)

This suggests the following road map for switching from conventional component databases to ontology-based engineering databases.

1. Define an ontology that consists of a single class to host those generic properties that need to be available for describing any existing component. Definition of these generic properties must take into account both existing standard ontologies and the current content of the company conventional component database if any. Then, this ontology will be referenced by the main corporate ontology and all the classes where generic properties need to be used will be subsumed by this class (in PLIB, using case-of).
2. Define a proprietary overall classification of the various component domains until class nodes where generic search would make sense (e.g., metric screw, circular bearing).
3. At the level of each of these classes, define the technical properties needed for characterizing their components, importing as many properties as possible from existing standard ontologies using subsumption (in PLIB, using case-of).
4. If some needed properties require more precise class for defining their application domain, refine the existing classes using subsumption relationship from corporate classes, and possibly from standard classes when properties of which they define the domain need to be imported.
5. Use this ontology structure for defining the logical schema of the new corporate engineering database, implemented either on top of an OBDB (ontology within the database) or on a relational or object relational DBMS.
6. Extend progressively the existing schema when new needs, and possibly new standard ontologies, emerge.
7. If automatic exchange of component information appears both feasible and useful, define mapping from proprietary class and property onto standard class and property when the latter become available.

7 Related Work

We discuss below three research threads deeply connected with the material presented in this paper: (1) the role of context representation in data integration, (2) context representation in some ontology models, and (3) some proposed approaches for ontology-based data integration.

7.1 Context Representation for Semantic Integration

Importance of context representation for data integration was identified by several researchers in the field of multidatabase system in the 90's. Kashyap and al. [19] proposed to represent the intentional definition context, at the schema level, as a set of meta-attributes expressing intentional properties, and in particular the constraints each object must fulfill. They proposed to use description logic (DL) to reason over such a context. But, in this work, the evaluation context of property values was only informally defined. Sciore and al. [31] proposed to represent value context at the value level by means of another set of meta-attributes. For these authors, a semantic value is a piece of data together with its associated context. This context may be represented, e.g., as a LISP-like list of meta-attribute-value pairs, or a set of environment variables. Following this work, the COntext INterchange project (COIN) was developed in MIT [13,14]. This project noted that a number of property values depends both of the evaluation context in which they are evaluated, and on the way in which they are represented. They proposed to associate with properties both *attributes* and *modifiers*. Attributes characterize the evaluation context of property values (e.g., the *date* where some financial property was evaluated). Modifiers characterize how property values should be interpreted (e.g., the *currency* in which it is represented, and possibly the *scaling factor* used to encode the value). In an integration process, both the information source and the information receiver specify their respective context for all the properties of some shared ontology. Then, a *context mediator* ensures the conversion of data from the export context to the import context to achieve interoperability at the semantic layer.

The idea to associate to each source the context of all its information element as a set of meta-data was also followed by Ziegler et al. [35] in the SIRUP project. The SIRUP system assumes the existence of one or several shared ontologies, but these ontologies are not supposed to explicitly define in which context properties are evaluated and represented. Therefore, source owner must build an intermediate model, called IConcepts (intermediate concepts), where each ontology concept is associated with "extensive meta-data ...(attribute data types, measurement unit, precision, constraints, etc)" [35].

In the context of data warehousing, a powerful data integration and reconciliation approach based on value context representation was proposed by. Calvanese et al. [5]. In this approach, domain conceptual model and source conceptual models, similar to ontologies, are formalized using a specific description logic, called $\mathcal{DLR}$, which supports n-ary relations. Articulations between global model and source models are specified by means of inter-model assertions, and the links between conceptual and logical levels is formally defined by associating with each relational table a query over the conceptual model that describes its content. This query is adorned by annotations that represent the local value context of each table column (e.g., the currency used for a price). Data conflicts are avoided by declaratively specifying suitable matching, conversion and data reconciliation operations by means of non-materialized views adorned by the name of a program able to compute the view. Then, a re-writing algorithm is able to compute automatically (or semi-automatically) the query allowing to load the various data warehouse relations.

If all these contributions developed efficient integration algorithms once value contexts are made explicit, up to now, few ontology models provided the necessary meta-attributes. Thus, context representation could not be provided by source owners. It needed to be done at source integration time, thus preventing automatic integration. Extending ontology models to support extensive context representation, as proposed by this paper, would constitute a major step toward automatic integration of heterogeneous data sources.

7.2 Context Representation in Ontology Models

Currently, most ontology models, and in particular OIL [11], DAML [6] and OWL [20] are based on DL. The main focus of these ontology languages is semantic annotations of Web resources using terms, and inferences over these terms. As a rule, DL-based ontologies consist of two parts. The TBox specifies class-level and property-level axioms. Class, and possibly properties, are structured as a subsumption lattice. The ABox (that may be empty) consists of a number of individual assertions. A class lattice is a powerful means for representing class definition context as it supports two important reasoning tasks [1]. Subsumption checking amounts to check whether a class is a subclass of another class. Class membership inference allows to checking whether an individual is a member of a specific class.

Concerning property definition context, most formalisms allow (but do not require) that a property is associated with a domain. Provided that this capability is systematically used in each source ontology and that ontology-level information may be accessed at integration time, an integration system may be able to distinguish, e.g., *department.name* and *employee.name* and to know that these two attributes are not semantically equivalent. Moreover, the C-OWL extension of OWL [4] allows to contextualize the interpretation of OWL constructs when they are imported from an ontology into another one. In such a case, the classical OWL semantics [25] assumes the existence of a unique interpretation domain used both for the referencing ontology and the referenced ontologies. This may lead to inconsistency, in particular when imported ontologies evolve. To the contrary, C-OWL associates with each ontology its own local domain [4]. The various domains may overlap but they are different. For the importing ontology, the local interpretation of an imported construct, i.e., concept or role, is different from its interpretation in its source ontology. This interpretation is restricted to the set of objets that belong to the local interpretation domain of the importing ontology. Bridge rules may be defined between imported and importing ontology constructs, thus controlling how object may be mapped, or migrated, from an imported ontology domain to a local domain. Such a domain contextualisation provides the required autonomy for corporate ontology to implement the road map proposed in section 6 also in OWL.

So, DL-based ontologies allow to represent important aspects of schema definition context and to contextualize interpretation domain. But they are much less efficient for representing context at the extensional level. Indeed, most DL languages support only unary (classes) and binary (properties) predicates. And binary predicates may only have class as a domain. Therefore, it is impossible, in DL-based ontologies, to connect formally two properties. It is neither possible e.g., to define, like in COIN, that the value of a *financial property* depends upon a *date*, or that a *length* depends upon a *temperature*, nor to express that the *financial value* is represented in *billions* of *Euros*, the *length* in *millimeters*, and the *temperature* in *degree Celsius*. These drawbacks of DL-based ontology languages, that exist also for OWL, require evolution of these languages, as suggested in this paper, for making them really usable in domains like engineering.

7.3 Ontology-Based Integration of Information

Various approaches have been developed for ontology-based integration of information [33]. In the single ontology approach each source is related to the same global domain ontology (e.g., PICSEL [12], COIN [14]). As a result, a new source cannot bring any new or specific concept without requiring change in the global ontology. In the multiple ontologies approach (e.g., Observer [21]), each source has its own ontology developed without respect of other sources. In this case the inter-ontology mapping is very difficult to define. This is because the different ontologies may use different aggregation and granularity of the ontology concept [33]. To overcome the drawback of single or multiple ontology approaches, several researches have proposed an hybrid approach where each source has its own ontology, but where all ontologies are connected by some means to a common shared vocabulary. For instance, BUSTER system [32] assumes that local ontologies are only restrictions of the global ontology. PLIB-based integration follows the hybrid approach and proposes a formal model for ontologies and ontology mappings. But, unlike BUSTER it does not restrict source autonomy and sovereignty: each source may define its own classes and completely re-structure the class subsumption hierarchy. It may also add whatever properties. To give modeling autonomy to the local sources, we use the same kind of ontology articulation as ONION [23]. But, unlike ONION, we suppose that articulation between local and shared ontology is done *a priori* by the local source administrator (as done in another context in e.g., [35]). As a result, our integration approach is completely automatic and it scales to any number of data sources [2]. Note that the PLIB ontology model is the first model we know that explicitly represents ontology mapping within a local ontology as a first class citizen (see 4.2: *case_of* and *imported_properties* attributes) as suggested by model management vision [3].

8 Conclusion

The concept of a domain ontology was mainly studied in computer science since early 90's. Its intent is to capture and to represent the essential nature of things of a domain through class structures and properties. In a number of computer disciplines, such an explicit representation of semantics appeared like some kind of philosopher's stone and a lot of languages, understandings, models and approaches were developed. Not surprisingly, differences in approaches reflect differences in the addressed problems, and it is often unclear how the various approaches and languages fit with each other and how they may be used for addressing a particular problem.

In this paper, we have investigated the use of ontology in a structured data integration perspective. First we have proposed a taxonomy of ontologies. Linguistic ontologies (LO) represent words and words relationships. They are natural language-oriented. They provide, in particular, for intelligent structuring, modeling and querying set of documents, such as those available on the Web. But they may also be used for defining a canonic human vocabulary for a particular domain, or for searching for equivalence between concepts through relationships between their linguistic descriptions. Conceptual ontologies (CO) represent concepts, as they are manipulated in the structured data universe like database or data engineering, and concept properties. Like for LO, two slightly different but complementary problems may be addressed using CO. The first one is to define a set of concepts allowing software systems, databases or agents existing within some community to exchange unambiguously information about a domain. For this purpose, concept equivalence should be avoided and canonical conceptual ontology (CCO) are needed. The second one is to also map different conceptualizations over the same domain. In this case, several CCOs need to be gathered within a unique non-canonical conceptual ontology (NCCO) that includes operators for reasoning over concept equivalence. In both cases however concept definitions and value interpretations must be unambiguous across their target community, and we have shown that this requests, in turn, ontology models of which context sensitivity has been explicitly represented and minimized. We have defined five principles to ensure that the definitions and value representations within an ontology are not context-sensitive and may thus be used to support semantic integration of data while leaving enough autonomy to the various sources. We have also shown how these principles have been implemented within the PLIB model, a CCO model developed to support integration of industrial data. The goal was not to promote PLIB as an alternative ontology language, but to identify and to illustrate those mechanisms that any ontology formalism should support to be usable for large-size integration of data. These principles are as follows:

- *Definition context representation.* Each property should be defined in the context of a class. Each class should define all its rigid properties, at least in some very broad context common to all the target data sources.
- *Point of view representation.* If several perspectives are needed over the domain, an ontology of perspectives should be defined and each needed perspective should correspond to a specific domain ontology.
- *Locality of interpretation context.* Resource importation between ontology should be feasible on a class per class basis, and then on a property per property basis. Interpretation domains of both referenced and referencing ontologies should be separated.
- *Value context representation.* Value dependency between property values should be explicit.
- *Value scaling representation* Unit and scaling of values should be explicit and computer interpretable.

A first version of the PLIB ontology model is now standardized, and a number of standard ontologies and of implementations are now emerging in various domains, and in particular in e-procurement and e-engineering that were the initial domains targeted by PLIB. Currently, most major manufacturing enterprises are switching from conventional component databases to ontology-based engineering databases that should allow to reduce useless component diversity, to improve component selection support and to facilitate integration of supplier catalogs, whatever the ontology model used. In this domain, our recommendation is not to use directly standard ontologies if they exist. It is to define a proprietary ontology and (1) to map classes onto standard classes if and when they exist, and (2) to import as much properties as needed properties from standard ontologies. Not only this approach may be followed immediately. But it also seems much more promising for the future.

Our current implementation of ontology-based databases are mainly based on the PLIB model with mapping onto this model of other ontology-based data [7]. We are now developing layered implementations [10] based on the CID model we have proposed and where various ontology models may cooperate. At the data level, all the context representation mechanisms are implemented together with a canonical data model. In the above layer, some concept equivalence operators from OWL and FLIGHT are implemented, providing for some ontology-level reasoning. In the upper layer, linguistic access is provided, in particular using ontology model-independent query language [17]. We are also further developing the PLIB model, adding integrity constraints and UML/XML [29] view over this model.

Acknowledgements

The author would like to thank the anonymous referees who provided helpful and valuable comments on an earlier version of this paper. The research reported here was supported in part by EU Project Esprit 8984 and IST-1999-12238 and by ANR grant 05RNTL02706.

References

1. Baader, F., Calvanese, D., McGuinness, D.L., Nardi, D., Patel-Schneider, P.F.: The description logic handbook. Cambridge University Press, Cambridge (2003)
2. Bellatreche, L., Dung, N.X., Pierra, G., Dehainsala, H.: Contribution of ontology-based data modeling to automatic integration of electronic catalogues within engineering databases. Computers in Industry 57(8-9), 711–724 (2006)
3. Bernstein, P.A., Havely, A.Y., Pottinger, R.A.: A vision of managament of complex models. SIGMOD Record 29(4), 55–63 (2000)
4. Bouquet, P., Giunchiglia, F., van Harmelen, F., Serafini, L., Stuckenschmidt, H.: Contextualizing ontologies. Journal of Web Semantics 1(4), 325–343 (2004)
5. Calvanese, D., De Giacomo, G., Lenzerini, M., Nardi, D., Rosati, R.: A principled approach to data integration and reconciliation in data warehousing. In: DMDW 1999. Proceedings of the Intl. Workshop on Design and Management of Data Warehouses, Heidelberg, Germany (June 14-15, 1999)
6. Connolly, D., Stein, L., McGuinness, D.: Daml-ont initial release (2000), www.daml.org/2000/10/daml-ont.html
7. Dehainsala, H., Pierra, G., Bellatreche, L.: OntoDB: An ontology-based database for data intensive applications. In: Kotagiri, et al. (eds.) DASFAA 2007. LNCS, vol. 4443, pp. 497–508. Springer, Heidelberg (2007)
8. Elmagarmid, A., Rusinkiewicz, M.: Heterogeneous Autonomous Database Systems. Morgan Kaufmann, San Francisco (1999)
9. Everett, J.O., Bobrow, D.G., Stolle, R., Crouch, R.S., de Paiva, V., Condoravdi, C., van den Berg, M., Polanyi, L.: Making ontologies work for resolving redundancies across documents. Communication of ACM 45(2), 55–60 (2002)
10. Fankam, C., Aït-Ameur, Y., Pierra, G.: Exploitation of ontology languages for both persistence and reasoning purposes: Mapping PLIB, OWL and flight ontology models. In: WEBIST 2007. Proc. of Third International Conference on Web Information Systems and Technologies, pp. 254–262 (2007)
11. Fensel, D., van Harmelen, F., Horrocks, I., McGuinness, D.L., Patel-Schneider, P.F: Oil: an ontology infrastructure for the semantic web. IEEE Intelligent Systems 16(2), 38–45 (2001)
12. Goasdoué, F., Lattès, V., Rousset, M.C.: The use of carin language and algorithms for information integration: The picsel system. International Journal of Cooperative Information Systems (IJCIS) 9(4), 383–401 (2000)
13. Goh, C.H., Madnick, S.E., Siegel, M.: Context interchange: Overcoming the challenges of large-scale interoperable database systems in a dynamic environment. In: CIKM 1994. Proceedings of the Third International Conference on Information and Knowledge Management, pp. 337–346 (December 1994)
14. Goh, C.H., Bressan, S., Madnick, E., Siegel, M.D.: Context interchange: New features and formalisms for the intelligent integration of information. ACM Transactions on Information Systems 17(3), 270–293 (1999)
15. Gruber, T.: Toward principles for the design of ontologies used for knowledge sharing in formal ontology. In: Guarino, N., Poli, R. (eds.) Conceptual Analysis and Knowledge Representation, Kluwer Academic, Dordrecht (1993)
16. Guarino, N., Welty, C.A.: Evaluating ontological decisions with ontoclean. Communications of the ACM 45(2), 61–65 (2002)

17. Jean, S., Aït Ameur, Y., Pierra, G.: Querying ontology based databases using ontoql (an ontology query language). In: ODBASE, pp. 704–721 (2006)
18. Jean, S., Pierra, G., Ameur, Y.A.: Domain ontologies: A database-oriented analysis. In: Filipe, J., Cordeiro, J., Pedrosa, V. (eds.) WEBIST (Selected Papers). Lecture Notes in Business Information Processing, vol. 1, pp. 238–254. Springer, Heidelberg (2006)
19. Kashyap, V., Sheth, A.P.: Semantic and schematic similarities between database objects: A context-based approach. VLDB Journal 5(4), 276–304 (1996)
20. McGuinness, D.L., Harmelen, F.: OWL web ontology language overview. W3C Recommendation (February 10, 2004)
21. Mena, E., Kashyap, V., Illarramendi, A., Sheth, A.P.: Managing multiple information sources through ontologies: Relationship between vocabulary heterogeneity and loss of information. In: Proceedings of Third Workshop on Knowledge Representation Meets Databases (August 1996)
22. Minsky, M.: Matter, mind and models. International Federation of Information Processing Congress 1, 45–49 (1965)
23. Mitra, P., Wiederhold, G., Kersten, M.: A graph-oriented model for articulation of ontology interdependencies. In: Zaniolo, C., Grust, T., Scholl, M.H., Lockemann, P.C. (eds.) EDBT 2000. LNCS, vol. 1777, Springer, Heidelberg (2000)
24. Noy, N.F., McGuinness, D.L.: Ontology development: A guide to creating your first ontology. Technical report ksl-01-05 and stanford medical informatics technical report smi-2001-0880, stanford Knowledge Systems Laboratory (April 2001)
25. Patel-Schneider, P.F., Hayes, P., Horrocks, I.: OWL web ontology language semantics and abstract syntax. W3C Recommendation (February 2004)
26. Pierra, G.: An object oriented approach to ensure portability of cad standard parts libraries. In: Eurographics 1990. Proceedings of the European Computer Graphics Conference and Exhibition, pp. 205–214 (1990)
27. Pierra, G.: A multiple perspective object oriented model for engineering design. In: New Advances in Computer Aided Design & Computer Graphics, pp. 368–373. International Academic Publishers, Beijing (1993)
28. Pierra, G., Dehainsala, H., Aït-Ameur, Y., Bellatreche, L.: Base de données à base ontologique: principe et mise en oeuvre. Ingénierie des systèmes d'information 10(2), 91–115 (2005)
29. Pierra, G., Sardet, E.: Proposal for a XML representation of the PLIB ontology model: Ontoml. Research Report RR 07-01, p. 188 (2007), http://www.lisi.ensma.fr/ftp/pub/documents/reports/2007/2007-LISI-2007-01.pdf
30. Schenck, D., Wilson, P.: Information modelling: The express way. Oxford University Press, Oxford (1994)
31. Sciore, E., Siegel, M., Rosenthal, A.: Using semantic values to facilitate interoperability among heterogeneous information systems. ACM Transactions on Database Systems 19(2), 254–290 (1994)
32. Stuckenschmidt, H., Vögele, T., Visser, U., Meyer, R.: Intelligent brokering of environmental information with the buster system. In: Proceedings of the 5th International Conference "Wirtschaftsinformatik", Physica-Verlag, pp. 15–20 (2001)
33. Wache, H., Vögele, T., Visser, U., Stuckenschmidt, H., Schuster, G., Neumann, H., Hübner, S.: Ontology-based integration of information - a survey of existing approaches. In: Proceedings of the International Workshop on Ontologies and Information Sharing, pp. 108–117 (August 2001)

34. Wiederhold, G.: Mediators in the architecture of future information systems. IEEE Computer 25(3), 38–49 (1992)
35. Ziegler, P., Dittrich, K.R.: User-specific semantic integration of heterogeneous data: The sirup approach. In: Bouzeghoub, M., Goble, C.A., Kashyap, V., Spaccapietra, S. (eds.) ICSNW 2004. LNCS, vol. 3226, pp. 44–64. Springer, Heidelberg (2004)

A   Annex: PLIB-Related Standards

Some standard numbers are quoted throughout the paper. Formal designations and some descriptions of these standards may be found at :

- *http://www.iso.org/iso/en/CatalogueListPage.CatalogueList*;
- *http://www.iec.ch*;
- *http://www.plib.ensma.fr* .

This annex gives a short overview of international standardization activities around PLIB.

One may distinguish four categories of standards.

A.1   Ontology Model

The standard ontology model was developed as a joint effort of ISO (International Organization for Standardization) and IEC (International electro technical commission) and published as the ISO 13584 and IEC 61360 standard series. The ontology model was first published in ISO 13584-42 and IEC 61360-2, as an EXPRESS specification, further extended in ISO 13584-25. A new edition is currently in process. An UML / XML self-contained view of the model, called OntoML (ISO 13584-32), is currently under ballot. Both should be published in 2008.

A.2   Ontology-Based Data

Capability to model and to exchange real world objects as ontology individuals (e.g., electronic catalogues, ontology-based database content) was specified in some other parts of ISO 13584, mainly part 20, 24 and 25 that provide both for static description (i.e., property value pairs) and dynamic behavioral description by meta-modelling of expressions and functions.

A.3   Methodological Aspect

Over the last two years, a guide for using PLIB ontology model for specification of product properties and classes was developed. It will be published as ISO/IEC Guide 77 in 2007, and recommended for use by all ISO and IEC product standardization committees.

A.4 Standard Ontologies

Several standard domain ontologies have been developed or are currently under development. Some of them are associated with maintenance agencies allowing to update continuously these ontologies. Examples of already standardized domain ontologies include : Electronic Components (IEC 61360-4), Laboratory Measuring Instruments (ISO 13584-501), Machining Tools (ISO 13399), Mechanical Fasteners (ISO 13584-511). Examples of domain ontologies under development include: Optics and Optronic (ISO 23584), Bearing (ISO 23768).

Semantically Processing Parallel Colour Descriptions[(*)]

Shenghui Wang[1] and Jeff Z. Pan[2]

[1] School of Computer Science, University of Manchester, UK
[2] Department of Computing Science, University of Aberdeen, UK

Abstract. Information integration and retrieval are useful tasks in many information systems. In these systems, it is far from an easy task to directly integrate information from natural language (NL) sources, because precisely capturing NL semantics is not a trivial issue in the first place. In this paper, we choose the botanical domain to investigate this issue. While most existing systems in this domain support only keyword-based search, this paper introduces an ontology-based approach to process parallel colour descriptions from botanical documents. Based on a semantic model, it takes advantage of ontologies so as to represent the semantics of colour descriptions precisely, to integrate parallel descriptions according to their semantic distances, and to answer colour-related species identification queries. To evaluate this approach, we implement a colour reasoner based on the FaCT-DG Description Logic reasoner, and present some results of our experiments on integrating parallel descriptions and species identification queries. From this highly specialised domain, we learn a set of more general methodological rules.

1 Introduction

Automatic information integration and retrieval have become desirable features for many information systems. The information which these systems have to process is often *descriptive* (written in natural language) and *parallel* (multiple sources describing the same objects or phenomena). Parallel descriptions may emphasise different aspects of the same object; they may represent the same information in different ways, or they may plainly disagree with each other. It is far from an easy task to directly integrate information from natural language (NL) sources, because capturing NL semantics precisely is not a trivial task.

In this paper, we choose the botanical domain to investigate this issue. As one of the premier descriptive sciences, botany offers a wealth of material on which to test our methods. For instance, in our dataset, the species *Origanum vulgare* (Marjoram) has four descriptions of its flowers' colour:

[(*)] This is an extended and revised version of the paper "Ontology-based Representation and Query of Colour Descriptions from Botanical Documents," which was published in the 4th International Conference on Ontologies, DataBases, and Applications of Semantics (ODBASE-2005). This work is partially supported by the FP6 Network of Excellence EU project Knowledge Web (IST-2004-507842).

- "violet-purple" in *Flora of the British Isles* [1],
- "reddish-purple, rarely white" in *New Flora of the British Isles* [2],
- "white or purplish-red" in *Flora Europaea* [3],
- "purple-red to pale pink" in *Gray's Manual of Botany* [4].

It has been demonstrated by Wood et. al. [5] that extracting and collecting parallel information from different sources can produce more complete results. Some current projects, such as eFloras[1] and the PLANTS database,[2] attempt to store knowledge from natural language documents in electronic form. These projects generally allow keyword-based queries but fail to process information directly based on their semantics.

This paper makes the following contributions towards semantically processing parallel colour descriptions:

1. It introduces an ontology-based approach to processing parallel colour descriptions from botanical documents. Ideally, an *ontology* captures a shared understanding of certain aspects of a domain: it provides a common *vocabulary*, including important concepts, properties and their definitions, and *constraints* regarding the intended meaning of the vocabulary, sometimes referred to as background assumptions. One of the main advantages of using ontologies is that parallel information can be extracted and represented in a uniform ontology. The explicitly written information can be accessed easily and the implicit knowledge can also be deduced naturally by applying reasoning on the whole ontology. Some earlier work [6,7] has indicated that an ontology could help in extracting, collecting and organising parallel information.
2. It proposes to use a well known colour model, namely the Hue Saturation Lightness (HSL) Model, to model basic colour terms. Based on this semantic model, complex colour descriptions are precisely quantified by applying common morpho-syntactic rules, including adjective modifiers, ranges, conjunctions and disjunctions indicated by NL constructions (see Section 3 for more details). It should be noted that our approach is a general one, and using the HSL model is just one example of a semantic model that can be applied to our approach.
3. It proposes to use the OWL-Eu ontology language [8] to represent the quantitative semantics in the model. OWL-Eu is an extension of the W3C OWL DL [9] standard with unary datatype expressions, which can be used, e.g., to capture the intended quantitative semantics in the HSL Model. The formal representation brings computational and reasoning benefits [10]. For example, subsumption reasoning of the OWL-Eu language can be used to check if one colour description is more general than another one.
4. It presents a framework to support species identification queries. It substantially extends our previous conference paper [11] with the following aspects: (1) For the first time, it proposes two distance functions to calculate distances between parallel information (e.g., the distance between "light blue

---

[1] http://www.efloras.org
[2] http://plants.usda.gov/

to purple" and "violet-blue to pink"). The first distance function d_1 is based on the hue dimension only, and the second distance function d_3 is based on all three HSL dimensions. The main advantage of these two distance functions is that they are designed for measuring distances between ranges, while existing distance functions can only measure distances between points. These are on the one hand not precise enough to capture the semantic colour model and on the other hand not expressive enough to capture the distance between colour descriptions. (2) Based on the distance functions, an algorithm is provided for integrating parallel colour descriptions. (3) the OWL-Eu subsumption reasoning service can then be used to query the integrated colour descriptions, and the distance functions can be used to rank the answers to such queries.

5. Most importantly, it presents our colour reasoner, which is based on the FaCT-DG DL reasoner, and experiments on species identification queries, including comparing our semantic query with existing keyword-based search. The colour reasoner provides the following functionalities: (1) with the help of a NL parser, it transforms the semantics of colour descriptions into their ontological representations; (2) it collaborates with the FaCT-DG reasoner to answer colour-related species identification queries; (3) it calculates distances of parallel information for integration and also infers some probabilistic conclusions. Furthermore, we present some results of our experiments with the colour reasoner on integrating parallel descriptions and species identification queries (see Section 6 and 8 for more details).

We argue that the ontology-based approach is effective in the colour domain, and we have been investigating its applicability to other domains. We believe that it can also be successfully applied to other domains, as long as an appropriate semantic model is chosen and the domain-dependent aspects are well studied.

The rest of the paper is structured as follows. Section 2 introduces some technical background knowledge of multi-dimensional colour models and the OWL-Eu ontology language. Section 3 presents the morpho-syntactic rules that are used to build complex colour descriptions. Section 4 describes how the semantics of colour descriptions are represented in the OWL-Eu language. Section 5 investigates how to answer species identification queries. Section 6 gives primary experimental results of such queries. Sections 7 and 8 introduce the collaboration of distance measuring and DL reasoning, with some interesting integration results. Some related work is described in Section 9. Finally, Section 10 concludes this paper and discusses some of our future work.

2 Technical Background

2.1 The Colour Model

Several colour representations using a multi-dimensional space (CIE XYZ, L*a*b*, L*u*v*, RGB, CMYK, YIQ, HSV, HSL, etc.) have been employed in computer graphics and image processing. Colours are quantified as points

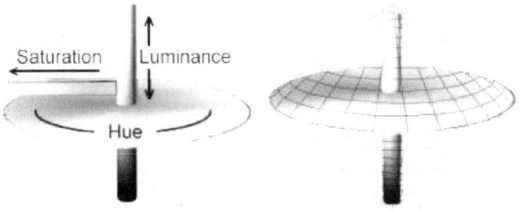

Fig. 1. HSL Colour Model

(or regions) in those spaces. Naming of physically represented colours has been thoroughly investigated [12].

The HSL (Hue Saturation Lightness) model is psychologically based. It corresponds to human's use of colour terms more naturally than machine-oriented colour models, such as the RGB (Red Green Blue) model. In colour notation, it is second only to natural language [13]. The HSL model was therefore chosen to represent basic colour terms. Its colour space is a double cone (see Figure 1).

In the HSL model, a colour is represented by the following three parameters:

- *Hue* is a measure of the colour tint. In fact, it is a circle ranging from 0 (red) to 100 (red again), passing through 16 (yellow), 33 (green), 50 (cyan), 66 (blue) and 83 (magenta).
- *Saturation* is a measure of the amount of colour present. A saturation of 0 is a total absence of colour (i.e. black, grey or white), a saturation of 100 is a pure colour tint.
- *Lightness* (also Luminance or Luminosity) is the brightness of a colour. A lightness of 0 is black, and 100 is white, between 0 and 100 are shades of grey. A lightness of 50 is used to generate a pure colour.

Each basic colour term corresponds to a small space in the double cone whose centre is the particular point representing its HSL value; that is, instead of a point, we represent a colour term by a cuboid space, defined by a range triplet (hueRange, satRange, ligRange). For instance, "purple" is normally defined as the HSL point (83, 50, 25), but is represented by adding a certain range to each parameter, as the region (78–88, 45–55, 20–30).[3]

2.2 OWL DL and Its Datatype Extension OWL-Eu

The OWL Web Ontology Language [15] is a W3C recommendation for expressing ontologies in the Semantic Web. OWL DL is a key sub-language of OWL. Datatype support [16,17] is one of the most useful features that OWL is expected to provide, and has brought extensive discussions in the RDF-Logic mailing list [18] and Semantic Web Best Practices mailing list [19]. Although OWL provides considerable expressive power to the Semantic Web, the OWL datatype

---

[3] Referring to the NBS/ISCC Color System [14], giving a 100-point hue scale, each major hue is placed at the middle of its 10-point spread, or at division 5.

formalism (or simply *OWL datatyping*) is much too weak for many applications. In particular, OWL datatyping does not provide a general framework for customised datatypes, such as XML Schema user-defined datatypes.

To solve the problem, Pan and Horrocks proposed OWL-Eu [8], a small but necessary extension to OWL DL. OWL-Eu supports customised datatypes through unary datatype expressions (or simply datatype expressions) based on unary datatype groups. OWL-Eu extends OWL DL by extending datatype expressions with OWL data ranges.[4] Let $\mathcal{G}$ be a unary datatype group. The set of $\mathcal{G}$-*datatype expressions*, $\mathbf{Dexp}(\mathcal{G})$, is inductively defined in abstract syntax as follows [8]:

1. *atomic expressions*: if u is a datatype URIref, then $u \in \mathbf{Dexp}(\mathcal{G})$;
2. *relativised negated expressions*: if u is a datatype URIref, then $\mathtt{not}(u) \in \mathbf{Dexp}(\mathcal{G})$;
3. *enumerated datatypes*: if $l_1, \ldots, l_n$ are literals, then $\mathtt{oneOf}(l_1, \ldots, l_n) \in \mathbf{Dexp}(\mathcal{G})$; with arity 1, where {} is called the oneOf constructor;
4. *conjunctive expressions*: if $\{E_1, \ldots, E_n\} \subseteq \mathbf{Dexp}(\mathcal{G})$, then $\mathtt{and}(E_1, \ldots, E_n) \in \mathbf{Dexp}(\mathcal{G})$;
5. *disjunctive expressions*: if $\{E_1, \ldots, E_n\} \subseteq \mathbf{Dexp}(\mathcal{G})$, then $\mathtt{or}(E_1, \ldots, E_n) \in \mathbf{Dexp}(\mathcal{G})$.

For example, the following XML Schema user-defined datatype
<simpleType name = "HueRange">
 <restriction base = "xsd:integer">
  <minInclusive value = "0"/>
  <maxInclusive value = "100"/>
 </restriction>
</simpleType>
can be represented by the following conjunctive datatype expression:

and(xsd:nonNegativeInteger, xsdx:integerLessThanOrEqualTo100),

where xsdx:integerLessThanOrEqualTo100 is the URIrefs for the user-defined datatype $\leq_{100}$. Note that *Uniform Resource Identifiers* (URIs) are short strings that identify Web resources [20]. A *URI reference* (or URIref) is a URI, together with an optional fragment identifier at the end. In OWL, URIrefs are used as symbols for classes, properties and datatypes, etc.

Similarly to an OWL DL ontology, an OWL-Eu ontology typically contains a set of class axioms, property axioms and individual axioms. FaCT-DG, a datatype group extension of the FaCT DL reasoner, supports OWL-Eu ontologies.[5] In Section 5, we will use the FaCT-DG reasoner to help answering queries.

3 NL Processing

A close observation of the descriptions in floras shows that colour descriptions are mostly complex phrases, so that they can cover the variations of plant individuals in the field (see the example in Section 1). Complex colour descriptions are built

---

[4] This is the *only* extension OWL-Eu brings to OWL DL.
[5] To be more precise, FaCT-DG supports the $\mathcal{SHIQ}(\mathcal{G})$ DL, i.e., OWL-Eu without nominals, which are not used in the paper.

Table 1. Colour description patterns and their relative frequencies of occurrence, where X, Y and Z each represent a single colour term or an atomic colour phrase, A is a degree adjective and P is a probability adverb

Description patterns	Frequency of occurrence	Example
X	25.5%	"orange"
A X	36.5%	"pale blue"
X to Y (to Z...)	25.9%	"white to pink to red to purple"
X-Y	19.9%	"rose-pink"
X+ish(-)Y	13.2%	"reddish-purple"
X(, Y) or Z	6.5%	"white or violet"
X(, Y), P Z	6.4%	"reddish-purple, rarely white"
X/Y	4.6%	"pink/white"
X, Y	2.8%	"lavender, white-pink"
X(, Y), and Z	2.3%	"white and green"

from several basic colour terms by applying certain morpho-syntactic rules. In order to be represented correctly, a complex colour description has to be analysed by using the same rules.

We carried out a morpho-syntactic analysis on 227 colour descriptions of 170 species from five floras.[6] Different description patterns and their relative frequencies of occurrence in the data set are summarised in Table 1. Table 3 gives the corresponding BNF syntax for colour descriptions. As shown in Table 1, most patterns describe colour ranges that are built from several atomic colour phrases, such as "blue," "blue-purple" or "bright yellow."

There are two steps in our text processing. Firstly, we construct the following *atomic* colour phrases as basic colour spaces:

X: This is a single colour space, i.e. (hueRange, satRange, ligRange).[7]

A X: We need to modify the space of X according to the meaning of A, as shown in Table 2. For example, "light blue" is represented as (61–71, 70–80, 65–75) where "blue" is (61–71, 90–100, 45–55).

X-Y: This represents an intermediate colour between the two colours X and Y [22]. For example, "blue-purple" is generated as the halfway colour between "blue" (66, 100, 50) and "purple" (83, 50, 25), that is, the colour with HSL value of (75, 75, 38). The hue is calculated by the following formula (with similar calculations for saturation and lightness):

$$Hue_{X-Y} = \frac{Hue_X + Hue_Y}{2} \quad (1)$$

---

[6] They are *Flora of the British Isles* [1], *Flora Europaea* [3], *The New Britton and Brown Illustrated Flora of the Northeastern United States and Adjacent Canada* [4], *New Flora of the British Isles* [2] and *Gray's Manual of Botany* [21].

[7] According to the Colour Naming System (CNS) [22], given a 100-point hue scale, each major Munsell hue placed at the middle of its 10-point spread, or at division 5. Therefore, for each basic term, a 5-point spread along each side of the prototypical values builds up a reasonable space. This setting is inherited by some of the following operations.

Table 2. Meanings of modifiers and their corresponding operations on a colour space

Adjective	Meaning[a]	Operation[b]
strong	high in chroma	satRange + 20
pale	deficient in chroma	satRange - 20, ligRange + 20
bright	of high saturation or brilliance	satRange + 20, ligRange + 20
deep	high in saturation and low in lightness	satRange + 20, ligRange - 20
dull	low in saturation and low in lightness	satRange - 20, ligRange - 20
light	medium in saturation and high in lightness	satRange - 20, ligRange + 20
dark	of low or very low lightness	ligRange - 20

[a] Referring to Merriam-Webster online dictionary.
[b] Referring to the specifications from the Colour Naming System (CNS) [22], saturation and lightness are each divided into 5 levels, which causes a range/ranges to change by 20 (100/5).

Finally it is represented by the range triple (70–80, 70–80, 33–43), by adding 5-point spread in each dimension from the centre.

Xish-Y: Specified in CNS [22], this denotes a quarterway value between the two colours, closer to the latter colour term. For instance, "reddish-purple" means it is basically purple (83, 50, 25) but reflecting a quarterway deviation to red (100, 100, 50), so the hue range for "reddish-purple" is centred on 87, calculated by the following formula (similar formulae for saturation and lightness):

$$Hue_{X_{ish}-Y} = Hue_Y + \frac{Hue_X - Hue_Y}{4} \quad (2)$$

and the colour is finally represented as (82–92, 58–68, 29–39).

Secondly, we build up combined colour spaces based on basic ones. Specifically, combined colour spaces are built up by a colour reasoner, according to the following morpho-syntactic rules:

1. If atomic colour phrases are connected by one or more "to"s, the final colour space should be the whole range from the first colour to the last one. For instance, if "light blue" is (66, 80, 70) and "purple" is (83, 50, 25), "light blue to purple" should be the whole range (66–83, 50–80, 25–70), which contains any colour in between.

   Note that special care is needed for ranges starting or ending with a grey colour, such as "white to purple." In the HSL model, colours ranging from white, through different levels of grey, to black have no hue and saturation values. For instance, the HSL value of "white" is (0, 0, 100), while "red" also has a hue value of 0 but its saturation is 100. A special rule for building such ranges has to be followed; that is, a range from colour A $(0, 0, l_a)$ to colour B (h_b, s_b, l_b) should be $(\overline{h_b - 5} \text{-} \overline{h_b + 5}, 0 \text{-} s_b, l_a \text{-} l_b)$, where the hue value does not range from 0 to h_b which is actually from red to colour B. For example, the range from "purple" (83, 50, 25) to "white" (0, 0, 100) should

Table 3. BNF syntax of colour descriptions

$<Cterm>\ ::=\ red\|yellow\|green\|\ldots$
$<Dmodifier>\ ::=\ strong\|pale\|bright\|deep\|dull\|light\|dark\|\ldots$
$<Pmodifier>\ ::=\ usually\|often\|sometimes\|occasionally\|rarely\|never\|\ldots$
$<Cphrase>\ ::=\ <Cterm>$
$\mid\ <Cterm>\ [ish][-\mid\ ]\ <Cterm>$
$\mid\ <Cphrase>\ -\ <Cphrase>$
$\mid\ <Dmodifier>\ <Cterm>$
$<Cdescription>\ ::=\ <Cphrase>$
$\mid\ <Cphrase>\ \{\ to\ <Cphrase>\}$
$\mid\ <Cphrase>,\ <Cphrase>$
$\mid\ <Cphrase>\ /\ <Cphrase>$
$\mid\ <Cphrase>\ \{,<Cphrase>\}\ or\ <Cphrase>$
$\mid\ <Cphrase>\ \{,<Cphrase>\}\ and\ <Cphrase>$
$\mid\ <Cphrase>\ \{,<Cphrase>\},\ <Pmodifier>\ <Cphrase>$

be represented by the triple (78–88, 0–50, 25–100), so that the hue range (78–88) keeps the purple tint when the colour changes from purple to white.

2. If atomic colour phrases are connected by any of these symbols: "or," "and," comma (",") or slash ("/"), they are treated as separate colour spaces; that is, they are disjoint from each other. For instance, "white, lilac or yellow" means that the colour of this flower could be either white or lilac or yellow, not a colour in between.

Notice that "and" is treated as a disjunction symbol because, in floras, it normally means several colours can be found in the same species, instead of indicating a normal logical conjunction. For instance, flowers of species *Rumex crispus* (Curled Dock) are described as "red and green," which means that both red and green flowers may occur in the same species, but it does not mean that one colour is both red and green.

By using an NL parser based on our BNF syntax, we can generate an OWL-Eu ontology to model complex colour information.

4 Representation of Colour Descriptions in OWL-Eu

Based on the morpho-syntactic rules introduced in the last section, we can decompose the semantics of colour descriptions into several quantifiable components, which can be represented as DL datatype expressions. In this section, we will show how to use the OWL-Eu ontology language to represent the semantics of a colour description.

The fragment of our plant ontology $\mathcal{O}_C$ contains Colour as a primitive class. Important primitive classes in $\mathcal{O}_C$ include

Class(Species), Class(Flower), Class(Colour);

important object properties in $\mathcal{O}_C$ include

ObjectProperty(*hasPart*), ObjectProperty(*hasColour*);

important datatype properties in $\mathcal{O}_C$ include

DatatypeProperty(*hasHue* Functional
 range(and(xsd:nonNegativeInteger, xsdx:integerLessThanOrEqualTo100))),
DatatypeProperty(*hasSaturation* Functional
 range(and(xsd:nonNegativeInteger, xsdx:integerLessThanOrEqualTo100))),
DatatypeProperty(*hasLightness* Functional
 range(and(xsd:nonNegativeInteger, xsdx:integerLessThanOrEqualTo100))),

which are all functional properties. A *functional* datatype property relates an object with at most one data value. Note that the datatype expression
 and(xsd:nonNegativeInteger, xsdx:integerLessThanOrEqualTo100)
is used as the range of the above datatype properties.

Based on the above primitive classes and properties, we can define specific colours, such as Purple, as OWL-Eu defined classes (indicated by the keyword "complete").

Class(Purple complete Colour
 restriction(*hasHue* someValuesFrom
            (and(xsdx:integerGreaterThanOrEqualTo78,
                 xsdx:integerLessThanOrEqualTo88)))
 restriction(*hasSaturation* someValuesFrom
            (and(xsdx:integerGreaterThanOrEqualTo47,
                 xsdx:integerLessThanOrEqualTo52)))
 restriction(*hasLightness* someValuesFrom
            (and(xsdx:integerGreaterThanOrEqualTo20,
                 xsdx:integerLessThanOrEqualTo30))))

In the above class definition, datatype expressions are used to restrict the values of the datatype properties *hasHue*, *hasSaturation* and *hasLightness*. Note that not only colour terms but complex colour descriptions can be also represented in OWL-Eu classes, as long as they can be transformed into proper colour subspaces with constraints on their hue, saturation and lightness.

As colour descriptions are represented by OWL-Eu classes, we can use the subsumption checking service provided by the FaCT-DG reasoner to check if one colour description is more general than another. Namely, if ColourA is subsumed by ColourB, we say that ColourB is more general than ColourA. With the help of the FaCT-DG DL reasoner, the formal representation of colour descriptions makes it possible to express a query about a range of colours, such as to retrieve all species which have "bright rose-pink" or "light blue to purple" flowers.

5 Domain-Oriented Queries

The flower colour of an individual plant is an important distinguishing feature for identifying which species it belongs to. The species identification that botanists are interested in can be written as a query: "Given a certain colour, tell me all the possible species whose flowers have such a colour." We would like to point out that, from a botanical point of view, one has to take the variations between individuals in nature into account. In other words, botanists rarely use colour as a strict criterion. It is more appropriate to answer such species identification queries in an fuzzy manner, that is, returning a list which contains all species that *could* match the query. We call this kind of query, which is particularly suitable for domain interests, *domain-oriented* queries.

We can answer species identification queries based on subsumption queries that are supported by the FaCT-DG DL reasoner. For example, if the plant ontology contains the following class axioms:

```
Class(SpeciesA restriction(hasPart someValueFrom(FlowerA)))
Class(FlowerA restriction(hasColour someValueFrom(ColourA)))
Class(SpeciesB restriction(hasPart someValueFrom(FlowerB)))
Class(FlowerB restriction(hasColour someValueFrom(ColourB)))
```

and if from the definitions of ColourA and ColourB we can conclude that ColourA is subsumed by ColourB, when we ask our DL reasoner whether the above ontology entails that SpeciesA is subsumed by SpeciesB, the reasoner will return "yes." By using this kind of subsumption query, we can, for example, conclude that a species having "golden" flowers is subsumed by a more general species which has "yellow" flowers, which again is subsumed by another species which has "orange to yellow" flowers. Therefore, if one asks "Which species might have yellow flowers," our colour reasoner will return all these three species.

For species identification, this hierarchical subsumption matching is very useful for shortening the possible species list. After classification reasoning, we have already had three different levels of matchings:

- **Exact** matching (Class$_{RealSpecies}$ ≡ Class$_{QuerySpecies}$),
- **PlugIn** matching (Class$_{RealSpecies}$ ⊑ Class$_{QuerySpecies}$)
- **Subsume** matching (Class$_{RealSpecies}$ ⊒ Class$_{QuerySpecies}$)

Actually there is another possible species list, which is not covered by the above three kinds of matchings, that is, **Intersecting** matching ($\neg$(Class$_{RealSpecies}$ ⊓ Class$_{QuerySpecies}$ ⊑ $\bot$)) [23,24]. For example, if a species has "greenish-yellow" flowers, it would also be possible to find in the field an individual which has "yellow" flowers. Although this latter list has a lower probability to contain the correct answers, it is still helpful from botanical point of view.

Our colour reasoner reduces our domain problems into standard DLs reasoning problems. In fact, in order to answer domain-oriented queries, it interacts with the FaCT-DG reasoner. First, the colour in a query is represented by an OWL-Eu class Q with datatype constraints about its hue, saturation and lightness.

Secondly, the colour reasoner calculates the complete set of colours $complete_Q$ which satisfies the above four levels of matching. Specifically, $complete_Q$ consists of the following four sets.

- $equiv_Q$: all elements are equivalent to the class Q, such as "yellow;"
- sub_Q: all elements are subsumed by the class Q, such as "golden;"

- $super_Q$: all elements subsume the class Q, such as "yellow to orange to red;"
- $intersection_Q$: all elements intersect with the class Q, such as "greenish-yellow."

Note that the first two contain answers with 100% confidence, while the latter two contain those with less confidence. Thirdly, in order to find all species that have flowers whose colour satisfies the query, the colour reasoner interacts with the Fact-DG reasoner to return those species which have flowers whose colour is contained in $complete_Q$ set.

6 Experiments on Representation and Query

In this section, we will present some experiments, based on our plant ontology, of species identification queries.

We chose 100 colour terms which are commonly found in floras, as basic colour terms. For each basic term, we obtained its RGB value by referring to the X11 Colour Names,[8] converted this into its corresponding HSL value and finally defined it as ranges in hue, saturation and lightness (as described in Section 4).

A simple plant ontology, mentioned in Section 4, was constructed using the OWL-Eu language. This ontology contains 1154 species, selected from five floras, mentioned before, and the online eFloras.[9], each of which has a flower part which has a colour property. The colour property is represented by a datatype expression, representing the colour spaces transformed from the original colour descriptions,

For example, species *Viola adunca* has "light blue to purple" flowers.

```
Class(Viola_adunca complete Species
    restriction(hasPart someValuesFrom(Viola_adunca_flower))),
Class(Viola_adunca_flower complete Flower
    restriction(hasColour someValuesFrom(Viola_adunca_flower_colour))),
Class(Viola_adunca_flower_colour complete Colour
    restriction(hasHue someValuesFrom
                (and(xsdx:integerGreaterThanOrEqualTo66,
                     xsdx:integerLessThanOrEqualTo83)))
    restriction(hasSaturation someValuesFrom
                (and(xsdx:integerGreaterThanOrEqualTo50,
                     xsdx:integerLessThanOrEqualTo100)))
    restriction(hasLightness someValuesFrom
                (and(xsdx:integerGreaterThanOrEqualTo25,
                     xsdx:integerLessThanOrEqualTo70))))
```

In our experiments, 10 species identification queries based flower colours were

---

[8] http://en.wikipedia.org/wiki/X11_Color_Names
[9] This is an international project which collects plant taxonomy data from several main floras, such as *Flora of China, Flora of North America, Flora of Pakistan*, etc. Plant species descriptions are available in electronic form, but still written in the common style of floras, i.e. semi-NL.

Table 4. Query results (partial) of species having "yellow," "light blue" and "light blue to purple" flowers

Species	Flower colour	Matching type
Amsinckia menziessi	yellow	Exact matching
Ranunculus acris	golden	PlugIn matching
Eucalyptus globulus	creamy-white to yellow	Subsume matching
Tropaeolum majus	yellow to orange to red	Subsume matching
Rhodiola sherriffii	greenish-yellow	Intersection matching
Eschscholzia californica	deep orange to pale yellow	Intersection matching

(a) "yellow"

Species	Flower colour	Matching type
Aster chilensis	light blue	Exact matching
Heliotropium curassavicum	white to bluish	Subsume matching
Linum bienne	pale blue to lavender	Subsume matching
Triteleia laxa	blue to violet	Intersection matching
Dichelostemma congestum	pink to blue	Intersection matching

(b) "light blue"

Species	Flower colour	Matching type
Viola adunca	light blue to purple	Exact matching
Linum bienne	pale blue to lavender	PlugIn matching
Verbena lasiostachys	blue-purple	PlugIn matching
Lupinus eximus	blue to purple, sometimes lavender	Intersection matching
Stachys bullata	light purple to pink to white	Intersection matching
Triteleia laxa	blue to violet	Intersection matching

(c) "light blue to purple"

carried out. The queries consist of basic terms, range phrases and others with different levels of complexity (as shown in Table 1). Each query finished in 1–2 seconds on a 2G Hz Pentium 4 PC. Some of the results are presented in Tables 4, in the order of complexity of colours: "yellow," "light blue," "light blue to purple."

We can query in a specific manner, for example to find species which have "light blue" flowers but excluding those with "dark blue" flowers (see Table 4 (b)); or in a more general style, to query all species which could have flowers ranging from "light blue to purple" (see Table 4 (c)). All of these facilities use our quantitative model which makes it possible to compare and reason with classes at a semantic level.

As stated in Section 5, the resulting list is from four different levels of matching, which gives a complete list for species identification. We can also specify to stop at certain levels of matching to get results with different confidences, such as only returning those species which fully satisfy the query.

The semantics of a colour term or a complex colour description is decomposed and represented by a group of ranges in multiple numerical parameters, which is a small subspace in a multi-dimensional space. Numerical representation makes

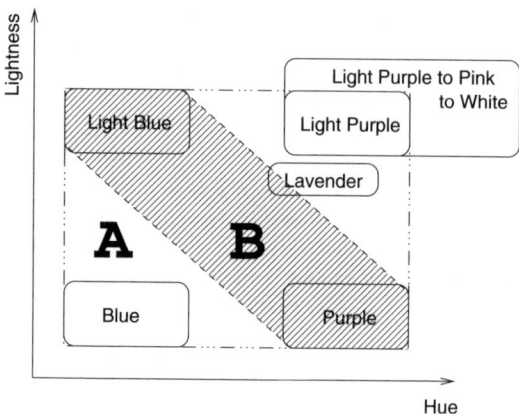

Fig. 2. Range between "light blue" and "purple"

Table 5. Performance comparison between semantic matching and keyword matching

Method	Precision	Recall
Semantic matching	98.2%	81.1%
Keyword matching	84.8%	71.9%

it easy to build ranges between colours, but a further observation shows that this is not as obvious as we thought. For example, there could be different ways of interpreting the meaning of "light blue *to* purple" (see Figure 2):

- light blue to purple directly (area B),
- light blue to blue then to purple,
- light blue to light purple then to purple,
- the whole rectangle (area A).

In our experiment (see Table 4 (c)), we used the last option (the whole rectangle) for the sake of simplicity and computation cost. It is open to extend our work and to allow the users to pick up one of the above options when they query with the keyword "to."

We further compared our semantics-based query with the simple keyword matching. The standard precision and recall[10] were use to measure the performance. Here, if the distance of returned answer to the query is less than a threshold used for integration, as we will introduce later, then this answer is considered correct. Table 5 gives the comparison results of the performance of these two methods.

---

[10] The precision indicates the proportion of answers in the returned list which are correct, while the recall is all the correct answers in the whole dataset that were found.

7 Integration of Parallel Colour Descriptions

In the previous sections, we have shown that, by using a multi-dimensional colour model, we can precisely represent the semantics of complex colour descriptions. Represented in the OWL-Eu language, this quantitative representation enables reasoning on the real semantics of NL information and provides more practical query results.

However, the reality does not stop here. As the example in Section 1 shows, a species is often observed by different botanists, that is, parallel descriptions of the same species are easily found cross different floras. Since they describe the same species, these parallel colour descriptions are expected to be similar to or compatible with each other. Most importantly, as demonstrated in [5], extracting and collecting parallel information from different sources can produce more complete results.

A close observation of real data shows that, even using a standard naming system, botanists use their personally preferred patterns to describe what they observe, so as to cover the variations of plant individuals in nature. Accordingly, parallel colour descriptions are rarely exactly the same; sometimes they vary a lot, especially when the species itself has a relatively wide variation. Here we do not focus on some genuine geographic or temporal influences on species variation or some literary errors; instead, we are only concerned linguistic differences between parallel information. We assume that information from different sources is correct but probably incomplete; i.e. different sources are never considered contradictory, only complementary, possibly with a certain degree of overlap.

The key task is to find good strategies to integrate parallel colour descriptions; otherwise, we could end up producing incomplete or redundant results. A simple *conjunction* (or *intersection*) would cause information loss. For example, if one flora says that a flower is "white" while another says it is "white or purplish, sometimes yellow," the result of their intersection is "white"—"purple" and "yellow" would be removed. Another logic operation, *disjunction* (or *union*), does not work ideally either. For example, there are two descriptions of the same flower: "reddish-purple, rarely white" and "white or purplish-red." Each of them is represented by two separate colour subspaces. The union operation results in

White ⊔ Purplish-red ⊔ Reddish-purple

Note that the other "white" is omitted because two "white"s are identical. The result is complete but there is a redundant overlap between "reddish-purple" and "purplish-red;" while people can easily infer from the original texts that actually any colour between red and purple is possible for this species.

The above observations show that naive use of logic operations cannot produce the integration results as we really expect, indicating that it is not appropriate to simply mix information without careful studies of how similar or how different they are. Along this line, investigations of the similarities of parallel information seem to be a good integration strategy. To a large degree, similarities of their semantics can tell how much different descriptions agree with each other,

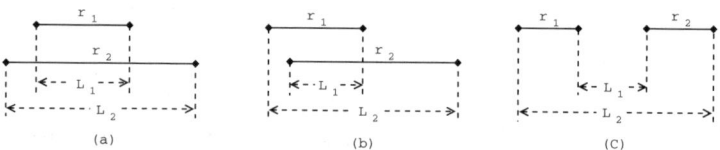

Fig. 3. Three different relations between two ranges

namely, the more similar two descriptions are, the more compatible they are. Thus, given similarities are quantified properly, if two descriptions are similar enough, although they might not be exactly the same (due to various reasons), it is better to combine them as one single "super-description" and remove redundancies; otherwise, it is safer to leave them separate because they are both likely to provide partial information of the same object.

The similarity of two objects is often closely related to the distance between their representations in certain underlying spaces [25]. More specifically, similarity is a decaying function of distance. Ideally, since colour is a common perceptual phenomenon, any distance function for colours should be able to capture the real differences perceived by human eyes. However, how to find perfect colour distances in different colour models is beyond the scope of this paper. Here, we claim that any perceptually acceptable distance function $d(x,y)$ (for a metric space $\mathcal{S}$) which satisfies the following conditions (for all points x, y in $\mathcal{S}$) will suffice.

Minimality: $d(x, y) = 0 \implies x = y$;
Symmetry: $d(x, y) = d(y, x)$.

In what follows, we will present two ways to define the distance function $d(x, y)$; we will also show that both distances satisfy the above two conditions.

Inspired by Tversky's feature contrast and ratio model [26], given two ranges r_1 and r_2, the distance of r_1 and r_2, i.e. $d(r_1, r_2)$, is equal to the "non-common part of r_1 and r_2" divided by "the minimal super-range that contains both r_1 and r_2".

Distance Function $d1$. We start to consider a simple distance function: distance w.r.t. the hue-range only. Obviously, hue differences is always the first and the most prominent aspect when people try to compare colours.

There are 3 different types of relations between two ranges, shown in Figure 3. With the help of the FaCT-DG DL reasoner, we can tell whether one range subsumes the other ($r_1 \sqsubseteq r_2$), or they intersect with each other ($\neg(r_1 \sqcap r_2) \sqsubseteq \bot$), or they are disjoint from each other ($(r_1 \sqcap r_2) \sqsubseteq \bot$). Accordingly, we define the following distance function for two arbitrary ranges r_1 and r_2:

$$d1(r_1, r_2) = \begin{cases} 1 - \frac{L_1}{L_2} & \text{if } r_1 \text{ and } r_2 \text{ overlap} \\ 1 + \frac{L_1}{L_2} & \text{otherwise}; \end{cases} \quad (3)$$

where L_2 is the length of minimal super-range which contains both r_1 and r_2, and L_1 is defined as follows: when r_1 and r_2 overlap (see (a) and (b)), L_1 is the length of the overlap part of two ranges; otherwise, for (c), L_1 is the length of the gap between two ranges. If two ranges r_1 and r_2 only share one point, we say they *meet* each other and $L_1 = 0$

The distance $d1(r_1, r_2)$ is continuous and nicely scaled into the range $[0, 2)$: if $d1(r_1, r_2) = 0$, r_1 equals r_2; if $0 < d1(r_1, r_2) < 1$, r_1 and r_2 overlap; if $d1(r_1, r_2) = 1$, r_1 meets r_2; if $1 < d1(r_1, r_2) < 2$, r_1 and r_2 are disjoint; as two ranges move further apart from each other, the distance gets closer to 2.

Distance Function $d3$. As we know, hue, saturation and lightness values should be assigned to a colour at the same time because they are *integral* dimensions [27]. In order to have a more sensible distance measure, it might be better to take the other two dimensions into account.

We still use the overlap/gap ratio to measure distances. Instead of comparing the length of ranges in one dimension, we measure the volume of the overlap/gap space. Similarly, the FaCT-DG DL reasoner helps to classify the relation between two colour spaces, which would be subsumption, intersection or disjunction. Accordingly, we define the function $d3$ for two colour spaces cs_1 and cs_2:[11]

$$d3(cs_1, cs_2) = \begin{cases} 1 - \frac{V_1}{V_2} & \text{if } cs_1 \text{ and } cs_2 \text{ overlap} \\ 1 + \frac{V_1}{V_2} & \text{otherwise} \end{cases} \quad (4)$$

where V_2 is the volume of minimal cuboid space which contains both cs_1 and cs_2, and V_1 is defined as follows: when cs_1 and cs_2 overlap with each other, V_1 is the volume of the overlap space of the two spaces; otherwise, V_1 is the volume of the gap between two spaces in terms of their "super-space" V_2. It is easy to show that the distance function 4 has exactly the same properties as the distance function 3 has.

Once the distances of any two colour descriptions are calculated, users can have a better overview of all parallel information from different sources. Based on such an overview, they can therefore decide whether it is necessary to combine two pieces of information or just to leave them as separate as they are. If a reasonable distance threshold is given,[12] our colour reasoner automatically combines two descriptions if they are close/similar enough or keeps them separate otherwise.

The integration process is recursive as follows:

Step 1. Use the FaCT-DG DL reasoner to classify the relations between any two colour spaces generated from parallel descriptions of the same species, and then use our colour reasoner to calculate their distances (by using either Formula 3 or 4).

Step 2. Select two closest colour spaces and check whether they are "similar-enough," i.e. their distance is less than the distance threshold.

---

[11] Here, $d3$ means the distance function considers all three dimensions, instead of only the hue is considered as $d1$ measures.

[12] See Section 8 for more detail.

Step 3. If they are not similar enough then the integration stops; otherwise, the smallest cuboid space which contains them is generated and substitutes them as their integrated space (the same operation as building "to" ranges in Section 3).

Step 4. Go back to Step 1 to check the updated colour spaces.

In the final results, not only the integrated colour spaces are stored, but also those generated from parallel sources are kept for further references. For each disjoint colour space rcs_i in the final results, we check how many of the original colour spaces intersect with it.

$$Prob_{rcs_i} = \frac{\text{Count of original colour spaces that intersect with } rcs_i}{\text{Count of original colour spaces}} \quad (5)$$

According to the *Prob* value of each original colour space, we can see how many authors agree on one particular range of colours, which reflects how likely people will find such coloured plant individuals in the field. Therefore, some interesting frequency inferences can be deduced from parallel information integration, which will be illustrated in the next section.

8 Experiments on Integration

In this section, we present some results of our experiments on the integration of parallel colour descriptions. These experiments illustrate how the collaboration of DL reasoning and similarity measuring helps to integrate parallel information. Interestingly, our results can also be used to evaluate the performance of the two similarity functions in a real application.

We further selected 656 species, each of which has at least two parallel descriptions. Note that due to geographic influences, i.e. some species only exist in some particular regions, parallel information is not guaranteed for each species.

We extended the NL parser introduced in Section 3 in order that it can parse a whole botanical document and extract flower colour descriptions before it deeply parses these colour descriptions by using morpho-syntactic rules (see Table 3). All data is extracted by the parser automatically and double-checked manually.

In order to calculate the threshold for the integration, we selected a group of parallel descriptions from the whole dataset, which are not identical yet are still considered to be similar enough to be combined. The average distance of these parallel descriptions is used as the threshold. Interestingly, we got slightly different thresholds for two similarity functions, i.e. 1.5 for $d1$ and 1.4 for $d3$.

To simplify the presentation, here we use two species to illustrate our experiments. According to three different authors, *Linum bienne* (Pale Flax) has "pale blue to lavender," or "pale lilac-blue" or "pale blue" flowers. In the 3D HSL-space, the FaCT-DG DL reasoner classifies their relations as follows:

- $\neg(CS_{pale\ blue\ to\ lavender} \sqcap CS_{pale\ blue}) \sqsubseteq \bot$ ("pale blue to lavender" intersects with "pale blue"),
- $(CS_{pale\ blue\ to\ lavender} \sqcap CS_{pale\ lilac-blue}) \sqsubseteq \bot$ ("pale blue to lavender" is disjoint from "pale lilac-blue"), and

- $(CS_{pale\ blue} \sqcap CS_{pale\ lilac-blue}) \sqsubseteq \bot$ ("pale blue" is disjoint from "pale lilac-blue").

According to their logic relations, their distances are calculated differently. By using function $d3$, distances between these colour spaces are:

- $d3(CS_{pale\ blue\ to\ lavender}, CS_{pale\ blue}) = 0.55$,
- $d3(CS_{pale\ blue\ to\ lavender}, CS_{pale\ lilac-blue}) = 1.26$,
- $d3(CS_{pale\ blue}, CS_{pale\ lilac-blue}) = 1.77$.

$CS_{pale\ blue\ to\ lavender}$ and $CS_{pale\ blue}$ are combined first because they are close enough (actually, $CS_{pale\ blue} \sqsubseteq CS_{pale\ blue\ to\ lavender}$, so $CS_{pale\ blue\ to\ lavender}$ is kept as their integrated space), then the integration process goes back to check the newly updated colour spaces. This time, $CS_{pale\ lilac-blue}$ is close enough (1.26 is less than the threshold for $d3$, which is 1.4) to the newly integrated colour space ($CS_{pale\ blue\ to\ lavender}$), they are combined too although they do not overlap with each other directly. Therefore, three slightly different NL descriptions are finally combined as one single and unified colour space.

Differently, the species *Allium dichlamydeum* (Coast Onion) has two descriptions about its flower colour: "pink to rose" and "deep reddish-purple". They are obviously disjoint from each other; their distance is 1.63 which is higher than the threshold, so they are kept separately.[13] Table 7 shows more examples of parallel data and their integration results.

Our experiments confirm that the different effects of two distance functions $d1$ (based on hue dimension only) and $d3$ (based on all three HSL dimensions). Again taking *Allium dichlamydeum* (Coast Onion) for example, if only the hue dimension is considered, the two descriptions would be combined as a single colour space because their hue ranges are actually quite similar. However, after taking saturation and lightness into account, the HSL-space similarity function successfully keeps them separate, which seems more acceptable to human perception. Other similar cases are shown in Table 6.

It might be expected that using all three HSL dimensions would lead to very different integration results to those using the distances in the single hue dimension. Interestingly, these two distance functions give almost the same results in most cases. Only 20% of the parallel data give different results; for example, in Table 7, both distance functions (with different thresholds) give exactly the same integrated results. The more complicated HSL-space distance function ($d3$) does not produce as much advantage as we had expected. One possible reason is, as we mentioned in Section 7, that although people use different modifiers to distinguish colours' saturation and lightness, hue is still the most prominent aspect which really counts for describing flower colours. Therefore we choose to use the simpler hue-range distance as the default criterion for integration, while HSL-space distance is used for some advanced comparisons.

As stated in Section 7, one of the advantages of processing parallel information is that we can infer some probabilistic conclusions by observing how often certain information is mentioned by different authors, as the last column in

---

[13] It has been checked out that this species has slightly different flower colour according to its geographic distribution.

Table 6. Comparison of integration results from two different distance functions

Species	Parallel Descriptions	Distance Function	Integration Results		
			H	S	L
Allium dichlamydeum	pink to rose deep reddish-purple	$d1$	84–0	13–61	6–87
		$d3$	84–90	22–61	6–16
			97–0	13–24	45–87
Iris laevigata	blue dark blue or violet	$d1$	63–86	39–100	25–77
		$d3$	80–86	39–45	67–77
			63–69	60–100	25–55
Hylotelephium ewersii	pink or light purple purplish-red	$d1$	80–0	22–50	20–92
		$d3$	84–0	22–26	82–92
			80–86	35–50	20–50

Table 7 shows. Looking back to the example mentioned in Section 1, flowers of *Origanum vulgare* (marjoram) have been described by four different authors. After integration, "violet-purple," "purplish-red," "purple-red to pale pink" and "reddish-purple" are combined and substituted by the colour space whose hue ranges from 80 to 99, saturation from 18 to 88 and lightness from 26 to 100; "white" is kept as a disjoint colour space found from parallel sources. The former colour space has a higher probability value (66.7%) than the latter one (33.3%), from which a reasonable inference can be deduced that *white* marjoram flowers are less likely to be found in nature.

Table 7. Examples of parallel descriptions and their integration results

Species	Parallel Descriptions	Integration Results			
		H	S	L	Prob
Lathyrus latifolius	bright rose-pink vivid magenta-pink rose-pink	87–2	13–50	61–91	100%
Linum bienne	pale blue to lavender pale lilac-blue pale blue	63–78	3–80	65–94	100%
Raphanus sativus	lavender, white-pink white or violet white, lilac or violet, rarely purple/yellow	63–0 0–0 13–19	5–50 0–0 95–100	20–99 95–100 45–55	66.7% 22.2% 11.1%
Ranunculus arvensis	lemon-yellow pale greenish-yellow	12–23	60–96	46–75	100%
Origanum vulgare	violet-purple white or purplish-red purple-red to pale pink reddish-purple, rarely white	80–99 0–0	18–88 0–0	26–100 95–100	66.7% 33.3%

9 Related Work

Automatically integrating information from a variety of sources has become a necessary feature for many information systems [10]. Compared to structured or semi-structured data sources, information in natural language documents is more cumbersome to access [28]. Our work focuses mainly on parallel information extraction and integration from homogeneous monolingual (English) botanical documents.

Information Extraction (IE) [29] is a common Natural Language Processing (NLP) technique which can extract information or knowledge from documents. Ontologies, containing various semantics expressions of domain knowledge, have recently been adopted in many IE systems [30,31,32]. Semantics embedded in ontologies can boost the performance of IE in terms of precision and recall [33]. Since they can be shared by different sources, ontologies also play an important role in the area of information integration [10,34,28]. Ontology reasoning is also introduced into the extraction, representation and integration processes [35,36,33]. We have shown that reasoning support for ontologies with customised datatypes is very useful for answering species identification queries and integration of parallel colour descriptions.

One of our main contributions is to capture the NL semantics as precisely as possible. In other research areas, many methods have been tried to solve similar problems. Semantic differential [37] measures people's reactions to words or concepts in terms of ratings on bipolar scales defined with contrasting adjectives at each end, such as "good–bad". Individuals' connotations are captured in a multidimensional space and thus the psychological "distance" between words or concepts are measured. Lexical Decomposition [38] attempts to break the meanings of words down to several basic categories, hoping to find some internal structure for words' meaning. Multidimensional modelling was also employed in several areas of cognitive science [25]. Spatial or geometrical structures are exploited in concept formation and learning, and also in studies in cognitive linguistics [39]. The limitations of their methods are either the dimensions are difficult to interpret or they are most qualitative which prevents to capture semantics precisely.

The quantitative semantic model can produce more useful results for real domain purposes. Specifically, in the botanical domain, many current plant databases can only support keyword-based query, such as the ActKey,[14] ePIC project,[15] the PLANTS database,[16] etc. They rely heavily on the occurrence of keywords. As demonstrated in Section 6, our method uses real semantics matching, instead of pure keyword matching, which supports more flexible-styled queries, especially range-based ones.

Another important related research area is semantic similarity measurement. Obviously, similarity is an important criterion for integration. Depending on how

---

[14] http://flora.huh.harvard.edu:8080/actkey/
[15] http://www.rbgkew.org.uk/epic/
[16] http://plants.usda.gov/

they are represented in different models, similarity between objects is calculated differently, such as the ratio of common/distinct features in *feature models* [26], the vector distances in multidimensional *spacial models* [25,40], the path-length in *network models* [41,42], etc. In NL research, corpus-based methods are often used to measure similarities between concepts by comparing their information content [43]. Unfortunately, these methods only focus on relations between basic terms, but rarely pay enough attention to more complex expressions, such as regions or ranges. In other words, they are probably able to find the similarity between "lilac" and "purple," but cannot tell how close "lilac to pale blue" is to "deep reddish-purple," which is much more common in the real world. Our method uses a 3D-space as a basic representation of basic colour terms and maps all common linguistics rules into operations on such spaces. Complex NL descriptions are represented by one or several subspaces. By calculating the distances between these subspaces, the similarities between their original NL descriptions are successfully quantified and therefore used as a crucial criterion for the integration.

10 Conclusion and Outlook

This paper has presented and evaluated an ontology-based approach which facilitates representing, integrating and querying colour information from parallel floras. It turns out that, even in this limited domain, formally representing the semantics of colour descriptions is not a trivial problem. Based on a multi-dimensional semantic model and certain morpho-syntactic rules, we have implemented an NL parser which translates complex colour descriptions into quantitative representations written in the OWL-Eu ontology language. A colour reasoner is implemented to interact with the FaCT-DG DL reasoner in order to integrate parallel information and carry out queries for real botanical applications.

We have shown that our approach outperforms keyword-based approaches, which are widely used in this domain. Firstly, our quantifiable model enables automatic reasoning on the real semantic level. Relations between colour descriptions are captured precisely. For example, yellow is between red and green in terms of hue, lilac is lighter than purple although they have the same hue. Furthermore, based on the rules of processing adjective modifiers and ranges, we can query in a detailed manner, such as "light blue," which excludes pure blue and dark blue. We can also query on a fuzzy manner, such as "light blue to purple", as required for particular domain purposes.

Furthermore, we have also addressed a common but crucial problem for integration systems: semantic similarities between information from different sources. Two reasonable distance functions are proposed. The distance measuring collaborates with the FaCT-DG DL reasoner to give complete but not redundant results. From our experiments, the simpler distance function (i.e. $d1$) works well enough in a real-world application. By comparing integrated results with their original descriptions, some useful probabilistic conclusions can be inferred, which are especially useful for, e.g., the botanical domain.

Encouraged by the existing results, we plan to extend our work further on ontology-based species identification queries. Firstly, as suggested in Section 6, a future version of our colour reasoner should provide several options so as to allow users to decide on their intended meaning of the "to" keyword. Technically, this requires the use of not only unary but also n-ary datatype expressions as constrains on datatype properties *hasHue*, *hasSaturation* and *hasLightness*. To capture these constraints, we need to use the OWL-E [44,24] ontology language, which is the n-ary extension of OWL-Eu.

Another possible future work is to represent the probabilistic information in the ontology. There are many descriptions with adverbs of quantification, such as "sometimes," "rarely," "often," etc., which also indicate the probability of certain colour information. Because current ontology languages do not support the annotation of classes with probabilities, the probabilistic aspect is ignored in the text processing. This obviously affects the interpretation of integration results. However, there are several attempts to extend DL languages with fuzzy expressions [45,46,47], which, in the future, may be used to enable our logic representation to capture more of the real semantics implied by its original NL descriptions.

Most importantly, from this highly specialised domain, we have learnt a set of more general methodological rules. Key tasks we identified in our study include: (1) modelling the primitive terms (2) based on the semantic model, the effect of modifiers has to be defined and ranges have to be built properly; (3) in order to integrate parallel information, a proper distance measurement is crucial to quantify the similarities among information from multiple sources; (4) depending on the application, more expressive representation and additional reasoning may be necessary to solve real problems. This has proved itself a successful combination, not only in the evaluation but also in its computational tractability, providing us with a semantic basis for information integration and knowledge retrieval. Under this light, many continuous quantities occurring in botany and other descriptive domains, such as leaf shapes, texture, sound, spatial and temporal arrangements, appear to fit fairly straightforwardly into this framework. It is clear that much more development is possible in this very practical area and a holistic system is our future task.

References

1. Clapham, A., Tutin, T., Moore, D.: Flora of the British Isles. Cambridge University Press, Cambridge (1987)
2. Stace, C.: New Flora of the British Isles. Cambridge University Press, Cambridge (1997)
3. Tutin, T.G., Heywood, V.H., Burges, N.A., Valentine, D.II., Moore, D.M. (eds.): Flora Europaea. Cambridge University Press, Cambridge (1993)
4. Gleason, H.: The New Britton and Brown Illustrated Flora of the Northeastern United States and Adjacent Canada. Hafner Publishing Company, New York (1963)
5. Wood, M.M., Lydon, S.J., Tablan, V., Maynard, D., Cunningham, H.: Using parallel texts to improve recall in IE. In: RANLP 2003. Proceedings of Recent Advances in Natural Language Processing, Borovetz, Bulgaria, pp. 505–512 (2003)

6. Wood, M., Lydon, S., Tablan, V., Maynard, D., Cunningham, H.: Populating a database from parallel texts using ontology-based information extraction. In: Meziane, F., Métais, E. (eds.) NLDB 2004. LNCS, vol. 3136, pp. 254–264. Springer, Heidelberg (2004)
7. Wood, M., Wang, S.: Motivation for "ontology" in parallel-text information extraction. In: ECAI-OLP. Proceedings of ECAI-2004 Workshop on Ontology Learning and Population, Poster, Valencia, Spain (2004)
8. Pan, J.Z., Horrocks, I.: OWL-Eu: Adding Customised Datatypes into OWL. In: Gómez-Pérez, A., Euzenat, J. (eds.) ESWC 2005, LNCS, vol. 3532, Springer, Heidelberg (2005), An extended version is published in the Journal of Web Semantics(to appear)
9. Patel-Schneider, P.F., Hayes, P., Horrocks, I.: OWL Web Ontology Language Semantics and Abstract Syntax. Technical report, W3C, W3C Recommendation (2004)
10. Wache, H., Voegele, T., Visser, U., Stuckenschmidt, H., Schuster, G., Neumann, H., Huebner, S.: Ontology-based integration of information - a survey of existing approaches. In: Proceedings of the IJCAI-01 Workshop: Ontologies and Information Sharing, Seattle, WA, pp. 108–117 (2001)
11. Wang, S., Pan, J.Z.: Ontology-based representation and query colour descriptions from botanical documents. In: Meersman, R., Tari, Z. (eds.) OTM 2005. LNCS, vol. 3761, pp. 1279–1295. Springer, Heidelberg (2005)
12. Lammens, J.M.: A computational model of color perception and color naming. Ph.D. thesis, State University of New York (1994)
13. Berk, T., Brownston, L., Kaufman, A.: A human factors study of color notation systems for computer graphics. Communications of the ACM 25(8), 547–550 (1982)
14. U.S. Department of Commerce, National Bureau of Standards: Color: Universal Language and Dictionary of Names. NBS Special Publication 440. U.S. Government Printing Office, Washington D.C. (1976) (S.D. Catalog No. C13.10:440)
15. Bechhofer, S., van Harmelen, F., Hendler, J., Horrocks, I., McGuinness, D.L., Patel-Schneider, P.F. (eds.): L.A.S.: OWL Web Ontology Language Reference (2004), http://www.w3.org/TR/owl-ref/
16. Pan, J.Z., Horrocks, I.: Extending Datatype Support in Web Ontology Reasoning. In: Meersman, R., Tari, Z., et al. (eds.) ODBASE 2002. LNCS, vol. 2519, pp. 1067–1081. Springer, Heidelberg (2002)
17. Pan, J.Z., Horrocks, I.: Web Ontology Reasoning with Datatype Groups. In: Fensel, D., Sycara, K.P., Mylopoulos, J. (eds.) ISWC 2003. LNCS, vol. 2870, Springer, Heidelberg (2003)
18. W3C Mailing List (starts from 2001), http://lists.w3.org/archives/public/www-rdf-logic/
19. W3C Mailing List (starts from 2004) (2004), http://lists.w3.org/archives/public/public-swbp-wg/
20. Group, J.W.U.P.I.: URIs, URLs, and URNs: Clarifications and Recommendations 1.0., W3C Note (2001), http://www.w3.org/TR/uri-clarification/
21. Fernald, M.: Gray's Manual of Botany. American Book Company, New York (1950)
22. Berk, T., Brownston, L., Kaufman, A.: A new color-naming system for graphics languages. IEEE Computer Graphics and Applications 2(3), 37–44 (1982)
23. Li, L., Horrocks, I.: A Software Framework For Matchmaking Based on Semantic Web Technology. In: WWW 2003. Proc. of the Twelfth International World Wide Web Conference, pp. 331–339. ACM Press, New York (2003)
24. Pan, J.Z.: Description Logics: Reasoning Support for the Semantic Web. PhD thesis, School of Computer Science, The University of Manchester (2004)

25. Gärdenfors, P.: Conceptual Spaces: the geometry of thought. MIT Press, Cambridge (2000)
26. Tversky, A.: Features of similarity. Psychological Review 84(4), 327–352 (1977)
27. Melara, R.: The concept of perceptual similarity: from psychophysics to cognitive psychology. In: Algom, D. (ed.) Psychophysical Approaches to Cognition, pp. 303–388. Elsevier, Amsterdam (1992)
28. Williams, D., Poulovassilis, A.: Combining data integration with natural language technology for the semantic web. In: Fensel, D., Sycara, K.P., Mylopoulos, J. (eds.) ISWC 2003. LNCS, vol. 2870, Springer, Heidelberg (2003)
29. Gaizauskas, R., Wilks, Y.: Information extraction: Beyond document retrieval. Journal of Documentation 54(1), 70–105 (1998)
30. Embley, D., Campbell, D., Liddle, S., Smith, R.: Ontology-based extraction and structuring of information from data-rich unstructured documents. In: Proceedings of International Conference On Information And Knowledge Management, Bethesda, 7, Maryland, USA, (1998)
31. Maedche, A., Neumann, G., Staab, S.: Bootstrapping an ontology-based information extraction system. studies in fuzziness and soft computing. In: Szczepaniak, P., Segovia, J., Kacprzyk, J., Zadeh, L.A. (eds.) Intelligent Exploration of the Web, Springer, Berlin (2002)
32. Alani, H., Kim, S., Millard, D.E., Weal, M.J., Hall, W., Lewis, P.H., Shadbolt, N.R.: Automatic ontology-based knowledge extraction from web documents. IEEE Intelligent Systems 18(1), 14–21 (2003)
33. Ferrucci, D., Lally, A.: UIMA: an architectural approach to unstructured information processing in the corporate research environment. Journal of Natural Language Engineering 10(3-4), 327–348 (2004)
34. Goble, C., Stevens, R., Ng, G., Bechhofer, S., Paton, N., Baker, P., Peim, M., Brass, A.: Transparent access to multiple bioinformatics information sources. IBM Systems Journal Special issue on deep computing for the life sciences 40(2), 532–552 (2001)
35. Calvanese, D., Giuseppe, D.G., Lenzerini, M.: Description logics for information integration. In: Kakas, A.C., Sadri, F. (eds.) Computational Logic: Logic Programming and Beyond. LNCS (LNAI), vol. 2408, pp. 41–60. Springer, Heidelberg (2002)
36. Maier, A., Schnurr, H.P., Sure, Y.: Ontology-based information integration in the automotive industry. In: Fensel, D., Sycara, K.P., Mylopoulos, J. (eds.) ISWC 2003. LNCS, vol. 2870, pp. 897–912. Springer, Heidelberg (2003)
37. Osgood, C., Suci, G., Tannenbaum, P.: The measurement of meaning. University of Illinois Press, Urbana (1957)
38. Dowty, D.R.: Word Meaning and Montague Grammar. D. Reidel Publishing, Dordrecht (1979)
39. Lakoff, G.: Women, fire, and dangerous things: what categories reveal about the mind. University of Chicago Press, Chicago (1987)
40. Landauer, T.K., Foltz, P.W., Laham, D.: Introduction to latent semantic analysis. Discourse Processes 25, 259–284 (1998)
41. Rada, R., Mili, H., Bicknell, E., Blettner, M.: Development and application of a metric on semantic nets. IEEE Transactions on Systems, Man and Cybernetics 19(1), 17–30 (1989)
42. Wu, Z., Palmer, M.: Verb semantics and lexical selection. In: The 32th Annual Meeting of the Association for Computational Linguistics, Las Cruces, Mexico, pp. 133–138 (1994)

43. Resnik, P.: Using information content to evaluate semantic similarity in a taxonomy. In: The 14th International Joint Conference on Artificial Intelligence, Montreal, vol. 1, pp. 448–453 (1995)
44. Pan, J.Z.: Reasoning Support for OWL-E (Extended Abstract). In: Basin, D., Rusinowitch, M. (eds.) IJCAR 2004. LNCS (LNAI), vol. 3097, Springer, Heidelberg (2004)
45. Tresp, C., Molitor, R.: A description logic for vague knowledge. In: ECAI 1998. Proceedings of the 13th biennial European Conference on Artificial Intelligence, pp. 361–365. John Wiley and Sons, Chichester (1998)
46. Straccia, U.: Transforming fuzzy description logics into classical description logics. In: Alferes, J.J., Leite, J.A. (eds.) JELIA 2004. LNCS (LNAI), vol. 3229, pp. 385–399. Springer, Heidelberg (2004)
47. Stoilos, G., Stamou, G., Tzouvaras, V., Pan, J.Z., Horrock, I.: A Fuzzy Description Logic for Multimedia Knowledge Representation. In: Proc. of the International Workshop on Multimedia and the Semantic Web, Crete (2005)

A Cooperative Approach for Composite Ontology Mapping

Cássia Trojahn[1], Márcia Moraes[2], Paulo Quaresma[1], and Renata Vieira[3]

[1] Departamento de Informática, Universidade de Évora, Portugal
[2] Faculdade de Informática, Pontifícia Universidade Católica do Rio Grande do Sul, Brazil
[3] Pós-Graduação em Computação Aplicada, Universidade do Vale do Rio dos Sinos, Brazil
cassia@di.uevora.pt, mmoraes@pucrs.br, pq@di.uevora.pt, renatav@unisinos.br

Abstract. This paper proposes a cooperative approach for composite ontology mapping. We first present an extended classification of automated ontology matching and propose an automatic composite solution for the matching problem based on cooperation. In our proposal, agents apply individual mapping algorithms and cooperate in order to change their individual results. We assume that the approaches are complementary to each other and their combination produces better results than the individual ones. Next, we compare our model with three state of the art matching systems. The results are promising specially for what concerns precision and recall. Finally, we propose an argumentation formalism as an extension of our initial model. We compare our argumentation model with the matching systems, showing improvements on the results.

1 Introduction

Ontology mapping is the process of linking corresponding terms from different ontologies. The mapping result can be used for ontology merging, agent communication, query answering, or for navigation on the Semantic Web.

There are many different approaches to the mapping problem. Whereas lexical approaches consider measures of lexical similarity; semantic ones consider semantic relations usually on the basis of semantic oriented linguistic resources. Other approaches consider term positions in the ontology hierarchy. Indeed, taxonomies of the different mapping approaches have been proposed in the literature, see for example [28][30] and [31]. However, the use of a single technique for a large variety of schemes is unlikely to be successful[7]. Since these approaches are complementary to each other their combination should lead to high matching accuracies than those provided by each one individually.

We consider that different agents working on the basis of particular approaches arrive to distinct matching results that must be shared, compared, chosen and agreed. In order to deal with this problem, we present a composite mapping approach based on cooperative agents, which negotiate on a final matching result.

We compare our model with three state of the art schema-based matching systems, namely Cupid[19], COMA[7], and S-Match[14]. The results are promising specially for what concerns precision and recall.

To deal with some mapping conflicts, which are not resolved by our negotiation model, we propose an argument formalism for composite ontology mapping. We extend a state of art argumentation framework, namely the Value-based Argumentation Framework (VAF)[3], in order to represent arguments with confidence degrees. The VAF allows to determine which arguments are acceptable, with respect to the different *audiences* represented by different agents. We then associate to each argument a confidence degree, representing the confidence that a specific agent has in that argument.

In our novel proposal, cooperative agents apply individual mapping algorithms and cooperate in order to change theirs local results (arguments). Next, based on their preferences and confidence of the arguments, the agents compute their preferred mapping sets. The arguments in such preferred mapping sets are viewed as the set of globally acceptable arguments. This is a more formal presentation for composite mapping. We also compare our argumentation model with the Cupid, COMA, and S-Match systems. The results are better than when using our negotiation model.

The paper is structured as follows. The next section briefly reviews the state of the art in ontology mapping. Section 3 comments on cooperative negotiation. Section 4 presents our negotiation model. Section 5 presents the results using the negotiation model. Section 6 presents the argumentation formalism and section 7 presents our argumentation model. Section 8 compares the results of the argumentation model and previous approaches. In section 9, related work are commented. Finally, section 10 presents the final remarks and the future work.

2 Ontology Mapping Approaches

The previous work of [28], [30] and [31] present a broad overview of the various approaches on automated ontology matching, classifying the mapping approaches in terms of input and techniques utilized in the mapping process. We propose a revision of the classification of mapping approaches presented in previous work, and we complement their proposals, including new elements in these classification. We point out that [20] presents other style of ontology mapping classification that is based on frameworks, methods and tools, translators, mediators, etc. We are not including these aspects in the classification presented here.

[28] distinguishes between individual and combining matchers. Individual matchers comprise schema-based and instance-based, element and structure levels, linguistic and constrained-based matching techniques. Combining matchers comprise hybrid and composite matchers.

Based on this previous taxonomy, [30] distinguishes between heuristic and formal techniques at schema-level; and implicit and explicit techniques at element- and structure-level. [31] introduces new criterias which are based on (i) general properties of matching techniques, i.e., approximate and exact techniques;

(ii) interpretation of input information, i.e., syntactic, external, and semantic techniques at element and structure levels; and (iii) the kind of input information, i.e., terminological, structural, and semantic techniques.

Moreover, [13] distinguishes between weak semantics and strong semantics element-level techniques. Weak semantics techniques are syntax-driven techniques (e.g., techniques which consider labels as strings, or analyze data types, or soundex of schema elements) while strong semantics techniques exploit, at the element level, the semantics of labels (e.g., based on the use of thesaurus).

We present a revised classification in Figure 1 (our modifications are in bold font). As in [28], we distinguish between individual and combining matchers. However, we divided the individual matchers on data level, ontology level, or context level, but we kept the combining matcher divided on hybrid or composite.

At the data level, data instances are used as input to the matching process. At the ontology level, the terms of the ontology structure and the hierarchy are taking into account. Then, as [28], we distinguish between element-level matcher and structure level matcher. Finally, the ontology's application context can be used, i.e, how the ontology entities are used in some external context. This is specially interesting, for instance, to identify WordNet sense that must be considered to specific terms.

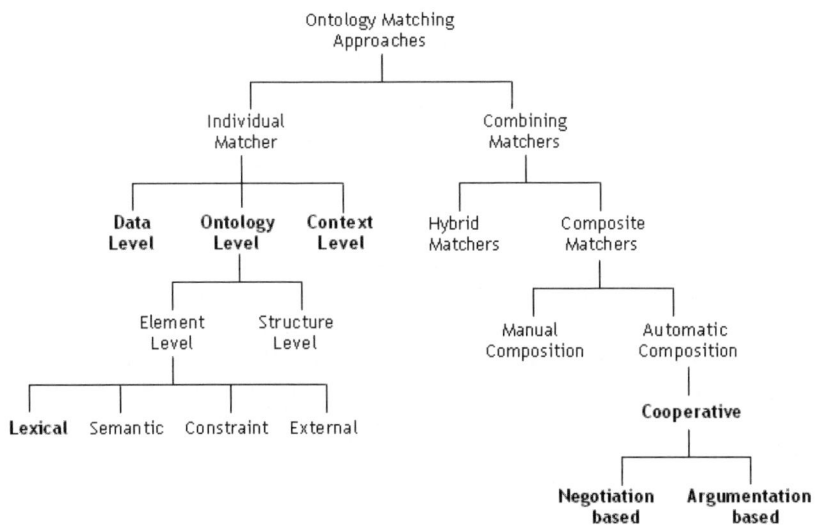

Fig. 1. Our classification of matching approaches

At the element level we consider, according to [31], semantic and external matchers. However, we replaced the syntactic by lexical and added a constraint-based matchers. We assume that the term "syntactic" refers to morpho-syntactic categories of words (i.e., implicating some word annotation). We consider that the term "lexical" is more appropriated to refer to the category of approaches based on string similarity.

The lexical approaches use metrics to compare string similarity. One well-known measure is the Levenshtein distance or edit distance [23], which is given by the minimum number of operations (insertion, deletion, or substitution of a single character) needed to transform one string into another. Based on Levenshtein measure, [25] proposes a lexical similarity measure for strings, the String Matching (SM), that considers the number of changes that must be made to change one string into the other and weighs the number of these changes against the length of the shortest string of these two. Other common metrics are: the Smith-Waterman[34], which additionally uses an alphabet mapping to costs; and the [11] which searches for the largest common substring.

Semantic matchers consider semantic relations between concepts to measure the similarity between them, usually on the basis of one thesaurus or similar semantic oriented linguistic resources. The well-known WordNet[1] database, a large repository of English items, has been used to provide these relations. This kind of mapping is complementary to the pure string similarity metrics. Cases where string metrics fail to identify high similarity between strings that represent completely different concepts are common. For example, for the words "score" and "store" the Levenshtein metric returns 0.68, which is a high metric if we consider that the they represent very different concepts. On the other hand terms like "student" and "learner" are semantically similar although they are lexically distant from each other.

Constraint-based matchers are based on data types, value ranges, uniqueness, cardinalities, and other information constraints in the matching process. For example, the similarity between two terms can be based on the equivalence of data types and domains, of key characteristics (e.g., unique, primary, foreign), or relationship cardinality (e.g., 1:1 relationships) [28].

Finally, at the element-level, we consider that external matchers consider some type of external information, such as user input or previous matching results.

Structural matchers use the ontology structure as input to the matching process (i.e., the positions of the terms in the ontology hierarchy are considered). Several approaches using this intuition have been proposed: super(sub)-concept rules consider that if super or sub concepts are the same, the actual concepts are similar to each other ([5][10]); bounded path matching takes two paths with links between classes defined by the hierarchical relations, compare terms and their positions along these paths, and identify similar terms (see, for instance, Anchor-prompt algorithm [27][16]); leaves-rules, where two non-leaf schema elements are structurally similar if their leaf sets are highly similar, even if their immediate children are not, see, for example[19].

We also consider, as [28], hybrid and composite matchers, at combining matcher level. Hybrid matchers use multiple matching criteria (e.g., name and type equality) within an integrated matcher; and composite matchers (which can use a manual or automatic process) combine multiple match results produced by different match algorithms. Our approach is an automatic composite matcher and then we add a cooperative approach at automatic level, which can be based on negotia-

---

[1] http://www.wordnet.princeton.edu

tion or argumentation. We point out that an automatic mapping approach can be also based on machine learning techniques, as presented by [8], which combines multiple matchers using a learning approach.

Due to the complexity of the problem using only one approach is usually not satisfactory. These approaches are complementary to each other. Combining different approaches must reflect a better solution when compared to the solutions of individual approaches. Our first proposal is to use a cooperative negotiation model, where agents apply individual mapping algorithms and negotiate on a final mapping result.

3 Cooperative Negotiation

Negotiation is a process by which two or more parties make a joint decision [38]. It is a key form of interaction that enables groups of agents to arrive at mutual agreement regarding beliefs, goals or plans [2]. Hence the basic idea behind negotiation is reaching a consensus [15].

Negotiation usually proceeds in a series of rounds, with every agent making a proposal at each round [37]. The process can be described as follow, based on [22]. One agent generates a proposal and other agents review it. If some other agent does not like the proposal, it rejects the proposal and might generate a counter-proposal. If so, the other agents (including the agent that generated the first proposal) review the counter-proposal and the process is repeated. It is assumed that a proposal becomes a solution when it is accepted by all agents.

Cooperative negotiation is a particular kind of negotiation where agents cooperate and collaborate to obtain a common objective. In cooperative negotiation, each agent has a partial view of the problem and the results are put together via negotiation trying to solve the conflicts posed by having only partial views [12].

This kind of negotiation has been currently adopted in resource and task allocation fields [4][26][38]. In these approaches, the agents try to reach the maximum global utility that takes into account the worth of all their activities. In our approach the cooperative negotiation is a form of interaction that enables the agents to arrive to mutual agreement regarding the result of different ontology mapping approaches.

4 Cooperative Negotiation Model for Composite Ontology Mapping

In our model, the agents use lexical, semantic and structural approaches to map terms of two different ontologies. The distinct mapping results are shared, compared, chosen and agreed, and a final mapping result is obtained. This approach aims to overcome the drawbacks of the using individual ontology mapping approaches. First, we present the organization of the agent society and next we detail the negotiation process.

4.1 Organization of the Agent Society

We describe our model according to an agent society (Figure 2), using the Moise+ model [18]. This model proposes three dimensions for the organization of agent societies: structural, functional and deontic. The structural dimension defines what agents could do in their environment (theirs roles). The functional dimension defines how agents execute their goals. The deontic dimension defines the permissions and obligations of a role in a goal. This paper focuses on the first dimension.

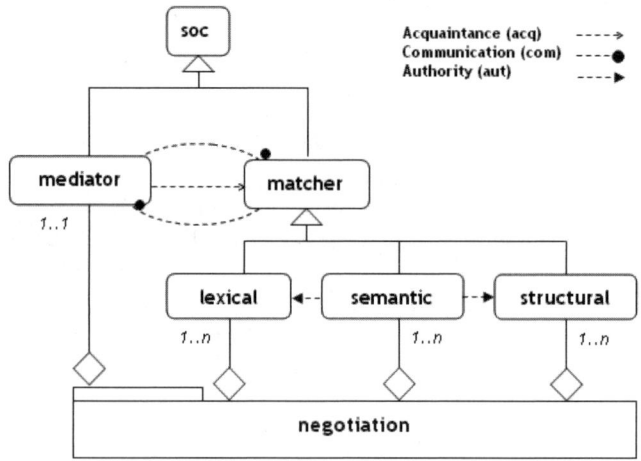

Fig. 2. Organizational model

According to [18] and [17], structural specification has three main concepts, roles, role relations and groups that are used to build, respectively, the individual, social and collective structural levels of an organization. The individual level is composed by the roles of the organization. A role means a set of constraints that an agent ought to follow when it accepts to play that role in a group. The following roles are identified in the proposed organization:

- Mediator: this role is responsible for mediating the negotiation process, sending and receiving messages to and from the mapping agents.
- Matcher: this role is responsible for giving an output between two ontology mappings (i.e., encapsulates the mapping algorithms). One matcher could assume the lexical, semantic or structural role. On the lexical role, the matcher makes the mapping using algorithms based on string similarity. On the semantic role, the agent search by corresponding terms in a semantic oriented linguistic database. On the structural role, the agent is based on the intuition that if super-classes are the same, the compared classes are similar to each other. If sub-classes are the same, the compared classes are also similar.

In the social level are defined the kinds of relations among roles that directly constrain the agents. Some of the possible relations are:

- Acquaintance (acq): agents playing a source role are allowed to have a representation of the agents playing the destination role. In Figure 2, this kind of relation is present between the source role mediator and the destination role matcher.
- Communication (com): agents playing a source role are allowed to communicate with agents that play the destination role. In Figure 2 this kind of relation is present between the source role mediator and the destination role matcher (by heritage, lexical, semantic and structural).
- Authority (aut): agents playing a source role has authority upon agent playing destination role. In Figure 2 this kind of relation is present between the source role semantic and the destination roles lexical and structural.

The collective level specifies the group formation inside the organization. A group is composed by the roles that the system could assume, the sub-groups that could be created inside a group, the links (relations) valid for agent and by the cardinality. A group can have intra-groups links and inter-groups links. The intra-group links state that an agent playing the link source role in a group is linked to all agents playing the destination role in the same group or in its sub-groups. The inter-group links state that an agent playing the source role is linked to all agents playing the destination role despite the groups these agents belong to [18]. Links intra-group are represented by a hatched line and links inter-groups are represented by a continue line. This specification defines only a group called negotiation and all links are intra-group.

Based on the structural specification of the proposed organization, our society is composed by one agent that assumes the mediator role and three agents that assume the matcher role. One of the matcher agents is assuming the lexical role, one is assuming the semantic role, and one is assuming the structural role.

4.2 Negotiation Process

Basically, the negotiation process involves two phases. First, the agents work in an independent manner, applying a specific mapping approach and generating a set of negotiation objects. A negotiation object is a 3-tuple $O = (t_1, t_2, C)$, where t_1 corresponds to a term in the ontology 1, t_2 corresponds to a term in the ontology 2, and C is the mapping category resulting from the mapping for these two terms. Second, the set of negotiation objects, that compose the mapping is negotiated among the agents. The negotiation process involves one mediator and several matcher agents.

In order to facilitate the negotiation process (i.e, reduce the number of negotiation rules), we define four mapping categories according to the output of the matcher agents. Table 1 shows the categories and the corresponding mapping results.

Lexical agent. The output of the lexical agents is a value from the interval [0,1], where 1 indicates high similarity between two terms (i.e, the strings are identical). The Levenshtein metric is used. For example, the words "reference" and "citation" have a Levenshtein value equals to 0.0. This way, if the output is 1, a "mapping with certainty" is obtained. If the output is 0, the agent has a "not mapping with certainty". A threshold is used to classify the output in uncertain categories. The threshold value is specified by the user.

Semantic agent. The semantic agents consider semantic relations between terms according to the WordNet database. Relations such as synonym, antonym, holonym, meronym, hyponym, and hypernym can be returned for a given pair of terms. For instance, the semantic agent searches the relations between the terms "reference" and "citation" in the WordNet database and can assume that these terms are synonymous. Synonymous terms are considered as mapping with certainty; terms related by holonym, meronym, hyponym, or hypernym are considered mapping with uncertainty; when the terms can not be related by the WordNet (the terms are unknown for the WordNet database), the terms are considered as not mappings with uncertainty.

Structural agent. The structural agent uses the super-classes intuition to verify if the terms can be considered similar. First, it is verified if the super-classes are lexically similar. Otherwise, the semantic similarity is used. If the super-classes are lexically or semantically similar, the terms are similar to each other. For instance, when mapping the terms "reference/thesis" (where "reference" is the super-class of "thesis") and "citation/proceeding", the structural agent indicates that the terms can be mapped because the super-classes are semantically similar. The matching category corresponds the output of the lexical or semantic comparison (e.g, if super-classes are not lexically similar, but they are considered synonymous, a "mapping with certainty" is returned).

We point out that semantic and structural mappings are complex problems, and in this paper we simple adopted state-of-art semantic and structural approaches. Therefore, we are composing on what is now generally available. We consider that using richer semantic and structural mappings is relevant, but our emphasis for this paper is in combining state of art approaches.

Figure 3 shows an AUML interaction diagram with the messages changed between the agents during a negotiation round. We use an extension of AUML-2 standard to represent agents' actions (the actions are placed centered over the

Table 1. Mapping categories

Category	Lexical	Semantic
Mapping (certainty)	1	synonym
Mapping (uncertainty)	$1 > r > t$	related
Not mapping (uncertainty)	$0 < r <= t$	unknown
Not mapping (certainty)	0	

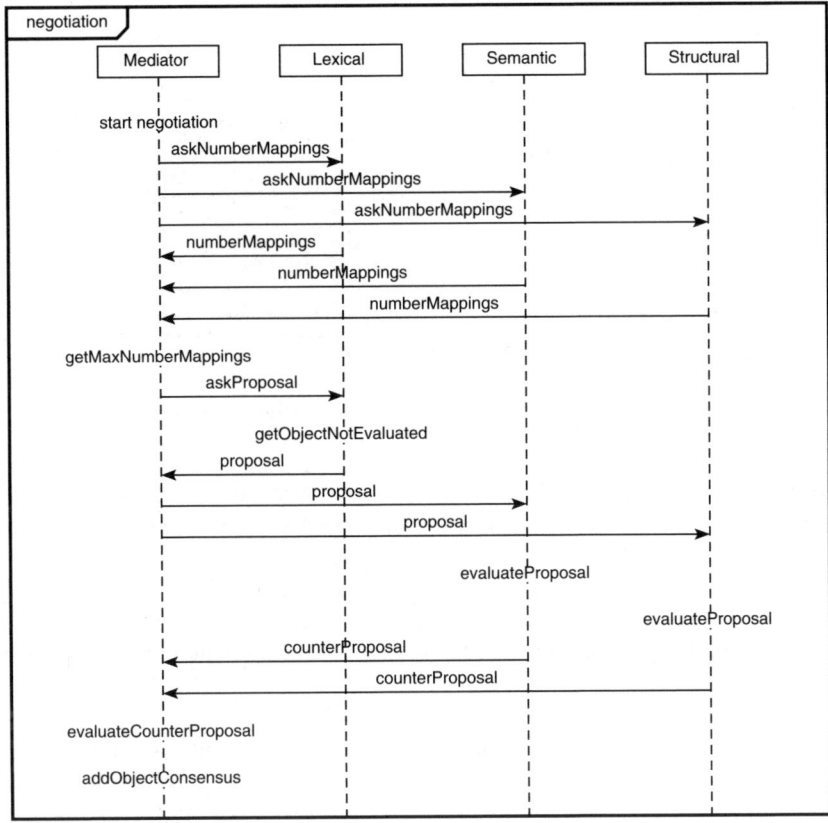

Fig. 3. AUML negotiation interaction

lifeline of the named agent). The interaction diagram refers to negotiation of the mapping between the classes "personal computer " and "pc" (Figures 4 and 5)[2].

The negotiation process starts with the mediator agent asking to the matcher agents for its number of "mappings with certainty". The first matcher agent to generate a proposal is one that has the greatest number of "mappings with certainty" (lexical agent, in the specific example).

The proposal contains the first negotiation object that still wasn't evaluated by the agent. This proposal is then sent to the mediator agent, which sends it to other agents (in the specific example, the lexical agent proposes a "not mapping with certainty" to the mapping between the classes "personal computer " and "pc"). Each agent then evaluates the proposal, searching for an equivalent negotiation object. One negotiation object is equivalent to another when both refers to same terms which are being compared in the two ontologies.

If an equivalent negotiation object has the same category, the agent accepts the proposal. Otherwise, if the agent has a different category for the compared

---

[2] Ontologies available in http://dit.unitn.it/ accord/Experimentaldesign.html(Test 4).

```
<owl:Class rdf:ID="Electronic"> </owl:Class>

<owl:Class rdf:ID="PC">
  <rdfs:subClassOf rdf:resource="#Electronic"/>
</owl:Class>
```

```
<owl:Class rdf:ID="Electronics"> </owl:Class>

<owl:Class rdf:ID="Personal_Computers">
  <rdfs:subClassOf rdf:resource="#Electronics"/>
</owl:Class>

<owl:Class rdf:ID="Microprocessors">
  <rdfs:subClassOf rdf:resource="#Personal_Computers"/>
</owl:Class>

<owl:Class rdf:ID="Photo_and_Cameras">
  <rdfs:subClassOf rdf:resource="#Eletronics"/>
</owl:Class>

<owl:Class rdf:ID="Accessories">
  <rdfs:subClassOf rdf:resource="#Microprocessors"/>
</owl:Class>
```

```
<owl:Class rdf:ID="PC_board">
  <rdfs:subClassOf rdf:resource="#PC"/>
</owl:Class>

<owl:Class rdf:ID="Camera_and_Photo">
  <rdfs:subClassOf rdf:resource="#Electronic"/>
</owl:Class>

<owl:Class rdf:ID="Accessory">
  <rdfs:subClassOf rdf:resource="#Camera_and_Photo"/>
</owl:Class>

<owl:Class rdf:ID="Digital_Camera">
  <rdfs:subClassOf rdf:resource="#Camera_and_Photo"/>
</owl:Class>
```

Fig. 4. Ontology 1   **Fig. 5.** Ontology 2

terms in the negotiation object, its object negotiation is sent as a counter-proposal to the mediator agent, which evaluates the several counter-proposals received (several agents can send a counter-proposal). In the example, semantic and structural agents have generated counter-proposals, indicating a "mapping with certainty" between the compared terms. The semantic agent identifies that the terms are synonymous in WordNet, and structural agent identifies terms having the same super-class (electronics).

The mediator selects one counter-proposal that has the greater number of hits. If two categories receive equals number of hits, the category indicated by the semantic agent is considered as the negotiation consensus. When a proposal is accepted by all agents or a counter-proposal consensus is obtained, the mediator adds the corresponding negotiation object in a consensus negotiation set and the matcher agents mark its equivalent one as evaluated. The negotiation ends when all negotiation objects are evaluated.

5 Experiments Using the Negotiation Model

We applied our negotiation model to link corresponding class names in two different ontologies. The results produced by our negotiation model were compared with manual matches[3] (expert mappings). The manual matches specified between the attributes of the ontologies were not considered in this set of experiments.

Previous experiments using our negotiation model were presented in [36]. This current work extends that previous one in many aspects. First, there we used only lexical and semantic agents in the negotiation process. Second, the resulting mapping category was obtained by majority, where the semantic agent had authority over the lexical agents (when two mapping categories received the equal number of hits, the semantic agent decides the resulting mapping cate-

---

[3] Obtained from http://dit.unitn.it/ accord/Experimentaldesign.html

gory). Third, we used only two other ontologies related to bibliography domain to evaluate that initial proposal.

The negotiation model was implemented in Java for Windows, version 1.5.0, and the experiments ran on Pentium(R) 4, UCP 3.20GHz, 512MB. The lexical agent was implemented using the edit distance measure (Levenshtein measure). We used the algorithm available in the API for ontology alignment (INRIA)[4] (EditDistNameAlignment). The semantic agent uses the JWordNet API[5], which is an interface to the WordNet database. For each WordNet synset, we retrieved the synonymous terms and considered the hypernym, hyponym, member-holonym, member-meronym, part-holonym, and part-meronym as related terms. The structural agent is based on super-classes similarity.

The threshold used to classify the matcher agents output was 0.6. A preprocessing step was made, where special (e.g., _) and stop words (e.g., "and", "or", "of") were removed.

We have used four groups of ontologies: parts of Google and Yahoo web directories[6], product schemas[7], course university catalogs[8], and company profiles[9]. We considered the "mappings with certainty" and the "mappings with uncertainty" as examples of the positive classes. As a mapping quality measure, the well-know measures of precision, recall, and f–measure were used.

First, we compared the results obtained from our model with the results from expert mapping (Table 2 – the column "Others" contains mappings identified as corrects by our model, which where not identified by the experts). We also indicated the number of terms for each group of ontologies (only class names).

The negotiation consensus identified correctly all mappings defined by the expert, for all groups – all mappings defined by the expert were returned as "mappings with certainty" by our model. When considering the other mappings ("Others"), for the "Google and Yahoo", 3 "mappings with certainty" and 5 "mappings with uncertainty" have been returned. For instance, a "mapping with uncertainty" between the terms "/Arts/Visual_Arts" (where "Arts" is the superclass of "Visual_Arts") and "/Arts_Humanities/Design_ Art" has seen identified. This mapping was not defined by expert, however it could be considered as correct. This kind of "mapping with uncertainty" has been observed in the other examples. In "Product schemas", only one new mapping has been returned, being a "mapping with certainty", but incorrectly (i.e., "/Electronics/Personal _Computers/Accessories" and "/Electronic/Cameras_and_Photos/Accessories"). Finally, for the "Course catalogs", 3 new mappings were categorized as "mappings with uncertainty" (e.g., "/Courses/College_of_ engineering" and "/Courses/ College_of_Arts_and _Sciences").

---

[4] http://alignapi.gforce.inria.fr
[5] http://jwn.sourceforge.net (using WordNet 2.1).
[6] http://dit.unitn.it/āccord/Experimentaldesign.html (Test 3).
[7] http://dit.unitn.it/āccord/Experimentaldesign.html (Test 4).
[8] http://dit.unitn.it/āccord/Experimentaldesign.html (Test 7).
[9] http://dit.unitn.it/āccord/Experimentaldesign.html (Test 8).

Table 2. Expert mapping and consensus results

Ontology	Expert mapping	Consensus Correct	Others
Google and Yahoo directories (54)	4	4	8
Product schemas (30)	4	4	1
Course catalogs (48)	6	6	3
Company profiles (9)	3	3	0

Second, we compared the output of all agents (Table 3). Using lexical or structural individual agents was not sufficient to obtain all corrects mappings. These agents did not classify correctly all positive classes (0.64 and 0.68, respectively, for recall, and 0.67 and 0.71, for f–measure), although having good precision measures. The consensus resulting from negotiation was better than the individual results obtained by these agents, having identified correctly all positive classes (recall equals 1 for all groups of ontologies). The semantic agent had better performance than lexical and structural agents (recall equals 1 and f–measure equals 0.78), and it produces similar results when compared with the negotiation consensus. For ontologies which are lexically and structurally simple (e.g., "Company profiles"), all agents produce equivalent results.

Table 3. Matcher agents and consensus results

Ontology	Consensus			Lexical			Semantic			Structural		
	P	R	F	P	R	F	P	R	F	P	R	F
Google-Yahoo dir. (54)	0.33	1.0	0.49	0.50	0.25	0.33	0.28	1.0	0.43	1.0	0.50	0.66
Product schemas (30)	0.80	1.0	0.88	0.40	0.50	0.44	0.80	1.0	0.88	0.60	0.75	0.66
Course catalogs (48)	0.66	1.0	0.79	1.0	0.83	0.90	0.66	1.0	0.79	0.60	0.50	0.54
Company profiles (9)	1.0	1.0	1.0	1.0	1.0	1.0	1.0	1.0	1.0	1.0	1.0	1.0
Average	0.69	1.0	0.79	0.72	0.64	0.67	0.68	1.0	0.78	0.80	0.68	0.71

The similar results between semantic agent and negotiation consensus occurs because the labels mapped by experts have strong semantic correspondence, identified as "mappings with certainty" by the semantic agent. In these cases, the structural agent returned "mappings with uncertainty", while the lexical agent returned "not mappings with certainty" (e.g., the correct mapping between "/Arts/Arts_History" and "/Architecture/History" terms). Then, the semantic agent decides the final category. However, for the "Google and Yahoo" ontologies, which have greater number of terms (54) when compared with the other groups of ontologies, the consensus returned better precision (0.33) than semantic agent (0.28). As a concluding result, the consensus had better behavior than lexical, semantic and structural individual agents, with f–measure value equals 0.79 against 0.67, 0.78 and 0.71, respectively.

We also identified cases where conflicts occur, which are not resolved by our model and the semantic agent is not sufficient to identify them. Considering the terms "Music/History" and "Architecture/History" ("Google and Yahoo" ontologies), the semantic and lexical agents returned a "mapping with certainty", differently of the structural agent. However, this is not a correct mapping. As will be commented in section 7, we are working on argument-based negotiation, in order to solve this kind of conflict. An argument for accepting the mapping may be that the terms are synonymous and an argument against may be that some of their super-concepts are not mapped.

Third, we compared our negotiation model with three state of the art matching systems: Cupid[19], COMA[7], and S-Match[14]. The comparative results among these three systems are available in [14]. We utilized these test results as criteria to evaluate our proposal, but the details of these tests (implementations, time of run, processor, etc) are not available. Following, we describe each system.

The Cupid algorithm is based on linguistic and structural approaches. In a first phase, called linguistic matching, it matches individual schema elements based on their names, data types, domains, etc. A thesaurus is used to help match names by identifying short-forms (for instance, Qty for Quantity), acronyms, and synonyms. The result is a linguistic similarity coefficient, lsim, between each pair of elements. The second phase is the structural matching of schema elements based on the similarity of their contexts or vicinities. The structural match depends in part on linguistic matches calculated in phase one and the result is a structural similarity coefficient, ssim, for each pair of elements. The weighted similarity (wsim) is a mean of lsim and ssim: wsim = wstruct × ssim + (1−wstruct) × lsim, where the constant wstruct is in the range 0 to 1.

The COMA represents a generic system to combine match results. The match result is a set of mapping elements specifying the matching schema elements together with a similarity value between 0 (strong dissimilarity) and 1 (strong similarity) indicating the plausibility of their correspondence. The matchers currently supported fall into three classes: simple, hybrid and reuse-oriented matchers. They exploit different kinds of schema information, such as names, data types, and structural properties, or auxiliary information, such as synonym tables and previous match results.

The S-Match algorithm is based on two main steps. First, the meaning of each concept of the ontologies is captured, using the WordNet database to obtain the senses of them (element-level). Second, the structural schema properties are taken into account, where the path to the root is computed (structure-level). Element level semantic matchers provide the input to the structure level matcher, which is applied on to produce the set of semantic relations between concepts as the matching result.

Our proposal uses different techniques for composite mapping approaches from these previous work.

Our comparative results consider the mappings between attributes of the ontologies in order to compute the precision and recall measures. Then, we have added to our ontologies such attributes, which are viewed as specific sub-classes by our agents. Table 4 shows the comparative results. Considering the attributes

Table 4. Comparative mapping results – matching systems and negotiation model

Ontology	Consensus			Cupid			COMA			S-Match		
	P	R	F	P	R	F	P	R	F	P	R	F
Company profiles (160)	1	0.63	0.77	0.50	0.60	0.54	0.80	0.70	0.74	1.0	0.65	0.78

of the ontologies, the number of terms to be compared is 160 (i.e., 10 terms in the first ontology with 16 terms in the second ontology).

As shown in Table 4, our model returned better precision than Cupid and COMA, and similar precision when compared to the S-Match, having returned as "mapping with certainty" only the correct expert mappings (precision equals to 1). When comparing the F-measure values, our model had similar result than COMA and S-Match and better result than Cupid.

In order to obtain better results than our negotiation model, we propose extend the model using the argumentation formalism. In the following sections, we first introduce the argumentation formalism. Next, we present our novel argumentation model and its evaluation. using it.

6 Argumentation Framework

Our argumentation model is based on the Value-based Argumentation Frameworks (VAF)[3], a development of the classical argument system of Dung [9]. First, we present the Dung's framework, upon which a VAF rely. Next, we present a VAF and our extended framework.

6.1 Classical Argumentation Framework

Dung [9]defines an argumentation framework as follows.

Definition 2.1.1 An Argumentation Framework is a pair $AF = (AR, attacks)$, where AR is a set of arguments and *attacks* is a binary relation on AR, i.e., $attacks \subseteq AR \times AR$. An *attack*(A,B) means that the argument A attacks the argument B. A set of arguments S attacks an argument B if B is attacked by an argument in S.

The key question about the framework is whether a given argument A, $A \in AR$, should be accepted. One reasonable view is that an argument should be accepted only if every attack on it is rebutted by an accepted argument [3]. This notion produces the following definitions:

Definition 2.1.2 An argument $A \in AR$ is *acceptable* with respect to set arguments $S(acceptable(A,S))$, if $(\forall x)(x \in AR)$ & $(attacks(x,A)) \longrightarrow (\exists y)(y \in S)$ & $attacks(y,x)$

Definition 2.1.3 A set S of arguments is *conflict-free* if $\neg(\exists x)(\exists y)((x \in S)$ & $(y \in S)$ & $attacks(x,y))$

Definition 2.1.4 A conflict-free set of arguments S is *admissible* if $(\forall x)(x \in S)$ $\longrightarrow acceptable(x,S)$

Definition 2.1.5 A set of arguments S in an argumentation framework AF is a *preferred extension* if it is a maximal (with respect to set inclusion) admissible set of AR.

A *preferred extension* represent a consistent position within AF, which can defend itself against all attacks and which cannot be further extended without introducing a conflict.

The purpose in extending the AF is to allow to distinguish between one argument attacking another, and that attack succeeding, so that the attacked argument is defeated.

6.2 Value-Based Argumentation Framework

In Dung's frameworks, attacks always succeed. However, in many domains, including the one under consideration, arguments lack this coercive force: they provide reasons which may be more or less persuasive [21]. Moreover, their persuasiveness may vary according to their audience. The VAF is able to distinguish attacks from successful attacks, those which defeat the attacked argument. It allows relate strengths of arguments to their motivations and accommodate different audiences with different interests and preferences.

Definition 2.2.1 A Value-based Argumentation Framework (VAF) is a 5-tuple $VAF = (AR, attacks, V, val, P)$ where $(AR, attacks)$ is an argumentation framework, V is a nonempty set of values, val is a function which maps from elements of AR to elements of V and P is a set of possible audiences. For each $A \in AF$, $val(A) \in V$.

Definition 2.2.2 An audience-specific value based argumentation framework (AVAF) is a 5-tuple $VAF_a = (AR, attacks, V, val, Valpref_a)$ where AR, $attacks, V$ and val are as for the VAF, a is an audience and $Valpref_a$ is a preference relation (transitive, irreflexive and asymmetric) $Valpref_a \subseteq V \times V$, reflecting the value preferences of audience a. $Valpref(v_1, v_2)$ means v_1 is preferred to v_2.

Definition 2.2.3 An argument $A \in AF$ defeats$_a$ (or *successful attacks*) an argument $B \in AF$ for audience a if and only if both $attacks(A,B)$ and not $valpref(val(B), val(A))$.

An attack succeeds if both arguments relate to the same value, or if no preference value between the values has been defined.

Definition 2.2.4 An argument $A \in AR$ is *acceptable* to audience a ($acceptable_a$) with respect to set of arguments S, $acceptable_a(A,S)$ if $(\forall\ x)\ ((x \in AR\ \&\ defeats_a\ (x,A)) \longrightarrow (\exists y)((y \in S)\ \&\ defeats_a(y,x)))$.

Definition 2.2.5 A set S of arguments is *conflict-free* for audience a if $(\forall x)(\forall y)((x \in S \ \& \ y \in S) \longrightarrow (\neg attacks(x,y) \lor valpref(val(y),val(x)) \in valpref_a))$.

Definition 2.2.6 A *conflict-free* for audience a set of argument S is *admissible* for an audience a if $(\forall x)(x \in S \longrightarrow acceptable_a(s,S))$.

Definition 2.2.7 A set of argument S in the VAF is a *preferred extension* for audience a (*preferred$_a$*) if it is a maximal (with respect to set inclusion) admissible for audience a of AR.

In order to determine the preferred extension with respect to a value ordering promoted by distinct audiences, [3] introduces the notion of *objective* and *subjective* acceptance.

Definition 2.2.8 An argument $x \in AR$ is *subjectively* acceptable if and only if x appears in the preferred extension for some specific audiences but not all. An argument $x \in AR$ is *objectively* acceptable if and only if, x appears in the preferred extension for every specific audience.
An argument which is neither objectively nor subjectively acceptable is said to be *indefensible*.

6.3 An Extended Value-Based Argumentation Framework

We extend the VAF in order to represent arguments with confidence degrees. Two elements have been added to VAF: a set with confidence degrees and a function which maps from confidence degrees to arguments. The confidence value represents the confidence that a specific agent has in some argument. We assumed that the confidence degrees compose a second axis which is necessary to represent a problem domain, such as the ontology mapping.

Definition 2.3.1 An Extended Value-based Argumentation Framework (E-VAF) is a 7-tuple $E\text{-}VAF = (AR, attacks, V, val, P, C, valC)$ where $(AR, attacks, V, val, P)$ is a value-based argumentation framework, C is a nonempty set of values representing the confidence degrees, $valC$ is a function which maps from elements of AR to elements of C. $valC \subseteq C \times C$ and $valprefC(c_1, c_2)$ means c_1 is preferred to c_2.

Definition 2.3.2 An argument $A \in AF$ *defeats$_a$* (or *successful attacks*) an argument $B \in AF$ for audience a if and only if $attacks(A,B)$ and $(valprefC(valC(A),valC(B))$ or $(\neg \ valpref(val(B),val(A))$ and $\neg \ valprefC(valC(B), valC(A))))$.

An attack succeeds if (a) the confidence degree of the attacking argument is greater than the confidence degree of the argument being attacked; or if (b) the argument being attacked does not have greater preference value than attacking argument (or if both arguments relate to the same preference values) and the confidence degree of the argument being attacked is not greater than the attacking argument.

Definition 2.3.4 A set S of arguments is *conflict-free* for audience a if $(\forall A)(\forall B)$ $((A \in S\ \&\ B \in S) \longrightarrow (\neg attacks(A, B) \vee (\neg valprefC(valC(A),valC(B))$ and $(valpref(val(B), val(A)) \vee valprefC(valC(B),valC(A)))))$.

7 E-VAF for Composite Ontology Mapping

In our model, dedicated agents encapsulate different mapping approaches which represent different audiences in an E-VAF, i.e, the agents' preferences are based on specific approach used by the agent. In this paper we will consider three argumentive audiences: lexical (L), semantic (S), and structural (E) (i.e. $P = \{L, S, E\}$, where $P \in$ E-AVF). We point out that our model is extensible to others audiences.

First, we present the re-organization of the agents society and next we detail the argumentation process.

7.1 Organization of the Agents Society

We use the Moise+ model to describe our novel argumentation model (Figure 6). In this society, only the matcher role is identified, which is responsible for giving an output between two ontology mappings (i.e., encapsulate the mapping algorithms). One matcher could assume the lexical, semantic or structural role. Differently from our negotiation model, there is no role responsible for mediating the argumentation process. The mediator role has been eliminated.

The possible relation between the agents is the communication, where the agents playing a source role are allowed to communicate with agents playing the destination role. This kind of relation is present through the communication among the three matcher agents within an agent society.

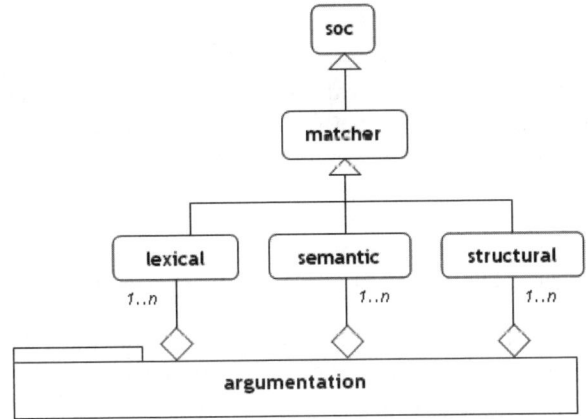

Fig. 6. Organizational model

7.2 Argumentation Generation

First, the agents work in an independent manner, applying the mapping approaches and generating mapping sets. The mapping result will consist of a set of all possible correspondences between terms of two ontologies. A mapping can be described as a 3-tuple $m = (t_1, t_2, R)$, where t_1 corresponds to a term in the ontology 1, t_2 corresponds to a term in the ontology 2, and R is the mapping relation resulting from the mapping for these two terms. The lexical and semantic agents are able to return *equivalence* values to R, while the structural agents returns *sub-class* or *super-class* values to R.

Each mapping m is represented as a argument. Now, we can define arguments as follows:

Definition 4.1 An *argument* $\in AF$ is a 4-tuple $x = (m,a,c,h)$, where m is a mapping; $a \in P$ is the agent's audience generating that argument; $c \in C$ is the confidence degree associated to that mapping; h is one of $\{-,+\}$ depending on whether the argument is that m does or does not hold.

The confidence degree is defined by the agent when applying the specific mapping approach. Here, we assumed $C = \{\text{certainty, uncertainty}\}$, where $C \in$ E-VAF.

Table 5 shows the possible values to h and c, according to the agent's audiences. The agents generate theirs arguments based on rules from Table 5.

Table 5. h and c to audiences

		Audiences	
h	c	Lexical	Semantic
+	certainty	1	synonym
+	uncertainty	1 > r > t	related
-	certainty	0 < r <= t	
-	uncertainty	0	unknown

Lexical agent. The output of lexical agents (r) is a value from the interval [0,1], where 1 indicates high similarity between two terms. This way, if the output is 1, the lexical agent generates an argument $x = (m, L, certainty, +)$, where $m = (t_1, t_2, equivalence)$.

If the output is 0, the agent generates an argument $x = (m, L, certainty, -)$, where $m = (t_1, t_2, equivalence)$. A threshold ($t$) is used to classify the output in uncertain categories. The threshold value can be specified by the user.

Semantic agent. The semantic agents consider semantic relations between terms, such as synonym, antonym, holonym, meronym, hyponym, and hypernym (i.e., such as in WordNet database). When the terms being mapped are synonymous, the agent generates an argument $x = (m, S, certainty, +)$, where $m = (t_1, t_2, equivalence)$.

The terms related by holonym, meronym, hyponym, or hypernym are considered related and an argument $x = (m, S, uncertainty, +)$ is generated, where

$m = (t_1, t_2, equivalence)$; when the terms can not be related by the WordNet (the terms are unknown for the WordNet database), an argument $x = (m, L, uncertainty, -)$, where $m = (t_1, t_2, equivalence)$, is then generated.

Structural agent. The structural agents consider the super-classes (or sub-classes) intuition to verify if the terms can be mapped. First, it is verified if the super-classes are lexically similar. If not, the semantic similarity is used. If the super-classes are lexically or semantically similar, the terms are equivalent to each other. The argument will be generated according to the lexical or semantic comparison.

For instance, if super-classes are not lexically similar, but the terms are considered synonymous, an argument $x = (m, E, certainty, +)$, where $m = (t_1, t_2, super\text{-}class)$, is generated.

7.3 Preferred Extension Generation

After generating their set of arguments, the agents change with each other their arguments. Following a well-defined protocol, an agent asks the others about theirs arguments. The other agents then, send their arguments to the first agent. An *ack* sign is then sent to requesting agents, in order to indicate that the arguments have been correctly received. Otherwise, an *error* sign is sent. Figure 7 shows an AUML interaction diagram with the messages exchanged between the agents during the argumentation process.

When all agents have received the set of argument of each other, they generate their *attacks* set. An *attack* (or counter-argument) will arise when we have arguments for the mapping between the same terms, but with conflicting values of h. For instance, an argument $x = (m_1, L, certainty, +)$ have as an *attack* an argument $y = (m_2, E, certainty, -)$, where m_1 and m_2 have the same terms in the ontologies. The argument y also represents an *attack* to the argument x.

As an example, consider the mapping between the terms "Reference/ Dissertation" and "Citation/Thesis" and the lexical and structural agents. The lexical agent generates an argument $x = (m, L, uncertainty, -)$, where $m =$ (dissertation, thesis, *equivalence*); and the structural agent generates an argument $y = (m, E, certainty, +)$, where $m =$ (dissertation, thesis, *super-class*). For both lexical and structural audiences, the set of arguments is $AR = \{x, y\}$ and the *attacks* $= \{(x, y), (y, x)\}$. However, the relations of *successful attacks* will be defined according to specific audience (see *Definition 2.3.2*), as it is commented below.

When the set of arguments and attacks have been produced, it is necessary for the agents to consider which of them they should accept. To do this, the agents compute their preferred extension, according to the audiences and confidence degrees. A set of arguments is *globally subjectively acceptable* if each element appears in the preferred extension for some agent. A set of arguments is *globally objectively acceptable* if each element appears in the preferred extension for every agent. The arguments which are neither objectively nor subjectively acceptable are considered *indefensible*.

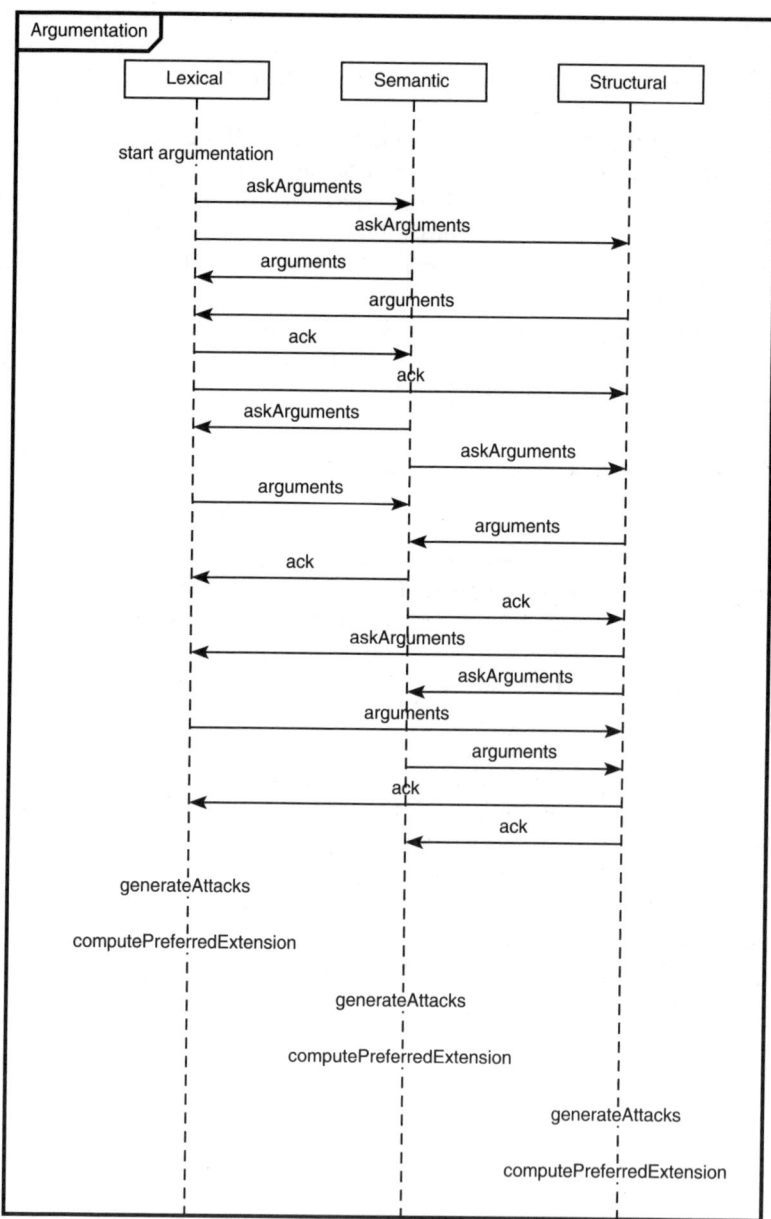

Fig. 7. AUML interaction diagram

In the example above, considering the lexical(L) and structural(E) audiences, where L ≻ E and E ≻ L, respectively. For the lexical audience, the argument y successful attacks the argument x, while the argument x does not successful attack the argument y for the structural audience. Then, the preferred extension of both lexical and structural agents is composed by the argument y, which can be seen as globally *objectively* acceptable. The mapping between the terms "Reference/ Dissertation" and "Citation/Thesis", indicated by y is correct.

8 Experiments Using the E-VAF

Let us consider that three agents need to obtain a consensus about mappings that link corresponding class names in two different ontologies.

First, we considered part of the ontology of Google and Yahoo web directories[10], and the argumentation model output have been compared with manual matches[11] (expert mappings).

We considered lexical (L), semantic (S), and structural (E) audiences in order to verify the behavior of our argumentation model. These agents were implemented in Java, and the experiments ran on Pentium(R) 4, UCP 3.20GHz, 512MB. The argumentation model, however, was not fully implemented. In order to have its practical evaluation, the output of the agents were used as input for a manual simulation of the argumentation protocol.

The threshold used to classify the matcher agents output was 0.6. We have selected three possible mappings between terms of the ontologies: "Music/History" and "Architecture/History", "Art/ArtHistory" and "ArtHumanity/ArtHistory", and "Art" and "ArtHumanity". Table 6 shows arguments and attacks (counter-arguments) generated for each audience. The mappings between these terms have been selected because they were identified as conflicting cases when using our negotiation model.

Table 6. Arguments and attacks

ID	Argument	Attacks
1	(history,history,*equivalence*,L,*certainty*,+)	3
2	(history,history,*equivalence*,S,*certainty*,+)	3
3	(history,history,*super-class*,E,*certainty*,-)	1,2
4	(art-history,art-history,*equivalence*,L,*certainty*,+)	-
5	(art-history,art-history,*equivalence*,S,*certainty*,+)	-
6	(art-history,art-history,*super-class*,E,*certainty*,+)	-
7	(art,art-humanity,L,*equivalence*,*uncertainty*,-)	8,9
8	(art,art-humanity,S,*equivalence*,*certainty*,+)	7
9	(art,art-humanity,E,*super-class*,*uncertainty*,+)	7

For the mapping between the terms "Music/History" and "Architecture/ History", each agent has as arguments $AR = \{1,2,3\}$ and as relations of attack $attacks = \{(3,1), (3,2), (1,3), (2,3)\}$. These sets are generated by each agent, after receiving the arguments of the other agents. After, the arguments that defeat

---

[10] http://dit.unitn.it/ãccord/Experimentaldesign.html (Test 3).
[11] http://dit.unitn.it/ accord/Experimentaldesign.html

each other are computed. For the lexical audience, where L ≻ S and L ≻ E, there is no arguments that successful attack each other, because all agent have certainty in the mappings. The same occurs for the semantic (S ≻ L and S ≻ E) and structural (E ≻ L and E ≻ S) audiences.

Then, the preferred extensions of the agents are composed by the arguments generated by the corresponding agent (i.e, the preferred extension of the lexical agent is {1}; the preferred extension of the semantic agent is {2}; and the preferred extension of the structural agent is {3}). This way, there is no argument globally *objectively* acceptable. We can consider that the mapping between the terms is not possible, what is true according to the manual mapping.

Using our negotiation model, the final mapping between the "Music/History" and "Architecture/ History" terms was incorrect. The semantic and lexical agents returned mappings with certainty, while the structural agent returned a not mapping with certainty. By majority, the mapping with certainty was obtained. This conflict is then resolved by our argumentation model.

For the mapping between the terms "Art/ArtHistory" and "ArtHumanity/ArtHistory", each agent has as arguments $AR = \{4,5,6\}$, but there are not relations of attack. Then, all agents accept the mapping with certainty between these terms. This mapping is considered a correct mapping by the manual mapping.

Finally, for the mapping between the terms "Art" and "ArtHumanity", each agent has as arguments $AR = \{7,8,9\}$ and as relations of attack $attacks = \{(8,7), (9,7), (7,8), (7,9)\}$. For the lexical audience, the argument 8 successful attacks the argument 7. Then, the preferred extension has the argument 8. For the semantic audience, the argument 8 also successful attacks the argument 7, and for audience structural, the arguments 8 and 9 successful attack theirs counter-arguments. Then, the preferred extension of the structural agent is {8,9}. The argument 8 is present in all preferred extension, then it is globally *objectively* acceptable, confirming the mapping indicated by manual mapping.

We have used different agents' output which use distinct mapping algorithms in order to verify the behavior of our model. Our argumentation model has identified correctly the three mappings defined by expert mappings, being two mapping positives (h is +) and one negative (h is -).

Second, we compared the argumentation output with the results obtained by a cooperative negotiation model. Table 7 shows the comparative results. Although the negotiation model having obtained better precision than argumentation model, the F-measure of the argumentation model is better than negotiation model. The negotiation model identified 7 true positive mappings and it did not classify correctly 4 true positive mappings. The argumentation model identified 8 true positive, returning 1 false positive mapping not identifying 3 true positives mappings.

Third, we compared our argumentation model with Cupid, COMA, and S-Match systems. We consider the class and the attribute names of the ontologies in the comparison. Table 8 shows the results. Our argumentation model had better F-measures than all others systems.

Table 7. Argumentation vs. negotiation

Ontology	Argumentation			Negotiation		
	P	R	F	P	R	F
Company profiles (160)	0.88	0.72	0.79	1	0.63	0.77

Table 8. Comparative mapping results – argumentation model

Ontology	Arg			Cupid			COMA			S-Match		
	P	R	F	P	R	F	P	R	F	P	R	F
Company profiles (160)	0.88	0.72	0.79	0.50	0.60	0.54	0.80	0.70	0.74	1.0	0.65	0.78

9 Related Work

In the field of ontology negotiation we find distinct proposals. [35] presents an ontology to serve as the basis for agent negotiation, the ontology itself is not the object being negotiated. A similar approach is proposed by [6], where ontologies are integrated to support the communication among heterogeneous agents.

[1] presents an ontology negotiation model which aims to arrive at a common ontology which the agents can use in their particular interaction. We, on the other hand, are concerned with delivering mapping pairs found by a group of agents using the argumentation formalism. The links between related concepts are the result of the preferred mappings of each agent, instead of an integrated ontology upon which the agents will be able to communicate for a specific purpose. We do not consider negotiation steps such as the ones presented in [1], namely clarification and explanation. But we consider different mapping methods represented by different audiences selecting by argumentation the best solution for the mapping problem.

[32] describes an approach for ontology mapping negotiation, where the mapping is composed by a set of semantic bridges and their inter-relations, as proposed in [24]. The agents are able to achieve a consensus about the mapping through the evaluation of a confidence value that is obtained by utility functions. According to the confidence value the mapping rule is accepted, rejected or negotiated. Differently from [32], we do not use utility functions. Our model is based on cooperation and argumentation, where the agents change their arguments and by argumentation they select the preferred mapping. The arguments in each preferred set are considered globally acceptable.

[21] proposes to use an argument framework to deal with arguments that support or oppose candidate correspondences between ontologies. The mapping candidates are provided by a single service. The accepted mappings resulting from argumentation are used to agent communication. Differently from [21], the mappings are obtained by different agents specialized on different mapping algorithms and not only in a single service. In [21], the mappings are assumed to be correct, and we are interested in how to obtain mapping sets by combining

different approaches for ontology mapping. Moreover, in [21] it is assumed that arguments being negotiated have the same confidence. We are proposing to associate to each argument a confidence degree. This way, in order to compute the preferred mapping, the audiences and confidence degrees must be considered.

Semantic heterogeneity is an important problem for data bases and more recently it has been raised as one of the key problems to be solved for the development of the semantic web. We can find in the literature different approaches to the problem. The work presented in [29] provides an encoding of the extensible knowledge on commonly found semantic conflicts, providing an automatic way of comparing and manipulating contextual knowledge of different information sources, which is used for semantic transformation across heterogeneous databases. In [33], the MAFRA Toolkit is presented, the tool helps a domain expert to work on ontology mapping tasks. Whereas these previous approaches are concerned with the specification of semantic conflicts that arise between different sources, ours is concerned with the particular problem of identifying pairs of corresponding terms in different ontologies. In the future we will see these various approaches in an integrated way.

10 Final Remarks

This paper presented the use of cooperative agents for composite ontology mapping. We first presented an extended classification on automated ontology matching and proposed an automatic composite solution for the matching problem based on cooperative approach. Our agents encapsulate different mapping approaches (lexical, semantic and structural) and a consensual result from cooperative negotiation of these agents. This model is fully implemented. We compared our results with expert mappings, for four ontologies in different domains. The negotiation result was better than lexical and structural agents and it returned better F-measure value than the semantic agent. When comparing our model with other state of the art matching systems, our model obtained better F-measure than Cupid and COMA and similar results if compared with the S-Match system.

Next, we proposed an extension of our negotiation model, which is based on argumentation formalism. With this we were able to give a formal presentation of our composite mapping approach. Our proposal extends the Value-based Argumentation Framework, in order to represent arguments with confidence degrees. We assumed that the confidence degrees compose a second axis which is necessary to represent a problem domain, such as the ontology mapping. We initially evaluated the argumentation model considering the mapping identified as conflicting cases when using the negotiation model. This model has obtained satisfactory results for the conflicting cases. We also compared the argumentation model with the Cupid, COMA, and S-Match. Our model obtained better F-measure values than these systems. The contribution of the argumentation model, which is the only one that is not implemented resides in the formal presentation of the problem, which was given with its practical evaluation.

As future work we plan to improve the semantic and structural approaches. We also intend to develop further tests considering also agents using constraint-based approaches; and use the ontology's ap- plication context in our matching approach. Another goal is to evaluate our proposal against systems based on machine learning techniques, such as the system proposed by [8]. Finally, we plan to use the mapping result as input to an ontology merging process in the question answering domain.

Acknowledgments

The first author is supported by the Programme Alban, the European Union Programme of High Level Scholarships for Latin America, scholarship no.E05D059374BR.

References

1. Bailin, S., Truszkowski, W.: Ontology negotiation between intelligent information agents. The Knowledge Engineering Review 17(1), 7–19 (2002)
2. Beer, M., d'Inverno, M., Luck, M., Jennings, N., Preist, C., Schroeder, M.: Negotiation in multi-agent systems. In: Workshop of the UK Special Interest Group on Multi-Agent Systems (1998)
3. Bench-Capon, T.: Persuasion in practical argument using value-based argumentation frameworks. Journal of Logic and Computation 13, 429–448 (2003)
4. Bigham, J., Du, L.: Cooperative negotiation in a multi-agent system for real-time load balancing of a mobile cellular network. In: Proceedings of the Second International Joint Conference on Autonomous Agents and Multiagent Systems, pp. 568–575. ACM Press, New York (2003)
5. Dieng, R., Hug, S.: Comparison of personal ontologies represented through conceptual graphs. In: ECAI. Proceedings of the European Conference on Artificial Intelligence, p.341 (1998)
6. Diggelen, J.v., Beun, R., Dignum, F., Eijk, v.R., Meyer, J.C.: Anemone: An effective minimal ontology negotiation environment. In: Proceedings of the V International Conference on Autonomous Agents and Multi-Agent Systems, pp. 899–906 (2006)
7. Do, H.H., Rahm, E.: Coma - a system for flexible combination of schema matching approaches. In: Dressan, S., Chaudhri, A.B., Lee, M.L., Yu, J.X., Lacroix, Z. (eds.) VLDB 2002. LNCS, vol. 2590, Springer, Heidelberg (2003)
8. Doan, A., Madhaven, J., Dhamankar, R., Domingos, P., Helevy, A.: Learning to match ontologies on the semantic web. VLDB Journal (Special Issue on the Semantic Web) (2003)
9. Dung, P.: On the acceptability of arguments and its fundamental role in nonmonotonic reasoning, logic programming and n–person games. Artificial Intelligence 77, 321–358 (1995)
10. Ehrig, M., Sure, Y.: Ontology mapping - an integrated approach. In: Proceedings of the European Semantic Web Symposium, pp. 76–91 (2004)
11. Euzenat, J., Le Bach, T., Barrasa, J., Bouquet, P., De Bo, J., Dieng-Kuntz, R., Ehrig, M., Hauswirth, M., Jarrar, M., Lara, R., Maynard, D., Napoli, A., Stamou, G., Stuckenschmidt, H., Shvaiko, P., Tessaris, S., Van Acker, S., Zaihrayeu, I.: State of the art on ontology alignment. Technical report (2004)

12. Gatti, N., Amigoni, F.: A cooperative negotiation protocol for physiological model combination. In: Proceedings of the Third Internation Joint Conference on Automomous Agents and Multi-Agent Systems, pp. 655–662 (2004)
13. Giunchiglia, F., Shvaiko, P.: Semantic matching. Knowledge Engineering Review 18(3), 265–280 (2004)
14. Giunchiglia, F., Shvaiko, P., Yatskevich, M.: S-match: An algorithm and an implementation of semantic matching. In: First European Semantic Web Symposium (2004)
15. Green, S., Hurst, L., Nangle, B., Cunningham, P., Somers, F., Evans, R.: Software agents: A review. Technical report, Trinity College (1997)
16. Hovy, E.: Combining and standardizing large-scale, practical ontologies for machine translation and other uses. In: Proceedings of the First International conference on language resources and evaluation (1998)
17. Hubner, J.: Um Modelo de Reorganização de Sistemas Multiagentes. PhD thesis, Escola Politécnica da Universidades de São Paulo, Departamento de Engenharia da Computação e Sistemas Digitais (2003)
18. Hubner, J., Sichman, J., Boisser, O.: A model for structural, functional, and deontic specification of organizations in multiagent systems. Advances in Artificial Intelligence (2002)
19. Madhavan, P.B.J., Rahm, E.: Generic schema matching with cupid. In: VLDB 2001. Proceedings of the Very Large Data Bases Conference, p.49 (2001)
20. Kalfoglou, Y., Schorlemmer, W.M.: Ontology mapping: The state of the art. In: Semantic Interoperability and Integration (2005)
21. Laera, L., Tamma, V., Euzenat, J., Bench-Capon, T., Payne, T.R.: Reaching agreement over ontology alignments. In: Cruz, I., Decker, S., Allemang, D., Preist, C., Schwabe, D., Mika, P., Uschold, M., Aroyo, L. (eds.) ISWC 2006. LNCS, vol. 4273, Springer, Heidelberg (2006)
22. Lander, S., Lesser, V.: Understanding the role of negotiation in distributed search among heterogeneous agents. In: Proceedings of the International Joint Conference on Artificial Intelligence (1993)
23. Levenshtein, I.: Binary codes capable of correcting deletions, insertions an reversals. In: Cybernetics and Control Theory (1966)
24. Maedche, A., Motik, B., Silva, N., Volz, R.: Mafra - a mapping framework for distributed ontologies. In: 13th International Conference on Knowledge Engineering and Knowledge Management, pp. 235–250 (2002)
25. Maedche, A., Staab, S.: Measuring similarity between ontologies. In: Proceedings of the European Conference on Knowledge Acquisition and Management, pp. 251–263 (2002)
26. Mailler, M., Lesser, V., Horling, B.: Cooperative negotiation for soft real-time distributed resource allocation. In: Proceedings of the second international joint conference on Autonomous agents and multiagent systems, pp. 576–583. ACM Press, New York (2003)
27. Noy, N., Musen, M.: Anchor-prompt: using non-local context for semantic matching. In: IJCAI. Proceedings of the workshop on Ontologies and Information Sharing at the International Joint Conference on Artificial Intelligence, pp. 63–70 (2001)
28. Rahm, E., Bernstein, P.A.: A survey of approaches to automatic schema matching. VLDB 10, 334–350 (2001)
29. Ram, S., Park, J.: Semantic conflict resolution ontology (scrol): An ontology for detecting and resolving data and schema-level semantic conflicts. IEEE Transactions on Knowledge and Data Engineering 16(2), 189–202 (2004)

30. Shvaiko, P.: A classification of schema-based matching approaches. Technical report, Informatica e Telecomunicazioni, University of Trento (2004)
31. Shvaiko, P., Euzenat, J.: A survey of schema-based matching approaches. Technical report, Informatica e Telecomunicazioni, University of Trento (2004)
32. Silva, N., Maio, P., Rocha, J.: An approach to ontology mapping negotiation. In: Proceedings of the K-CAP Workshop on Integrating Ontologies
33. Silva, N., Rocha, J.: Semantic web complex ontology mapping. In: WI 2003. Proc. of IEEE/WIC Web Intelligence Conference, pp. 82–88 (2003)
34. Smith, T., Waterman, M.: Identification of common molecular subsequences. Journal of Molecular Biology 147, 195–197 (1981)
35. Tamma, V., Wooldridge, M., Blacoe, I., Dickinson, I.: An ontology based approach to automated negotiation. In: Proceedings of the IV Workshop on Agent Mediated Electronic Commerce, pp. 219–237 (2002)
36. Trojahn, C., Moraes, M., Quaresma, P., Vieira, R.: A negotiation model for ontology mapping. In: Proceedings of the IEEE/WIC/ACM International Conference on Intelligent Agent Technology (2006)
37. Wooldridge, M.: An Introduction to Multiagent Systems. John Wiley and Sons, Chichester (2002)
38. Zhang, X., Lesser, V., Podorozhny, R.: Multi-dimensional, multistep negoriation for task allocation in a cooperative system. Autonomous Agents and Multi-Agent Systems 10, 5–40 (2005)

Author Index

Albertoni, Riccardo   1

Cabral, Liliana   96
Calvanese, Diego   133

Davies, Rob   96
De Giacomo, Giuseppe   133
De Martino, Monica   1
Domingue, John   96

Galizia, Stefania   96
Gugliotta, Alessio   96
Gutierrez Villarias, Leticia   96

Hurtado, Carlos A.   31

Lam, Joey Sik Chun   62
Lembo, Domenico   133
Lenzerini, Maurizio   133

Moraes, Márcia   237

Pan, Jeff Z.   62, 212
Pierra, Guy   174
Poggi, Antonella   133
Poulovassilis, Alexandra   31

Quaresma, Paulo   237

Richardson, Marc   96
Rosati, Riccardo   133
Rowlatt, Mary   96

Sleeman, Derek   62
Stincic, Sandra   96

Tanasescu, Vlad   96
Trojahn, Cássia   237

Vasconcelos, Wamberto   62
Vieira, Renata   237

Wang, Shenghui   212
Wood, Peter T.   31

Printing: Mercedes-Druck, Berlin
Binding: Stein+Lehmann, Berlin

Lecture Notes in Computer Science

Sublibrary 3: Information Systems and Application, incl. Internet/Web and HCI

For information about Vols. 1– 4519
please contact your bookseller or Springer

Vol. 4903: S. Satoh, F. Nack, M. Etoh (Eds.), Advances in Multimedia Modeling. XIX, 510 pages. 2007.

Vol. 4900: S. Spaccapietra (Ed.), Journal on Data Semantics X. XIII, 265 pages. 2008.

Vol. 4882: T. Janowski, H. Mohanty (Eds.), Distributed Computing and Internet Technology. XIII, 346 pages. 2007.

Vol. 4881: H. Yin, P. Tino, E. Corchado, W. Byrne, X. Yao (Eds.), Intelligent Data Engineering and Automated Learning - IDEAL 2007. XX, 1174 pages. 2007.

Vol. 4877: C. Thanos, F. Borri, L. Candela (Eds.), Digital Libraries: Research and Development. XII, 350 pages. 2007.

Vol. 4872: D. Mery, L. Rueda (Eds.), Advances in Image and Video Technology. XXI, 961 pages. 2007.

Vol. 4871: M. Cavazza, S. Donikian (Eds.), Virtual Storytelling. XIII, 219 pages. 2007.

Vol. 4858: X. Deng, F.C. Graham (Eds.), Internet and Network Economics. XVI, 598 pages. 2007.

Vol. 4857: J.M. Ware, G.E. Taylor (Eds.), Web and Wireless Geographical Information Systems. XI, 293 pages. 2007.

Vol. 4853: F. Fonseca, M.A. Rodríguez, S. Levashkin (Eds.), GeoSpatial Semantics. X, 289 pages. 2007.

Vol. 4836: H. Ichikawa, W.-D. Cho, I. Satoh, H.Y. Youn (Eds.), Ubiquitous Computing Systems. XIII, 307 pages. 2007.

Vol. 4832: M. Weske, M.-S. Hacid, C. Godart (Eds.), Web Information Systems Engineering – WISE 2007 Workshops. XV, 518 pages. 2007.

Vol. 4831: B. Benatallah, F. Casati, D. Georgakopoulos, C. Bartolini, W. Sadiq, C. Godart (Eds.), Web Information Systems Engineering – WISE 2007. XVI, 675 pages. 2007.

Vol. 4825: K. Aberer, K.-S. Choi, N. Noy, D. Allemang, K.-I. Lee, L. Nixon, J. Golbeck, P. Mika, D. Maynard, R. Mizoguchi, G. Schreiber, P. Cudré-Mauroux (Eds.), The Semantic Web. XXVII, 973 pages. 2007.

Vol. 4822: D.H.-L. Goh, T.H. Cao, I.T. Sølvberg, E. Rasmussen (Eds.), Asian Digital Libraries. XVII, 519 pages. 2007.

Vol. 4816: B. Falcidieno, M. Spagnuolo, Y. Avrithis, I. Kompatsiaris, P. Buitelaar (Eds.), Semantic Multimedia. XII, 306 pages. 2007.

Vol. 4813: I. Oakley, S.A. Brewster (Eds.), Haptic and Audio Interaction Design. XIV, 145 pages. 2007.

Vol. 4810: H.H.-S. Ip, O.C. Au, H. Leung, M.-T. Sun, W.-Y. Ma, S.-M. Hu (Eds.), Advances in Multimedia Information Processing – PCM 2007. XXI, 834 pages. 2007.

Vol. 4809: M.K. Denko, C.-s. Shih, K.-C. Li, S.-L. Tsao, Q.-A. Zeng, S.H. Park, Y.-B. Ko, S.-H. Hung, J.H. Park (Eds.), Emerging Directions in Embedded and Ubiquitous Computing. XXXV, 823 pages. 2007.

Vol. 4808: T.-W. Kuo, E. Sha, M. Guo, L.T. Yang, Z. Shao (Eds.), Embedded and Ubiquitous Computing. XXI, 769 pages. 2007.

Vol. 4806: R. Meersman, Z. Tari, P. Herrero (Eds.), On the Move to Meaningful Internet Systems 2007: OTM 2007 Workshops, Part II. XXXIV, 611 pages. 2007.

Vol. 4805: R. Meersman, Z. Tari, P. Herrero (Eds.), On the Move to Meaningful Internet Systems 2007: OTM 2007 Workshops, Part I. XXXIV, 757 pages. 2007.

Vol. 4804: R. Meersman, Z. Tari (Eds.), On the Move to Meaningful Internet Systems 2007: CoopIS, DOA, ODBASE, GADA, and IS, Part II. XXIX, 683 pages. 2007.

Vol. 4803: R. Meersman, Z. Tari (Eds.), On the Move to Meaningful Internet Systems 2007: CoopIS, DOA, ODBASE, GADA, and IS, Part I. XXIX, 1173 pages. 2007.

Vol. 4802: J.-L. Hainaut, E.A. Rundensteiner, M. Kirchberg, M. Bertolotto, M. Brochhausen, Y.-P.P. Chen, S.S.-S. Cherfi, M. Doerr, H. Han, S. Hartmann, J. Parsons, G. Poels, C. Rolland, J. Trujillo, E. Yu, E. Zimányie (Eds.), Advances in Conceptual Modeling – Foundations and Applications. XIX, 420 pages. 2007.

Vol. 4801: C. Parent, K.-D. Schewe, V.C. Storey, B. Thalheim (Eds.), Conceptual Modeling - ER 2007. XVI, 616 pages. 2007.

Vol. 4797: M. Arenas, M.I. Schwartzbach (Eds.), Database Programming Languages. VIII, 261 pages. 2007.

Vol. 4796: M. Lew, N. Sebe, T.S. Huang, E.M. Bakker (Eds.), Human–Computer Interaction. X, 157 pages. 2007.

Vol. 4794: B. Schiele, A.K. Dey, H. Gellersen, B. de Ruyter, M. Tscheligi, R. Wichert, E. Aarts, A. Buchmann (Eds.), Ambient Intelligence. XV, 375 pages. 2007.

Vol. 4777: S. Bhalla (Ed.), Databases in Networked Information Systems. X, 329 pages. 2007.

Vol. 4761: R. Obermaisser, Y. Nah, P. Puschner, F.J. Rammig (Eds.), Software Technologies for Embedded and Ubiquitous Systems. XIV, 563 pages. 2007.

Vol. 4747: S. Džeroski, J. Struyf (Eds.), Knowledge Discovery in Inductive Databases. X, 301 pages. 2007.

Vol. 4744: Y. de Kort, W. IJsselsteijn, C. Midden, B. Eggen, B.J. Fogg (Eds.), Persuasive Technology. XIV, 316 pages. 2007.

Vol. 4740: L. Ma, M. Rauterberg, R. Nakatsu (Eds.), Entertainment Computing – ICEC 2007. XXX, 480 pages. 2007.

Vol. 4730: C. Peters, P. Clough, F.C. Gey, J. Karlgren, B. Magnini, D.W. Oard, M. de Rijke, M. Stempfhuber (Eds.), Evaluation of Multilingual and Multi-modal Information Retrieval. XXIV, 998 pages. 2007.

Vol. 4723: M. R. Berthold, J. Shawe-Taylor, N. Lavrač (Eds.), Advances in Intelligent Data Analysis VII. XIV, 380 pages. 2007.

Vol. 4721: W. Jonker, M. Petković (Eds.), Secure Data Management. X, 213 pages. 2007.

Vol. 4718: J. Hightower, B. Schiele, T. Strang (Eds.), Location- and Context-Awareness. X, 297 pages. 2007.

Vol. 4717: J. Krumm, G.D. Abowd, A. Seneviratne, T. Strang (Eds.), UbiComp 2007: Ubiquitous Computing. XIX, 520 pages. 2007.

Vol. 4715: J.M. Haake, S.F. Ochoa, A. Cechich (Eds.), Groupware: Design, Implementation, and Use. XIII, 355 pages. 2007.

Vol. 4714: G. Alonso, P. Dadam, M. Rosemann (Eds.), Business Process Management. XIII, 418 pages. 2007.

Vol. 4704: D. Barbosa, A. Bonifati, Z. Bellahsène, E. Hunt, R. Unland (Eds.), Database and XML Technologies. X, 141 pages. 2007.

Vol. 4690: Y. Ioannidis, B. Novikov, B. Rachev (Eds.), Advances in Databases and Information Systems. XIII, 377 pages. 2007.

Vol. 4675: L. Kovács, N. Fuhr, C. Meghini (Eds.), Research and Advanced Technology for Digital Libraries. XVII, 585 pages. 2007.

Vol. 4674: Y. Luo (Ed.), Cooperative Design, Visualization, and Engineering. XIII, 431 pages. 2007.

Vol. 4663: C. Baranauskas, P. Palanque, J. Abascal, S.D.J. Barbosa (Eds.), Human-Computer Interaction – INTERACT 2007, Part II. XXXIII, 735 pages. 2007.

Vol. 4662: C. Baranauskas, P. Palanque, J. Abascal, S.D.J. Barbosa (Eds.), Human-Computer Interaction – INTERACT 2007, Part I. XXXIII, 637 pages. 2007.

Vol. 4658: T. Enokido, L. Barolli, M. Takizawa (Eds.), Network-Based Information Systems. XIII, 544 pages. 2007.

Vol. 4656: M.A. Wimmer, J. Scholl, Å. Grönlund (Eds.), Electronic Government. XIV, 450 pages. 2007.

Vol. 4655: G. Psaila, R. Wagner (Eds.), E-Commerce and Web Technologies. VII, 229 pages. 2007.

Vol. 4654: I.-Y. Song, J. Eder, T.M. Nguyen (Eds.), Data Warehousing and Knowledge Discovery. XVI, 482 pages. 2007.

Vol. 4653: R. Wagner, N. Revell, G. Pernul (Eds.), Database and Expert Systems Applications. XXII, 907 pages. 2007.

Vol. 4636: G. Antoniou, U. Aßmann, C. Baroglio, S. Decker, N. Henze, P.-L. Patranjan, R. Tolksdorf (Eds.), Reasoning Web. IX, 345 pages. 2007.

Vol. 4611: J. Indulska, J. Ma, L.T. Yang, T. Ungerer, J. Cao (Eds.), Ubiquitous Intelligence and Computing. XXIII, 1257 pages. 2007.

Vol. 4607: L. Baresi, P. Fraternali, G.-J. Houben (Eds.), Web Engineering. XVI, 576 pages. 2007.

Vol. 4606: A. Pras, M. van Sinderen (Eds.), Dependable and Adaptable Networks and Services. XIV, 149 pages. 2007.

Vol. 4605: D. Papadias, D. Zhang, G. Kollios (Eds.), Advances in Spatial and Temporal Databases. X, 479 pages. 2007.

Vol. 4602: S. Barker, G.-J. Ahn (Eds.), Data and Applications Security XXI. X, 291 pages. 2007.

Vol. 4601: S. Spaccapietra, P. Atzeni, F. Fages, M.-S. Hacid, M. Kifer, J. Mylopoulos, B. Pernici, P. Shvaiko, J. Trujillo, I. Zaihrayeu (Eds.), Journal on Data Semantics IX. XV, 197 pages. 2007.

Vol. 4592: Z. Kedad, N. Lammari, E. Métais, F. Meziane, Y. Rezgui (Eds.), Natural Language Processing and Information Systems. XIV, 442 pages. 2007.

Vol. 4587: R. Cooper, J. Kennedy (Eds.), Data Management. XIII, 259 pages. 2007.

Vol. 4577: N. Sebe, Y. Liu, Y.-t. Zhuang, T.S. Huang (Eds.), Multimedia Content Analysis and Mining. XIII, 513 pages. 2007.

Vol. 4568: T. Ishida, S. R. Fussell, P. T. J. M. Vossen (Eds.), Intercultural Collaboration. XIII, 395 pages. 2007.

Vol. 4566: M.J. Dainoff (Ed.), Ergonomics and Health Aspects of Work with Computers. XVIII, 390 pages. 2007.

Vol. 4564: D. Schuler (Ed.), Online Communities and Social Computing. XVII, 520 pages. 2007.

Vol. 4563: R. Shumaker (Ed.), Virtual Reality. XXII, 762 pages. 2007.

Vol. 4561: V.G. Duffy (Ed.), Digital Human Modeling. XXIII, 1068 pages. 2007.

Vol. 4560: N. Aykin (Ed.), Usability and Internationalization, Part II. XVIII, 576 pages. 2007.

Vol. 4559: N. Aykin (Ed.), Usability and Internationalization, Part I. XVIII, 661 pages. 2007.

Vol. 4558: M.J. Smith, G. Salvendy (Eds.), Human Interface and the Management of Information, Part II. XXIII, 1162 pages. 2007.

Vol. 4557: M.J. Smith, G. Salvendy (Eds.), Human Interface and the Management of Information, Part I. XXII, 1030 pages. 2007.

Vol. 4541: T. Okadome, T. Yamazaki, M. Makhtari (Eds.), Pervasive Computing for Quality of Life Enhancement. IX, 248 pages. 2007.

Vol. 4537: K.C.-C. Chang, W. Wang, L. Chen, C.A. Ellis, C.-H. Hsu, A.C. Tsoi, H. Wang (Eds.), Advances in Web and Network Technologies, and Information Management. XXIII, 707 pages. 2007.

Vol. 4531: J. Indulska, K. Raymond (Eds.), Distributed Applications and Interoperable Systems. XI, 337 pages. 2007.

Vol. 4526: M. Malek, M. Reitenspieß, A. van Moorsel (Eds.), Service Availability. X, 155 pages. 2007.

Vol. 4524: M. Marchiori, J.Z. Pan, C.d.S. Marie (Eds.), Web Reasoning and Rule Systems. XI, 382 pages. 2007.